Diversity in Disney Films

Diversity in Disney Films

*Critical Essays on Race, Ethnicity,
Gender, Sexuality and Disability*

EDITED BY JOHNSON CHEU

McFarland & Company, Inc., Publishers
Jefferson, North Carolina, and London

Library of Congress Cataloguing-in-Publication Data

Diversity in Disney films : critical essays on race, ethnicity,
    gender, sexuality and disability / edited by Johnson Cheu.
        p.   cm.
    Includes bibliographical references and index.

    ISBN 978-0-7864-4601-8
    softcover : acid free paper .

    1. Walt Disney Productions.   2. Pixar (Firm)   3. Motion
pictures—United States—History and criticism.   4. Animated
films—United States—History and criticism.   5. Race in
motion pictures.   6. Ethnicity in motion pictures.   7. Sex
role in motion pictures.   8. Disabilities in motion pictures.
9. People with disabilities in motion pictures.   I. Cheu,
Johnson, 1969–
PN1999.W27D58 2013
791.43'6552—dc23   2012044136

British Library cataloguing data are available

Front cover image © 2013 Shutterstock

Manufactured in the United States of America

*McFarland & Company, Inc., Publishers
    Box 611, Jefferson, North Carolina 28640
    www.mcfarlandpub.com*

For May and Anne
and everyone who was young once

Acknowledgments

I am grateful to all of my contributors who took this journey with me and who believed in the importance of the work. My colleagues at Michigan State, present and former, for their support and encouragement; in particular John Bratzel, who said, "If you can't find the book you need, then you need to make one." Also Cheryl Caesar and Deborah Carmichael who lent their ears without fail, along with Jeff Charnley, Kitty Geissler, Gary Hoppenstand, Douglas Noverr, Richard Manderfield and Benjamin Urish. A very special thanks to John A. Dowell, Michigan State's Technology Literacy Specialist, for his friendship and his invaluable expertise and contributions in manuscript preparation. Christine Levecq of Kettering University gave of her time and wisdom. My thanks to Randall W. Scott, indexer extraordinaire, Michael Rodriguez, and all the librarians at Michigan State. Further thanks to Diana Shank and Marsha Edington for their administrative support. My thanks to all my students at Michigan State, particularly those who took my Disney course.

This project had its beginnings back when I was a graduate student doing work on disability and Disney's *The Hunchback of Notre Dame*. My thanks to the good people there who worked with me on my early musings: Brenda Brueggemann, Kay Halasek, Valerie Lee (for the Doll Theory articles), Linda Mizjewski, Debra Moddelmog, Jim Phelan, and Thomas Piontek.

Good friends and family gave of their time and support. The Barbosa-Topetes, and the Collins-Sullivan clan for the trip to the Disney Family Museum in San Francisco and friendship beyond measure. For their love, advice, and support: John McCombe, Edna Poore, and Carolyn Tyjewski. Thanks to my family: my parents, my sister and brother-in-law, and my nieces, May and Anne, who were so good when uncle needed to watch something by Disney yet again, but who also knew enough to distract him when he didn't.

Table of Contents

Introduction: Re-casting and Diversifying Disney in the Age of Globalization

JOHNSON CHEU

In 2011, Disney unveiled Annie Liebowitz photos from their Disney Dreams campaign featuring celebrities in "classic" Disney film poses such as Roger Federer as King Arthur from *The Sword in the Stone* (1963), Scarlett Johansson as Cinderella (1950) running away from the ball, Penelope Cruz and Jeff Bridges as Belle and the Beast, Mark Anthony and Jennifer Lopez as Jasmine and Aladdin, Whoopi Goldberg as the Genie from *Aladdin* (1992), and Queen Latifah as Ursula from *The Little Mermaid* (1989).[1] The inclusion of international as well as ethnic celebrities perhaps signifies very little in our multicultural and global world at present. Yet, it's hard to believe that Disney, one of the largest media conglomerates in the world, was not aware of such shrewd marketing, for the re-casting of Disney characters largely identified as Caucasian (*Aladdin* [1992] notwithstanding) with mostly celebrities of color can clearly be seen as a nod toward a more inclusive pluralistic society.

Whether or not Disney *intended* from the start a more muticultural out-look and representation in its films and ads is debatable (and depends perhaps on how well the Dreams campaign is ultimately received), but there can be no doubt that with such characters and films as the Asian American boy Russell in *Up* (2009)—a film that also contains an explicit reference to divorce—Princess Tiana, the first African American princess introduced in *The Princess and the Frog* (2009), *Pocahontas* (1995), *Mulan* (1998), and *Aladdin*, Disney is, in fact, becoming more multicultural in its filmic fare and its image. The latest *Toy Story* installment, *Toy Story 3* (2010), contains "Spanish–mode" Buzz Lightyear, a futuristic Latin-Lover-type-Tim Allen/Antonio Banderas hybrid, meant to assuage Woody's fears of leaving Annie, as Annie gushes to Woody,

1

"It's all right Woody, now that I know about Buzz's Spanish switch." *Toy Story 3* also has what one might call "ambiguously gay Ken" or, at least, "metrosexual Ken," a Ken more into clothes than Barbie (the scene where she's about to tear apart his Nehru jacket), and who signs his letters with hearts and flowers. In the age where so-called "children's movies" have become more infused with humor aimed at adults—Mike Meyers' *Cat in the Hat* (2003) holding a rake and breaking the fourth wall proclaiming "dirty hoe" or a panning of Fiona's room in *Shrek 2* (2004) showing a drawing of Sir Justin on the wall, alluding to the then-real-life Justin Timberlake/Cameron Diaz romance— such wink-wink humor aimed at adults in *Toy Story 3* seems like a bit of harmless fun to keep the adults entertained while they sit through yet another viewing of *Toy Story 3*. Yet these representations of minority groups, of diversity, are anything but mindless fun in our digital-download-video-streaming age where these images can be viewed repeatedly. The critic Jack Zipes, in "Breaking the Disney Spell," states that Disney has replaced the original fairy tales in our popular and collective imaginations; Disney has become the cultural touchstone (an apropos reference to its Touchstone film division) for generations. Zipes writes, "If children or adults think of the great, classic fairy tales today ... they will think of Walt Disney. Their first and perhaps lasting impression of these tales and others will have emanated from a Disney film, book, or artifact."[2] With the premiere of two new television series—*Grimm* and *Once Upon a Time*—on United States television networks in the fall of 2011 as well as two large-screen adaptations of *Snow White* premiering in 2012, popular interest in fairy tales, the cornerstone upon which Walt Disney built his empire beginning with *Snow White and the Seven Dwarves*, has grown and so has consumption of Disney and Disney–esque media.

I was surprised to see how little critical attention has been paid to the preeminent thing that Disney made: his films. Doing research for a class I was putting together in 2008, I found that the vast majority of our university's holdings on Disney concerned his business practices or the global impact of his empire. Relative to the fifty or so books on business and commercialism and childhood psychology, little attention had been paid to his films, and books that did, such as Ward and Christian's *Mouse Morality*, were out of print. To be sure, some books such as Janet Wasko's *Understanding Disney* contained film criticism and certainly specialized books such as Amy Davis's *Good Girls and Wicked Witches* and Sean Griffin's *Tinkerbells and Evil Queens* existed, as well as the Bell et al. collection *From Mouse to Mermaid*, but still, it seemed as though Disney the Man/Mogul or Disney the global conglomerate loomed large in scholarship while scholarship on his artistic output remained relatively scant.

Within the film scholarship that was in print, the amount that concerned representations of diversity were largely located in specialized books such as the ones mentioned above or in specialized journal issues. There could be a myriad of reasons for this, none the least of which is academia's current push toward STEM research and, within film and animation studies, toward production. Whatever the reason or reasons for the trends in film and animation studies that seem to be occurring, the reality is that within academia and outside of it, there remains a growing emphasis on globalization. Yet, the fact that that emphasis requires *more* interest and attention paid to issues of diversity rather than less, seems somehow lost in the swirl of things, as though *bibbity, boppity boo,* and we all just know how to get along, how to act as global citizens.

Disney's global empire and reach and its commercialization of world ethnic cultures via its EPCOT centers around the globe are already well documented and critiqued so I will not advance those arguments here.[3] In looking at the Disney company's filmic output in regards to ethnic and other kinds of cultural diversity, there were holes in the critical scholarship which this collection seeks to address.

This book really begins with Peter Pan and the childhood game of Cowboys and Indians. In searching for scholarly criticism to address the depiction of the "Red Man," a.k.a. Native Americans, in both song and character, neither I nor the university librarians could find any. An email and phone buzz of Native American specialist colleagues at various universities across the U.S. yielded nothing. Nothing on Disney's 1958 Sal Mineo film *Tonka,* in which Mineo plays a Sioux who tames a stallion named Tonka, turned up. Yet, there were articles critiquing *Pocahontas.* In looking further, I discovered something similar with *Mulan,* for which there were a number of scholarly articles, including some in Chinese, and yet there was nothing about the Siamese Cats in *Lady and the Tramp* (1955), which, as mentioned in the documentary *Mickey Mouse Monopoly* (2002) are commonly held to be stereotypes of Asian Americans. Likewise, when it came to gender, there was much criticism on the Princess phenomenon (everything from more mainstream criticism such as Peggy Orenstein's *Cinderella Ate My Daughter,* to more traditional academic scholarship in journals such as *Woman's Communication Quarterly*), but relatively scant scholarship on masculinity studies. Though princes are relatively one-note characters in many of Disney's films, there can be little doubt that without the presence of princes, the princesses and the growth and change one sees from *Snow White* to *Tangled* in character development would not be possible. When it came to coverage of newer fields of scholarship such as queer studies, critical whiteness studies and disability studies respectively, the coverage and range of topics was even more narrow.

Even the abstracts and proposals submitted for this collection exhibited certain trends. There were, for example, many proposals about *Mulan* but little else concerning Asian American representations. Likewise with disability: much on *The Hunchback of Notre Dame,* but little else. Perhaps academicians are swayed by their childhoods, by the most obvious kinds of representations and impressions, just as much as everyone else? Perhaps it is a calculation of what seems publishable, as something more obscure might not be. Or perhaps it's as simple as personal interest. Whatever the reason or reasons, the necessity for examining diversity and a wider range of it within Disney appears pertinent in our age of globalization. For my part as editor, I've chosen essays which encompass a wide range of films as well as being cognizant of fresh theoretical approaches.

Every author in the collection has his or her own approach to the filmic history of Disney as it relates to the films they are examining. A broad overview of who Disney is or a chronological overview of the nearly hundred years of Disney's filmic output is unnecessary here. There are also, it should be noted, differences in formality of tone among the essays, some being more formal or personal than others. Letting the authors' unique voices shine through helps, I would suggest, to show the authors' perspective and relationship to the films. In the end, cohesiveness of argument won out over tone.

* * *

The essays in Section I, on issues of race and ethnicity, challenge older representations of ethnicity as well as looking at newer fare. Some of Disney's earliest depictions of race occurred in his *Oswald the Rabbit* (pre–Mickey Mouse) shorts, and beyond with his employment of blackface. Kheli R. Willetts' essay, "Cannibals and Coons: Blackness in the Early Days of Walt Disney," gives a historical overview of Disney's early representations of blacks and blackness and looks at reverberations of such portrayals to the present day. The essay also breaks new ground as little critical attention has been paid to race in these early works. Karen S. Goldman in her essay, "*Saludos Amigos* and *The Three Caballeros*: The Representation of Latin America in Disney's 'Good Neighbor' Films," looks anew at Disney's travelogue films (1942 and 1944) from his journey to Latin America during the unionization strife at his studio. The 1950s saw a return to more traditional fare with *Peter Pan* (1953). Prajna Parasher's essay, "Mapping the Imaginary: The *Neverland* of Disney Indians," examines portrayals of American Indians in *Peter Pan* and *Brother Bear* (2003). Both Goldman and Parasher use the iconography of maps and mapping to trace historical understandings of Latin American and American Indian identity and their impact on current popular culture. While Parasher's essay uses Orientalist theory to understand American Indian imagery, Kimiko Akita and Rick Kenney's essay, "A 'Vexing Implication': Siamese Cats and Orientalist Mischief-Making," uses Orientalism to dissect depictions of Asian Americans in *Lady and the Tramp*, *The Aristocats* (1970) and others. Natchee Blu Barnd's essay, "White Man's Best Friend: Race and Privilege in *Oliver and Company*" (1988), ties together many of the ideas explored in the previous essays and connects them to class and privilege and critical Whiteness studies, tying it to ideas of social justice. And lastly, Sarah E. Turner's essay, "Blackness, Bayous and Gumbo: Encoding and Decoding Race in a Colorblind World," looks at

Disney's current portrayal of African Americans in *The Princess and the Frog*, using the theory of "colorblind racism" to argue that perhaps America has not progressed as much as it may believe regarding issues of race, class and gender.

In examining gender and sexuality, the idea of traditions and transformations that Turner's essay and others touch upon reverberate as the authors examine and question what it means to be a boy, and what it means to be a girl. Danielle Glassmeyer's essay, "Fighting the Cold War with *Pinocchio, Bambi* and *Dumbo*" (1940, 1942 and 1941, respectively), opens Section II by using classic Disney to make a case for how such films shaped boys into the men who fought the Cold War. Gwendolyn Limbach's essay, "'You the Man, Well, Sorta': Gender Binaries and Liminality in *Mulan*," tackles traditional notions of masculinity and femininity by examining issues of cross-dressing in *Mulan*. Gael Sweeney's essay, "'What Do You Want Me to Do? Dress in Drag and Do the Hula?': Timon and Pumbaa's Alternative Lifestyle Dilemma in *The Lion King*," queers Timon and Pumbaa articulating their life as a couple. Amanda Putnam's essay, "Mean Ladies: Transgendered Villains in Disney Films," ties together issues of villainy, and by extension, goodness, with transgenderism, helping us to re-conceptualize all of those issues, creating broader notions of gender, goodness and evilness.

The field of disability studies as a cultural studies discipline is relatively new compared to race, gender, and sexuality. As the essays in Section III reflect, it asks us to re-conceptualize disability beyond medical impairment or bodily materiality to a more socially and culturally constructed definition of Disability Identity, examining, among other things, mainstream representations of disability. As such, a trope disability studies critiques is the idea of disability as punishment for evilness from Oedipus to Richard III and more current representations. Martin F. Norden's essay, "'You're a Surprise from Every Angle': Disability, Identity and Otherness in *The Hunchback of Notre Dame*," looks at Quasimodo from a disability studies perspective, examining the Disney company's motives and its creation of the character and its impact on both a disabled and nondisabled audience. Karen Schwartz, Zana Marie Lutfiyya and Nancy Hansen's essay, "Dopey's Legacy: Stereotypical Portrayals of Intellectual Disability in the Classic Animated Films," looks at representations of intellectual disability, a subject not often studied from a cultural vantage point, articulating the damage caused by the innocent child-like stereotype. Tammy Berberi and Viktor Berberi's essay, "A Place at the Table: On Being Human in the *Beauty and the Beast* Tradition," compares and contrasts filmic and literary representations of *Beauty and the Beast*, revealing Disney's version as sanitized from the French cinema's classic version by Cocteau.

Finally, the essays in Section IV take on the ideas of reimaginings and new visions in the films they examine, offering glimpses of where Disney may be headed, literally and figuratively, with issues of diversity. All of the essays have to do with traveling, quite literally, as Disney, (re)imagines the past and envisions the future. William Verrone's essay, "Is Disney Avant-Garde? A Comparative Analysis of *Alice in Wonderland* and Jan Svankmajer's *Alice*," opens the section looking at Disney's *Alice in Wonderland* (1951) and Svankmajer's *Alice* (1989), questioning the popular reception of Disney's *Alice in Wonderland* and the subversive nature of both films. Ana Salzberg's "(Indivi)duality in *Return to Oz*: Reflection and Revision" takes a lesser-known Disney film, *Return to Oz*, and looks at the ethereal and the physical world, the bodies and identities within, to understand transformations in identity and memory, while adding to the growing body of *Oz*–related scholarship. Michael Green's "Securing the Virtual Frontier for Whiteness in *Tron*" questions why race (beyond whiteness) is virtually absent in the futuristic world of *Tron* and what Tron ultimately teaches us about racial issues in our future. (I should note that in *Tron: Legacy* the one and only time an African American appears on the screen, another character, ostensibly referring to their numerical status, calls the African American the racially-imbued term "primitive.") Walter C. Metz's essay, "A Womb with a Phew! Post-Humanist Theory and Pixar's *Wall-E*," looks at disability and the post-human body in the futuristic world of *Wall-E*. Finally, Dennis Tyler's "Home Is Where the Heart Is: Pixar's *Up*" examines gender, race, and domesticity in *Up*. Of note is his analysis of the meanings implied in the ways things are literally drawn on the page, citing film theorist Sergi Eisenstein's essay on Disney and his use of space and movement.

* * *

In *Ratatouille* (2007), the critic Anton Ego says (in the voice of Peter O'Toole), "In many ways, the work of a critic is easy. We risk very little, yet enjoy a position over those who offer up their work and their selves to our judgment. We thrive on negative criticism which is fun to write and to read.... But there are times when a critic truly risks something, and that is in the discovery and the defense of the new." Critiquing the work of Disney certainly is not new, but *how* we look at and understand movies in the wake of the Culture Wars and the Digital Age we are in, in many ways, is. As such, the work of scholars is literally easier, as movies are accessible for repeat viewings via a disc or download, the poor film subjected to endless viewings and arguments. But in ways the work of the critic is harder now, not only because film studies in the academy is creeping towards production and, to some degree, away from criticism, but also because everyone can offer up his or her own critique of the film via a blog, Facebook, or Twitter feed. The voice of the academic critic is diminished perhaps in the cacophony of voices competing for attention, particularly in the backlash against negative criticism. The job of the critic is not simply to be negative, but to help people—students, the public, whomever— discover new ways of seeing and understanding the text at hand, be it print, visual, or digital. The critic and teacher's job is to offer new ways of seeing to enrich the understanding of the text, to enhance its appreciation. The critics in this volume all share, at their core, a love of Disney, the art that he made, that his company continues to create, the legacy he left behind. Otherwise, we wouldn't spend time critiquing work that others find trivial, "child's fare" and unworthy of attention. Sure, we may want the representations of diversity to be different from what we see, but that is only because we understand the reach and impact Disney has, its cultural importance upon shaping our global citizenry. As we move further and further into the 21st century, as technology makes media more accessible to all, it is not far fetched to wish for us all to become more cognizant of what we and our children see and consume. Whether this book enriches or detracts from a reader and viewer's experience of Disney is beyond the reach of what the writers here can control. We hope, though, that you'll encounter something new.

Notes

1. See http://www.popeater.com/2011/03/03/Annie-Leibovitz-disney-celebrities/
2. Zipes, Jack. "Breaking the Disney Spell"; Sells, et al. *From Mouse to Mermaid*, 21.
3. See Meehan, et al. *Dazzled by Disney? The Global Disney Audiences Project.*

Bibliography

Bell, Elizabeth, Lynda Haas and Laura Sells, eds. *From Mouse to Mermaid: The Politics of Film, Gender, and Culture.* Bloomington: Indiana University Press, 1995.
Meehan, Eileen R., Mark Philips, and Janet Wasko, eds. *Dazzled by Disney? The Global Audiences Project.* Leicester: Leicester University Press, 2005.
Von Glinow, Kiki. "Annie Leibovitz Photographs Celebrity Disney Scenes." http://www.popeater.com/2011/03/03/Annie-Leibovitz-disney-celebrities/ (accessed June 3, 2011)
Zipes, Jack. "Breaking the Disney Spell," in *From Mouse to Mermaid*, 21–42.

SECTION I—BEYOND THE FAIREST: ESSAYS ON RACE AND ETHNICITY

Cannibals and Coons: Blackness in the Early Days of Walt Disney

KHELI R. WILLETTS

Wish Upon a Star

There is little doubt that for the young and young at heart, Disney is synonymous with magic and fantasy, a wish factory if you will. It is an alternate universe that operates at the pleasure of young children, centering their world view, creating a place where animals speak, one never grows old and the possibility of becoming a prince or princess seems far more attainable than becoming a scientist or teacher. Mickey is the unofficial *wishmaster*. He and his animated entourage are interwoven into the fabric of this nation and the lives of many families who pass their love for Disney and its magic from one generation to the next. Yet for all of its allure, Disney's world is not magic for everyone. Although many may cite *The Princess and the Frog* (2009) as evidence to the contrary, the arrival of a Disney–born black princess—more than 70 years after the appearance of their first effort to create an animated fairytale with *Snow White*—offers little consolation to people like me who spent their childhood on a quest for a reflection of myself in the world of Disney.

Growing up I searched for characters who mirrored the people in my community and reflected the values and aesthetics of the Other, in this case, African, Latino, Asian and First Nations Diasporas. Instead, Disney gave me caricatured representations of the diversity of my world. Disney's diversity was often channeled not with cartoon characters but through animals whose speech and mannerisms reflected animated minstrelsy. Self-proclaimed *injuns*, complete with red skin, exaggerated features and eagle feathers share a *peace pipe* with Peter Pan, Wendy and the crew as *the natives* tell their story through

9

stereotypical dance while singing, *What Made the Red Man Red* (1953). *Song of the South* (1946), Disney's first live-action musical drama, offers us Bre'r Rabbit, Fox and Bear. These core characters of African American folktales are transformed into shady imposters of their authentic selves, into classic coons physically and verbally, complete with the standard speech of "dees," "dems" and "dose."[1] These characters were the rule instead of the exception. The portrayals were presented during the ascent of America's favorite mouse with images that dashed my girlhood wishes for Disney magic that looked, and felt, familiar and beautiful.

The Legacy of Caricatured Blackness

Shortly after the birth of Mickey Mouse in the animated short *Steamboat Willie* (1928), caricatured illustrations of Africans and African Americans began to appear in Disney animated films.[2] Disney's images were the latest in a history of drawings informed by racism that had been in existence for almost 500 years. Since the first explorers began traveling to Africa in the mid–15th century renderings of Africans have been included as a part of their travel diaries and official records of their journeys.[3]

Many of the drawings were ethnographic recordings of various cultural groups and nations and used for anthropological studies. In addition to the images being used as visual references for scientific investigations, illustrations of men, women and children appeared in a variety of other ways ranging from decorative elements along of the border of maps that detailed the continent and countries of Africa, to portraits featuring them in the service of Europeans. Irrespective of the manner of portrayal the intent was the same: to illustrate the differences between the races, thereby validating the notion of Africana people as direct descendants of "the missing link," more closely related to primates in ancestry, appearance and behavior than humans (Europeans).[4] Scientists, scholars and the leaders of nations utilized the discourse of difference as a means to justify the morality of the Transatlantic Slave Trade.[5]

It must be noted, however, that not all of the drawings were anthropological in nature. One of the earliest non-scientific illustrations can be found in Milan featuring a male servant as one of the assassins of a Milanese Duke, Galeazzo Maria Sforza, in a 1476 frontispiece of Giovanni Andrea da Lampugnano's *Lament of the Duke Galeazzo Maria.*[6] Paintings and sculptures of African descended kings, traders and religious figures housed in the world's museums demonstrate that there were a number of artists working during the same 500 year period who were more interested in portraying realistic representations of the aesthetics and cultures of the sitters as opposed to stylized stereotypical interpretations.

Nevertheless a large majority of the images continued to highlight the differences between Africans and Europeans and create a dichotomous relationship that presented Europeans as good, pretty, intellectual, refined and driven, commonly articulated as *whiteness,* juxtaposed against bad, ugly, emotional, savage and lazy Africans, representing *blackness.*[7] It was the racialization of humanity that served as the foundation for many theories related to the validity of inherent *inhumanness* of black people, thereby grounding the argument for enslavement, segregation, oppression and genocide. Almost 200 years after da Lampugnano's work was published, the United States joined Europe in the slave trade, as well as their propagandistic pursuit to justify their endeavor.

Even Thomas Jefferson (1743–1826), third president of the United States, formally comments on the differences between the races in his book *Notes on the State of Virginia,* first published in 1781. In this text Jefferson uses physical differences between blacks and whites to justify the continued enslavement of Africans:

> The first difference which strikes us is that of colour. Whether the black of the negro resides in the reticular membrane between the skin and scarf-skin, or in the scarf-skin itself; whether it proceeds from the colour of the blood, the colour of the bile, or from that of some other secretion, the difference is fixed in nature, and is as real as if its seat and cause were better known to us. And is this difference of no importance? Is it not the foundation of a greater or less share of beauty in the two races? Are not the fine mixtures of red and white, the expressions of every passion by greater or less suffusions of colour in the one, preferable to that eternal monotony, which reigns in the countenances, that immoveable veil of black which covers all the emotions of the other race.[8]

Jefferson also believed that there was a connection between color and countenance. Unifying complexion and character was a part of the discourse employed by pro-slavery advocates and served as a rallying point for their cause. Although less than 100 years after Jefferson's observations, enslavement would come to a formal end, the battle over Blackness and the humanity of African Diasporan people would continue. The rhetoric of difference, however, was now infused into the fabric of this nation, impacting all aspects of society from policy to public engagement, from education to entertainment.

In the 19th century, illustrator Edward Williams Clay (1799–1857) drew caricatured black figures in a series entitled *Life in Philadelphia* (1828–1830). According to the University of Michigan's Clements Library exhibition, *Reframing the Color Line: Race and the Visual Culture in the Atlantic World,*

> Clay deployed caricature to pose questions about who African Americans, many of them former slaves, could be in a nation that relied upon race and slavery to signal inequality and difference. Clay invented black figures that uttered malapropisms, wore clothing of exaggerated proportions, struck ungraceful poses,

and thereby failed to measure up to the demands of freedom and citizenship. His ideas were cruel, yet enduring.[9]

Caricaturists Arthur Burdett Frost (1851–1928) and Edward Windsor Kemble (1861–1933), known for their illustrations in the Joel Chandler Harris series featuring *Uncle Remus*,[10] continued Clay's legacy of black caricatures reifying the stereotypical interpretations of people of African descent.

The works of Clay, Frost and Kemble are not unique in their imagery or intent. Artists working in a variety of media incorporated stereotypical representations of black people into their work. Yet the illustrations and cartoons found in books, magazines and newspapers made the largest impact by normalizing these caricatured perspectives largely due to the accessibility of the media. In addition most of these images were accompanied by text in the form of captions or descriptive commentaries. The text was often written in what was considered an accurate encapsulation of the manner in which black people spoke, or *black dialect*, further perpetuating and cementing society's perceptions about the ignorance and limited educability of blacks.

Although the impact of cartoons and illustrations was far-reaching, the advent of animated cartoons ushered in by Winsor McCay (1871–1934), who transformed his comic strip *Little Nemo in Slumberland* into an animated short in 1911, brought messages and images to broad audience regardless of literacy, education and exposure (Crawford, 2007). With animation, accessibility of these images dramatically increased well beyond the reach attained through books, magazines and newspapers. As a result, caricatured imagery became embodied through animation so when McCay's character *Little Nemo* was introduced to the nation through his short, so were his black maid and the enslaved Africans who were in the service of King Morpheus, ruler of all Slumberland (Heer, 2006).

Prior to McCay and other early animators working in studios like Bray Productions (1914) and the Pat Sullivan Studio (1916), the images presented by Disney Brothers Cartoon Studio (1923) signaled the emergence of the next generation in animation as well as racist characterizations of black people, offering a visual justification for their continued segregation and oppression.

Here Comes the Rabbit ... I Mean the Mouse

Disney Brothers Cartoon Studio was renamed Walt Disney Studios shortly after its founding. Named after Walt at the urging of his brother Roy, their studio would quickly emerge as an innovator in the burgeoning field of cartoon animation. Disney improved upon existing techniques created by other animators, including Max Fleischer who first used live action and animated characters in the same scene, as well as the synchronization of the sound and character originally attempted by Warner Brothers' production of the first "talky" in the live action film, *The Jazz Singer* (1927*)*. However it was Disney's creative and progressive approach to their animation technique and storytelling that laid the foundation upon which the Disney empire now rests, confirming their current standing as a cultural icon.

Oswald the Lucky Rabbit, Mickey's animated forefather, was the first Disney character to enamor himself to America. Co-created by Walt Disney and his friend and fellow animator Ub Iwerks, Oswald starred in 26 cartoon shorts from 1927 to 1928, guided by Disney's and Iwerk's vision. Oswald became the first character to generate a fan base as well as marketing merchandise.[11] Although Disney and Iwerks created Oswald as well as the *Alice Comedies*, the work was being produced for and marketed by Universal Pictures.

With the success of Oswald, Walt Disney sought to renegotiate his contract only to be denied and subsequently informed that almost everyone with exception to Iwerks and animator Les Clark had signed contracts with Universal in anticipation of their continued success. Walt Disney, Iwerks and Clark decided to leave it all behind, including Oswald who was owned by Universal. In 2006 Oswald returned home (via a trade between Disney and NBC/Universal) to the Disney family after a 78-year separation.[12]

Although Walt Disney's utilization of stereotypical imagery was not as overt in his early work as it would later become once Mickey arrived, the Oswald series was not exempt. In *Africa Before Dark* (1928) Oswald journeys to Africa as a big game hunter. One can only speculate what the trip is about because it is among the Disney–inspired Oswald shorts that are considered lost. However there are other Oswald cartoons that offer caricatured representations of Blackness.

In *Bright Lights* (1928), Oswald attempts to sneak into a theater. The opening scene featuring a lighted marquee with the word *Vodvil*, with four high-kicking women in the center above the name of the headliner, *Mlle. Zulu Shimmy Queen,* alludes to Paris and its headliner Josephine Baker, who became an overnight sensation with her banana dance when she performed it at the Folies Bergère two years earlier in 1926. Baker's dance would have been known to Walt Disney and his peers and his decision to racialize the headliner by using Zulu as her surname leaves little question as to implied cultural heritage of the featured act. In *Bright Lights*, Oswald's Josephine is portrayed by his feline girlfriend, who in the Oswald series is not offered the courtesy of a fixed identity, and as a result goes by a number of names or sometimes no name at all.

The short continues with Oswald attempting to sneak into the theater literally in the shadow of a high roller outfitted in a full-length fur, bowler cap and fat cigar. His ruse is discovered when the bellhop, while taking the coat and the shadow, reveals a very skinny man underneath the coat and Oswald beneath the shadow. In this scene, the bellhop is portrayed as an orangutan, the only one among the rabbits, cats, bears and other *animalesque* characters that make up Oswald's world. In the early part of the 20th century, African American men often worked as bellhops and in other service staff positions, often by circumstance rather than choice. Although the bellhop's appearance is brief, it is significant because Oswald's world was an anthropomorphic interpretation of reality, one in which Blackness was viewed through the lens of exoticism and societal bias.

When Walt Disney lost the rights to Oswald because of his refusal to sign the Universal contract that dramatically cut his salary and impacted his autonomy, the end result was a parting of ways, making room for the emergence of a new Disney character, free from what could be described as *animation sharecropping* under Universal. Although there are competing theories surrounding the genesis of Mickey, with some of the stories coming directly from Walt's own revisionist recollections himself, the one thing that is indisputable is once the mouse was in the house, animation, American culture and the world would never be the same.

In the article "Mickey Mouse at Seventy-Five," written on the occasion of Mickey's birthday, author Garry Apgar details the diversity of Mickey's fan base and how he was woven into popular culture (2003). Apgar notes how Mickey was adored by mainstream society as well as the rich, famous and influential. His greatest supporters included *The New York Times,* Charlie Chaplin and American writer and cultural critic Gilbert Seldes. Mickey was also referenced in a Cole Porter lyric for the song *You're the Top* (1934) and in a scene from *Bringing Up Baby* (1938), starring Katharine Hepburn and Cary Grant. American regionalist painter Thomas Hart Benton also featured him in a set of murals in 1932 for the Whitney Museum Library.[13] Scholar Robert W. Brockway in his article, "The Masks of Mickey Mouse: Symbol of a Generation," provides additional commentary about the global appeal of Mickey.

> By 1933 the Mickey Mouse craze was global. George V decreed that there must be a Mickey Mouse cartoon at all film performances attended by the royal family and their guests. The Emperor of Japan wore a Mickey Mouse watch.... Mickey was adored by the whole world. He was listed in *Who's Who* and *Encyclopedia Britannica* devoted an entire article to him.[14]

Less than 10 years after his New York City debut, Mickey went global. It is his swift rise to international iconic status that makes Disney's visual commentary on Blackness so complicated and problematic. Mickey's worldwide appeal spread perspectives about Black people that went unchallenged because a counter-narrative did not exist. African Americans were little more than one generation removed from enslavement, which had been in existence in the United States since 1619 and the world since the 15th century. It is nearly impossible to compete with hundreds of years of propagandistic portrayals of African Diasporan people as a justification for oppression and enslavement. It is that understanding coupled with the subtlety of these images that results in them remaining largely unnoticed or ignored, in mainstream society, from the very beginning until today.

Cannibals and Coons

As previously mentioned, stereotypical portrayals of Blackness in Disney animation were present from the very beginning. However in the Oswald shorts that are available, Blackness was not used as comical fodder as a means to move the plotline along until Mickey took center stage. One of the earliest examples of this technique is in *The Grocery Boy* (1932).

In this short Mickey finds himself trying to prevent Pluto from completely destroying Minnie's house in an effort to eat the elaborate meal she has prepared. During the course of Pluto's many attempts to escape with a cooked turkey clenched in his teeth, Pluto knocks over a pedestal, sending a statue of Napoleon in the air to land on Mickey's head, completely encasing his body and leaving only his legs showing. Shortly thereafter, Pluto runs toward Mickey and scoops him up onto his back, transforming Mickey into Napoleon riding his trusty steed (Pluto). They eventually crash into a potbellied stove and transform the statue of Napoleon wearing his classic bicorn hat and uniform into a man in blackface wearing a bowler hat and overcoat. In other words, Mickey goes from conqueror to coon.

Disney's technique of using blackface continues in *Trader Mickey* (1932), except in this short, the role of Blackness moves beyond the blackface found in *The Grocery Boy* into creating an entire film inspired by racism for the amusement of viewers. In this short, Disney offers the audience visual illustrations for a virtually endless menu of stereotypes, caricatures and cultural perceptions about African people and Blackness. Set to the sounds of Shelton Brooks' *The Darktown Strutter's Ball* (1917), Mickey and Pluto find themselves sailing down the coast of Africa, established by the presence of hippos (indigenous to this continent), with cargo containing various items including musical instruments.

The trouble begins for Mickey and Pluto shortly after disembarking when they are captured by what could be characterized as *wild-eyed Africans,* quite literally, evidenced by their swirling eyeballs, as they gaze upon the intruders. Portrayed by animals most closely resembling primates, their facial features are reminiscent of chimpanzees and silverback gorillas. Historically, in film and literature, primates and Black people have been interchangeable. Not only have Africans been viewed, and portrayed, as the most apparent ancestor of monkeys, Disney's deliberate decision to animalize Blacks is evidenced in his films. Crows—presented as black men in *Dumbo*—are widely regarded as urban irritants, producers of raucous noises and more disturbing than their rural, less maligned cousins, the raven. When Blacks appear as donkeys in *Fantasia*, they define rough beasts of burden: ugly and obstinate—certainly no child's pined-for pony. And here, with *Trader Mickey*, Disney's chimp-likc *natives* replete with grass skirts, nose rings, spears and shields communicate through grunts and babbling ... that is when they are not laughing.

Disney's *natives* replete with grass skirts, nose rings, spears and shields communicate through grunts and babbling ... that is when they are not laughing. The *Africans* are immediately established as cannibals by the presence of an overabundance of skulls used as decorative elements and trophies. This sentiment is soon confirmed when Mickey and Pluto are brought to the chief and he and the cook decide that they will be the main course for dinner. While Mickey and Pluto are slowly simmering in cauldrons, the natives raid Mickey's boat and its contents. The items in the crates, including instruments, fascinate them although it is clear that they don't know what anything is used for as demonstrated by the chief who places a corset on his head or the suspenders that a mother with over-exaggerated lips, courtesy of a lip plate, uses to strap in all four of her children she is carrying on her back like a possum.

Capitalizing on the ignorance of the natives and a bit angry that the cook is using a saxophone to stir the pot he is in and also taste the broth, Mickey snatches the saxophone and begins to play it. The moment the music begins the natives respond with wide eyes and even wider smiles, eventually joining in using other instruments. Although they play them from the wrong end it presents little problem due to their big lips that are amazingly able to stretch over the end of all the instruments, even those that aren't played by mouth. In addition to the instruments, they also utilize their bodies to make all kinds of music.

One particularly disturbing example presents three women dancing in unison, in a sort of hula style dance more closely associated with South Pacific Island cultures. While the women are dancing they clap their lips together rhythmically. Shortly thereafter, the women turn revealing a baby strapped to each of their backs. These babies, wearing classic pickaninny, electrified hairstyles, turn away from their mothers' backs toward their rear ends and begin to play them with their hands keeping time with the syncopated rhythms made by their mothers' mouths.

In little more than seven minutes, Disney equates Blackness with ignorance and buffoonery and declares that African society and intellect are rudimentary at best. This is illustrated by Mickey's ability to adapt to the music and dance styles of his former kidnappers, transforming himself from captive to colonialist the moment he grabs the horn and begins to play. Disney also highlights and exaggerates the physical attributes of these so-called Africans, in a manner that suggests large lips and ample hips are grotesque and abhorrent.

The overtly racist *Trader Mickey* is a direct representation of Disney's views on African people and Blackness. These portrayals continued to be incorporated throughout Disney's films although they were not always integral to the plot. *Fantasia* (1940) was one of Disney's most successful animated films featuring these types of characters. It is the only film where Disney responded to the criticisms about their racist characters, by modifying or eliminating elements from the *Pastoral Symphony* scene in subsequent releases.[15] Set to the sounds of the world's best classical musicians including Igor Stravinsky, Pyotr Illyich Tchaikovsky and Johann Sebastian Bach, *Fantasia* is a visual and aural feast and by today's standards would also be considered a concert film. Featuring Ludwig Van Beethoven's *Symphony No. 6 in F, Op. 68 "Pastorale,"* Disney's *Pastoral Symphony* creates a mythological world featuring gods, satyrs, cupids, centaurs, and pegasi preparing for a visit from some young centaur men on their coming to take part in the celebration of Dionysus, the Greek god of wine.[16] Keeping with tradition, Disney continues to equate Blackness with servitude and Otherness.

In beginning of this scene we find the beautiful and colorful centaur women getting ready, with the help of very creative cupids, for the arrival of the dashing and equally colorful male centaurs. The only centaur not being prepared by these cupids, but rather assisting in the process, is their Black servant aptly named Sunflower. Named after a member of *asteraceae* or *compositae* family, sunflowers are known by a number of common names including "Black-eyed Susan," "Yellow Daisy" and "Golden Jerusalem," but this flower is also known as a Niggerhead.[17] Given the visual conversation that Disney engages regarding Blackness, it unlikely that their choice of name was coincidental. Sunflower reflects quintessential coon features: dark skin, big lips, wide eyes and a pickaninny hairstyle. She is a pseudo-centaur because she is part donkey, not horse. The choice of a donkey is yet another not-so-subtle commentary on race as the scientific name for donkey is *equus africanus asinus* (2008). Referencing its undomesticated ancestor, Disney's animated Darwinism makes it clear that Sunflower could only be a servant because she is aesthetically, physically and genetically inferior to the women she serves. Sunflower's main job is to assist in the beautification rituals of the women she serves by polishing hooves, decorating tails and holding a flower bridle while the more beautiful and refined centaur women jockey for position to see the approaching men.

We meet the two other Black centaurs in the latter half of *Pastoral* with the arrival of Dionysus. The god of wine arrives to great fanfare and in his own parade, which in modern terms looks more like an entourage. Dionysus enters this centaur community with a Black servant on each side. Their main role is to ensure that he stays cool through continuous fanning and that his wine never runs out. Unlike Sunflower, these nameless women who are part-zebra, which are indigenous to Africa, are brown-skinned, their hair is coiffed to perfection and aesthetically they more closely resemble their White centaur counterparts. Given that they do not possess all of the qualities of Sunflower nor the women she serves, these servants present the embodiment of the exotic

Other. Although they are there to serve the god of wine, by making them beautiful, Disney seems to be suggesting that these women literally work for the pleasure of Dionysus who by nature is passionate and overindulgent.

Earlier in this chapter I addressed Disney's overtly racist characterization of Blackness. When Disney addressed the same issue, it was no less demeaning nor damaging as evidenced by the film *Dumbo* (1941). On its face *Dumbo* tells the endearing story about the trials and tribulations of baby circus elephant Jumbo Jr., renamed Dumbo by Mrs. Jumbo's persnickety girlfriends, who is born with enormous ears. But it is also a tale about embracing difference, and how a seemingly simple gesture can change the attitude of the people around you. However that concept does not appear to apply to African Americans. In *Dumbo*, Disney offers viewers their standard caricatured portrayals of Blackness in addition to mocking legislation aimed at moving African Americans closer to first-class citizenship in the United States.

Early in the film we see African American laborers in song while erecting the circus tents during a storm. Disney's portrayal of this scene reads more like inmates on the chain gang than hardworking men earning a living. In tune to the rhythm of clanking metal, broad-backed men pound stakes into the mud. Although working in the dark and the rain with the help of elephants may seem tough, they chant with irrational joy. They invoke a common African American colloquialism known as "can't see to can't see," which refers to the notion of working from before the sun rises till after the sun sets. The phrase was most often used by the African American community since enslavement. Even the workers toil ceaselessly, even though they are illiterates who don't just work but "slave" and even though they admittedly waste their money on payday, they are—pause for a full-toothed grin here—oh, so happy!

Traditionally, laborers travel with carnivals and circuses to build and break down the tents. However, when you take into consideration the historically limited positive portrayals of Black men in cinema, for them to proclaim their lack of education and celebrate their seemingly never-ending work day with childlike joy paints a picture of Blackness commonly found on the silver screen. As scholar Donald Bogle details in his text, *Toms, Coons, Mulattoes, Mammies & Bucks: An Interpretive History of Blacks in American Films:* "Fun was poked at the American Negro by presenting him as either a nitwit or a childlike lackey."[18]

Disney continues their critique of Blackness through caricatures, but in the following scene they also make a mockery of African Americans' efforts towards attaining equality. Toward the end of the film we are introduced to a motley crew of characters in the form of black crows in the scene where Dumbo is sleeping it off after inadvertently drinking water from a bucket into which a group of circus performers engaging in a post-performance celebration knocked a full champagne bottle earlier that evening. Led by the main crow *Jim*, referencing racial segregation laws enacted in the late 19th and early 20th centuries, he and the other crows, which remain nameless, offer a performance reminiscent of turn-of-the-century minstrel shows.

The crows are culturally identified through Disney's efforts to reproduce authentic African American speech through word choice, phonology and mannerisms. One of the crows, dressed in a hat and vest from a zoot suit, starts it off by declaring, *"My my, why dis is mose eeregulah,"* as they sit on a tree limb above speculating about a sleeping Dumbo and his mouse friend Timothy. In response, a bespectacled crow asks: *"Dey ain't dead is dey?"* His rotund partner responds, *"Nooo! Dead people don't snore ... or do dey?"* At this point they stop looking below and turn to each other and chatter among themselves about the possible scenarios that landed an elephant and a mouse on a branch below theirs.

The conspiracy theories only end when Jim lands on the branch, wearing a tiny bowler hat, shirt, vest and spats with no shoes while asking, *"Uh, wut's all the rookus? C'mon step aside brotha,"* as he clears the limb so he can parade back and forth peppering his *crow*nies with questions as he smokes a big stogie. Calling each other *brotha* points more to Walt Disney's affection for Joel Chandler Harris' *Uncle Remus* (1904) series featuring Bre'r Fox, and Bre'r Rabbit, as opposed to kinship. Jim even calls Timothy "brotha," although the mouse vehemently rejects that label. Ultimately they fall to the ground and when Timothy suggests that Dumbo can fly as a rationale for waking up in such a unique location, Jim and his homeboys laugh and make fun of the very idea. As the music builds for Jim to begin his song, "When I See an Elephant Fly," he lists all the unusual things he has seen but declares, *"But I be dun seen 'bout everything, when I see an elephant fly."* His declaration is quickly questioned by one of the other crows off camera, *"Wut chu say, boy?"* Calling Jim Crow *"boy"* offers a commentary on Disney's views about *de facto* segregation legislation. Given the history of terrorism and violence experienced by men, women and children in pursuit of their rights as citizens of this country, reducing a significant part of African American—dare I say, American—history to a bunch of coons masquerading as crows led by a leader who responds to being called "boy" is problematic at best.

Still Wishing Upon a Star

Ultimately Disney's use of caricatured representations of Blackness serves to confirm the status quo perceptions about Black people, post–Reconstruction, and set the stage for a pattern of racist portrayals that continue through the 21st century. The impact of this imagery not only affects the perceptions of the people portrayed in this manner, but it also impacts how these same people view their own culture. Disney's *Song of the South* (1946) is an excellent illustration of how a film plays such a role of self-critique. This film's concept and execution are based upon racist discourse about African Americans.

Specifically it is the bastardization of characters taken from traditional African folktales that survived the Middle Passage and were transformed by enslaved Africans in this country. Disney's re-interpretation of these treasured folkloric characters is so offensive that it forever changed how African Americans view them. As a result, characters including Bre'r Rabbit and Bre'r Fox, originally celebrated by African Diasporan people for their endlessly cunning ways of outwitting abusive whites, were later depicted by white writers as simply lazy and foolish. These centuries-old characters, born in ancient Africa as animal metaphors for crafty, sage survivalists, have been silenced and are no longer an active part of African American folklore and culture.

Disney continues their utilization of caricatured representations, although today's images also include diverse communities who often share the designation of Other. Over time their portrayals have become even subtler and more sophisticated such as King Louis, the jive talking orangutan whose self-hatred and desire to become a white man is on display when he proclaims "I want to be like you" in *The Jungle Book* (1967). Also exemplified are Disney's Sebastian, the ambiguous Caribbean crustacean and servant to King Triton in *The Little Mermaid* (1989), and Frozone, the one-dimensional brutal Black buck superhero sidekick to Mr. Incredible in *The Incredibles* (2004). Disney's 2009 *The Princess and the Frog* earned its share of criticism about the garbled English of Cajun fireflies and a princess who spends most of the movie as an amphibian. I still search for images of myself, and now, my daughter, in Disney; I still long to see diverse representations of diverse people. I imagine a blockbuster film featuring everyday people—Latinas without sass, Asians without choppy English and Africans without rhythm or rage. This is my *Fantasia*, perfectly suitable for animation, with villains and heroines characterized by their character and not misrepresented by caricatures, color or culture. Perhaps, one day, Disney will make new magic, complete with enough sparkle for everyone, and finally fulfill my wish for images that look, and feel, familiar and beautiful.

Notes

1. Disney's African American characters as well as those coded as Black are often marked by speech patterns that are meant to convey what is believed to be African American English (also described as African American Black Vernacular), but are often distorted and employed in a manner to illustrate deficiencies; e.g., lack of education. For further reading on this topic please see: Green, Lisa. *African American English: A Linguistic Introduction.* MA: Cambridge University Press; Billings, Andrew. "Beyond the Ebonics Debate: Attitudes about Black and Standard American English." *Journal of Black Studies* 36.1 (2005) 68–81.

2. *Plane Crazy* and *Gallopin' Gaucho*, both released in 1928, were the first and second films that featured Mickey Mouse. However both films were silent. It was Disney's debut of *Steamboat Willie*, the first animated feature with sound, that same year at the Colony Theater in Manhattan that is credited with the arrival of Mickey.

3. Deborah Willis and Carla Williams, *The Black Female Body: A Photographic History.* Philadelphia: Temple University Press, 2002.

4. For purposes of this essay, Black, African American and African Diasporan/African

Descended are used interchangeably although each term suggests a different emphasis on terms that are utilized. Black indicates political and cultural emphasis from a nationalist perspective, African American is used as a continental identity where politically and culturally their views may not emanate from a nationalist paradigm. African Disaporan/African Descended is both continental and political due to its direct identification with Africa but also denotes kinship with all peoples whose identity emerges from their African heritage, by birth, kinship or the legacy of the transatlantic slave trade.

5. August F. Saint-Aubin, "A Grammar of Black Masculinity: A Body of Science." *The Journal of Men's Studies* 10.3 (2002), 247–270.

6. http://commons.wikimedia.org/wiki/File:Frontespizio_Lamento_del_duca_Galeazzo_Maria_-Sforza,_1444–1473-,_1476.jpg. The web address suggests that this is a frontispiece, but, according to the file information, the image is on the title page.

7. Here, the words "bad, ugly, emotional, savage and lazy" become synonymous with "Blackness" when explained from a racially-biased view. "Blackness" here—unlike the "Blackness" often juxtaposed with "African-American" or used as an identity of pride—also becomes code for an impure, dirty, underworld racial identifier.

8. Thomas Jefferson, *Notes on the State of Virginia*. Philadelphia: Pritchard and Hall, 1788, 264–265.

9. "Reframing the Color Line: Race and the Visual Culture in the Atlantic World." Exhibition, William L. Clements Library and Center for Afroamerican and African Studies, University of Michigan, Oct. 19, 2009–Feb. 19, 2010.

10. Joel Chandler Harris' "Uncle Remus" books became classics for their supposed authentic offerings of African American vernacular, storytelling and cultural detail. The heroic trickster tales of "Bre'r Rabbit, Bre'r Bear and Bre'r Coon," for example, emerged from his writings.

11. The official licensed items were a stencil set, candy bar and button.

12. http://disney.go.com/vault/archives/characters/oswald/oswald.html

13. When the Whitney Museum relocated uptown in 1953, five of the murals were sold to the New Britain Museum of American Art in Connecticut.

14. Robert W. Brockway, "The Mask of Mickey Mouse: Symbol of a Generation," *The Journal of Popular Culture* 22.4 (1989), 25.

15. *Fantasia* was re-released in 1946, 1956, 1963, 1969, 1977, 1982, 1985 and 1990, then released on video in 1991. In 2000 Disney released *Fantasia 2000*, a new version of *Fantasia*, on DVD.

16. Also known by his Roman name, Bacchus.

17. http://www.nature-and-flower-pictures.com/black-eyed-susan.html

18. Donald Bogle, *Toms, Coons, Mulattoes, Mammies & Bucks: An Interpretive History of Blacks in American Films*, 4th ed. New York: Continuum, 2001, 4.

Bibliography

Apgar, Garry. "Mickey Mouse at Seventy-Five." *The Weekly Standard* 224 (Nov. 2003): 31–34.

Beethoven, Ludwig van. *Symphony No. 6 in F, Op.68*, 1808.

Bogle, Donald. *Toms, Coons, Mulattoes, Mammies and Bucks: An Interpretive History of Blacks in American Films*. New York: Continuum, 2002.

Brockway, Robert W. "The Masks of Mickey Mouse: Symbol of a Generation." *Journal of Popular Culture* 22:4 (1989): 25–34.

Brooks, Shelton. *Darktown Strutter's Ball*. Vinyl recording. Leo Feist, 1917.

Crawford, Philip C. "Oooh! I Must Be Dreaming: The Delightfully Strange and Marvelous Worlds of America's Great Fantasist, Winsor McCay." *Knowledge Quest* 35:5 (2007): 58–61.

Da Lampugnano, Giovanni Andrea. *Lamento del duca Galeazzo Maria–Sforza*, 1476. Wikimedia Commons, 23 July 2009.

Documenting the American South. University Library, University of North Carolina at

Chapel Hill, accessed 1 Aug. 2009. <http://docsouth.unc.edu/southlit/jefferson/menu.html>.

Fain, Sammy, orch. "What Made the Red Man Red." By Sammy Cahn. 1953.

Harris, Joel Chandler. *The Tar Baby and Other Rhymes of Uncle Remus.* Bedford: D. Applewood and Company, 1904.

Heer, Jeet. "Little Nemo in Comicsland." *Virginia Quarterly Review* 82:2 (2006): 104–21.

Jefferson, Thomas. *Notes on the State of Virginia.* Philadelphia: Prichard and Hall, 1788.

Porter, Cole. "You're the Top." *Anything Goes.* Alfred Publishing, 1934. Vinyl recording.

"Reframing the Color Line: Race and the Visual Culture in the Atlantic World." Clements Library, University of Michigan. http://theclementslibrary.blogspot.com/2009/10/exhibition-and-symposium-reframing.html. October 19 2009–February 19, 2010.

Reitz, Elizabeth J., and Elizabeth S. Wing. *Zooarchaeology.* Cambridge: Cambridge University Press, 2008.

Saint-Aubin, August F. "A Grammar of Black Masculinity: A Body of Science." *The Journal of Men's Studies.* 10:3 (2002): 247–270.

Willis, Deborah, and Carla Williams. *The Black Female Body: A Photographic History.* Philadelphia: Temple University Press, 2002.

Saludos Amigos *and* The Three Caballeros: *The Representation of Latin America in Disney's "Good Neighbor" Films*

KAREN S. GOLDMAN

This essay examines representations of Latin America and situational Latin American identities in the feature-length Disney films *Saludos Amigos* (1942) and *The Three Caballeros* (1945). These films have come to be known as "Good Neighbor" films because, in contrast to earlier Disney animations that focused on children's stories and family entertainment, they were produced with a clear political and public relations mandate: to foster goodwill between U.S. and Latin American audiences. In a notable scene from the 16mm documentary short *South of the Border with Disney*, cartoonist Norm Ferguson is shown in Santiago, furiously sketching page after page of Pluto drawings to give away to a seemingly endless line of Chilean children. The footage, shot by Walt himself in 1942, represents a concise visual summary of the underlying set of relationships between the Disney Studio and its Latin American subjects. While the artist provides cartoon images from a widely recognized compendium of characters, the filmmaker captures new, "authentic" images of inhabitants of an exotic locale. These are in turn framed for consumption, and repackaged as a Hollywood product for U.S. consumers as well as those same exotic Others that the films putatively seek to represent.

From a structural point of view, the films are divided into discrete segments, which in *Saludos Amigos* are linked by the travel footage of Disney and his entourage, or "El grupo." In *The Three Caballeros*, the narrative is more organically connected by the travels of Disney's cartoon surrogate, Donald Duck, and his avian friends. In both, we can identify several central strategies

23

that allow the narrative to contain the largely unfamiliar and potentially threatening degree of difference that the Latin American world signified to U.S.
audiences. First, the "Good Neighbor" films are intertextual: that is, they rely
on the audience's familiarity with a variety of external sources. The literary
term "intertextuality" was introduced by Julia Kristeva, who describes two axes
for each cultural text: a horizontal axis that connects the author and reader,
and a vertical axis, which locates the text in an infinite dialogue with other
texts.[1] Robert Stam, referring to the intertextuality of cinematic texts remarks
that it is "as if both filmmaker and spectator were members of a vast audio-
visual library."[2] Both films contain references to a diversity of texts and genres
from this "library," calling on the spectator's previously garnered knowledge
of film genres and characters. *Saludos Amigos* provides, for example, a satirical
wink at then-popular film travelogues, and also presents itself as a quasi-
ethnographic documentary, in the style of Robert Flaherty, Merian C. Cooper
and Ernest Schoedsack, to bolster its claim to realism. Both films also draw
on Disney's collection of widely recognized characters as well as the Disney
brand itself. The spectator's previously-established expectations of Disney animation endow these films with an aura of legitimacy and perceived quality to
which no other filmmaker of the time could lay claim.

In addition, and in an effort to both personalize the films (making them
appear to come directly from Walt Disney's authorial hand) and to de-
personalize them (ultimately reflecting the Disney model of keeping the actual
artists anonymous), *Saludos Amigos* and *The Three Caballeros* exhibit a surprisingly high degree of reflexivity, underscoring their own means of production,
and intentionally uncovering the nature of cartoon illusion itself. Reflexivity
blurs the divisions along the vertical axis of a text, and make visible what by
generic custom had largely been invisible: the presence of the author in the
text itself. Self-reflexivity in animation was certainly not new to audiences in
the 1940s. References to the "real" cartoonist and/or the cartoon genre itself
can be found from the early days of animation. Characters from Max Fleish-
man's 1930s "Out of the Inkwell" series and Otto Mesmer's "Krazy Kat" often
interacted with the animated "cartoonist." Similarly, in Tex Avery's cartoons,
spectators are occasionally addressed directly, and asides are often spoken
specifically to the complicit spectator, without the knowledge of the other
characters.

Early Disney cartoons were also sometimes self-reflexive, including interventions by the animator's voice or hand in cartoon shorts. But the technique
of self-reflexivity was first introduced in an animated feature in 1941 with Disney's *The Reluctant Dragon*. Contrary to the traditional and unstated "rules"
of animated film, *The Reluctant Dragon* is deliberately and self-consciously
reflexive. It begins by depicting in live-action the animator, Robert Benchley.
Benchley, who, in the scripted process of searching for Walt Disney himself
to pitch his cartoon idea, learns about the workings of animation and the

process of converting written narrative into cartoons. The film then launches into the actual cartoon featuring the dragon. Perhaps what is most remarkable about the inclusion of the cartoonist in *The Reluctant Dragon* is that the film's production coincides with the animator's strike that was taking place at the Disney studios. The strike was principally about dissatisfaction over unpaid work, overtime and job security, but another very central issue for the strikers was the lack of attribution and credit for individual artists. All work produced at the Disney studios was signed by only one creator, and that was Walt Disney, in the unmistakable signature that has become the international logo of the company.

And while *Saludos Amigos* and *The Three Caballeros* were commissioned, in part, to dispel negative stereotyping of Latin Americans in Hollywood cinema, close analysis reveals that the films actually promote other, no less inaccurate stereotypes, and, in particular, underscore the longstanding unequal relationship between the U.S. and Latin America. They continue to depict the flow of cultural texts from north to south as natural and unequivocal. Furthermore, *Saludos Amigos* and *The Three Caballeros* code the nations and people of Latin America as exotic, idealized and sexualized. This last category, especially, has been the focus of numerous commentators and critics. Film and cultural critics José Piedra, Jean Franco and Julianne Burton have, from different perspectives, all analyzed the many segmented sequences of *The Three Caballeros* as the staging ground for a gendered narrative of U.S. masculine-identified hegemony vis à vis a highly feminized representation of Latin America. Piedra focuses on the sexualization of Latin America as an extension of U.S. financial interests in the region, the real motor behind this libidinal economy:

> Ultimately the U.S., self-styled as a good neighbor, stands as an incestuous *padre de familias* who, while ostensibly teaching his Pan-American children to forge their own nations, libidinally encourages their dependency. The system even teaches us Latin Americans how to become the "child brides" of the United States. Thus we Latins in and around the U.S. backyard become not only the poor live-in neighbor but the tantalizing girl-next-door—not to mention the fruit-next-door—so dear to the United Fruit Company's heart.[3]

Burton, on the other hand, likens Disney animation to an unmediated reality beyond objective experience that "can also be the site of unbridled expressions of the individual and collective unconscious ... cartoons in this sense can be understood as a kind of dreamer's dreaming, the unconscious of the unconscious."[4]

In their landmark 1971 study *How to Read Donald Duck: Imperialist Ideology in the Disney Comic*, Ariel Dorfman and Armand Mattelart pointed out that Disney represents another kind of dream, more a reflection of the way Disney products work to construct meanings, and ultimately reproduce, in the words of Henry A. Giroux, "ideologically loaded fantasies."[5] According to

Dorfman and Mattelart, this invitation to fantasize about the Other represents a grave threat to the cultural autonomy of Latin American nations. The threat is not so much that Disney products embody the "American way of life" as the "American Dream of Life":

> It is the manner in which the U.S. dreams and redeems itself, and then imposes that dream upon others for its own salvation, which poses the danger for the dependent countries. It forces us Latin Americans to see ourselves *as they see us*.[6]

While Dorfman and Mattelart's analysis is primarily focused on the Donald Duck comic strip, and their interpretation of Donald may seem limited today, the point of their latter statement is central to understanding the "Good Neighbor" films. Even at their most authentic, the films offer up an externally-constructed, highly condensed and almost parodical representation of Latin American national identities *for* Latin American audiences. Both films situate Latin Americans as exotic Others in contrast to a normative (U.S.) hegemonic culture, which is always eager to incorporate them—literally, through the figures that are "animated," literally brought to life through the magic of animation, and figuratively, through the many ways that they are framed as "real" by the film narrative.

The question of realism in Disney cartoons has always been a complicated one, since from the moment the studio embarked on the production of its first animated feature, *Snow White*, the Disney studio strove to produce cartoons that rival live action footage in their ability to depict realistic characters and backgrounds, all while maintaining the "magic" of animation. The emphasis on producing animation that closely approximated the look and movement of live humans and animals came to be known in the Disney context as "the illusion of life." It is described in detail in both a 1981 book and "Wonderful World of Disney" television special.[7] In the 1940s, cartoons were generally flat and characters lacked personality and depth. Disney's aim was to create an animated scene that presented an almost photographic fidelity to "real" life and therefore could "forge that emotional bond with the audience-an animated universe he called 'the plausible impossible' that stretched natural laws without actually breaking them."[8] To achieve this aim, Disney artists studied photographs, live models and live action film to accurately reproduce the look of landscapes and backgrounds and especially the seamless, natural way that bodies (human and animal) moved. The studio had already been making use of the Disney–developed technology of the multi-plane camera, which created the illusion of depth by layering animation cels[9] one over another and photographing them from above. The desire to animate as realistically as possible even led to the use of the "rotoscope," a device that allows live action footage to be traced and used for animation drawings.

Disney's "illusion of life" animation as a form of cinema art has been widely commented and frequently criticized. In the opinion of film theorist

Sigfried Kracauer, animation is a form of cinema that does not depend on a photographic reproduction of the real; i.e., nothing in the cartoon exists in real life, except in the very literal sense that the camera photographically records a collection of drawings. Thus, animators do not actually reproduce life or reality and therefore do not make use of what Kracauer terms the cinema's "inherent affinities." Kracauer continues:

> Unlike photographs or live action, animation is called upon to picture what is not real—that which never happens. (....) Walt Disney's increasing attempts to express fantasy in realistic terms are aesthetically questionable precisely because they comply with the cinematic approach. There is a growing tendency toward camera-reality in his later full length films. Peopled with the counterparts of real landscapes and real human beings, they are not so much "drawings brought to life" as life reproduced in drawings.[10]

In Kracauer's view, animation is an inherently fantastic form of cinema and therefore Disney's attempt to depict cinematic realism, either by the "illusion of life" techniques or by creating hybrid forms, such as those featured in the "Good Neighbor" films, was necessarily a poor format to exploit the aesthetic qualities of the medium. And while Kracauer's estimation of Disney's "realism" is wholly negative, his description of the realism that characterizes these films is quite accurate. Disney's intent was indeed to "reproduce life in drawings" as well as in live-action and hybrid forms.

But the assumption that this reflects a deliberate aesthetic decision with regard to the "Good Neighbor" Disney films is questionable. The live action footage, by virtue of its photographic realism clearly endowed the films with an aura of authenticity. But the inclusion of live action footage was, in the end, a financial decision. The highly realistic animation such as that featured in the early, "illusion of life" films—*Snow White, Pinocchio, Fantasia, Dumbo* and *Bambi*—was extremely labor-intensive and very expensive. It required thousands of individual cels to be hand drawn and inked. In contrast, live action sequences shot on location allowed the films to be extended significantly in length without the additional cost of animation or filming on a studio set. Thus, the preference for hybrid forms and the use of live-action footage in *Saludos Amigos* and *The Three Caballeros* point to a central priority of the Disney Studios at the time: keeping production costs low while maintaining quality and assuring a profit. The studio had been experiencing continued financial troubles due in part to Walt's mismanagement, and in part to the high cost of producing its recent cartoon features, which left the Disney with a deficit of more than a half of a million dollars in 1942.[11] In addition, as mentioned above, in 1941 the Disney studio was in the throes of a bitter strike led by the animators union. The company was facing, for the first time since its establishment in 1923, the prospect of pay cuts and layoffs. Disgruntled animators picketed the studio daily and refused to work, creating an even more dire financial outlook for Disney. In short, the company was in need of a way to continue making films quickly and with a reduced labor pool. The combination of live action and animation was one response to this problem. Another was to rely on external funding to cover the production costs. The U.S. government's "Good Neighbor" policy was just the thing to afford Disney the opportunity to turn a profit with little capital investment.

Although the "Good Neighbor Policy" dates back to the presidency of Herbert Hoover, it was President Franklin Delano Roosevelt in 1933, who, determined to improve relations with the nations of Central and South America, adopted the "Good Neighbor" as the official U.S. foreign policy vis-à-vis Latin America. Its stated mission was to emphasize cooperation and trade rather than military force to maintain stability in the hemisphere. In his inaugural address on March 4, 1933, Roosevelt stated: "In the field of world policy I would dedicate this nation to the policy of the good neighbor—the neighbor who resolutely respects himself and, because he does so, respects the rights of others." Roosevelt's Secretary of State, Cordell Hull, participated in the Montevideo Conference of December 1933, where he backed a declaration favored by most nations of the Western Hemisphere: "No state has the right to intervene in the internal or external affairs of another." In December Roosevelt stated, "The definite policy of the United States from now on is one opposed to armed intervention."[12] Obviously, this emphasis on good neighborliness versus interventionism is open to question, given the continued U.S. military operations in Latin America. But the policy did address a number of economic issues that had been troublesome for U.S-Latin American relations. Hull's policies of low tariffs improved the economies of the Latin American countries that had been hurt by the protectionist Hawley-Smoot Tariff of 1930, especially in Cuba, where low prices on sugar had previously made it difficult to sell to the United States.

Near the end of the 1930s, the U.S. government encountered reason to fear that the Nazi communications machine was making inroads in Latin America. Already disconcerting was the fact that in the early 1940s German interests held ownership or majority control over the telephone systems in Argentina, Ecuador, Uruguay, Paraguay, southern Chile and Mexico.[13] Anatole Litvak's 1939 anti–Nazi film *Confessions of a Nazi Spy* had been banned in eighteen Latin American countries. In 1940, most Latin American governments also banned Charles Chaplin's *The Great Dictator*, understood universally as an exhortation to oppose Hilter's tyranny, and many were allowing Nazi propaganda films (such as the fictional film described in Argentine writer Manuel Puig's novel *The Kiss of the Spider Woman*) to be shown freely in commercial cinemas. To counter that troubling trend, President Roosevelt in 1940 named Nelson Rockefeller, who had extensive experience in Latin America because of the many business holdings he possessed there, to head the Office of the Coordinator of Inter-American Affairs. One of Rockefeller's first actions was to create a Motion Picture Division that would concentrate its efforts on seeing that Hollywood films, which had presented almost exclusively negative stereotypical images of Latin Americans, would now present positive ones. The goal of the Motion Picture Division would be to present assumedly more authentic images of Latin America and Latin Americans. To head this division, Rockefeller chose John Hay Whitney, a vice-president of the Museum of Modern Art, a financial backer of many films, and, like Walt Disney himself, an enthusiastic polo player.

The Coordinator's office sent various Hollywood celebrities to visit Latin American countries to take advantage of their celebrity and charisma to win over this public. Hollywood producers were even asked to include Latin American themes in their movies to attract Spanish–speaking viewers and to bolster good will between the continents. Twentieth Century–Fox released a string of films highlighting Latin American topics, including *Down Argentine Way* (1940), *That Night in Rio* and *Weekend in Havana* (both 1941). Following Fox's success, other studios followed suit. Latin music soared in popularity, and U.S. audiences across the nation became familiar with entertainers like Xavier Cugat and Desi Arnaz. Nonetheless, it was clear that the strategy of advancing the "Good Neighbor" policy by including Latin American themes in Hollywood films was, by any measure, a dismal failure. Instead of promoting a sense of pride and good will in Latin American audiences, the inaccurate and stereotypical images enraged them. J.B. Kaufman, one of Disney's official historians, commented on Universal Pictures' *Argentine Nights*: "When the film was shown in Buenos Aires, with its wildly inaccurate portrayal of Argentina and its jumble of Spanish dialects, audiences were so infuriated that riot police were called to quell the disturbance, and the feature was pulled after two days."[14]

In an effort to stave off this kind of blatant and insensitive inaccuracies, the Office of the Coordinator of Inter-American Affairs agreed to finance not only the Disney Studio's "Good Neighbor" film production itself, but also travel for Disney and a group of 15 artists through Latin America to research, draw and generally familiarize themselves with the cultures and the geography of the continent. Disney artists, musicians and other employees received instruction in the history, customs, music, art and literature of the various regions as though they were completing a research seminar on the topic. Perhaps most important, the Office arranged visits with Latin American comics, artists and musicians. J.B. Kaufman, one of the Walt Disney Family Foundation's official historians, commented glowingly on Disney's efforts at depicting an authentic Latin American reality:

> Walt was already on the right track with in-depth research on individual countries. (....) Let other Hollywood studios commit their careless cultural mistakes: the Disney studio would consistently strike a responsive chord with Latin American audiences by picturing their cultures in authentic detail.[15]

Did Disney in fact, provide a more authentic representation by providing attention to detail, or manage to avoid committing "careless cultural mistakes" as Kaufman asserts the other studios did? In response, I note that that the representations of the diverse Other in the Disney animations are far from careless, and do not project the non-intentionality of the term "mistake." The Latin Americans in the "Good Neighbor" films are without exception depicted as happy, friendly and frequently child-like. Disney's gaze at the indigenous Other is clearly an idealized and exoticizing one, which aims less to provide a faithful representation of an historical reality than to make it attractive and as such to render it less threatening: that which is diverse becomes positive. And the inclusion of diverse elements in the films are highly selective: some indigenous elements are presented (such as the Andean populations around Lake Titicaca in *Saludos Amigos*) and others elided (such as any intimation of African heritage in any of the Brazilian segments). With the sole exception of the documentary scenes in *Saludos Amigos*, which offer a picture-postcard representation of "modern" cities such as Rio de Janeiro and Buenos Aires, neither history, nor political or social reality infects the idealized and exoticized universe of Disney's Latin America. As Jean Franco notes: "This was a Latin America that people could live with...."[16]

This idealized celebration of the idealized Other, and its positioning in a timeless, faceless, classless context, however, is in fact simply the other face of its polar opposite: ethnocentrism. Débora Krischke Leitão's remarks regarding Brazilian exoticism in French fashion are applicable here:

> Ranging from suspicion to hostility, [ethnocentrism] rejects all cultural forms that are different from one's own. In this regard, ethnocentrism and exoticism are drawn closer together. Even if different in content—one valuing, the other repealing—both attitudes are less a statement about the *other* than about oneself.[17]

Ethnocentrism can be described as the understanding of one's own culture as hegemonic, the dominant standard against which, from the perspective of the creator/viewer, all others are measured. Consumption of the exotic is not only the process of consuming products from *elsewhere*; it is also a process of differentiating between *us* and *them*.

And indeed the opening shot of *Saludos Amigos* could not be more direct in its positioning of Latin America as Other in relation to the dominant position of Disney—the enunciative "I" in the "Saludos" of the title. The opening screen is dominated by a written message, superimposed on an outline map of Latin America, and signed by Walt himself: "With sincere appreciation for the courtesy and cooperation shown us by the artists, musicians, and our many friends in Latin America." An animated airplane flies over the map, standing in stark contrast to the subsequent live-action scene of a gleaming silver Pam Am airplane that Walt and his artists are boarding (a scene that, in keeping with the simulacrum that characterized many subsequent Disney products, was actually shot in the parking lot of the Disney Studio in Burbank). The animated airplane flies over the map, showing all of Latin America as a colorful region of tidy cities, quaint villages, mountains and rivers, all fitting nicely into a camera frame. When the plane arrives at Lake Titicaca, the format suddenly switches to live-action. Like the popular Fox Movietone newsreels and travelogues, the subsequent scenes are accompanied by an authoritative male voice-over. This is the intertextual cue for the viewer to switch into the documentary mode: the live action sequences resemble nothing so much as Disney's 1950s nature documentaries such as *The Living Desert* and *The Vanishing Prairie*, which feature footage of real animals and flora. In addition, by showing the animators who are the same creative force behind the film we are watching, the film reflects back on itself, and invites the audience to observe the creative presence behind the animation they are watching.

While this self-reflexive technique is often employed as a distancing technique by modernist authors and filmmakers to "elicit an active thinking spectator rather than a passive consumer,"[18] the effect here is rather the opposite. By couching the exotic Other in a generic format that is familiar for audiences, and exposing the American artists as the "authors" of the segment, the diverse elements are contained in the narrative and rendered less threatening.

To complement the neutralization of the exotic difference of the Other, the U.S. "visitor" not only encounters, but also appropriates the exotic cultural artifacts. The first Latin American people we see in the film are the Bolivian inhabitants of the *altiplano* assembled for market day. A Bolivian woman, dressed in a traditional colorful *pollera* and an undersized bowler hat, carries a large bowl on her head and a baby, wrapped in a long shawl, on her back. The live action is magically and self-reflexively transformed into a pastel drawing, showing the freckled hand of the artist filling in the color of the now mimetically-rendered woman. As strains of an Andean flute are introduced in the soundtrack and the image returns to a live action frame, the voice-over remarks: "Their music is strange and exotic." This statement summarizes the representation of the Latin American Other throughout the film, which is appropriated by Disney's various surrogates, and adjusted to suit the perceptions of the hegemonic "us" of the narration. The point is unambiguously exemplified in the following scene, in which Donald Duck permits us to see "The land of the Incas through the eyes of a celebrated North American tourist." (Contemporary viewers will recognize the depictions of the Andean landscape, the llamas, and even the people from 2000s Disney feature *The Emperor's New Groove*.) Wearing an explorer's helmet in the style of H.M. Stanley, Donald, golf clubs in tow, engages in a series of visual gags on the shores of Lake Titicaca. Donald produces a still camera and begins photographing examples of "local color," injecting yet another moment of reflexivity, and pointing again to the unseen presence of both the filmmakers and the animators introduced at the beginning of the film. In one of many moments of cultural appropriation, Donald exchanges the young "Incan" boy's wool cap, poncho and *flauta* for his own helmet and camera. "The visitor is never satisfied until he tries on the native costume," quips the voice-over. Donald initially plays the "strange exotic music" of the *altiplano*, but then switches to a jazzy tune that is sounds unmistakably like a lively Hollywood sound track. This small example again illustrates the dynamic underlying the "Good Neighbor" films: The image of the exotic Other (the boy) is captured by a familiar character (Donald's camera), rendered unthreatening through cultural appropriation (Donald's Americanization of the strange, exotic music) and then repackaged for international consumption as a Hollywood product by a studio that represents the best of American capitalism (the feature itself).

There are numerous additional examples of this pattern of intertextuality, reflexivity and cultural appropriation in the remainder of the film, but suffice it here to point out a most compelling one: the Argentine segment, and especially the representation of Goofy as gaucho. The segment begins with live action "postcard" shots of Buenos Aires, but quickly moves to the "lush, windswept plains of the Pampas." This is followed by a segment introducing Argentine artist, F. Molina Campos, best known for his folkloric paintings of gauchos. Disney's pre-production collaboration with Campos was supposed to assure an authentic representation of the gaucho. But, in the end, the camera only briefly focuses on Campos' paintings during a visit to his studio. In contrast, it is the Disney animator who is shown sketching the dancing gauchos. John Rose, Disney's liaison to the Office of the Coordinator for Inter-American Affairs, in a private memo to the New York office remarked: "The frank truth of the matter is that we don't *need* the guy at all- and that blunt fact applies to all the other South American talent we had lined up."[19]

The next segment, again underscoring the *us/them* structure of the film, "compares the life of the Argentine gaucho to that of our own cowboy." Goofy begins the segment as a stereotypical cowboy figure in Texas, flies over the map of Latin America to the Pampas, and, like Donald in the previous segment, dons a traditional gaucho costume. Again, what follows is a series of visual gags punctuated by descriptions of gaucho dances. In the end, Goofy flies safely back to "his prairie homeland" and the "natural" order of things is restored. Again, the exotic Other is neutralized through its elision with a familiar intertextual figure. The self-reflexive format emphasizes the fact that the normative position of the film is "us," and not "them." The last segment of *Saludos Amigos* points forward toward *The Three Caballeros*, with the introduction of both the figure of the seductive (and anonymous) Latin Beauty, and Donald's second caballero, the Brazilian parrot Zé Carioca.

The Three Caballeros begins with Donald Duck tearing open a series of wrapped boxes. Donald (Disney's best-known character after Mickey Mouse), like Goofy in *Saludos Amigos* appeals to the audience's intertextual familiarity, providing an unequivocally U.S. perspective from which to venture into the unknown. The boxes are labeled in Spanish: "Best wishes to Donald Duck on his birthday, Friday the 13th, from his friends in Latin America." Self-reflexivity makes its first appearance here, as the first box contains a movie projector, a screen and a film reel. As he subsequently screens these films, Donald repositions himself: no longer just a cartoon subject but a spectator; focusing his "all-American" gaze at a collection of tropical cartoon birds, followed by the unlikely stories of a penguin who loves warm weather and a young gaucho's flying donkey.

At this point, the film-inside-a-film concludes and Donald opens the next gift. This time, the intertextual "container" is a large encyclopedia-like book entitled *Brazil,* out of which, when opened, pop a collection of Brazilian sequences. The most significant of these, from the point of view of diversity in Disney, is the scene that features the first "Latin Baby," of the film: a live-action Aurora Miranda, singing "Os quindins de Yayá." This is the first instance in this film of a hybrid format, and the first one in Disney since the 1923 production of a very primitive *Alice in Wonderland* featuring a superimposed live action Alice. Miranda appears over a cartoon background of the quaint colonial streets of Bahia. Again, we encounter the key strategy of intertextuality: with her exaggerated headdress and long, flowing skirt, it would be nearly impossible for audiences not to associate Aurora with Carmen, her more famous sister. Carmen Miranda had already become an iconic signifier, both for her flamboyant, tropical style and her positioning as the "Brazilian Bombshell" in many Hollywood films. Myra Mendible demonstrated how Miranda's body came to serve as a "synecdoche for Latin America." Identified as she eventually became with the Chiquita Banana trademark, Miranda ultimately functioned "as an ethnic commodity—and unwitting marketing rep for U.S. corporate exploitation of Latin American labor and natural resources."[20] The fact that Aurora Miranda is portrayed as a Bahian sweets-seller only underscores her insertion in the economy of sexual and material consumption that underlies the representations in *The Three Caballeros.* The commodification of the Latina body is paralleled in an unequivocal manner here with Miranda's depiction as purveyor of authentic Brazilian "goods" (especially the sexually suggestive "cookies") and her positioning as the object of both the Anglo (Donald's) and the Brazilian (Zé's) eroticizing gaze. The fact that she is dancing in the scene gives added weight to the stereotype of the hypersexual Latina, given that even this simple act is "loaded with gendered, racialized baggage."[21]

It is in this scene, accordingly, that Donald reveals himself for the first time as a *rara avis*: "a wolf in Duck's clothing." He lusts after women to the point of having to be restrained by his parrot friend, who exclaims: "Donald, you are a wolf! Take it easy!" This characterization is affirmed in a subsequent scene, as well as in the text that appears in one of the first posters advertising the film. Located in a cartoon balloon above Donald's sombrero'd head it says

Imagine me and all my pals singing, dancing, romancing in the same scenes, with real, live, three-dimensional (and what dimensions!) luscious latin beauties like Aurora Miranda, Dora Luz, Carmen Molina! We're twice as torrid as a hot foot on the equator—and even more fun! Just change the name girls, from Donald Duck to Donald El Wolf, sí, sí, and wooooooooo-woooooo!"

With the depiction of Donald exhibiting this traditional (Latin–associated) macho behavior, another stereotype is reinforced; this time in the all–American character, who, recalling his role as tourist at Lake Titicaca in *Saludos Amigos*, now engages in a frenzy of real and symbolic cross-dressing, code-switching and "slumming with the natives."

Out of the next gift box, the largest of all, emerges Panchito, a Mexican cock dressed as a traditional *charro*. He is easily identified as the gun-toting, pistol-shooting *bandito*—another negative Latin stereotype familiar to Hollywood audiences. He yells loudly, dances, sings and leads the trio in panting over the silhouette of a shapely woman. The three take off on a magic flying serape to tour Mexico. After a series of cultural sidetrips that feature Mexican customs and folklore, they end up flying over the beach in Veracruz—again, this scene was actually simulated in the Burbank studio parking lot.[22] In this scene the telescope that Donald looks through self-reflexively becomes the subjective circular iris of the camera's "eye." The all-female sunbathers wave at the visitors, but then scatter and run, as Donald tries in various ways to catch them, even playing an improvised game of blind-man's bluff (called, significantly, in Spanish, "the blind hen"). In the end, the women escape, leaving Donald, still blindfolded, kissing an imagined woman, but actually in the arms of Zé Carioca. "No, Donald, don't do that!" exclaims the parrot. While transgendered characters, gender ambiguity and hints of homoeroticism occur throughout the film (Piedra), like the threatening degree of difference represented in the native Others, this is quickly neutralized as the trio continues on its serape ride. As if to compensate for this lapse in normative heterosexuality, the remainder of the film features Donald rapturously entranced by a number of Mexican women, and variously framed by flowers, animated lips, disembodied legs, stars, sombreros and an army of phallic cacti. These in turn transform into a series of miniature Donalds. The reference here to sexual reproduction could not be more unambiguous. Even the original meaning of the term "animation" becomes relevant here, as the cartoon quite literally becomes a life-giving agent of creation. And not surprisingly, the creative mechanism here is purely a masculine undertaking—the phallic cacti beget the baby ducks. The female component is relegated to the background, or played out mimetically by the male birds. *The Three Caballeros* concludes with a frenzied bullfight scene, in which Donald plays the bull, and an orgasmic fireworks finale, in which all restraint is abandoned and the three cartoon birds sing, dance, and morph from one figure into another. The concluding scenes show the three "amigos" with Donald in the middle, synecdochically channeling his apparent ultimate contrition for his bawdy behavior, again, through costume: he wears the serape over his head like a Madonna, and looks angelically heavenwards, while his sailor's cap floats gently above his head in the guise of a halo. But the final ending, over which the words "The End" appear, is a cataclysmic explosion. In the end, neither the framing of the camera nor the sturdy boxes can contain the difference that Latin America, with its irrepressible birds, maps, colorful dancers and especially Latin women represents.

Saludos Amigos and *The Three Caballeros* both signal a turning point in the history of Disney's cinema. They mark the beginning of the Disney foray into the documentary mode that characterized much of its later production, especially in the educational animated and live-action shorts that rounded out Walt's commitment to the "Good Neighbor" program. They introduced the highly stereotypical representations of Latin America and Latin Americans that remained stubbornly consistent throughout subsequent productions, including the colorful, exotic Latins that appear in the feature-length 1988 film *Oliver and Company*, the 1990 animated film and television show *Duck Tales*, the 2000 release *The Emperor's New Groove* and even the cartoon map of Latin America that makes a brief appearance in the 2009 feature *Up*. These early films also set the stage for the introduction of a longstanding Disney animation staple: the offensive and condescending treatment of the exotic and diverse Other that can be observed in the subsequent representations of African Americans in *Song of the South* and other ethnic characters in later films. As Jean Franco points out, the Disney cartoon "vies with the real and forecasts the power of the simulacrum that today draws millions of Latin Americans to Disneyland and Disneyworld."[23] Among those many consumers, viewers and visitors, there are many who either learned to see their Latin neighbors, or indeed to see *themselves*, through Disney's "Good Neighbor" treatment of difference.

Notes

1. Julia Kristeva, *Desire in Language: A Semiotic Approach to Literature and Art*. Leon S. Roudiez, ed. Thomas Gora, Alice Jardine and Leon S. Roudiez, trans. (New York: Columbia University Press, 1980), 66.

2. Robert Stam, *Reflexivity in Film and Literature from Don Quixote to Jean-Luc Goddard*. (New York: Columbia University Press, 1992), 21.

3. José Piedra, "The Three Caballeros": Pato Donald's Gender Ducking. *Jump Cut: A Review of Contemporary Media* no. 39 (June 1994) 23, 112.

4. Julianne Burton, "Don (Juanito) Duck and the Imperial-Patriarchal Unconscious: Disney Studios, the Good Neighbor Policy, and the Packaging of Latin America" in: *Nationalisms & Sexualities* , Andrew Parker ... [et al.], eds. (New York: Routledge, 1992), 31.

5. Henry A. Giroux, "Are Disney Movies Good for Your Kids?" in *Kinder Culture: The Corporate Construction of Childhood*. Steinberg, Shirley and Joe L. Kincheloe, eds. (Boulder, Colorado: Westview Press, 1997), 57.

6. Ariel Dorfman and Armand Mattelart. *How to Read Donald Duck: Imperialist Ideology in the Disney Comic*. David Kunzle, ed. (New York: International General, 1991), 95. Emphasis mine.

7. Ollie Johnston, Frank Thomas. *The Illusion of Life: Disney Animation*. (New York: Disney Editions, 1981).

8. Neal Gabler. *Walt Disney: The Triumph of the American Imagination.* (New York: Knopf, 2006), 173.

9. A "cel" in animation, short for "celluloid" is a transparent sheet on which objects are drawn or painted. See Tim Dirk's FilmSite: http://www.filmsite.org/animatedfilms.html.

10. Siegfried Kracauer. *Theory of Film.* (Princeton, N.J.: Princeton University Press, 1960), 89–90.

11. Gaizka S. de Usabel. *The High Noon of American Films in Latin America.* (Ann Arbor, Michigan: UMI Research Press, 1982), 164.

12. Fredrick B. Pike. *FDR's Good Neighbor Policy: Sixty Years of Generally Gentle Chaos.* (Austin: University of Texas Press, 1995).

13. Rodolfo Vidal González. *La actividad propagandística de Walt Disney durante la Segunda Guerra Mundial.* (Salamanca: Publicaciones Universidad Pontífica de Salamanca, 2006) 114.

14. J.B. Kaufman. *South of the Border with Disney: Walt Disney and the Good Neighbor Program, 1941–1948.* (New York: Disney Editions, 2009), 19.

15. *Ibid.,* 24.

16. Jean Franco. *The Decline and Fall of the Lettered City: Latin America in the Cold War* (Cambridge, Mass: Harvard University Press, 2001), 26.

17. Débora Krischke Leitão. "We, the Others: Construction of the Exotic and Consumption of Brazilian Fashion in France." *Horizontes Antropológicos,* Vol.4 no. se Porto Alegre, 2008, 7.

18. Robert Stam, *Reflexivity in Film and Literature from Don Quixote to Jean-Luc Goddard* (New York: Columbia University Press, 1992), 16.

19. Kaufman, *South of the Border with Disney,* 73.

20. Myra Mendible, ed. *From Bananas to Buttocks: The Latina Body in Popular Film and Culture.* (Austin: University of Texas Press, 2007), 10, 12.

21. *Ibid.,* 20.

22. Kaufman, *South of the Border with Disney,* 221.

23. Franco, *The Decline and Fall of the Lettered City,* 28.

Bibliography

Adams, Dale. "Saludos Amigos: Hollywood and FDR's Good Neighbor Policy." *Quarterly Review of Film and Video,* 24: 2007. pp.289–295.

Black, George. *The Good Neighbor: How the United States Wrote the History of Central America and the Caribbean.* New York: Pantheon, 1988.

Brode, Douglas. *Multiculturalism and the Mouse :Race and Sex in Disney Entertainment.* Austin: University of Texas Press, 2005.

Burton, Julianne. "Don (Juanito) Duck and the Imperial-Patriarchal Unconscious: Disney Studios, the Good Neighbor Policy, and the Packaging of Latin America." In *Nationalisms & Sexualities.* Andrew Parker, et al., eds. New York: Routledge, 1992.

Dorfman, Ariel. *How to Read Donald Duck: Imperialist Ideology in the Disney Comic.* David Kunzle, ed. New York: International General, 1991.

Gabler, Neal. *Walt Disney: The Triumph of the American Imagination.* New York: Knopf, 2006.

Giroux, Henry A. "Are Disney Movies Good for Your Kids?" In *Kinder Culture: The Corporate Construction of Childhood.* Steinberg, Shirley and Joe L. Kincheloe, eds. Boulder, Colorado: Westview Press, 1997. Pp. 53–67.

Kaufman: J.B. *South of the Border with Disney: Walt Disney and the Good Neighbor Program, 1941–1948.* New York: Disney Editions, 2009.

Kristeva, Julia. *Desire in Language: A Semiotic Approach to Literature and Art.* Leon S. Roudiez, ed. Thomas Gora, Alice Jardine and Leon S. Roudiez, trans. New York: Columbia University Press, 1980.

Kracauer, Siegfried. *Theory of Film.* Princeton: Princeton University Press, 1960.

Leitão, Débora Krischke. "We, the Others: Construction of the Exotic and Consumption of Brazilian Fashion in France." *Horizontes Antropológicos* vol.4, Selected Edition, 2008.

Mendible, Myra, ed. *From Bananas to Buttocks: The Latina Body in Popular Film and Culture.* Austin: University of Texas Press, 2007.

Piedra, José. "The Three Caballeros:" Pato Donald's Gender Ducking. *Jump Cut: A Review of Contemporary Media*, no. 39, June 1994, 112. 1994, 2006, pp. 72–82.

Pike, Fredrick B. *FDR's Good Neighbor Policy: Sixty Years of Generally Gentle Chaos.* Austin: University of Texas Press, 1995.

Richard, Alfred Charles, Jr. *Censorship and Hollywood's Hispanic Image: An Interpretive Filmography, 1936–1955.* Westport, Conn.: Greenwood, 1993.

Sherman, Sharon and Mike J. Koven. *Folklore/Cinema: Popular Film as Vernacular Culture.* Logan, Utah: Utah State University Press, 2007.

Smoodin Eric, ed. *Disney Discourse: Producing the Magic Kingdom.* New York: Routledge, 1994.

Stam, Robert. *Reflexivity in Film and Literature from Don Quixote to Jean-Luc Goddard.* New York: Columbia University Press. 1992.

Telotte, J.P. "The Changing Space of Animation: Disney's Hybrid Films of the 1940s." *Animation*, Vol. 2, No. 3 (Nov. 2007), pp. 245–258.

Thomas, Frank Ollie Johnston, Ollie Johnson and Cllie Johnston. *Illusion of Life: Disney Animation, Vol. 1.* New York: Disney Editions, 1995.

Todorov, Tzvetan. *Nosotros y los otros.* Buenos Aires: Siglo XXI, 2005.

Usabel, Gaizka S. de. *The High Noon of American Films in Latin America.* Ann Arbor, Michigan: UMI Research Press, 1982.

U.S. Department of State. "Diplomacy in Action: Good Neighbor Policy 1933." http://www.state.gov/r/pa/ho/time/id/17341.htm "Inaugural Speech of Franklin Delano Roosevelt," Washington, D.C. March 4th, 1933. http://www.hpol.org/fdr/inaug/

Vidal González, Rodolfo. *La actividad propagandística de Walt Disney durante la segunda Guerra Mundial.* Salamanca: Publicaciones Universidad Pontífica de Salamanca, 2006.

Watts, Steven. "Walt Disney: Art and Politics in the American Century. *The Journal of American History*, Vol. 82, No. 1 (Jun., 1995), pp. 84–110.

Mapping the Imaginary: The Neverland of Disney Indians

Prajna Parasher

Much of the discourse about Disney's *Peter Pan* has focused on the eternal boy child (now well inflected by Michael Jackson though the film predates him by a couple of decades). Barrie's imaginative leap into the mind of house-bound Edwardian boyhoods becomes in Disney's hands a map of already decaying white imperialist concepts masquerading as playful fantasies. Foppish Captain Hook, bumbling pirate crew, and a leering alligator people Neverland with images born of standard British childhood literature visualized through the American burlesque tradition of stagey exaggeration. It is in the Disney Indian camp, though, that the rupture of charming fun into racial hostility can be most obviously noted. Is a perception of wildness an antidote for the constraints of life in a Victorian nursery?

To begin to investigate how Disney's Indians came to be depicted as they are, it's necessary to trace their history in American popular culture. Going back at least to Buffalo Bill's Wild West, entertainers known as "Show Indians" participated in circus-like demonstrations of the usual dramas—stagecoach robbery, kidnapping, war dances—what was already understood through penny dreadful novels[1] as the narrative of European/American Indian interactions. Presented in places where large audiences could support the considerable expense, these circus productions were what we would now recognize as a market commodity; actors displaced from their cultural traditions took on work imitating themselves, depicting the image of the frontier as urban people in both America and Europe already understood it.[2]

While the studio could make use of these images without any concern over copyright, the same is not true of the title text. There were years of negotiation with the Great Ormond Street Hospital in London, which had inherited the royalties to the novel; part of buying the rights included front-loading the film with an acknowledgement of thanks.[3] It's useful to compare Barrie's text with the Disney one. There are fewer rewrites than one might expect; the primary difference is in weight of the various aspects of Neverland. In the original, Indians played a less significant role—one more of Peter's adventures but not so central as Hook. They disappear from the narrative after the first half of the book. When America of 1950 looks through the lens of London 1910, however, the camera might well find itself focused on an anonymous but identifiable malevolent enemy whose most identifiable characteristic is recognizable racialized difference. As McCarthyism badgered Hollywood into the reiteration of banalities and away from anything issue-driven,[4] the Indians would rise out of the underbrush like Gus from *Birth of a Nation*. While the studio was canny enough not to use Barrie's language, "the Piccaninny tribe, and not to be confused with the softer hearted Delawares or the Hurons,"[5] it reveals itself willing to make use of racialized cliché through filmic conventions. The hand-drawn chart or rutter,[6] so significant in the rise of the actual colonial experience, lives on in adventure stories which rewrite it into docility.

Maps are two-dimensional and have been constructed as accurate, fixed and objectively presented copies of a "real" world, at the same time they are socially constructed, ideologically engineered, and as a paradigm of colonial discourse, maps permit the national to "imagine" itself. In *Peter Pan*, maps do not reiterate a seemingly objective representation. Instead they represent a position of power that evokes a cartographer, giving Peter the means to transform land/maps according to his needs. With Peter we embark on an imaginary expedition in which maps and landscapes are mercurial instead of fixed, changing appearances according to where the Darling children, Peter, Tiger Lily and Tinker travel. Through this journey the audience becomes an imaginary cartographer who interacts through representation.

Disney's use of the map has multiple functions in transforming Barrie's Edwardian story to the needs of another decade. It replaces with a familiar iconography the collusive literary tone of the original. Barrie's coy asides are necessarily transformed into visualities and filmic readings as familiar to the film audiences of the 1950s as direct address to the novel's reader would have been to the young readers of the 1900s. The map chalked on John Darling's boiled shirt, not part of the original text, depends, like so much of the slapstick in the nursery scenes, on a physical comedy tradition sourced in American vaudeville, minstrelsy, and British working class music halls. To write the map into this tradition is to compound it with another theatrical convention familiar since Shakespeare, that of the distant tropical island. We know, as audience, that this remove will be to a place of license, magic, sexual ambiguity, low vulgar comedy and ultimate happy endings. Our position as audience/tourist is enhanced by recognition that we will also be voyeurs, forever wiser and more ahead of the game than the players. Disney studios' particular insertion into this trajectory included the need to maintain the apparent playful quality whilst overriding the lewd, cruel and jingoistic aspects by screening them, much as Barrie did previously, through a childish imagination. Both apologize for their colonial positioning by dismissing it as foolery and thus, in the tradition of the theater fool, make their most important statements in riddling reversals.

In the Disney film, the map first appears on the patriarch's body. When we see it next it is a series of transitional frames that allow us to visualize that we are leaving London for someplace else. Such coding was common, even expected, in films with "exotic" locations (*Casablanca* [1942], *King Kong* [1933], *The African Queen* [1951]). All of them depend on a schoolboy confidence that representation of the unknown bestows ownership. The pathetic fallacy obscured in dramatic or adventure genres is fore-grounded in fantasy, but the function doesn't change. "X" not only marks the spot, it confirms that the spot exists. Such mapping is reiterated when Tink, who is without voice but not without expression, uses it to trace a line to Peter's hideout amongst the Indians. In a polyglot visual language (melodrama's oily seducer and betrayed maiden mixed up with the bad girl's betrayal of her wholesome lover) Tink dips her feather-tipped mules in ink and catwalks over the map with a series of backward glances worthy of Betty Grable or maybe even Sisi of Habsburg. Her highly sexualized figure writes its own doom, as we well know even before Hook shuts her up in a lantern. Disney, cautious about the changes of sexual language, calls her a pixie and not a fairy, but in her Vegas gear, she is fairly equivalent to the Barrie original "exquisitely gowned in a skeleton leaf, cut low and square, through which her figure could be seen to the best advantage, She was slightly inclined to be *embonpoint*."[7] It is the Hollywood of the fifties.[8] She is female, selfish, willful, vapid and most damning of all, common; if she takes up a tool of power, she will carelessly destroy the Indians through her preoccupation with Peter. In a turn of the plot she shares with the tragic mulatto[9] and other female characters of color, she will have to offer her own life to correct this terrible error.

Depictions of female sexuality have always been fraught in English/American tradition but the coding changed with the era. So it is Tiger Lily who, while portrayed as sexually available in Barrie, becomes in Disney the epitome of the exoticized maiden/vamp. Almost as voiceless as Tinker Bell, a kettle mender whose name recalls Irish gypsies, the Indian Princess's gestural language is limited to an aloof, stubborn (but fetching) stare and a set of crossed arms. All she can say is "no," until we get to the dance scene, where it is suddenly "yes, yes, yes."

Within a postcolonial context we can recognize maps as the act of looking as well as guides to actual travel. Looking and exploring constantly fuel each other. Lines, borders and boundaries, are cached on the landscape, and within this swaying between looking and going maps become more fluid and acquire independent cartographical qualities separate from any reflection of political or geographical realities.[10] Mapping implies a 'shifting ground' that is subject to change, erasure, and new reworkings.[11] Mapped onto the animated body of Tiger Lily are some rudimentary markers of the American Indian, braided hair, headband, leather garments; she is equally represented though period expectations the Hollywood ingénue. She will take central place, backed by a male chorus, in the musical interlude. This cartography comes up as expected in "Why is the Red Man Red?" Some complaint has already been voiced by those who oppose stereotypical representation about this song, which affirms that he's red from a constant pursuit of red women.[12] It would be hard for the studio in 2010 to wriggle out from under this pre-civil rights era gaff particularly since the braves are indeed drawn in darker tones than Lily, and that's not the whole of it. The braves are not only bigger and darker than the maiden, but they are to a man clumsy, grotesque and with faces which have prominent noses and mouths but also no eyes at all. Does this elision of the return gaze suggest that they accept what has been written upon them? In trying to imagine what they were thinking in creating these characters, one of the ideas which occurs to this observer is that they were cognizant of the racist tradition into which they were drawing: these bodies, with different costuming, could easily be those of happy field hands or bush cannibals leaping around their fire. The google-eyed look contributing to black buck can be re-drawn as eyeless, producing instead the inscrutable slanty-eyed tribal.[13] That it also shifts the characters into a more completely passive role betrays an unconscious reflexivity visible in other parts of the sequence. Tiger Lily's dance maintains the toe-to-heel step we associate with Indian dance, and she bends forward as if in obeisance to something, but she is otherwise mapped into Western filmic codes. She dances alone, eventually with Peter, standing on a stump and with a fluid eroticized body meant to display her personal appeal, not her function as part of the group. The scene ends, as anyone might predict, with Lily and Peter rubbing noses, an "Indian Kiss." Language conventions ("how," "ugh," "red man") not only further characterize the Indians as buffoons but also make their way into the film's songs, further trivializing the silencing they mask.[14]

Peter in his war bonnet recalls the popular notion that significant whites such as Presidents were given this headdress as an honorific, a sign of inclusion into the tribe. It is, of course, another piece of show Indian behavior since the specific meaning of the bonnet, the materials in it and the rank of who might wear one, would have different meaning, if any, to those of the culture to which it belongs. In a non-reflexive playing out of the white man's hubris that he is welcomed and cherished by those he has conquered, the story line affirms that the Indians are grateful to Peter because he rescued Lily. In order to keep the patriarchal implications clear, Wendy is sidelined by being called "squaw" and asked to carry firewood. The wood business is original with Disney, but Barrie does say that the London miss does not like being called "squaw" recognizing it as insulting in the way that "brave" is not.

The book is Edwardian, the tracery of a slipping empire appearing as quaint charm in the ascendant America of the fifties. Barrie's revealingly money-preoccupied John Darling becomes transformed by Disney into one more in the procession of inept Hollywood fathers protected by competent, loving wives. In an era caught in the illusion of standardized family relations, it was a general paradigm that did not depend on external experience. In those early years of broadcast television, children played imitative games of house, and of cowboys and Indians. Cap guns, imitation Stetsons and other cowboy gear were significantly more popular toys than moccasins and bows and arrows. A friend who remembers this era says, "The girls and the little kids always had to be Indians." Jungian shadow space: America's own imperialism, already intuited if not understood by its children, underwent regular rehearsal.[15]

Maps spur imagination, discovery, travel, conquest, and migration. Scientific in their plan, maps reinscribe, enclose and create hierarchies of space for the acquisition, management and reinforcement of power articulated through practices of recording, labeling, naming and classifying. Disney's map of Neverland, apparently sourced in the "pirate map," easily found on a mid-century cereal box or luncheonette placemat, discovers itself to be real, the plat book of burgeoning Disneylands: corporate reality, virtual, national, global. A century ago it felt perfectly reasonable, and possible, that Cody could bring the Wild West to London. Now we go to it; winning football players in the lead, we can fly—Orlando the stopover—to a programmed, idealized environment which can be both adventurous and safe, permanently happy and never unpredictable. It is a map our children can read before they know their way to school. That Michael Jackson should not only identify this film as his favorite, but also name his home in its honor, might well have predicted another un- or sub-conscious reflexivity that only breaks the surface like the crocodile's tail; Jackson's brushes with fame, with gossip, with the law, and his early death by drugs have at this point mapped onto lived experience what can happen when your GPS is programmed "second to the right and straight on to morning." His story is the painful evidence of the dangers in inhabiting a commodity construction: a 50 year-old black millionaire died as a starveling white crone.

Disney's genius in the transformation of the story is in the technological use of Neverland as a dead space; not only are plot deaths reversible, but it all happens within childish imagination, the anxiety of an impossible nationalism coped with by a magical place with nebulous borders. Significantly, *Peter Pan*'s popularity does not stop with America's shores. It had and still has an international following. Peter's heroics defuse not only the sexual minefield but the racial one as well, and more significantly, sexualized racial lines where a preadolescent white boy (he still has his baby teeth) can outwit any threat, historical or geographical. Barrie, responding to the end of the great colonial period, dressed the lost (British–born if rough) boys in animal skins as a masquerade which they eventually escape but felt no need to give the grunting braves individual names, voices or futures.

The diverse, decimated communities that provided the material for this erasure became homogenized into Pidgin English, plains Indian teepees, and more than anything else, the substitution of the terror and horror of a warring exploitive past with a jokey, incompetent present: Jim Crow Indians. The animated version of *Peter Pan* incorporates a standing theatrical tradition; its own particular inflection is the lack of any shading or irony and, in the America of the 1950s, oblivion masquerading as innocence, something the upcoming '60s were about to dispel. The figures—braves, squaw, chief, princess—are immediately recognizable as Disney which in itself displays a caricature history that was at inception specifically racist (Little Black Sambo, et al.) and then transformed into animals (Goofy, Bugs, Porky) as the animal bodies upon which embedded stereotypes were subsequently written.[16] The illusions and elisions of 1953 were so ingenuous that much of this history is entirely evident. Princess Tiger Lily's name is English; whatever this flower is called in American Indian languages, it wouldn't reference an animal from other continents. Conventional uses of the exotic abound. When the chief is dancing, at one point his steps change from the campfire cadences we recognize to something between an Irish jig (vaudeville) and a Cossack squat-dance.... Cossacks were also a feature of William Cody's traveling shows. Concomitantly with the American Indians themselves taking jobs as show Indians as a form of acknowledgement that their own cultures were undergoing erasure, popular culture—majority culture—had to create an Indian to fill the emptied space and forestall any acknowledgement of living on stolen ground. It has often been said that slavery is the founding trauma of the nation; it may not be the only one. If we see this as a black and white issue, and certainly it was, Indians were dubbed "red" men but what that meant was that they were not white, and the white man's entitlements while not overtly questioned, benefited from, nay, required, the continuous propping up available through minimizing the humanity of any Other.[17]

A brief loop backward. While Disney Studios had their own traditions to work out of, they share more than might be expected with Peter Pan's original creator, Barrie. Buffalo Bill's company appeared in London in 1887 for Queen Victoria's Jubilee held in celebration of the semi-centennial of her reign. Held in Earl's Court, London, it was housed in a huge arena with a grandstand of 20,000 seating capacity. Her Majesty, making her first public appearance since Prince Albert's death twenty years previous, not only approved of the show but promoted it. Considering it an event of "educational superexcellence" she endorsed a performance for the entertainment of 3000 royal representatives assembled from every part of the empire. By royal fiat, Bill's Indians were as safely locked into the English psyche as the Kohinoor into the Tower. If we try to decode the emotional underpinnings of the Darling family in London, why a focus on Indians? What do they have to do with not growing up? If in America the various incarnations of the pop culture black man (Uncle Tom, Jim Crow, Zip Coon) were created to defuse changing mainstream fears in changing social milieus, could the "savage" be seen as the antithesis of English boyhood? Barrie's sexual anxieties are more covert than those revealed in the American minstrel tradition, doubly coded in childhood derring-do and oblique classical allusion. What Disney does with this is to elide subtlety (Pan's garments are more of theater Robin Hood than satyr) and to pretend—perhaps it's not a pretense—that we all see Indians as projections of our own personal losses of the chance to pillage and shout, not as a national loss of honor. The shift was as smooth as Yankee Doodle transforming into a patriotic song. Because the visual coding of blacks was already well-established in the Disney canon, it was inevitable that these stereotypes would be transferred to the Indian encampment in Neverland. The lost boys live underground and are dressed as animals. If the English children are reduced to animal forms, then hierarchy demands that the Indians be something less; they make their first appearance as marauding trees. Sign and signifier are one thing; more than at home in the wilderness, Indians are the land they inhabit. Even when out of their disguises, they look much alike, an ugly and monotonous parade of the big-nose Indian on the buffalo nickel.[18] Racial stereotyping requires not only a disempowering gaze but a unifying one as well. "The only good Indian is a dead Indian," or one reduced to unthreatening caricature. The hand-drawn figures are spookily similar to the cheap, angular cartoons of later digital productions.

It's possible to think of Disney's *Peter Pan* as a kind of innocence, not the "wholesome family entertainment" umbrella which has sheltered the studio's fatuous bigotry for so many years, but the innocence of an era not yet engaging in a critical look at the psychic damage made visible through popular culture. Walt Disney's own repeated attempts to make a film based on *Hiawatha* suggests that such a consideration never came up.[19]

The same thing cannot be said for more recent Disney show Indians, those in *Brother Bear* (2003). Set "respectfully" amongst the Inuit, the characters are generic enough to be Eskimos and with a nod toward the preoccupations of our era (multiculturalism, shamanism, totems, matriarchy, transformative power of love) move through a story line that struggles between Cartoon Network and religious docudrama. Unsettlingly like the thank you to the hospital in *Peter Pan*, but far more obfuscated, at its onset this film thanks unnamed experts and consults. Acknowledging real ownership is here transformed into self-created authority. As in *Peter Pan* the exploitation is of the image, not anything itself. The half century between the two products reveals, however, both an increase in the crassness with which "magic" is produced and a refusal to engage with the cultural assumptions that allow the ethnic Other to be conflated with an animal. Joseph Campbell, whose scholarship on the hero's quest helped to inspire *Star Wars,* would recognize the same framing in *Brother Bear* but here made campy and didactic. Not played for laughs like the Indians of *Peter Pan,* the primary characters, brothers Kenai, Denahi and Sitka, are undergoing manhood ordeals; rather than demonstrating competency in adult responsibility, though, what they do is rush around in life-risking adventures over rough terrain, ice-age retro Marvel heroes. A vague location in the distant past, glib truisms, adroit animation, and careful avoidance of any hot-button topics (no tarted-up maidens for instance) suggest that all the "creative" work had first to be vetted by a roomful of company lawyers. In response to a general increase of cultural sensitivity and discourses surrounding political correctness, Disney's 21st century peek outside Burbank is no less patronizing, only more bland. Very much like the worst of contemporary school history books, it is a philosophy of avoidance rather than engagement. If you can't find a non-controversial way to transform Pocahontas into Lady Rebecca, leave them both out. What is most revealing about *Brother Bear* is the way Disney is still locked into their original dodge from overt racism, that of pasting racial stereotypes onto anthropomorphized animals. This story line not only allows Kenai to become a bear, but finds that he prefers such a life, violating the superhero tradition where Clark Kent always in the end comes back to his recognizable human self.[20] It is hard to imagine that such liberties would have been taken with any contemporary urban character. Even Spiderman and Cat Woman revert to comforting office clothes after they have righted the world. To present the American Indian man as transferable (mercurial) to a bear is to equalize their value, not in the hokey transformative way the new ageist story asserts but as commoditized units well below white men in the Great Chain of Being. But there is more here....

Brother Bear's take on Ice Age man depends on the givens of commodity stereotype. The characters wear skins, have slanty eyes, carry stone weapons and write on cave walls. In a nod toward feminism, the wise character is a kind old female, but we are never allowed to forget this is a constructed world—moose, mammoths and bears are all in the same time and place, personified and cooperative with men. The animal figures have more individual personality than the humans, who are so similar we identify one from another mostly by haircut. The men's monotony recalls the indistinguishable braves of Neverland. They reveal commodity fetishism not only by their lack of individual person-ality but also with dialogue co-opted from New Age preoccupations and pasted onto an imagined hunter-gatherer society based on archeological evidence which offers very little such detail. Placing it in the distant past is no more effective than placing it on an imaginary island. While it may prevent any racial slurs from being actionable, it is bald racism nonetheless. Only in a play-ful film like *Harvey* (1950) would a contemporary white man be turned into an animal. Kenai's transformation into his totem happens in the radioactive half-life of a mainstream visual history going back at least to Edward S. Curtis' manipulated images of living American Indians costumed according to his idea of how they should look for the avid consumers of specular Otherness.[21] Such leather and feather Indians lived, as Bert Williams said about being a stage Negro, a very inconvenient life, providing simulacra for which there was indeed an original, but one known only to the actor in his private life and unavailable to, unwanted by, the paying audience.[22] Disney fits comfortably into this tradition. The tragedy we are now living in, concrete as part of Disneyland as an imaginary map which has created its own corporate real with tentacles into the most private parts of our consumerist lives, is yet another incarnation of Manifest Destiny, so alluring and so often repeated that it can and does overwrite lived experience.

The paradigm from which Disney studio Indians are drawn betrays its Orientalist perspective subtly as well as overtly. Kenai's name, innocuous in written letters, comes over somewhat differently as experienced in the film. Heard, not seen, it is pronounced "keen eye," directly evocative of "Hawkeye," James Fenimore Cooper's character and one of the earlier entertainment Indians sourced in the literary imagination of an urban writer using American material to embroider a novel based in the European tradition. That Cooper's works may have at last been removed from most curricula and that film versions of *Last of the Mohicans* have not been particularly successful does not have much impact on the persistence of Tontoesque characterizations pretending to acknowledge the presence of pre–Columbian civilizations.

In like ways, the map is present in *Brother Bear*, re-coded but not transformed. The transitional device here is cave-wall painting. Far more like those discovered in France than those in the Grand Canyon, it does not even pretend to any cultural specificity but uses familiar images rather like the pidgin English of non-white players in adventure films; the only thing it tells us about those who use it is that they are less than ourselves because they are not fluent in our language. The bear paw print, portrayed as produced by a man and presented in elaborate computer animation, is the mark of B'rer Fox in a terrifying new disguise. We are supposed to accept him as family.

Of course he's not really scary because we all know we're kidding. As with our lost past, the whole relationship of contemporary urban Americans with wild life is fraught with historical misunderstanding. American Indians, who both knew bears and depended on them, treated the animal with honor and respect. Pioneers, recognizing a dangerous but useful resource, of necessity maintained the respect even when their religious text obviated the honor. Now that our real relationship is through animation and the mall, it is more familiar to think of bears as adorable toys than as real creatures once at home in the spaces we now inhabit. In this way, outside of historical time and common sense, *Brother Bear* is a screen upon which the outline of erasure can play. The insult is in the way that lived trauma, orphanhood for instance, can be presented as repairable by theatrical magic.

American Indians as part of the consumerist menu are particularly available when we use those about whom we have no evidentiary trace. The mystery of the Ice Age allows us to pretend there never were any cigar store Indians or forced migrations or Carlisle training schools. We can print around this pretense of vacuum, Smokey paws on the wall, whatever history is convenient for this moment. One of the reasons this production was so mildly successful may well be the transparency of the conceptual base. As a film it falls flat. *Peter Pan's* century of interest depends on Barrie's ability to have intuited the unspeakable of his time. *Brother Bear* is locked into the acceptable of its time. Like the historical pageants springing up as part of historical sites and community celebrations, it does not pretend to be anything more than a series of signifiers allowing us to use the "past" to celebrate ourselves. That such productions are not successful as theater is unimportant. Mirror writing does not allow for the multiple reflections that serious psychic reflection drama requires. Multicultural discourse is a kind of therapeutic discourse, designed to work out the wrinkles of its creator; it can't be decentered without evaporating.

On his way to embodying Pan, Michael Jackson evoked another man/animal transformative tradition in *Thriller.* The extraordinary popularity of this video suggests that he did indeed tap into the same kind of subterranean racial and emotional material that Barrie discovered. The werewolf tradition is another European construct interestingly conflating the wild with the sexual. Originating in the need to cope with wilderness still surrounding evolving town and city culture, it becomes something else after crossing the Atlantic. In America this discourse always includes elements of race. *Thriller's* (1983) backdating itself into the fifties acknowledges the black and white B movies it is sourced in as a series of complex filmic jokes. The primary consumers for this product would have been anticipated as teenagers and young adults. At this point in his career, Jackson was still visibly African American so the incorporation of cultural fears about Black males needed no elaboration and could even be played for laughs at the same moment it was most serious. It also appeared when such material was open for discussion, activism and social change.[23] The recognition factor available here allows for viewer involvement in a way that pandering to "we are the world" iterations cannot.

What such things are useful for is to remind ourselves of the security of our position. The Indian is as safely dead as the werewolf and the bear. We claim ownership of his trace the same way we see his vacated places only as geographical points on a map. While we don't yet have shops where children can "Build an Indian" and watch while a machine opens his back and stuffs him with fluff, we can appropriate his image in similar fashion. The action at Wounded Knee was in 1973 yet we are still comfortable co-opting Indian tracery and Indian words as if they were part of the public domain, the imaginary.

Notes

1. Cheap American and British popular fiction of the 19th Century.
2. For more on how an entertainment spectacle is taken for "the real thing," see Joy Kaysson's book *Buffalo Bill's Wild West: Celebrity, Memory, and Popular History*. For cinematic representation of American Indians see Harry M. Benshoff and Sean Griffen's *America on Film: Representing Race, Class, Gender and Sexuality at the Movies*.
3. See the opening credit sequence in Walt Disney's *Peter Pan*.
4. Of course there were notable exceptions like *The Treasure of the Sierra Madre* (1948) and *To Kill a Mockingbird* (1962).
5. J.M. Barrie, p. 56
6. Rutters are hand-drawn charts or maps produced from the late 16th century to mid–19th century. These maps provided sailing directions and routes between destinations.
7. J.M. Barrie, p. 25
8. For an interesting thread of connection between Walt Disney, Marilyn Monroe and Tinker Bell see Douglas Brode's *Multiculturalism and the Mouse: Race and Sex in Disney Entertainment*, pp. 132–133.
9. Young woman of color or a woman of biracial heritage, who is inserted into the narrative in order to be the obvious victim. In American literature of the 19th and 20th centuries, the tragic mullato is a stereotypical character who can "pass" for white until her biracial status is revealed. Her story always ends in tragedy.
10. I have adopted De Certeau's correlation between maps, touring and looking.
11. For a discussion of the map as a "shifting ground" see Gilles Deleuze and Felix Guattari's *A Thousand Plateaus: Capitalism and Schizophrenia*. "The map," they write, "is open and connectable in all its dimensions; it is detachable, reversible, susceptible to constant modification. It can be torn, reversed, adapted to any kind of mounting, re-worked by an individual, group, or social formation. It can be drawn on the wall, conceived of as a work of art, constructed as a political action or as a meditation" (p. 12).
12. See American Indian activist websites and also University of California, Berkeley's library catalogue of books and articles on American Indian representation in the movies—"The Movies, Race and Ethnicity: Native Americans."
13. See Douglas Brode's discussion of caricatured representation in *Peter Pan*, pp. 25–26.
14. An interested person could compare this sequence of the Indians celebrating their mistaken identities with the way Uncle Remus does his, though finding a copy of *Song of the South* will require a more "scholarly" investigation than finding *Peter Pan*, which is still in general circulation.
15. Judith Butler's conception of the gendered and racialized body as constructed in terms of a corporeal style is useful to my argument here.
16. See Paul Wells' discussion in *The Animated Bestiary* of how animation uses animals to play out the conception of human animals.
17. For an understanding of the racial stereotype I have drawn on the work of Homi Bhabha who has called attention to the commodified, exploited and exoticized colored body from a psychoanalytic perspective.
18. Minted from 1913 to 1938 and withdrawn in the 1950s and 1960s.
19. See Brode, *Multiculturalism and the Mouse: Race and Sex in Disney Entertainment*, pp. 24–25.
20. For the meaning and cultural context of Superman through the changing mediums of comic books, television shows and film see Tom De Haven's *Our Hero: Superman on Earth*.
21. In 1900, Edward S. Curtis documented American Indian cultures on hand-pulled photogravures.
22. In Marlon Riggs' *Ethnic Notions*, choreographer Leni Sloan discusses the origins of blackface minstrels and the complexities of this form when black performers were allowed on the minstrel stage. In the film, Sloan pays homage to Bert Williams, the greatest and most successful African American blackface comedian of the Vaudeville era.
23. See Kobena Mercer's analysis of the racial and sexual ambiguity of Michael Jackson in *Thriller* (1983) in *Welcome to the Jungle: New Positions in Black Cultural Studies*.

Bibliography

Barrie, J.M. *Peter Pan.* New York: Charles Scribner's Sons, 1950.

Bhabha, Homi K. *The Location of Culture.* New York: Routledge, 1994.

Benshoff, Harry M., and Griffen, Sean. *America on Film: Representing Race, Class, Gender and Sexuality at the Movies.* Malden, MA: Blackwell, 2004.

Brode, Douglas. *Multiculturism and the Mouse: Race and Sex in Disney Entertainment.* Austin: University of Texas Press, 2005.

De Certeau, M. *The Practice of Everyday Life.* Berkeley: University of California Press, 1984.

De Haven, Tom. *Our Hero: Superman on Earth.* New Haven: Yale University Press, 2009.

Deleuze, Gilles, and Guattari, Felix. *A Thousand Plateaus: Capitalism and Schizophrenia.* Minneapolis: University of Minnesota Press, 1980.

Kasson, Joy S. *Buffalo Bill's Wild West: Celebrity, Memory, and Popular History.* New York: Hill and Wang, 2000.

Kilpatrick, Jacquelyn. *Celluloid Indians: Native Americans and Film.* Lincoln: University of Nebraska Press, 1999.

Mercer, Kobena. *Welcome to the Jungle: New Positions in Black Cultural Studies.* New York: Routledge, 1994.

Reddin, Paul. *Wild West Shows.* Urbana: University of Illinois Press, 1999.

Rutherford, Jonathan. *Forever England: Reflections on Masculinity and Empire.* London: Lawrence & Wishart, 1997.

A *"Vexing Implication": Siamese Cats and Orientalist Mischief-Making*

KIMIKO AKITA and RICK KENNEY

Si and Am, the slinky, sneaky, and ultimately sinister cartoon cats who appear in a cameo in the 1955 Walt Disney Productions animated film *Lady and the Tramp*, have long—and often—been identified as offensive caricatures, exemplary of the "yellow peril" stereotype popularized and perpetuated by U.S. mass media in the mid–20th century. In a brief appearance on screen, the cunning pair wreaks havoc during a visit to the uptown Manhattan household of Jim Dear and Darling, menacing a bird in a cage and a goldfish in a bowl, clawing through drapery, and conspiring to steal a baby's milk—and perhaps more. Central to the film's theme of the protagonists Lady and Tramp as archetypal heroes overcoming a series of challenges, Si and Am (*Siam*, the former name for Thailand) manage to compromise the cocker spaniel while literally chewing up the scenery. Scholars have noted the details that draw the cats as easy-to-identify *Orientalist* villains: their exaggeratedly slanted eyes, inscrutable grins, and heavily accented English speech—let alone their mischievousness.

We apply the idea of Orientalism to the study of the stereotypes used to flesh out these animated Siamese characters and the "vexing implication"[1] of villainous cats as Chinese, with American/Westerners as preferred reader of the film as text. We move beyond previous critical/cultural studies to situate the production, distribution, and audience for the initial theatrical release of *Lady and the Tramp* (1955) in its socio-historical/political context, as well as in the context of subsequent and derivative cultural texts. We trace the legacy of such popular stereotypes to draw parallels to later Orientalist phenomena involving Siamese cats: *The Aristocats* (1970) and Amy Tan's *The Chinese Siamese Cat* (1994). The enduring success of *Lady and the Tramp* and its influence not only signify the acceptance of these denigrations of the Oriental by the target audience but also tell us something about enduring American cultural perspectives on the Orient.

We begin with a brief explanation of Edward Said's notion of Orientalism,[2] the theoretical background that informs our perspective and which we will demonstrate at play in the representation of Asians—specifically, Siamese cats—in the aforementioned entertainment texts. We next provide necessary background against which the Siamese cat needs to be considered. We interrogate the text of Si and Am in *Lady* and interpret its meaning. Finally, we discuss the legacy of these Siamese cats and argue why the sphere of such cultural representations deserves our attention and remedy.

The Fictions of Orientalism

Said's concept of Orientalism asserts that the West regards the non–Western world as the Orient: strangers and outsiders.[3] Orient itself is a Western word and a Western construction. A social mechanism exists that sustains the hierarchal colonial power relationship between the colonizer and the colonized and between the West and the Orient: "The status of colonized people has been fixed in zones of dependency and peripherality, stigmatized in the designation of underdeveloped, less-developed, developing states, ruled by a superior, developed, or metropolitan colonizer who was theoretically posited as a categorically antithetical overlord."[4]

The West occupies the privileged position of interpreting culture through Western eyes; of having control in defining the reality of the world; and—in the case of texts—of being the preferred reader. This interpreted knowledge of the Orient over time represents how the Orient has been treated as an object that was collected, produced, and reproduced. Said argued that the Orient is only a representation of what we would hope the Orient to be.[5] Thus, Orientalism is a representation of what the West thinks the Orient is. The West describes the Orient by romantic and exotic expressions, but Orientalism hides the context beneath its scholarly and aesthetic idiom. Orientalism is pervasive and unavoidable.

Orientalism also "illustrates how the Western experience of order and truth, epitomized in the exhibition [representation], depended upon creating the very effect of an 'outside,' of an 'external reality' beyond all representation."[6] Orientalism tells us as much about American culture by how the Orient is treated (i.e., represented); if, as an object, it fits well with the external reality of American society, as Mitchell claimed.

We contend that Disney's *Lady and the Tramp* and other cultural products that followed unfold the Orientalism of decades. We will illustrate that its Orientalist devices specifically demonize Asians as villainous Others. The animated depictions of Siamese cats produce the Orient as a commodified Western object: a fiction of America, by America, and for America.[7] Fiction is engineered by commercialism, as it is an invented story, an object, a commodity for sale. Through fictionalization, exoticization, and mystification, *Lady and the Tramp* creates a distance between the Orient and the West, exaggerating an Us-Other (sometimes "Them") dichotomy and sustaining Orientals. The West will continue to understand the Orient as different and strange, and as objects.

Situating Disney

It has been estimated that 200 million people watch a Disney film each year.[8] The influence such fictional films have on children "has been increasingly recognized, and yet there has also been a tendency to avoid scrutinizing these mass media products too closely, to avoid asking the sort of hard questions that can yield disquieting answers."[9] Numerous researchers have deconstructed Disney films and their collateral cultural products to reveal messages about race, gender, sexuality, class, and ageism.[10]

The Disney culture industry has persevered, however, and remains a significant producer of texts to be consumed by American children, generation after generation, since the films are periodically rereleased. For example, the highly acclaimed and groundbreaking animated film *Fantasia* (1940) was rereleased in 1956, 1969, 1982, 1990, and 2000, the latter two years marking the 50th and 60th anniversaries, respectively. No longer is it necessary for the films to be shown only in theaters. Disney films also have been made available to new generations of children on new media as technologies have evolved. The film at issue in this essay, *Lady and the Tramp*, originally released June 22, 1955, was rereleased to theaters in 1962, 1971, 1980, and 1986. It was issued on VHS and Laserdisc in 1987 as part of Disney's *The Classics* video series; in 1998 in the Walt Disney Masterpiece Collection video series; and on the Disney Limited Issue series DVD in 1999. The film was remastered and restored as a Platinum Edition series DVD in 2006, when one million copies were sold.[11] Finally, a moratorium on further sales of the 2006 DVD and the 2006 reissue of *Lady and the Tramp II: Scamp's Adventure* was announced.[12] Therefore, Disney films and their characters are new again to each generation, and their significance has been reinforced since 1984, when legal changes in the industry made it possible for anyone to own a copy of a film and to watch it over and over.

Disney animated films provide an experience beyond mere moviegoing; they are connected to

> the rituals of consumption ... [to] provide a "marketplace of culture" where children can buy (into), not only the fun of the films themselves and the "fairytale" lives of the characters in them, but also can come very close to, at least materially, re-creating those "lives" in their own living rooms.[13]

The films' popularity suggests that the public's acceptance of and affinity for

Disney trumps scholars' criticism. Bell, Haas and Sells, for example, noted their own students' reluctance to criticize Disney because of their "pleasurable participation in Disney film and its apolitical agendas," citing that "it's only for children, it's only fantasy, it's only a cartoon, and it's just good business."[14] Silverman noted that the

> unwillingness to critically analyze children's films stems from the adult's difficulty in overcoming subjective perceptions of an object that relates to childhood in order to objectively view the same object as a product of a corporation. Deeming a product "for children" often strips it of its accepted ability to be critically analyzed.[15]

Giroux suggested that

> If educators and other cultural workers are to include the culture of children as an important site of contestation and struggle, then it becomes imperative to analyze how Disney's animated films powerfully influence the way America's cultural landscape is imagined.[16]

Disney's first animated representations stereotyping Asians date to World War II, when the company produced propaganda films for the U.S. military, but these have drawn little critical attention. The character Donald Duck was "Disney's star in the war years."[17] In *Commando Duck* (1944), which runs just under seven minutes long, Donald parachutes onto a remote Pacific island to destroy a Japanese base. Virtually oblivious of the dangers that surround him there, he dodges enemy fire from, among others, one soldier disguised as a rock and another embodied in a buck-toothed, slant-eyed tree, speaking in stereotypical dialect and advocating the firing of the first shot at a soldier's back. In the historical animated short *How to Be a Sailor*, Goofy is launched as a torpedo 6 minutes, 25 seconds into the 7:10-long film and crashes through a succession of Japanese ships that are also buck-toothed and slant-eyed before he crashes into the mainland on the distant horizon, represented by a stylized rising sun. Mission accomplished.

Previous Studies

Scholars have critiqued Disney animated films, and specifically *Lady and the Tramp* for the portrayal of the Siamese cats. Contemporary criticism has tended to focus on more recent animated films, such as *Mulan*,[18] but the present study focuses on Siamese cats. More general critiques do not discuss *Lady and the Tramp* or the cats but provide relevant contexts to consider in a more narrowly focused study.

General Studies

Giroux questioned the prevailing view of the "innocence" and "wholesome" fun of Disney animation:

The relevance of such films exceeded the boundaries of entertainment. Needless to say, the significance of animated films operates on many registers, but one of the most persuasive is the role they play as the new "teaching machines" ... [Disney films] help children understand who they are, what societies are about.[19]

Towbin, Haddock, Zimmerman, Lund, and Tanner examined the portrayals of the organizing societal principles of gender, race, age, and sexual orientation across a sample of 26 full-length animated Disney films and found gender, racial, and cultural stereotypes that have persisted over time.[20] Few positive portrayals emerged but were more common in later films; marginalized groups were portrayed negatively, rarely, or not at all.

Lacroix extended this thread of scholarly inquiry into Disney films by examining the second wave of animated features: those produced and released from 1989 on, beginning with *The Little Mermaid* in 1989.[21] As we do in this essay, Lacroix grounded her analysis of women of color in the context of Orientalism and noted "how representations of gender and cultural difference operated within Disney's consumerist framework."[22]

Specific Studies

Other scholars have commented on Si and Am in passing, but none has interrogated every aspect of their characterization. Most focused on their appearance and behavior. Booker noted that Si and Am were "slant-eyed, shifty-eyed, insidious, grinning creatures, wearing expressions of predatory obsequiousness ... conspiratorial, subversive, malign."[23] They have "slanted eyes and whiney voices [and] are bent on mischief and destruction"[24]; they are "wily, duplicitous, troublemaking, freeloading, Asian illegal immigrants"[25]; "cruel and criminal ... [with] stereotypical Asian features: slanted eyes, buck-teeth, and heavy accents ... mean, sly, greedy."[26]

The Current Study

This essay follows Williams (as cited by Lacroix) in attempting to look "both at the text and beyond it ... to see how it creates its own unity, to establish the 'class of truth' which determines its meaning because it is not an isolated object, but part, and product, of a combination of socio-historical forces.[27] Seeking to fill a gap in the research, we employ a similar lens to comment on representations of the Oriental in *Lady and the Tramp* and how their meanings connect to a larger cultural framework. We conduct here a textual analysis focused tightly on the representations of the Oriental embodied in the characters of Si and Am, Siamese cats who visit and disrupt the domestic bliss of the Dear household in the Disney animated film *Lady and the Tramp*. We examine these representations through the filter of four categories—*physical characteristics, posture and nonverbal communication, behaviors,* and *dialogue*—

in exploring Disney's construction of the Oriental. We undertake the challenge of critically analyzing the hegemony of Disney and will illuminate the danger in not doing so.

The Siamese Cat, in Context

BACKGROUND.   Siamese cats were introduced to the West in 1878, when David B. Sickels, a U.S. diplomat in Bangkok, shipped one to First Lady Lucy Hayes.[28] According to legend, Siamese cats were owned by royalty, lived in the palace, and served as guardians of Buddhist temples.[29] Within years of the Hayes adoption, Siamese cats were being exported to Britain, too. Siamese cats begin appearing in Western popular culture in the early 20th century. They may well have debuted as the enemies of Growltiger, the eponymous character in a poem by T.S. Eliot.[30] Growltiger hates the Siamese:

> *But most to Cats of foreign race his hatred had been vowed;*
> *To Cats of foreign name and race no quarter was allowed.*
> *The Persian and the Siamese regarded him with fear—*
> *Because it was a Siamese had mauled his missing ear.*

Although Growltiger is a fearsome and fearless cat, the Siamese, en masse, spring an attack on him and his lover, Griddlebone. The poem's narrator describes the Siamese as a "fierce Mongolian horde," "the enemy," and "the foe ... armed with ... cruel carving knives."

Yet, Siamese cats are actually considered among the tamest and friendliest of animals. (And no, they are not born as identical twins; the first human conjoined twins on record, however, Chang Bunker and Eng Bunker, were from Siam and spent most of their life—May 11, 1811–January 17, 1874—in the U.S.[31]) Siamese cats would seem a curious choice to play villains in a Disney animated film, except that the 1950s were a peak decade in the history of heights of American xenophobia. The cats conjured images of the Asian associated with World War II and Korean War propaganda.[32] Americans were coping, too, with "guilt feelings over the atomic bombings of Hiroshima and Nagasaki," which "gave this racism a new nervous edge in the long 1950s..." Si and Am threaten Lady's "domestic bliss," an experience shared by "many Americans in the mid–1950s that their comfortable lives were endangered by sinister foreigners."[33] Invading and imposing on the Dears' household, the cats represent illegal Asian immigrants. They visually represent a foreign "yellow menace."

> Although ostensibly domesticated their goal is to subvert and exploit the domestic scene to their own ends. Although aggressors, they pose as victims. Most important, in the lexicon of the 1950s, they are un–American, their un–Americanness emphasized from the outset, when they announce: "We are Siamese if you please; we are Siamese if you don't please."[34]

Good animals, such as Lady, come from higher classes—or, like heroic Tramp, who is a mixed breed, they possess strong moral character, unlike Si and Am, who will prove themselves scheming and untrustworthy.

Asian "Inscrutability"

Chinese-American author Maxine Hong Kingston has long noted that many reviews of her novel *The Woman Warrior* "praised the wrong things," using the "false standard" of the "exotic, inscrutable, mysterious oriental":

> What I did not foresee was the critics measuring the book and me against the stereotype of the exotic, inscrutable, mysterious oriental.... I had not calculated how blinding stereotyping is, how stupefying. The critics who said how the book was good because it was, or was not, like the oriental fantasy in their heads might as well have said how weak it was, since in fact it did not break through that fantasy.[35]

Chow noted that the Western inference of the "inscrutability" of the Chinese persists: "Pertinently for the present purposes, this stereotype hinges on a scrutiny by those who are outside the Chinese culture ... 'inscrutable Chinese' at the sociological level is often invoked in mockery against Asian people (hence its reputation as a racist or an orientalist stereotype)."[36]

Prasso, in writing about Americans' "continued willingness to believe that Asia and Asian people are somehow fundamentally different—exotic, enigmatic, and inscrutable," recalled that "perhaps the only humorously subversive relief came in the form of a television commercial" for a laundry detergent additive that aired ran throughout the 1970s[37]: "While still playing off the stereotypes of Asians in the service trade as tricky and inscrutable, this one has the Asian woman trumping both her secretive husband and their white customer." When the customer inquires of the laundry owner, "How do you get your shirts so clean, Mr. Lee?" he replies, "Ancient Chinese secret." In the next moment, Mrs. Lee shouts from the back room, "We need more Calgon!" The customer smirks, "Ancient Chinese secret, huh?"

Findings

THE TEXT.   The cats Si and Am, who are as yet unknown to Lady (a watchdog trained to be suspicious of anything unusual or out of place in her master's household), are brought into the Dear home and first appear on screen by lifting the lid of a picnic basket—a Trojan horse of sorts—in which they were brought. Initially, they are represented merely as two mysterious pairs of disembodied, slanted eyes. As the innocent and unsuspecting, but clearly worried Lady passes by, they peer at her from out of an artificial and impossible darkness (with the lid lifted, their faces should have been as illuminated as their surroundings). Quickly, they close the lid as she passes by, still unaware of their presence. Then, a slinky, black tail slips out, serpent like, from under the lid and taps Lady on her hindquarters before disappearing inside the box again. When she turns about to see what's there, she spies the closed box but hears the opening strains of a distinctly Asian song. As she approaches the box, the lid lifts again to reveal, again, only the eyes of Si and Am. Lady is startled; her eyes widen, her jaw drops, and her floppy ears stand straight up. She has never seen such a sight. Si and Am drop the lid to the accompanying sound of a gong. Lady has never heard such a sound. Frightened, she darts away, hiding around a corner wall and looking back at the picnic basket.

Now, we see Si and Am's tails have slipped out and are dancing like two charmed snakes. The near half of the lid lifts again to reveal their eyes once more. Their tails tap the lid shut as Lady returns to examine more closely, and both cats have now retreated into the picnic box altogether. They then pop up, head and shoulders, out of the back end of the basket and stare straight at Lady. They begin a dance synchronized to the music and to each other's movements and begin to approach Lady. As they near her, their image on screen grows considerably, until the frame can no longer contain them. With a knowing glance at each other, Si and Am begin to sing about being Siamese.

Lady stays still as they slink past her, rubbing, as friendly cats sometimes will, as they pass. They leave the room to explore another, and Lady follows. Immediately, Si and Am are drawn to a bird's cage and, with a sudden leap, one climbs the pole and reaches a paw inside the cage. Barking, Lady dashes to chase them off. Si and Am bound across a sofa and onto a piano on which sit a cloth and vase of roses. Skidding across the polished wood, the cats knock the vase—roses, water, and all—onto the open keyboard and bench. Lady arrives too late to stop the damage and looks upon it helplessly.

Quickly, however, Si and Am scale a tall armoire, and from their vantage point, spot a fishbowl next and plot to kill its inhabitant. They descend from their perch by rappelling down drapes, shredding them with their ominously extended sharp claws in the process. They crouch and sneak beneath furniture as they make their way to a credenza, on which sits their target: the fishbowl. They discuss how they'll divvy up their meal. This time, instead of jumping up on the furniture, they merely pull at a cloth, on which the fishbowl sits. It nears the edge and totters there precariously before Lady grabs the other end of the cloth with her teeth and engages in a tug of war. The cats release their grip, and the tension results in the cloth and fishbowl flinging off at Lady's end of the credenza.

The bowl spills, and the fish flops on the carpet toward the Siamese cats, who are now hiding under a chair but have their paws out to catch their meal. The fish proves slippery and elusive, though, giving Lady a chance to rescue it, snatching it away delicately between her teeth. She races the fish back to the safety (and remaining water) of the bowl, only to find that one of the Siamese lies in wait inside, its jaws wide open in line with the mouth of the bowl. At the last possible moment, as the cat slams its jaws shut, Lady pulls the fish away but loses her grip. The fish flops away again; meanwhile, the other cat has again climbed the pole to the bird cage and is reaching in with her paw when the two cats are distracted by the distant sound of a baby crying and go off to investigate, climbing the wide, carpeted stairs to the second-floor nursery since they know that, where there's a baby, there's milk nearby. Having finally restored the fish to its bowl, Lady bounds up the steps to the first landing and, barking, makes her stand and confronts Si and Am. They screech in protest and turn to run back down the stairs, Lady in pursuit. As she chases them through the house, they pull down drapes, knock over an end table, and evade Lady by climbing atop the armoire again. The ruckus has drawn the attention of Aunt Sarah, their owner, who enters the room to find Si and Am now crying and moaning and rolling on the floor in pretend agony. The old maid plucks up her cats and carries them upstairs, chastising Lady and soothing her own pets, who exchange smiles and lock their tails in secret solidarity behind her back.

Analysis

PHYSICAL CHARACTERISTICS.   Disney's animated villains are "preoccupied with their appearance, exhibiting a kind of vanity."[38] Animators created Si and Am to almost exacting standards in appearance of actual seal-point applehead Siamese cats. Their eyes are almond-shaped, as they should be, but they are pale blue; seal-point Siamese have the darkest blue eyes of the breed. The inscrutability of Si and Am also is pronounced in their physical characteristics. They are drawn to be sleek, giving them an air of sneakiness. Their eyes—sometimes the only visible manifestation of their presence—are slanted, in exaggerated stereotype of stylized representations of the Oriental.[39] They are also slender, and their necks extend like periscope to enable them to survey their surroundings, in contrast with the softer curves of the protagonist Lady. It cannot be determined whether they are female or male, although popular American singer Peggy Lee voiced the characters and sang their song. Their sensuous forms, however, fit the model Li-Vollmer and LaPointe described when they noted that below the neck, the physiques of animated villains also connote feminine forms.[40] Perhaps most striking about the cats' features is their exaggerated overbite, technically called *overjet*—a malocclusion in which the maxillary incisors (two upper front teeth) project forward at a prominent and obvious degree—and commonly called *buck teeth*. This feature has long been identified as an unfavorable stereotyped concept held by American children.[41] And Si and Am are, of course, yellow. Chang has traced exaggerated physical features such as "buck teeth, slit eyes, and yellow-tinted skin" as far back as American and British fears of a "yellow peril" invasion of Chinese immigrants at the turn of the 19th century, and to concerns before, during, and immediately after World War II, when the Japanese and then the Chinese filled Western imaginations with fear and loathing.[42] The timing of each of those hysterias coincides with the historical setting of *Lady and the Tramp*—circa 1909—and the initial release of the film—1955.

POSTURE AND NONVERBAL COMMUNICATION.   Villains signal deviance through their body movements and positioning.[43] Their tendency "to be erect and formal, their backs straight, neck elongated, and shoulders back ... as a well-bred lady" describe Si and Am. Their gender may be unrevealed to us, but they walk as villains—even males, such as Governor Ratcliffe in *Pocahontas* (1995) and Scar in *The Lion King* (1994)—in Disney animated films do: with a feminine gait. Spector described this in 1998 as "pranc[ing] around arrogantly in a Hollywood–invented style that is supposed to represent what the audience should assume are the mannerisms of aristocratic Siamese or Chinese."[44] Of the distinction between the nationalities, he noted: "Disney's films, like many Hollywood films, often tended to lump ethnic groups into a kind of undifferentiated mass—Asians, Chinese, Japanese, Siamese, for example..."

BEHAVIORS.   The Siamese cats wreck the parlor while Lady tries to prevent them from eating the bird and the goldfish and then from stealing the baby's milk. Si and Am's transgressions are recounted earlier in this essay, but they bear enumerating concisely for effect:

1. One of the cats climbs a pole and reaches a paw inside a bird cage unsuccessfully to extract its inhabitant.
2. Si and Am skid across a polished baby grand piano, knocking a vase of roses and water onto the open keyboard and bench.
3. They plot to drown and eat a fish they spy in a bowl and shred heavy drapes with their claws as they rappel toward the fish.
4. They yank on a cloth to pull the fishbowl off the credenza, then let go in a tug of war, causing the bowl to fly off the other end. One cat—we can't distinguish between Si and Am any better than a Westerner can tell the Chinese apart—lurks beneath a chair in wait for the flopping fish. The other assumes a position pretending to be the mouth of the bowl to swallow the fish.
5. One of the cats again climbs the pole to reach into the bird cage.
6. Si and Am climb a stairway to steal a crying baby's milk.
7. Chased through the house, they tear down drapes and knock over an end table.
8. They cry and moan and roll on the floor in mock agony to frame Lady as the troublemaker in the ruckus.

All in the space of 2 minutes, 34 seconds!

DIALOGUE.   There is no dialogue per se between the Siamese cats and other characters in Lady and the Tramp. For most of their time on screen, Si and Am sing their signature song, *We Are Siamese*, as a duet; sometimes to each other, sometimes to whoever is listening. They begin their song by way of introducing themselves to Lady and confronting her. Lady, it appears, cannot understand the tortured syntax of their non-native English speech. Nadel pointed out:

> Everything about this announcement—the insidious reversal ... [of the wording in the cats' lyrical phrase about "pleasing"] the false parallelism of the syntax, the clearly foreign accent of the voices and the music—everything tells us that these cats are double agents ... their accents put them in direct contrast with Tramp, who is, as his speech demonstrates, quintessentially domestic.[45]

Si and Am's lines are peppered with errors of grammar and syntax. Spector noted "the denigrating humor in listening to the Asiatic cats butcher the English language."[46] Ma described the cats' speech thusly:

> These lines are dominated by the long "e" sound, which arises from the assumption that the Chinese tend to end sentences with "e," such as the notoriously racist line "No tickee, no washee." The lyrics also suffer from unidiomatic expressions and a loss of be-verbs, all alleged characteristics of Chinese pidgin English.[47]

True, some state-of-being verbs are dropped, but not all. Given the inconsistency, one could cynically infer that the inclusion of the verbs arose only from the need to pad out lyrical lines for meter. The message: "Good animals speak with Western, British and American accents...."[48]

Legacy

Disney's Si and Am were only the first cartoon cats to be characterized as Siamese and to possess villainous or otherwise dubious traits. Although children's fictionalized animation since *Lady and the* Tramp was first released in 1955 has included depictions of other such Siamese cats, two particular cultural products are worth noting as heirs to a continuing legacy.

THE ARISTOCATS. In the 1970 Disney animated film *The Aristocats*, a Siamese cat named Shun Gon first appears 1 minute, 19 seconds into the song "Everybody Wants to Be a Cat." His back to the audience, he changes the tempo and tune as he bangs on the drums with chopsticks instead of drumsticks. His "l's," however, are clearly mispronounced—in what is derisively called *Engrish*—as "r's."[49] Shun Gon reappears at 1 minute, 47 seconds, now playing the pianos with chopsticks and singing and giggling his lines. And at 2 minutes, 13 seconds, reacting to a kitten's flat attempt on a trumpet, Shun Gon mispronounces the "l" in "blew."

THE CHINESE SIAMESE CAT. Ma asserted a connection among Orientalist stereotyping through a critique of Amy Tan's *The Chinese Siamese Cat.*[50] Ma described illustrator Gretchen Schields's graphics, juxtaposed with Tan's written texts as "an amalgamation of the style of *chinoiserie*, on the one hand, and of ethnic stereotypes of Chinese, on the other." Schields's chinoiserie idealizes a mythic China; ethnic stereotypes demonize the Chinese people. The "vexing implication" in all this, Ma asserted, was the lingering anthropomorphism of "Chinese as animals, whether cats or monkeys."[51] Siamese cats, "because of their namesake, seem to be one of the stock associations of Asians in the Western mind."[52] The "racial markers are transposed from humans to cats, not the other way around.

Disney cats may then be regarded as projections of the Western perception of Asians."[53] In making the connection to Shun Gon's references to *egg foo yung* and fortune cookies, Ma noted: "It is revealing that both kinds of food are Western concoctions of Chinese cuisine, just as the portrayal of Siamese cats is meant for Western consumption"[54]—a highly defined trait of Orientalism.

Conclusion

We set out to interrogate the text of *Lady and the Tramp* to uncover ethnic stereotyping in the representation of the Siamese cats, Si and Am, and to interpret those representations. We found both subtle and blatant instances of Orientalist stereotyping in *physical characteristics, posture and nonverbal communication, behaviors*, and *dialogue*. The evidence is overwhelming and understandable—though, we assert, not acceptable—in the context of the times and in the context of Disney animated films' consistent (and conservative) sociohistorical/political worldview. Although no single instance of stereotyping proves anything general about Orientalism in Disney's productions or its audiences' predisposed receptivity to the messages therein, the preponderance of evidence points toward an overarching Orientalist project that suits Western norms. The stereotypes we identified suggest an Orientalism at work in *Lady and the Tramp* and subsequent cultural artifacts.

The Orientalist characterizations of Si and Am are but the beginning of a continuous thread that has been woven through time. These stereotypes are consistent with other Orientalist representations in *The Aristocats* and *The Chinese Siamese Cat*. The exaggerations of *physical characteristics, posture*, and *nonverbal communication, behaviors*, and *dialogue* represent a legacy of Orientalist stereotyping. The archetype of Asian as inscrutable (and villainous) carries with it the "vexing implications"[55] of menace to the Western order of things.

We have explained several possible reasons for the Asian stereotype manifested in Si and Am and their cultural progeny, and two in particular seem most plausible: the a desire to distance the East, or Orient, from the West out of (1) guilt for the atrocities of Hiroshima and Nagasaki and (2) continuing fears of the Other (Chinese, Japanese, Siamese/Thai—in a word: "Asians") in the long post–World War II era of the Cold War, which continues to be played out not as a military enterprise, real or imagined or represented through agents acting on behalf of the principals, but rather in economic terms of global markets. We suggest that there ought to be some concern that Orientals in future Disney enterprises and similar cultural fictions may, in fact, become even more villainous in their representation as global conflicts on battlefields and in boardrooms.

The Orientalist projects discussed here reinforce norms in cultural reproductions that have been mostly unquestioned and accepted by Western, particularly U.S., audiences in the more than half a century since *Lady and the Tramp* established a standard for such ethnic stereotyping. Walt Disney stated that his only intention was to appeal to the inner child in everyone.[56] In counterpoint to the Disney company's self-proclaimed desire to promote diversity and unity—but also in response to Walt Disney's suggestion in a 1937 *Time* magazine interview that "We just try to make a good picture. And then the professors come along and tell us what we do"[57]—we contend that the portrayals of the Siamese cats in *Lady and the Tramp* and other mediated representations draw on and perpetuate demeaning stereotypes of Asians. The equation of villain with Asian reinforces Western fear of and attempted dominance over the Other and potentially raises nationalistic levels of xenophobia and its consequences.

Notes

1. Sheng-mei Ma, "Amy Tan's The Chinese Siamese Cat: Chinoiserie and Ethnic Stereotypes," *The Lion and the Unicorn* 23, no. 2 (1999): 202–218

2. Edward Said, *Orientalism* (New York: Pantheon, 1978).

3. Said, *Orientalism*, 1978.

4. Edward Said, "Representing the Colonized: Anthropology's Interlocutors," *Critical Inquiry* 15 (1989): 207.

5. Said, Orientalism, 1978.

6. Timothy Mitchell, "The World as Exhibition," *Comparative Studies in Society and History* 31, no. 2 (1989): 217–236.

7. Kimiko Akita, "Orientalism and the Binary of Fact and Fiction in Memoirs of a Geisha," *Global Media Journal* 5, no. 9 (2006): http://lass.calumet.purdue.edu/cca/gmj/fa06/gmj_fa06_akita.htm; Kimiko Akita, "Bloopers of a Geisha: Male Orientalism and Colonization of Women's Language," *Women and Language* 32 no. 1 (2009): 12–21.

8. Henry Giroux, *The Mouse That Roared: Disney and the End of Innocence* (Lanham, MD: Rowman & Littlefield, 1999).

9. Ariel Dorfman, *The Empire's Old Clothes* (New York: Pantheon Books, 1983).

10. Elizabeth Bell, Lynda Haas, Laura Sells, *From Mouse to Mermaid: The Politics of Film, Gender, and Culture* (Bloomington: Indiana University Press, 1995); Mike Budd and Max H. Kirsch, *Rethinking Disney: Private Control, Public Dimensions* (Middletown, NY: Wesleyan University Press, 2005); Eleanor Byrne and Martin McQuillan, *Deconstructing Disney* (London: Pluto Press, 1999); Rebecca-Anne C. Do Rozario, "The Princess and the Magic Kingdom: Beyond Nostalgia, the Function of the Disney Princess," *Women's Studies in Communication* 27, no. 1 (2004): http://search.rdsinc.com/texis/rds/suite/+cde7UC3ezxbtqzMommX_69KTFqn h1ccewx1qmwwwwewhanmeUqTpexhowww/showdoc.html?thisTbl=CWI (accessed July 20, 2009); Dorfman, *The Emperor's Old Clothes*; Sean Griffin, *Tinker Belles and Evil Queens: The Walt Disney Company from the Inside Out* (New York: New York University Press, 2000); Sylvia, Herbozo, Stavey Tatleff-Dunn, Jessica Gokee-Larose, and J. Kevin Thompson, "Beauty and Thinness Messages in Children's Media: A Content Analysis," *Eating Disorders* 12 (2004): 21–34; Nicholas Sammond, *Babes in Tomorrowland: Walt Disney and the Making of the American Child 1930–1960* (Durham, NC: Duke University Press, 2005); Mia Adessa Towbin, Shelley A. Haddock, Toni Schindler Zim-

merman, Lori K. Lund, and Litsa Renée Tanner, "Images of Gender, Race, Age, and Sexual Orientation in Disney Feature-Length Animated Films," *Journal of Feminist Family Therapy* 15, no. 4 (2004): 19–44.

11. Susanne Ault and Jennifer Netherby, "*Lady and the Tramp, Pride & Prejudice* Also Bow Well," *Video Business*. Posted March 2, 2006, http://www.videobusiness.com/article/CA6312352. html (accessed July 20, 2009).

12. David McCutcheon, "Disney Closes the Vault," ign.com. Posted September 29, 2006, http://dvd.ign.com/articles/736/736573p1.html (accessed July 20, 2009).

13. Henry Giroux, "Are Disney Movies Good for Your Kids?" in *The Politics of Early Childhood Education*, L.D. Soto, ed. (New York: Peter Lang, 1995): 99–114.

14. Bell et al; 4.

15. Rachel Anne Silverman, "New Dreams, Old Endings: Searching for 'A Whole New World' in Disney Second-Wave Animated Romance Films" (Honors thesis, Wesleyan University, 2009) 4.

16. Giroux, "Are Disney Movies Good for Your Kids?": 96.

17. Michael S. Shull and David E. Wilt, *Doing Their Bit: Wartime American Animated Short Films, 1939–1945*, 2d ed. (Jefferson, NC: McFarland, 2004): 141.

18. Weimin Mo, Wenju Shen, "A Mean Wink at Authenticity: Chinese Images in Disney's *Mulan*," *New Advocate* 13, no. 2 (2000): 129–142; Vincent E. Faherty, "Is the Mouse Sensitive? A Study of Race, Gender, and Social Vulnerability in Disney Animated Films," *SIMILE: Studies in Media & Information Literacy Education* 1, no. 3 (2001): 1–8; Georgette Wang and Emilie, Yueh-yu Yeh, "Globalization and Hybridization in Cultural Products: The Cases of *Mulan* and *Crouching Tiger, Hidden Dragon*," *International Journal of Cultural Studies* 8, no. 2 (2005): 175–193; Jun Tang, "A Cross-Cultural Perspective on Production and Reception of Disney's *Mulan* Through Its Chinese Subtitles," *European Journal of English Studies* 12, no. 2 (2008): 149–162.

19. Giroux, "Are Disney Movies Good for Your Kids?": 90.

20. Towbin et al.

21. Celeste Lacroix, "Images of Animated Others: The Orientalization of Disney's Cartoon Heroines from *The Little Mermaid* to *The Hunchback of Notre Dame*," *Popular Communication* 2, no. 4 (2004): 213–229.

22. Lacroix, 213.

23. M. Keith Booker, *The Post-Utopian Imagination: American Culture in the Long 1950s* (Westport, CT: Greenwood, 2002).

24. Mark I. Pinsky, *The Gospel According to Disney: Faith, Trust, and Pixie Dust* (Louisville, KY: Westminster John Knox Press, 2004): 71.

25. Byrne and McQuillan, 97.

26. Rebecca Rabison, "Deviance in Disney: Representations of Crime in Disney Films: A Qualitative Analysis" (Honors thesis, Wesleyan University, 2008): 77.

27. Patrick Williams, "Kim and Orientalism," in *Colonial Discourse and Postcolonial Theory: A Reader*, Patrick Williams and Laura Chrisman, eds. (New York: Columbia, 1994).

28. "Siam: America's First Siamese Cat: David B. Sickels' letter to Lucy Webb Hayes, November 1, 1878," Posted February 2004, http://www.rbhayes.org/hayes/manunews/paper_trail_display. asp?nid=65&subj=manunews (accessed July 20, 2009).

29. Marjorie McCann Collier and Karen Leigh Davis, "Siamese Cats: Everything About Acquisition, Care, Nutrition, Behavior, and Health," *Complete Pet Owner's Manual* (Barron's Educational Series, 2006).

30. Thomas Stearns Eliot, *Old Possum's Book of Practical Cats* (New York: Harcourt, Brace and Co., 1939). The poem "Growltiger's Last Stand" appeared in this book, which was the basis for the long-running Broadway musical *Cats*.

31. David R. Collins, *Eng & Chang: The Original Siamese Twins* (Boston, MA: Pearson, 1994).

32. Alan Nadel, *Containment Culture: American Narratives, Postmodernism, and the Atomic Age* (Durham, NC: Duke University Press, 1995).

33. Byrne and McQuillan, 97.

34. Nadel, 122.

35. Maxine Hong Kingston, "Cultural Misreadings by American Reviewers," in *Asian and Western Writers in Dialogue: New Cultural Identities*, Guy Amirthanayagam, ed. (London: Macmillan, 1982): 55–65.

36. Rey Chow, "How (the) Inscrutable Chinese Led to Globalized Theory," *PMLA* (Special Topic: Globalizing Literary Studies) 116, no. 1 (2001): 69–74.
37. Sheridan Prasso, *The Asian Mystique: Dragon Ladies, Geisha Girls, and Our Fantasies of the Exotic Orient* (New York: Public Affairs, 2005): 65.
38. Meredith Li-Vollmer and Mark E. LaPointe, "Gender Transgression and Villainy in Animated Film," *Popular Communication* 1, no. 2 (2003): 102.
39. Collier and Davis, 4.
40. Li-Vollmer and LaPointe, 98.
41. Rose Zeligs, "Children's Concepts and Stereotypes of American, Greek, English, German, and Japanese," *Journal of Educational Sociology* 28, no. 8 (1955): 360–368.
42. Michael Chang, *Racial Politics in an Era of Transnational Citizenship* (Hoboken, NJ: Blackwell Publishing, 2007).
43. Li-Vollmer and LaPointe, 100.
44. A. J. Spector, "Disney Does Diversity: The Social Context of Racial-Ethnic Imagery," in *Cultural Diversity and the U.S. Media*, Yahya R. Kamalipour and Teresa Carilli, eds. (State University of New York Press, 1998): 46.
45. Nadel, 123.
46. Spector, 46.
47. Ma, 202.
48. Rabison, 76.
49. "Speakers of many Oriental languages find it difficult to distinguish systematically between the /l/ and /r/ phonemes" (Roberts, 1976).
50. Ma, 202.
51. Ma, 213.
52. Ma, 215.
53. Ma, 216.
54. Ma, 215.
55. Ma, 213.
56. Steven Watts, *The Magic Kingdom: Walt Disney and the American Way of Life* (Columbia: University of Missouri Press, 1997).
57. Watts, i.

Bibliography

Akita, Kimiko. "Orientalism and the Binary of Fact and Fiction in *Memoirs of a Geisha.*" *Global Media Journal* 5, no. 9 (2006): http://lass.calumet.purdue.edu/cca/gmj/fa06/gmj_fa06_akita.htm
_____. "Bloopers of a *Geisha*: Male Orientalism and Colonization of Women's Language," *Women and Language* 32 no. 1 (2009): 12–21.
Ault, Susanne, and Jennifer Netherby. "*Lady and the Tramp, Pride & Prejudice Also Bow Well*," *Video Business*. Posted March 2, 2006, http://www.videobusiness.com/article/CA6312352.html (accessed July 20, 2009).
Bell, Elizabeth, Lynda Haas, and Laura Sells. *From Mouse to Mermaid: The Politics of Film, Gender, and Culture* (Bloomington: Indiana University Press, 1995).
Booker, M. Keith. *The Post-Utopian Imagination: American Culture in the Long 1950s* (Westport, CT: Greenwood, 2002).
Budd, Mike, and Max H. Kirsch. *Rethinking Disney: Private Control, Public Dimensions* (Middletown, NY: Wesleyan University Press, 2005).
Byrne, Eleanor, and Martin McQuillan. *Deconstructing Disney* (London: Pluto Press, 1999).
Chang, Michael. *Racial Politics in an Era of Transnational Citizenship* (Malden, MA: Blackwell Publishing, 2007).
Chow, Rey. "How (the) Inscrutable Chinese Led to Globalized Theory," *PMLA* (Special Topic: Globalizing Literary Studies) 116, no. 1 (2001): 69–74.

Collier, Marjorie McCann, and Karen Lee Davis. "Siamese Cats: Everything About Acquisition, Care, Nutrition, Behavior, and Health," *Complete Pet Owner's Manual* (Barron's Educational Series, 2006).

Collins, David R. *Eng & Chang: The Original Siamese Twins* (Boston, MA, Pearson, 1994).

Dorfman, Ariel. *The Empire's Old Clothes: What the Lone Ranger, Babar, and Other Innocent Heroes Do to Our Minds* (Durham: Duke University Press Books, 1996).

Do Rozario, Rebecca-Ann C. "The Princess and the Magic Kingdom: Beyond Nostalgia, the Function of the Disney Princess," *Women's Studies in Communication* 27, no. 1 (2004): http://search.rdsinc.com/texis/rds/suite/+cde7UC3ezxbtqzMommX_69KTFqn h1ccewx1qmwwwwewhanmeUqTpexhowww/showdoc.html?thisTbl=CWI (accessed July 20, 2009).

Eliot, T. S. *Old Possum's Book of Practical Cats* (New York: Harcourt, Brace and Co., 1939).

Faherty, Vincent E. "Is the Mouse Sensitive? A Study of Race, Gender, and Social Vulnerability in Disney Animated Films," *SIMILE: Studies in Media & Information Literacy Education* 1, no. 3 (2001): 1–8

Giroux, Henry. "Are Disney Movies Good for Your Kids?" in *The Politics of Early Childhood Education*, L.D. Soto, ed. (New York: Peter Lang, 1995): 99–114.

_____. *The Mouse That Roared: Disney and the End of Innocence* (Lanham, MD: Rowman & Littlefield, 1999).

Griffin, Sean. *Tinker Belles and Evil Queens: The Walt Disney Company from the Inside Out* (New York: New York University Press, 2000).

Herbozo, Sylvia, Stacey Tatleff-Dunn, Jessica Gokee-Larose, and J. Kevin Thompson. "Beauty and Thinness Messages in Children's Media: A Content Analysis," *Eating Disorders* 12 (2004): 21–34.

Hong Kingston, Maxine, "Cultural Misreadings by American Reviewers," in *Asian and Western Writers in Dialogue: New Cultural Identities*, Guy Amirthanayagam, ed. (New York: Macmillan, 1982): 55–65.

Lacroix, Celeste. "Images of Animated Others: The Orientalization of Disney's Cartoon Heroines from *The Little Mermaid* to *The Hunchback of Notre Dame*," *Popular Communication* 2, no. 4 (2004): 213–229.

Li-Vollmer, Meredith, and Mark E. LaPointe. "Gender Transgression and Villainy in Animated Film," *Popular Communication* 1, no. 2 (2003): 102.

Ma, Sheng-Mei. "Amy Tan's *The Chinese Siamese Cat:* Chinoiserie and Ethnic Stereotypes," *The Lion and the Unicorn* 23, no. 2 (1999): 202–218

McCutcheon, David. "Disney Closes the Vault," ign.com. Posted September 29, 2006, http://dvd.ign.com/articles/736/736573p1.html (accessed July 20, 2009).

Mitchell, Timothy. "The World as Exhibition," *Comparative Studies in Society and History* 31, no. 2 (1989): 217–236.

Mo, Weimin and Wenju Shen. "A Mean Wink at Authenticity: Chinese Images in Disney's *Mulan*," *New Advocate* 13, no. 2 (2000): 129–142.

Nadel, Alan. *Containment Culture: American Narratives, Postmodernism, and the Atomic Age* (Durham: Duke University Press, 1995).

Pinsky, Mark I. *The Gospel According to Disney: Faith, Trust, and Pixie Dust* (Louisville, KY: Westminster John Knox Press, 2004): 71.

Prasso, Sheridan. *The Asian Mystique: Dragon Ladies, Geisha Girls, and Our Fantasies of the Exotic Orient* (New York: Public Affairs, 2005): 65.

Rabison, Rebecca. "Deviance in Disney: Representations of Crime in Disney Films: A Qualitative Analysis." Honors thesis, Wesleyan University, 2008, 77.

Said, Edward. *Orientalism* (New York: Pantheon, 1978).

_____. "Representing the Colonized: Anthropology's Interlocutors," *Critical. Inquiry* 15 (1989): 207.

Sammond, Nicholas. *Babes in Tomorrowland: Walt Disney and the Making of the American Child, 1930–1960* (Durham: Duke University Press, 2005).

Shull, Michael S., and David E. Wilt. *Doing Their Bit: Wartime American Animated Short Films, 1939–1945*, 2d ed. (Jefferson, NC: McFarland, 2004).

Sickels, David B. "Siam: America's First Siamese Cat: David B. Sickels' letter to Lucy Webb Hayes, November 1, 1878," posted February 2004, http://www.rbhayes.org/hayes/manunews/paper_trail_display.asp?nid=65&subj=manunews (accessed July 20, 2009).

Silverman, Rachel Anne. "New Dreams, Old Endings: Searching for 'A Whole New World' in Disney Second-Wave Animated Romance Films." Honors thesis, Wesleyan University, 2009, 4.

Spector, Alan J. "Disney Does Diversity: The Social Context of Racial-Ethnic Imagery," in *Cultural Diversity and the U.S. Media*, Yahya R. Kamalipour and Teresa Carilli, eds. (Albany: SUNY Press, 1998): 46.

Tang, Jun. "A Cross-Cultural Perspective on Production and Reception of Disney's *Mulan* Through Its Chinese Subtitles," *European Journal of English Studies* 12, no. 2 (2008): 149–162.

Towbin, Mia Adessa, Shelley A. Haddock, Toni Schindler Zimmerman, Lori K. Lund, and Litsa Renée Tanner. "Images of Gender, Race, Age, and Sexual Orientation in Disney Feature-Length Animated Films," *Journal of Feminist Family Therapy* 15, no. 4 (2004): 19–44.

Wang, Georgette and Emilie Yueh-yu Yeh. "Globalization and Hybridization in Cultural Products: The Cases of *Mulan* and *Crouching Tiger, Hidden Dragon*," *International Journal of Cultural Studies* 8, no. 2 (2005): 175–193.

Watts, Steven. *The Magic Kingdom: Walt Disney and the American Way of Life* (Columbia: University of Missouri Press, 1997).

Williams, Patrick. "Kim and Orientalism," in *Colonial Discourse and Postcolonial Theory: A Reader*, P. Williams and L. Chrisman, eds. (New York: Columbia, 1994).

Zeligs, Rose. "Children's Concepts and Stereotypes of American, Greek, English, German, and Japanese," *Journal of Educational Sociology* 28, no. 8 (1955): 360–368.

White Man's Best Friend: Race and Privilege in Oliver and Company

NATCHEE BLU BARND

Introduction

At first glance *Oliver and Company* (1988) presents an opportunity to discuss representations of economic class and the relationships between poverty, wealth, and homelessness in a capitalistic society. Adapted from Charles Dickens' classic literary work *Oliver Twist* (1838), the story centers on the ascension of an orange kitten named Oliver from helpless orphan to member of a street family and finally to pampered pet for a lonely but wealthy girl living on New York City's posh Fifth Avenue. Like most Disney films, however, and despite the film's inspiration, *Oliver and Company* clearly sidesteps any direct questioning of inequality and poverty, instead pushing forward the much more palatable and marketable refrain of hope for eventual prosperity and recognition of one's rightful place among the economically and morally elite (a salve also contained in Dickens' version).

While *Oliver and Company's* clichéd rags-to-riches journey provides the general storyline, the subtext of the film offers a rich opportunity to explore Disney's narratives and representations of race and privilege during an era when multiculturalism was gaining widespread political and rhetorical support, as well as opposition.[1] Not surprisingly, Disney presents its viewers with a thoroughly normative depiction. Although the majority of the film's key characters are not human, the anthropomorphized dogs (and kitten) inevitably reflect dominant social constructions of race, sex, and sexual identity. Indeed, like most dominant narratives, the film constructs and presents its representations through a White male social lens, leaving the only treatment of difference to rhetorical questions of class and poverty; ostensibly asking, should the poor (characters) with self-initiative find success or wealth despite their downtrodden beginnings? In doing so, it centralizes men, assumes normative heterosexuality, and privileges Whiteness.

The story centers on male characters, with female characters as either the objects of male sexual desire, loyal sidekicks, or emotional and social wrecks.[2] The film also offers troubling representations of race that specifically construct Latinos as emotionally charged, criminal foreigners, African Americans as violent urban thugs, and European Americans as unmarked, normative, and singularly important figures.

Throughout my analysis, therefore, I draw pointed attention to this film's ability to convey and reproduce such social identities entirely through the deployment of animal characters. In particular, this essay examines how *Oliver and Company's* main characters are constructed as representations of heterosexual White male identities, and how the overarching narratives necessarily privilege this already dominant intersection of social identity categories. I argue that the film's question of class ultimately serves to elide any focus on other forms of difference or inequality, following a routine formula that leaves Whiteness un-interrogated. In addition, I outline how in order to reproduce dominant representations, this Disney production again relies on predictable representations of non-dominant identities that filmically reproduce and naturalize real world social inequalities.

Story Sketch

The central story consists of the elevation of the kitten Oliver from helpless orphan to elite pet. Oliver's journey is facilitated by a dog "gang" led by the savvy mutt Dodger.[3] Dodger's crew consists of a diverse collection of pedigrees, including his second-in-command Rita (an Afghan), an air-headed Great Dane named Einstein, and a pretentious bulldog named Francis.[4] The smallest, but most over-the-top member of the gang is Tito, a feisty Chihuahua aptly characterized by having a proverbial bark that is bigger than his bite. After Oliver is adopted by a wealthy pre-teen girl, Jenny Foxworth, the crew is temporarily joined by Georgette, Jenny's self-centered upper class show poodle who is determined to rid herself of Oliver. The story follows the crew's efforts to eek out living alongside their human caretaker Fagin, a quasi-homeless scavenger and small-time thief. Fagin's survival is threatened by his inability to repay debts owed a ruthless crime boss/shipping industrialist named Sykes, who is everywhere accompanied by two ferocious Doberman Pinschers, Roscoe and DeSoto. When Sykes kidnaps Oliver's owner-to-be (Jenny) in order to pay off Fagin's debt and garner substantial financial gain through her ransom, the dog crew sets into action to save the abducted child, free Fagin of his debt, secure Oliver's "rightful" place with Jenny, and end Sykes' tyranny of crime, intimidation, and violence.

The Dogged Persistence
of Race and White Privilege

While few of the characters are depicted in a fashion that explicitly references a racial or ethnic identity, all of the characters in *Oliver and Company* are nonetheless marked by the logic of racialization. Because the film mostly intends to construct "universal" characters, the filmmakers forge narratives that privilege dominant White, male, and heteronormative social perspectives, and thus render main characters that are—unless otherwise marked—effectively normative heterosexual White males.

My focus on the constructions of Whiteness in film reverses the "common sense" charge of examining race in film which usually focuses on representations of people of color. While attention to depictions of non–White images and narratives is necessary, it often excludes the "other side" of race and racism.[5] This neglect can unintentionally allow Whiteness to escape notice, something which ultimately serves to further entrench its force and power. Veteran scholar of Whiteness Studies Richard Dyer rightly points to the epistemological damage done by allowing Whiteness to stand in as normative. "Looking, with such passion and single-mindedness, at non-dominant groups," he reminds us, "has had the effect of reproducing the sense of the oddness, differentness, exceptionality of these groups, the feeling that they are departures from the norm. Meanwhile the norm has carried on as if it is the natural, inevitable, ordinary way of being human."[6] Taking active notice of Whiteness—noting its particularity and attendant privileges, as well as its modes of re-production—reduces its capacity to externalize difference. George Lipsitz precisely notes that, "as the unmarked category against which difference is constructed, whiteness never has to speak its name, never has to acknowledge its role as an organizing principle in social and cultural relations."[7] Thus, in order to deconstruct that fabricated invisibility, we must work to "see whiteness, see its power, its particularity and limitedness," despite its construction as normative or universal.[8] In *Oliver and Company* race is applied to clearly marked Others, while the central characters remain presumably free of marking, thus pointing to their presumed and invisible Whiteness. If we miss these constructions we also miss the implication of the power dynamics being naturalized through the character developments and narratives.

While Whiteness does not operate evenly for everyone and must be viewed through a matrix of privilege and power that accounts for class, sex, gender, sexuality, ability (among other factors), these intersections of identity do not negate the racially ordered material and social gains of those who may successfully benefit from Whiteness.[9] In *Oliver and Company*, however, the film's narrative framing around the lower class standing of the main characters threatens to undermine or overwhelm any productive attention to race and systems of privilege.

As one might expect, Disney regularly trades on the currency of Whiteness. In a recent study, Vincent Faherty found that more than forty seven percent of Disney's animated human characters were explicitly European or European American (read: White), while animals or objects comprised another forty percent.[10] Of the human characters, a full eighty-one percent are represented as White, a percentage that greatly increases when considering only the most substantial characters. The representations of animal or object characters, however, do not simply erase racial representations. Many characters are given clear ethnic and racial "markers," while others can be inferred based on non-visual factors, like speech pattern, relationship, or action. When characters lack any explicit racial markings they should be carefully examined for their potential to re-construct, presume, and thereby privilege dominant White identities. Instead of simply delving into how Disney creates characters explicitly marked by race (read: non–White), sex (read: female), and sexuality (read: non-heterosexual), we must also attend to the ways that the main characters and narratives privilege dominant, and therefore only implicitly marked social identities.

The central characters in *Oliver and Company* exemplify the reproduction of dominant White identities in animated filmmaking. Indeed, Oliver and Dodger articulate two variations of normative White identity in a nation increasingly confronted by and self-conscious of its ethnic and racial complexity during the 1980s. Further, the construction and emphasis of the main characters as lower-class (homeless; in poverty) mirrors the troubling White backlash against multiculturalism that works to render all differences equal. According to such logic, race is no longer an issue, and thus an irrelevant marker of difference. This denial allows White-identified persons to ignore or reject non–White racialized experiences, and instead attempt to deal only with issues of economic disparity. Such solitary attention to class reproduces the invisibility of Whiteness and ignores the very modes of its construction precisely through other, "irrelevant" differences.

Oliver is crafted as unexposed to the diversity of the city (and nation), and represents a notion of cultural innocence and naivety. Dodger, on the other hand, is fashioned as the savvy urban resident, representing firsthand experience with and a command over such multiplicity. Both, however, encounter "difference" outside of themselves, signaling their construction along the contours of dominant social identities. In essence, Oliver and Dodger are straight White males (one man/dog, and one boy/kitten) negotiating their way through a cosmopolitan and fluid urban environment.

The Disney team, by default, constructs these characters through their interaction with a diverse city and in their juxtaposition with other explicitly racialized characters. According to the narrative, their challenges are not just economic, but also cultural and racial. We are introduced to Oliver (voiced by European American child-actor Joey Lawrence), for example, in the film's opening scenes. He resides with a half-dozen siblings in a cardboard box being sold on the street by an anonymous character that is effectively depicted as White. By the end of the day the rest of the litter has been sold off, and only Oliver remains unclaimed, even after being offered for free. In effect, he becomes a homeless, unwanted child; an effective narrative tool for invoking audience sympathy for the cartoon kitten. Orphaned, Oliver struggles to find adequate shelter and safety from the dangers of the big city. Yet his abandonment is also shaped by his metaphorical expulsion from a safe White home, as his seller leaves him to fend for himself in a diverse city.

Oliver emerges from the traumatic night relatively unscathed, and awakens to find a bustling, vibrant urban street. Although the artists render most of the passing crowd of humans to appear White, the kitten's first direct interactions occur with explicitly ethnic or racialized characters. He is caressed by an Asian American infant character, who is promptly pulled away by his mother. A stereotypically voiced Italian American street vendor (who is also an obese, unkempt, hairy, and animal-hating cigar-smoker) aggressively shoos the hungry kitten away from his hot dog cart. In perhaps the most telling moment, Oliver is drawn to the sound of hip hop music played from a Black passerby who dances along with his radio. The kitten becomes enthralled, and mimics the dancing passerby, only to reveal his inadequacy as an urban denizen and hip hopper. After just a few struts he trips over his own paws and tumbles to the ground. These initial human characters clearly drive home the point of a culturally and ethnically diverse New York. More significantly, they signal Oliver's out-of-placeness, establishing the character's urban innocence, and productively marking him through the "unmarked" status of a standard "cultureless" Whiteness.

Although the early character development scene for Oliver establishes his initial lack of "street credentials," it also foreshadows his predictable overcoming of his "real," economic obstacles. By the end of the story, the helpless kitten will master street life and find his place both literally in the form of a home, and figuratively in the form of social belonging. The prefigured accomplishments assigned to Oliver likewise manifest in the construction of another character, the kitten's mentor to-be, Dodger. The story's symbolic transfer of "heritage" from Dodger to Oliver partly signifies the inherited social and material capital of racial privilege. Indeed, at the end of the film, Oliver has made his way into the elite of the city, a level of success built through the "inheritance" of his canine father figure's dominant racial, sexed, and sexualized identities.[11]

Where Oliver's social identities are revealed by the character's wide-eyed experience with a bustling New York City street, Dodger's identities are crafted through a combination of character traits and musical delineation. He is described and drawn as a terrier mutt, a dog ostensibly without clear or "pure" lineage. By constructing Dodger as a mixed-breed, the writers and artists of

Oliver and Company introduce the possibility of rendering the character's "ethnicity" productively elusive. On the one hand, his ambiguous heritage is clearly intended to allow a wider segment of the audience to identify with the protagonist. Yet, the abstraction of his heritage actually draws upon the force of assimilation theory aimed at wiping away ethnic identities in the cause of formulating new "American" ones.

The fatal flaw in ethnic assimilation theory, of course, has always been the violent constraints placed on racialized populations by a White dominated society; populations that despite whatever level of acculturation and amalgamation remain marked by phenotypic differentiation. In other words, only those who can pass as White are able to effectively participate and benefit from shedding their "old" identities and becoming "just" Americans. All other groups either carry doubled identities as both American citizens and members of racialized populations, or are simply denied recognition as citizens at all and are constantly and repeatedly marked only as racialized peoples (consider the "forever foreign" standing commonly proscribed to Asian Americans and Latinos).[12]

The mixed background of Dodger (voiced by European American soft rock singer-songwriter Billy Joel) could have been an analogy for mixed-race, except that mixed-race individuals must constantly confront their ethnic "ambiguousness," misrecognition, and the general discomfort their "elusive" identity causes for others. Harlon Dalton reminds us that "Whites who don't identify strongly with any ethnic group tend to take race for granted or to view it as somehow irrelevant"; a luxury not available to those who cannot easily claim Whiteness.[13] As SanSan Kwan and Kenneth Speirs point out, multiraciality has long been "a mark of shame and ignominy" in an American society which historically worked to "establish and sustain firm categories of race as a way to maintain White dominance."[14] The legacy and logic of those efforts to simplify racial identities still subjects mixed-race individuals to "exclusion from 'stable' racial categories, the enduring 'What are you?' question, continual misrecognition, accusations of passing, and so forth" as they navigate a world that does not readily acknowledge multiplicity or tolerate the disruption of supposedly fixed categories.[15]

Most importantly, non–White mixed individuals do not escape the process of racialization, just temporarily confound its streamlined social implementation. As an "unmarked" pedigree then, Dodger must be translated as a mix of White ethnicities. While his (hetero)sexuality is easily conveyed by quick scenes that show him crudely ogling or smooching at female dogs, his racialization as White is effectively secured by its very dismissal, and the absence of any explicit racial/ethnic reference. Quite unlike the construction of the characters Roscoe, Rita and Tito, the writers and animators do not supply their central mutt character with any distinctive "ethnic" characteristics. In the end, the force of his abstracted identity, which is usually only available to mixtures comprised of European heritages and White phenotypes, overshadows Dodger's potentially "racial" mixed-ness as a mutt.

By contrast, when the Imagineers turn their attention to creating *Oliver and Company's* non–White characters, the result is much less ambiguous. Although not nearly as explicitly as Tito's Latino construction (discussed below), the Disney production team effectively generate Roscoe and Rita as African American characters. These characters are crafted through visual and audio clues, by their contrast to Dodger and other characters, and through their curious relationship to one another. Let's consider Roscoe first. Both Roscoe and his partner DeSoto are drawn as Doberman Pinschers, popularly noted as highly athletic, loyal, and potentially vicious pets. Roscoe is Sykes' lead attack dog, and serves as proxy to his malevolence and ruthlessness. Indeed, the crime boss drives a large black sedan with a hood ornament of leaping chrome Dobermans, and personalized license plates reading "DOBR-MAN."

In the few scenes where the villainous dogs appear, the artists depict thick, well muscled and aggressive Pinschers in order to elicit the threat of violence, while Roscoe's voice artist deploys African American–inflected speech and tones (African American actor Taurean Blacque voices the lead Doberman).[16] The artists emphasize the dogs' predominantly black fur, in striking contrast to the mutt Dodger's predominantly white fur. In addition to their already dark fur color, the Dobermans always seem engulfed in shadow, an admittedly classic tactic for drawing animated villains, but also furthering the establishment of their uniquely dark "complexion." Also of significance, Roscoe and DeSoto are the only dog characters in *Oliver and Company* which do not have unique pedigrees. Dodger's five-dog crew consists of five distinct breeds, plus an interloping poodle (Georgette). All of the other dog "extras" drawn into the film are similarly unique. In contrast, Roscoe and DeSoto are indistinguishable. Their otherwise identical red (Roscoe) and blue (DeSoto) collars provide the only means by which the audience can differentiate between the two, in effect marking them with same kind of racially-coded "sameness" too often applied to Black males in accusations of criminal activity and during police lineups.

Rosina Lippi-Green's study of language use covering fifty years of Disney feature films reveals that any character's use of African American vernacular English (what Lippi-Green short hands as AAVE) or any other non-standard English dialect dramatically increases the chance the character will function as a villain, while only those characters that use mainstream US English serve as main characters or function as heroes. Her study documents that language consistently functions as a vehicle for conveying to audiences who is good and who is evil. The consequence is that the "overall representation of persons with foreign accents is far more negative than that of speakers of US or British English. About 20 percent of US English speakers are bad characters, while about 40 percent of non-native speakers of English are evil."[17] Further, using a limited data set she found that "all AAVE-speaking characters appear in animal rather than humanoid form," rousing troubling historical associations between Blackness and beastliness. Although nearly all of the characters in *Oliver and Company* are animals, the degree to which Roscoe's racialization is so readily apparent threatens to attach the character's menace as much to his Blackness as to his animated presentation.

Beyond their appearance and voice attributes, the film's narrative reproduces a troubling master-slave subtext which further suggests the two Dobermans are crafted through popular references to Blackness. Whereas Dodger and his crew are free to run the town and act in whatever manner they desire, Roscoe and DeSoto remain entirely under the control of their owner and "master" Sykes. During an initial encounter between Dodger's crew and the attack dogs, a brutal fight is abruptly halted after Sykes calls the dogs to return. As the Dobermans retreat, still making threats and regretting their inability to finish the fight, Rita (voiced by African American actor Sheryl Lee Ralph) derisively taunts the adversaries: "Run along Roscoe, your *master* is callin'" (emphasis original to voice talent). Indeed, Sykes himself assures a kidnapped Jenny Foxworth that the growling dogs encircling her "only eat when I tell them to," voicing the degree of command physically demonstrated by his finger snapping—which immediately sends them into attack mode, or instantly recalls them from their tasks.[18]

Rita, the sole female member of Dodger's crew is more muted in her apparent Blackness than Roscoe, filling the role of level-headed yet subservient lieutenant. At least one reviewer clearly discerned the intended racial construction, however, referring to the character as a "Motown Afghan."[19] Rita's linguistic racialization is most clearly noted when she inquires of Georgette about a framed picture of an anonymous male dog. Although referencing their shared heterosexual female-hood (straight "girl talk"), the writers also stake out Rita's and Georgette's racial distinctions through a subtle exploitation of dialectic Black English (or Lippi-Green's AAVE). "Excuse me, uh sistah, who's Rex?" Rita cautiously queries before being dismissed by the flabbergasted poodle. While the use of Black English is not nearly as pronounced as Br'er Rabbit's "Yes I is!" in Disney's 1946 *Br'er*, it clearly binds Roscoe and Rita together while also separating them from the other characters. Thus, another indicative scene that reveals both Roscoe's and Rita's implicit racialization occurs when Roscoe beckons Rita to leave Dodger's side and partner with him. "You know Rita, I can't figure out why you rather hang around a dump like this when you could be living uptown with a class act like myself."[20]

Although the filmmakers turn little attention to Rita, in one of her few featured scenes, she is again racially cast by the musical selection chosen to represent her. She predictably bursts into a pop/Motown-esque song that lasts only one stanza before the writers' abruptly interrupt the music and return the center of attention to Dodger and his ill-fated hit-and-run scheme. Just as Rita is about to launch into "Streets of Gold" she decides to help the fledgling Oliver gain some street smarts. In a stereotypical phrasing recalling the figure of the Black Mammy as childcare worker and house caretaker, the Afghan happily exclaims, "we gotta clean you up chile,' and give you some on-the-job trainin'!" While the racial identity of Disney's musical performers do not necessarily have to correspond to the animated characters purported identity, it seems compelling that European American recording artist Billy Joel sings Dodger's songs, and Ruth Pointer (now Pointer-Sayles), eldest sister of the then-popular Pointer Sisters R&B group, sings Rita's. Given that both of Rita's voice talents (Pointer and Ralph) are African American women, it seems extremely unlikely the Disney team did not intend to construct Rita as Black.

Unleashing Race

The construction of the film's most blatantly racialized and racist depiction—Tito—serves as the most indicative contrast with the main, White male protagonist Dodger. As the most clearly "ethnic" character, contemporary reviewers easily recognized the filmmakers' construction of the "ethnic stereotype" (Maslin 1988), referring to it variously as the "hairless Hispanic mutt,"[21] "peppery Chicano,"[22] or simply "Hispanic Chihuahua."[23] "Ignacio Alonzo Julio Federico de Tito" (voiced by Chicano actor and comedian Cheech Marin) effortlessly dances to Latin-Caribbean music, plays "congas," speaks with an unmistakable urban Chicano accent intermittently spliced with Spanish phrases, utters alarm at "aliens," anticipates dangerous "gang wars," rides on police cruisers, and assumes that any extraordinarily large home must naturally house "at least two hundred people."

Tito is presented as an over-sexualized, Latino male without the ability to self-regulate, and in serious need of paternal supervision and cultural refinement. He is a fast-talking, violence-prone, sexually predatory, and criminally inclined Chihuahua who overestimates his own prowess in predictably dramatic fashion. Sadly, these identities and characteristics are all predetermined by dominant representations of Latinos. In this film, the trope of the "spicy" Latino signals both sexual and physical aggression. These connected characteristics also feed one another, as Tito's oversexualization alludes to his propensity to excessively engage in criminal and violent behavior. In all, the film presents him as motivated entirely by passions and carnal desires, and thus incapable of self-restraint.

During the initial encounter between Dodger's crew and Jenny's show dog Georgette, for example, Dodger assures the poodle that he is not interested in her as sexual conquest/rape target after she immediately assumes such treatment from the "street" dogs. Referring to both the mission to recover Oliver and his genuine lack of interest in the coddled poodle, he reassures her that "You're barking up the wrong tree. It's not you I'm after." Tito, however, quickly interjects that he is "*very* impressed" (emphasis original to the voiceover) by the kept dog, inappropriately suggesting his sexual interest in the poodle. Disney, like much of popular culture, has long linked hypersexuality with Latinos. In a recent analysis of the challenges that Disney faced when trying to manage cultural and social hybridity with filmic hybridity (fused animation and live action) during the 1940s, J.P Telotte points out that representations of Latin America were "alluring yet also elusive."[24] During that era particularly, the combination of desire for the Other with the inability to craft solid understandings of and relationships with the Other manifested in the sexualization of Latinos, as was done with "Brazilian Bombshell" Carmen Miranda, her sister Aurora, singer Dora Luz, and dancer Carmen Molina.[25] In *The Three Caballeros* (1945), the embedded sexuality of Latinas is supposedly so great that it actually compels the animated Donald Duck into frantic although ultimately frustrated "romantic overtures" toward these real life women.[26] The filmmakers for *Oliver and Company* offer the masculine version of this racialized sexuality by emphasizing Tito's propensity to commit sexual assault. They craft the character forcing unwanted kisses upon the Georgette, and depict him having an erotic response after being slapped away: "Ooohh ... I think she likes me, man!"

When the Disney Imagineers are not depicting Tito as a sexual predator, they are featuring him as the main symbol of criminality.[27] Although the entire dog crew is ostensibly poor, dirty, and criminal to the extent that they survive by stealing food and accumulating resources to pawn, only Tito is consistently depicted engaging in illegal activities. When the audience is first introduced to the members of Dodger's crew, Tito extols the value of a shredded "primo" leather wallet he has contributed to the day's loot. While he holds his contribution in his mouth, defending its quality to Francis (the "stately" bulldog), the rest of the goods remain secure in a trunk, unattached to the other characters who have presumably also committed theft to obtain their items. Only Einstein—the character Dave Smith characterizes as "slow moving" (in reference to the speed of his mental processes)—suggests that he has a contribution; a ruined tennis racket that clearly has no use value and was more likely to be scavenged than stolen.[28]

In this simple scene, the writers and artists effectively link Tito to pickpocketing, burglary, or robbery, even if the thrashed wallet was simply found. The character's subtle criminalization is further entrenched by its juxtaposition against the comparative normalization of Francis (voiced by African American actor, and noted voice artist, Roscoe Lee Browne). While Tito's wallet tirade marks him as irrational, dangerous, and indiscriminate, the "British"-accented Francis passively watches a theatrical play on television while calmly reciting Shakespearean lines. Indeed, the next scene solidifies the contrasting characterizations, as it features the Chihuahua erupting into a frenzy and instigating a dogfight with his reserved bulldog colleague.

Tito's wallet fight effectively introduces a defining character trait that will be re-visited in later scenes. In the crew's first major caper, the dogs stage a fake hit-and-run with the wealthy Foxworth family car. When the family butler/chauffeur exits the vehicle to check on Francis, who is pretending to have been struck by the limousine (and practicing his "thespian" craft versus engaging in con-artistry), Dodger places Tito in charge of "electronics." This euphemism directs Tito to enter the car where he attempts to steal the car stereo. While he is ultimately unsuccessful, Tito's criminality is immediately punished, as he receives a massive jolt of electricity from biting into the stereo wires. Meanwhile, Oliver, who is bewildered as to how to be a "look out," is quickly rewarded by being claimed by the wealthy young Jenny Foxworth. Although the writers and artists clearly intended the electrocution as comedy-relief, this scene relegates Tito's character as the least morally upstanding member of a supposedly criminal dog crew. It clearly situates him as the most expendable and least worthy (animated) body in the crew, reflecting a national tradition of viewing Latinos as a necessary but undesirable, and thereby "throw-away" labor force. In later scenes, he again subjects himself to electrocution in order to benefit the crew's goals, further reiterating Tito's position and devaluing as "comedic" his constant subjection to physical punishment and pain.

Oliver and Company further deploys notions of Latino deficiency by suggesting Tito's need for cultural interventions. Specifically, the upper-class poodle Georgette attempts to bathe and groom the feisty Chihuahua against his wishes, while Francis tries to introduce him to high culture (Shakespeare, ballet, poetry). Tito's treatment recalls early twentieth century Americanization programs aimed at teaching European and Mexican immigrants (as well as many Mexican Americans), "proper" citizenship and cultural practices. In Los Angeles, for example, the programs presumed "Mexicans" culturally, morally, and racially deficient and therefore unapologetically sought to change how they ate, dressed, spoke, washed, worked, and played.[29] The consequences of these efforts were deemed deadly serious, as one proponent adamantly proclaimed that tortillas and beans (instead of bread and lettuce) would lead Mexican Americans into a life of crime. To reformers, Mexican American life "with no milk or fruit to whet the appetite" would necessarily lead the children to "take food from the lunch boxes of more fortunate children" whereupon the "initial step in a life of thievery [would be] taken."[30] Clearly, Georgette and Francis must have recognized that Tito had never been fed bread and lettuce growing up.

Same Old Song

Before concluding, I return to Disney's construction of a normative White heterosexual male narrative. In addition to the construction of Dodger using assimilation theories that privilege and reproduce Whiteness, the Disney team skillfully defined their lead character through its trademark use of song. As discussed above, the opening scene uses hip hop music, racialization, and notions of Blackness to fundamentally frame this Disney story of urban 1980s New York. Yet none of these facets figure in the explicit narrative of the urban storyline. In fact, the song created to encapsulate Dodger's character draws upon mainstream soft-rock and an outdated lyrical reference to 1950s bebop "cool" instead of the more unswerving, political messages of 1980s hip hop.[31] Given that 1988 (the year this film debuted) marked a pinnacle moment in hip hop, with New York artists such as Run DMC, Public Enemy, and Boogie Down Productions enjoying national and international audiences for giving voice to urban Black New York experiences, such a musical decision appears dangerously reticent, and smacks of mainstream White cultural insularity.[32]

Where groups like Public Enemy brazenly tell of anti–Black violence, segregation, and institutional racism in songs like "Black Steel in the Hour of Chaos," Billy Joel's performance of "Why Should I Worry?" articulates an understanding of social and spatial belonging clearly shaped by a dominant White experience. His only real obstacle remains an economic one. Thus, shortly after tricking Oliver into helping him steal food from the Italian American hot dog vendor, the Disney musical team launches Dodger into the film's feature (and Golden Globe nominated) song. The refrain indicates that he is worry free because he has possession of "street savior faire," which on the surface loosely translates into a kind of mastery of urban social life, and ease in relationships. Unlike the anger and angst in hip hop's articulation of the limits and challenges of urban Blackness and Latinidad, Dodger's soft-rock anthem celebrates individuality and casually dismisses social obstacles (read: class). According to the lyrics, no matter where this character travels in New York, he effectively fits in and succeeds. Indeed, despite the challenges posed by his proxy-homelessness (his owner Fagin squats in rickety boat) and economic standing, Dodger's transiency is re-scripted as a broad ownership over the entire cityscape.

The writers and song makers fashion Dodger as being comfortable in a wide variety of locales and lifestyles, specifically mentioning Central Park, Delancey Street, "the Bow'ry," St. Marks, Chelsea, and the Ritz. While much of this boast overtly focuses on class distinctions, it implicitly tell us about ethnic and racial difference as well. More pointedly, it highlights the unique spatial properties of heterosexual White maleness. As anti-racist, White activist-scholar Tim Wise points out, one of the key privileges of Whiteness is geographic freedom. It means "never being really out of place, about having access and, more to the point, the sense that wherever you are, you belong, and won't be likely to encounter much resistance to your presence."[33] Similar arguments can be made for being male, to the extent that anti-female violence and predatory sexuality renders many places unsafe for women to travel; and for heterosexuality, to the extent that anti-gay violence regulates the public display of non-normative sexual identities.

Again, quite unlike the narratives crafted by 1980s hip hop (as well as by some Motown artists), the final lyrics of the song suggest that none of Dodger's potential transgressions against the social order will impede the character's freedoms. This underlying spatial component of White heterosexual male privilege positions Dodger to croon that his savoir faire will mediate his social violations, suggesting that possession of the "right" or privileged set of social identities offers him protection against serious consequence. In other words, as Black and Latino men are arrested, imprisoned, and sometimes shot for serious offenses like driving, walking, and talking, the Dodger character expects to "own" the town. While young racialized urban residents are fitted with handcuffs, this character is confident he will wear a "crown."

Despite the limits on which racialized, gendered, and sexualized bodies can safely navigate New York City, let alone the degree to which they might make such claims over the space of the city and its people, the filmmakers intend for Dodger's song to become the mantra for the entire film, returning to close out the story with everyone invited to participate. "Why Should I Worry?, Why Should I Care?" begins exactly as before, with Dodger the sole performer and narrative subject. The lyrics abruptly and unexpectedly change as Rita leaps onto Dodger's makeshift stage and joins in the singing. In this moment Disney's multicultural dream of diverse characters romping around the nation in friendship and equality falls apart.

As Rita joins the closing song, the title lyrics are quickly modified from Dodger's singular "I" to "we," indicating a clear attempt to include all of the characters into the privileged position held thus far entirely by Dodger. Yet, as the "subordinate" dogs add their voices to the song the overall harmony and vocal skill quickly diminishes. Invoking the parody of off-key karaoke singers, the Frankie/bulldog character adds his brusque speak-sing contribution, before Tito interrupts everyone with his own scream-sing addition. As a quasi-parody, this revised song must remain a shadow of the original to the extent that it always references the original, and thus the original subject Dodger, or the heterosexual White male figure. The inequality of the singing fittingly mirrors the lesser character's inability to fully inhabit a position of privilege. Indeed, the crew's least memorable member, the "slow" Great Dane Einstein, is excluded altogether.

During an era of emergent and self-conscious multiculturalism, the Disney team clearly sought to generate an "inclusiveness" that spanned not just diverse personalities, but also diverse racial, ethnic, cultural, and gender backgrounds. Yet this convergence proposes an equality not evident anywhere in the film narrative nor in the reality of urban New York. As soon as second-in-command Rita joins Dodger in the song, the force of dominant male heterosexuality quickly acts to undercut her "ascension" as Tito and Dodger turn their attention to crudely ogling two random female dogs. Rita pulls Dodger away from his sexual advances, but the damage has been done. Dodger has reclaimed center stage and reasserted his importance to the film's narrative trajectory. As the new voices prove additive, this new version of the song re-centers the hetero-normative White male, who had traumatically lost his priv-ileged position for all of one musical refrain. As it turns out, with Disney in command of the pen and ink, Dodger truly did not need worry, nor care.

Conclusion

Oliver and Company follows a narrative trajectory well established in Dis-ney animated films. The central characters reflect dominant social identity categories, and thereby further privilege those already privileged perspectives. Even in a film which features mostly canine characters, the animators and writers effectively generated normative constructions of race, gender, and sex-uality. Whereas even the most apologetic viewer might understand the dangers inherent in the film's depiction of Tito, the feisty Chihuahua, the more subtle production of African American characters like Rita and Roscoe deserve equally critical attention. Moreover, the most powerful representations found in *Oliver and Company* draw on the unmarked, dominant categories of single White manhood which are effectively hidden through a discourse of economic struggle. It is only through careful delineation of these productions and their implications that we will ultimately begin to erase the social forces reflected and reinforced in Disney's restricted imagination, and start drawing on imag-inations better capable of envisioning social justice.

Notes

1. See Gordon and Newfield (1996).

2. Lippi-Green's study of 371 characters across twenty-four Disney movies between 1938 and 1994 found that just under seventy percent (69.8) of speaking roles were granted to male characters (1997: 87).

3. In the film, the application of the term "gang" to Dodger's crew clearly tends more toward the "group of friends" meaning than the "dangerous, organized crime group" definition. At one point in the film Dodger plainly states that "the gang means family."

4. Although Rita is sometimes described as a Saluki in digital forums like Wikipedia, Dave Smith—founder and longtime archivist for Walt Disney Archives—lists the character as an Afghan Hound in the official Disney encyclopedia (1996: 419).

5. See Rothenberg (2002).

6. Dyer (1988: 44).

7. Lipsitz (1998: 1).

8. Dyer (2002: 12).

9. Henry A. Giroux (1997) offers an intriguing meditation on "rethinking the subversive pos-sibility of 'Whiteness'" (91) in such a way that is both responsive to the diversity and intersec-tionality of White identities and productive toward generating a new, oppositional definition. This perspective is especially helpful for avoiding a simplistic association of White with dominance, racism, and systems of privilege.

10. Faherty (2001: 4).

11. This narrative ultimately naturalizes and downplays the significance of the continually

racially disparate accumulation of wealth available to families through inheritance. Consider Oliver and Shapiro's *Black Wealth/White Wealth* (1995) for a thorough documentation of the depth of our current economic divide, especially in the important articulation of the distinction between income and wealth.

12. For more on the notion of "forever foreign," see Lisa Lowe's Immigrant Acts.

13. Dalton (2002: 16).

14. Kwan and Speirs (2004: 1).

15. Ibid (2).

16. DeSoto is voice by European American actor Carl Weintraub.

17. Lippi-Green (1997: 92).

18. In the end, their blind aggression leads to early death. During the final fight/escape scene, the Dobermans each battle with Dodger, only to be shoved or forced to fall from Sykes' car, whereupon they are electrocuted by a subway tunnel's third rail.

19. Kemply (1988).

20. While this scene effectively neutralizes Rita's sexuality (at least in relation to Roscoe), the official Disney encyclopedia nevertheless explicitly describes the character in sexual terms; as a "sensuous" Afghan (Smith 1996: 419).

21. See Ansen (1988).

22. See Kempley (1988).

23. See Culhane (1988).

24. Telotte (2007: 113).

25. Ibid (111).

26. Although Telotte's focus is on the larger issues of cultural and political ambivalence and postmodern tension during an era of global uncertainty, the imposed sexuality serves as one of the key modes by which Disney represents this "dilemma" to Americans.

27. Dodger's initial theft of hotdogs functions mostly to establish that characters "street credibility," while Tito serves as primary actor in every major criminal or violent venture.

28. Smith (1996: 157).

29. Oliver and Company's writers hint at the tensions over English–only efforts when Tito admonishes Francis for using an extensive, intentionally haughty, vocabulary. In Cheech Marin's exaggerated Chicano accent, he demands that the "cultured" Francis "speak English." The irony of Tito's insistence on English also further marks him as foolish since it is clear that he is the most linguistically determined, non-standard character in the story.

30. Quoted in Sanchez (1993: 102). Although Americanization programs focused much of their attention on women—understood to be the bearers of culture and biggest influence on children and men—Tito's treatment recalls efforts to target men. Many European Americans feared an inherent threat of diseases, since they believed that "sanitary, hygienic, and dietic measures [were] not easily learned by the Mexican" (Sanchez 1993: 102). Tito's introductory scene depicts him scratching fleas, hair, and/or dirt off himself. He is the only dog explicitly marked as exceedingly dirty and unkempt, if not as an infested carrier of disease and parasites. Late in the film, the quasi-homeless, disheveled scavenger Fagin—at this point desperate and dejected—scrapes off similar-looking materials.

31. This should not be read to imply that bebop was not a critically-informed and reflective artistic form during the 1940s and early 1950s, only that it lacked such social force by the 1980s. Consider Amiri Baraka's (1963) Blues People, Eric Lott's (1988) "Double V, Double-Time: Bebop's Politics of Style" in Callaloo 11(3), Eric Porter's (1999) "'Dizzy Atmosphere': The Challenge of Bebop" in American Music 17(4), and John Lowney's (2000) "Langston Hughes and the 'Nonsense' of Bebop" in American Literature 72(2) for readings about the cultural and political force and potential of bebop during the World War II era.

32. In 1988, Run DMC released their fourth album, *Tougher than Leather*, Public Enemy dropped *It Takes a Nation of Millions to Hold Us Back*, and Boogie Down productions unveiled *By Any Means Necessary*. The release of Jazzy Jeff and the Fresh Prince's *He's the DJ, I'm the Rapper* in 1988 clearly signaled the widespread breakthrough of hip hop into suburban, White American life. This was also the year Los Angeles group Niggas With Attitude (NWA) garnered endless national controversy over the release of their album *Straight Outta Compton* and single "Fuck Tha Police."

33. Wise (2008: 48).

Bibliography

Ansen, David. 1988. "Cats and Dogs and Dinosaurs." *Newsweek,* 112 no. 22, 87.

Culhane, John. 1988. "*Oliver and Company* Gives Dickens a Disney Twist Urban Scene from an Appropriate Rooftop." *New York Times,* November 13, 1988.

Dalton, Harlon. 2002. "Failing to See." In *White Privilege: Essays on the Other Side of Racism.* Edited by Paula S. Rothenberg. New York: Worth Publishers.

Dyer, Richard. 2002. "The Matter of Whiteness." In *White Privilege: Essays on the Other Side of Racism,* edited by Paula S. Rothenberg. New York: Worth Publishers.

Dyer, Richard. 1988. "White." *Screen* 29 no. 4: 44–64.

Faherty, Vincent. 2001. "Is the Mouse Sensitive? A Study of Race, Gender, and Social Vulnerability in Disney Animated Films." *Studies in Media and Information Literacy Education* 1 no. 3: 1–8.

Giroux, Henry A. 1997. "White Noise: Racial Politics and the Pedagogy of Whiteness." In *Channel Surfing: Race Talk and the Destruction of Today's Youth.* New York: St. Martin's Press,.

Gordon, Avery F., and Christopher Newfield, eds. 1996. *Mapping Multiculturalism.* Minneapolis: University of Minnesota Press.

Kempley, Rita. 1988. "Oliver and Company." *Washington Post,* November 18, 1988.

Kwan, SanSan, and Kenneth Speirs, eds. 2004. "Introduction." In *Mixing it Up: Multiracial Subjects.* Austin: University of Texas Press.

Lippi-Green, Rosina. 1997. "Teaching Children How to Discriminate: What We Learn from the Big Bad Wolf." In *English with an Accent: Language, Ideology, and Discrimination in the United States.* London: Routledge.

Lipsitz, George. 1998. *The Possessive Investment in Whiteness: How White People Profit from Identity Politics.* Philadelphia: Temple University Press.

Lowe, Lisa. 1996. *Immigrant Acts: On Asian American Cultural Politics.* Durham, North Carolina: Duke University Press.

Maslin, Janet. 1988. "In Today's Animation, It's Dog Eat Doggie." *New York Times,* November 27, 1988.

Rothernberg, Paula S, ed. 2002. *White Privilege: Essays on the Other Side of Racism.* New York: Worth Publishers.

Sanchez, George J. 1993. *Becoming Mexican American: Ethnicity, Culture, and Identity in Chicano Los Angeles, 1900–1945.* New York: Oxford University Press.

Smith, Dave. 1996. *Disney A to Z: The Official Encyclopedia.* New York: Hyperion.

Telotte, J.P. 2007. "Crossing Borders and Opening Boxes: Disney and Hybrid Animation." *Quarterly Review of Film and Video* 24 no. 2: 107–116.

Wise, Tim. 2008. *White Like Me: Reflections on Race from a Privileged Son.* Brooklyn: Soft Skull Press.

Blackness, Bayous and Gumbo: Encoding and Decoding Race in a Colorblind World

Sarah E. Turner

Set in 1920s New Orleans, Disney's 2009 *The Princess and the Frog* release marks both the studio's return to hand-drawn animation and the arrival of their first Black princess in a feature-length film. Subject to criticism and speculation from the start, the much-anticipated project can be seen to both address and to erase race in its depiction of a black heroine and an ambiguously "brown" prince, not to mention the cast of swamp dwelling creatures, the choice of New Orleans as the setting, and the über-villain voodoo practicing Dr. Facilier. However, it is both too simplistic and too essentializing to read this film as yet another racist Disney production designed to further extend its $4 billion a year Princess line through the promotion of Princess Tiana products.[1] Instead, this film represents a complex moment in a culture steeped in political correctness and an adherence to the politics of colorblindness.

What this essay will do then is attempt to analyze the ways in which Disney and its audiences negotiate the complexities inherent within the readings of this film by drawing, in part, upon the theories of encoding and decoding as articulated by Stuart Hall in his seminal 1973 study.[2] It is possible to extend his analysis of production and reception, a central ideological argument in the field of cultural studies that focuses on audience reception, as a means to examine this film. Hall argues that "the 'object' of production practices and structures in [film] is the production of a message: that is, a sign-vehicle, or rather sign-vehicles of a specific kind organized, like any other form of communication or language, through the operation of codes, within the syntagmatic chains of a discourse."[3] Thus while the creators of the message "encode" a particular

83

ideology or reading into a text, an ideology that serves to reify the discourse of the hegemonic culture, there is a moment, the moment of "decoding," that enables an alternate reading (either negotiated or oppositional) in opposition to the dominant reading embedded within the discourse of the text. Dominant readings and readers fully share in the ideological codes of the text; negotiated readings and readers partly share the text's code but have some questions or reservations, while oppositional or counter-hegemonic readings and readers understand the intended or dominant reading but reject it.[4]

The dominant message encoded within this 21st century text is one of colorblindness, meaning that while Princess Tiana is clearly black, that is not the point of the text—she is simply a princess who "happens" to have black skin but is not representational of blackness or racially-prescribed tropes. Color-blind racism denies difference based on skin color by simply refusing to see color; therefore, Tiana is "just a princess," not a *black* princess. The rhetoric of color-blind racism enables an adherence to dominant ideologies and institutional practices by negating difference. Jeff Kurtti, author of *The Art of the Princess and the Frog*, articulates that desire to not "see" Tiana's blackness: she "stands apart from other Disney princesses not simply because of her race, but also because of her drive. 'It's ultimately more about *who* she is than *what* she is" [my emphasis].[5] While Kurtti's "who" signifies Tiana's drive and work ethic, it fails to also signify her color, clearly intrinsic to both "who" and "what" she is; his insistence that her drive displaces her race underscores the pernicious threat of viewing the world through a color-blind lens.

And yet, race was clearly foremost in Disney's mind with this project in that it both demonstrates their more recent intent to diversify their offerings and it responds to a recognizable paucity of black representation. Thus, Tiana must be black in the same way that Mulan was Chinese, Jasmine was Arabic, and Pocahontas was Native American. But, and herein lies the paradoxical nature of their project, she must also be simply another princess, albeit a more modern one, in a long line of Disney princesses. Audiences must simultaneously "see" her blackness and also overlook it in favor of her character and her desire to access the American dream. Disney's ability to both market her as their first black princess, and thus appeal to blacks and liberal whites, and use her as a means to engage a colorblind response to the film appeals to a wide-ranging audience and invites any number of complex readings of the film.

Recognizing the polemic nature of race and racial representation in American culture, Disney consulted representatives from the NAACP and Oprah during the production of the film and, in response to negative feedback, changed both the original name Maddy to Tiana and her employment from maid to waitress.[6] John Lasseter, Disney's chief creative officer, claims "we didn't want to do anything that might hurt anybody so we worked with a lot of African American leaders."[7] Even *EbonyJet*'s review of the film reifies this dominant colorblind reading through its claim that "the fact that both characters [Tiana and Naveen] are frogs underscores the post racial, why-can't-we-get-along attitude that everyone, no matter what color, is exactly the same underneath—that is green and slimy."[8] Film critic Roger Ebert adroitly exonerates Disney's racist past with his suggestion that *The Princess and the Frog* could have utilized the "innocent" song "Zip-a-dee Doo-Dah" while also celebrating the decision on the part of Disney to erase race in this text, recognizing tellingly that audiences don't want to see it:

> It is notable that this is Disney's first animated feature since *Song of the South* (1946) to feature African American characters, and if the studio really never is going to release that film on DVD, which seems more innocent by the day, perhaps they could have lifted "Zip-a-dee Doo-Dah" from it and plugged that song in here. Though the principal characters are all black (other than the rich man Big Daddy and the Prince, who is of undetermined ethnicity), race is not an issue because Disney adroitly sidesteps all the realities of being a poor girl in New Orleans in the early 1920s. Just as well, I suppose.[9]

Clearly the colorblind audience flocked to the film, resulting in a $25 million opening weekend in December 2009, and amassing $267,045,765 domestically as of the 28th of May 2011.[10] Interestingly, while *CNN.com* ran the headline "*Princess and the Frog* No. 1 at box office," *The New York Times* headline the following day claimed that "Disney's '*Princess*' Displays Limited Box Office Magic."[11] Did the more liberal *New York Times* imagine its readers flocking to the film as a means to demonstrate their liberalism and racial tolerance? As Angharad N. Valdivia so adroitly recognizes, "to be sure, Disney does not pursue new representational strategies unless it is certain that profits will increase without alienating the bulk of its audience."[12] If that audience exists in a colorblind world, then Disney's representational strategy must work to reify that adherence to what Eduardo Bonilla-Silvi refers to as the "central ideology of the post civil rights era"—that of color blind racism.[13] The ideology of color-blind racism,

> which acquired cohesiveness and dominance in the late 1960s, explains contemporary racial inequality as the outcome of nonracial dynamics ... it seems like "racism lite." Color-blind racism otherizes softly ... [and] serves today as the ideological armor for a covert and institutionalized system in the post–Civil Rights era. And the beauty of this new ideology is that it aids in the maintenance of white privilege without fanfare, without naming those who it subjects and those who it rewards.[14]

Thus Big Daddy La Bouff's mansion in the Garden Section of New Orleans is juxtaposed against the Ninth Ward shotgun style home of Tiana and her parents without questioning or problematizing the socio-economic disparity or difference encoded within the streetcar journey between the two.[15] Moreover, Tiana's Horatio Alger, rags-to-riches transformation in the film is read as indicative of an America where racism and racially coded stereotypes and glass ceilings are no more, at least in 1920s New Orleans. Look, says the dominant discourse, here is the story of a successful black girl/woman who, through hard work and perseverance, now has access to the American Dream; doesn't that construction of blackness suggest that America is now color-blind and magnanimously equal? Tiana didn't need affirmative action to succeed, just a good work ethic; such a portrayal of blackness appeals to all viewers—no one is alienated or threatened by Tiana or her gumbo restaurant. Writing for *The New York Times*, Manohla Dargis argues that "though the theme [of hard work] certainly serves the story—like her father, Tiana yearns to open a restaurant—it also displaces race, which the film, given the commercial stakes, cannot engage."[16] And her success re-affirms the dominant ideological tenets of hard work and capitalism, reifying their integral positioning in dominant American ideology while at the same time further marginalizing race and its role in that ideology.

The film is based upon the classic Grimm brothers fairy tale *The Frog Prince*, in which the main character, a prince, is turned into a frog and can only be returned to human form through the kiss of a beautiful princess. E.D. Baker re-wrote the story in the 2002 *The Frog Princess* to incorporate a more developed female character and it is this version that the Disney film loosely mimics. The film opens with a brief glimpse of Tiana as a child who, when she wishes upon a star, is reminded by her father that stars don't bring wishes, hard work does. Fast-forward to Tiana as a young woman working two jobs in order to save the down payment on the restaurant she dreams of opening. Juxtaposed against her work ethic is the prince of the tale, Prince Naveen, who arrives in New Orleans after being disinherited by his parents because of his absent work ethic. Quickly meeting up with Dr. Facilier, the Shadow Man, Naveen is turned into a frog, and his manservant is transformed into a replicant of Naveen who, Facilier hopes, will marry the wealthy Charlotte La Bouff thus giving Facilier access to her father's wealth. Naveen mistakes Tiana for a princess at the La Bouff masquerade ball, convinces her to kiss him, and, instead of him regaining his body, turns her into a frog as well. The bulk of the story details their journey to the bayou-dwelling Mama Odie, who, they believe, can turn them both back into people again.

The opening scene of the film works to situate the audience in the realm of fairy tales, princesses and the dreams of little girls. Charlotte's room, in the La Bouff mansion, serves as an homage to previous Disney princesses: there is a child-size carriage similar to that of Cinderella; an enormous, elaborate canopy bed echoing Sleeping Beauty; dolls and crowns, tea parties and dresses by the dozen. Moreover, this scene provides a clever inter-textual reference to the overarching storyline in that Tiana's mother Eudora, as voiced by Oprah, is telling young Tiana and Charlotte the story of *The Frog Prince*.[17] Audiences see the leather-bound text with the title embossed in gold; this serves to remind viewers that this is not Disney's original story but is instead a re-telling of a classic fairytale, albeit with a twist, that is, a black princess. What is intriguing about this scene is the oppositional reactions the two young girls have to the traditional fairy tale: young Charlotte, with her blond hair, wealthy father, absent mother and palatial home, embraces the tale, exclaiming "I would kiss a hundred frogs if it meant I could marry a prince and be a princess." Tiana, set up as the antithesis of Charlotte in so many ways, responds that "there is no way in this whole wide world I would ever, ever, ever, I mean never, kiss a frog!" On one hand, Charlotte is the classic Disney princess in a slightly less waif-like form, waiting for her prince to come, but, she brings a level of complexity to that princess role. Audiences recognize traditional Disney princess tropes in her character and locale, but, as an adult, her somewhat mercenary approach to finding her prince adds a level of irony to her desires; at the ball, she describes her carefully orchestrated conquest of Prince Naveen as going "back into the fray." The illustrations in the book from which Eudora is reading depict the more traditional/classic Disney couple: she is blond and he is white, a evocation echoed later in the film when Dr. Facilier shows Prince Naveen the marriage card from the tarot deck—that card places Charlotte and her father in the roles of eligible princess and King. Through such juxtapositions and illustrations, audiences are reminded again and again that this text, this princess, is something new and that Disney is working to de-stabilize or at least question their own princess status quo.

The opening images also work to locate the film historically, first in 1912, and then 1920s New Orleans both by having Eudora working for Big Daddy La Bouff as a seamstress and then showing the black mother and daughter sitting in the back of the streetcar when they leave. This "princess" lives in a shotgun style home in the Ninth Ward, where the neighborhood comes together over gumbo and hush puppies and where her father instills his work ethic in his young daughter. The coherent and loving family unit enables a point of identification for the audience—there are no wicked stepmothers here—and the eventual requisite dead parent is explained through a brief shot of a framed picture of Tiana's father in uniform, a medal hanging over one corner of the frame. In this way, patriotism and sacrifice subtly enter the ideological discourse of the film, again providing a point of connection or alignment for the audience. Grown-up Tiana works two jobs in order to amass the down payment needed for the abandoned building she has chosen for her restaurant. Duke's Café, her day job, is in the French Quarter; here audiences see a multicultural clientele although Tiana and the cook are black. The cook, presumably a business owner himself, undermines her dream when he tells her "you got about as much chance of getting that restaurant as I do of winning the Kentucky Derby." Whether his comments are grounded in race or gender is unclear; however, similar comments voiced by the white realtors, the Fenner Brothers, call to mind both: after telling her that another bid on the building has superseded hers, they tell her "a little woman of your background would've had her hands full ... you're better off where you're at." Whether such statements are grounded in sexism or racism, Tiana's desires to prove her naysayers wrong *do* work to provide a positive role model for many girls, not just black, and again appeal to a wide audience. However, the conflation of racism and sexism in a sense works again to erase race, to appeal to a colorblind reading since both black and white men make similar, deprecating comments.

   With the release of the DVD version of the film comes access to the deleted scenes, the first of which—"Advice from Mama"—reiterates Tiana's desire to be her own person, to place hard work over romance. Although only in storyboard format, the scene locates Tiana in the Horatio Algiers ideology, not the traditional princess role. Her mother, while using Tiana as a dress dummy as she works on Charlotte's elaborate princess dress for the upcoming ball, deprecates Tiana's "all work and no romance" lifestyle. In response, Tiana declares "Mama, I don't need a prince to sweep me off my feet and take me away to fairy tale land. I'm making my own fairy tales." Tiana promises her mother that she won't have to make any dresses once she opens her restaurant; in reply, her mother tells her that she has one more dress she wants to make: Tiana's wedding dress. This scene was dropped from the final version of the movie because the producers felt the restaurant scene and Tiana's first song "Almost There," a song about overcoming trials and tribulations through hard work, made such declarations "superfluous."[18]

   While her mother's desires clearly locate Tiana in the more traditional princess role, that of romance and marriage, the language of the movie marks a strong contrast to the rhetorical conventions of previous fairy tale films. In a 2003 study, sociologists Lori Baker-Sperry and Liz Grauerholz analyze the discourse practices of traditional fairy tales,[19] focusing on reprints and retellings of the classic Grimm brothers stories, including Disney's.[20] Their study concluded that

> Messages concerning feminine beauty pervade these fairy tales. Although the
> tales are not devoid of references to men's beauty, or handsomeness, it is
> women's beauty that is emphasized in terms of number of references to beauty,
> the ways it is portrayed, and the role feminine beauty plays in moving the story
> along.[21]

However, *The Princess and the Frog* is almost entirely devoid of references to Tiana's physical attributes; with the exception of one comment by Charlotte after she has dressed Tiana in one of her many princess gowns—describing her as "prettier than a magnolia in May"—there are no other discursive markers of feminine beauty until the penultimate scene, the wedding scene in the swamp, when Mama Odie refers to the now-human again Tiana as Prince Naveen's "lovely bride." Instead, the text references Tiana's work ethic, often as a negative attribute: her friends complain that "all you ever do is work;" her mother says it is a "shame you're working so hard;" Tiana herself acknowledges she "doesn't have time for dancing;" and, Naveen refers to her as a "stick in the mud." Indeed, the only time the audience hears Tiana refer to her physical self is immediately after she has transformed into a frog; she looks at herself in the mirror and laments "I'm green and I'm slimy." In contrast, Naveen frequently makes reference to his physical attributes, reminding Tiana that he is "charming and handsome" at one point, and then again when he informs Louis, who at this point has only seen Naveen as frog, that he is "unbelievably handsome." While a feminist reading of this absence of beauty references would suggest a positive and progressive shift, thus providing little girls with a role model more concerned with material success than physical beauty, the absence becomes more complex when race is introduced.

Although Directors John Musker and Ron Clements describe the film as "a kind of gumbo as well, mixing ingredients of the traditional Disney fairy tale with the rich fabric" of New Orleans,[22] those traditional elements do not incorporate race, or at least a way to talk about race in a culture steeped in colorblind racism. Jeff Kurtti's *The Art of The Princess and the Frog* is an amalgamation of quotations, storyboard sketches and explanations detailing the evolution of each character in the film. The artists and animators responsible for what audiences eventually see in the movie provide commentary and insights about the process. Thus, Charlotte is described as "Daddy's Little Princess," his "blonde, blue-eyed dear one."[23] Color styling supervisor Maria Gonzales effuses: "I love Charlotte. She's just got a lot of character to her—and the *look* that we've been able to get. We kind of went over the top when she's in her princess dress ... and that's intentional. We just wanted her to *glow*"[24] [original emphasis].

Frog Naveen is described as "pretty good-looking for a frog" while Prince Naveen is said to have "an irresistible charm and *joie de vivre*" in a "handsome and suave" physicality.[25] Even Ray, the Cajun firefly, is described in terms of the physical: a "lumpy, gap-toothed, goofy-looking little guy."[26] The rhetoric used to describe Tiana is fascinating in its avoidance of all things physical: moreover, she is described only in relation to other Disney "maidens"—in a 279 word "introduction" to Tiana in Kurtti's book, a mere seventy-seven words apply directly to Tiana, and of those words, the only adjectives are "vulnerable, interesting, and sympathetic."[27] When my class of university students was asked to describe a typical Disney princess, their list of adjectives included blond, beautiful, elegant, wealthy, stupid, busty, light-skinned, of European descent, having a "normal" American look. If this is their collective experience of Disney princesses, a fairly representative experience for contemporary Disney audiences, where in that rhetoric can Tiana be inscribed? Why can't Disney's discursive practices articulate black beauty and the black body? No mention is made of her appearance in Kurtti's book; unlike Charlotte, whose hair and eyes are described, or Naveen or Ray, both of whom are grounded in physical rhetoric, Tiana seems to exist in a world where her corporeality and her race are non-existent.

Many critics have pointed to the fact that Tiana in human form actually takes up very little screen time; the more prevalent image of Tiana and Naveen is as frogs.[28] In fact, human Tiana is only on the screen for the first twenty-nine minutes; frog Tiana takes up the next fifty-nine minutes, leaving only the final three and a half minutes for Tiana and Naveen to reappear in human form: "They say it ain't easy bein' green, but it's certainly a hell of a lot easier than being black."[29] The black female body evokes socially and historically constructed tropes of black women as either mammies or hyper-sexualized figures, tropes with which Disney cannot engage without seeming to participate in the dominant ideology that "others" difference as a means to reify the hegemonic culture.[30] Negotiating among these tropes explains Disney's studious avoidance of any rhetoric of the body and demonstrates once again their adherence to the politics of colorblindness. The most overt illustration of Disney's desires to encode a colorblind ideology in the film can be found in Mama Odie's song "Dig a Little Deeper:" Tiana and Naveen, and by extension the audience, are told that it doesn't matter what you look like or what you are. Once again, race, and physiognomy, don't matter; Tiana's blackness and Naveen's brownness are effectively erased, allowing the audience to focus instead on other aspects of the film such as her dream of the restaurant.

While Disney no doubt encoded a message of color-blindness for an audience willing to embrace the notion, oppositional readings abound in the decoding process, which is itself informed by a multiplicity of lenses and ideologies including race, class, sex, sexual orientation, age, and politics. Decoding is an active process, more an act of communication than of simple reception,[31] and so, the decoding of this film entails a moment of engagement and critical analysis for those who read the film through an oppositional perspective. One such oppositional reading comes from Scott Foundas, film editor and critic for *LA Weekly*, writing for the *Village Voice*: in his article "Disney's *Princess and the Frog* Can't Escape the Ghetto," Foundas criticizes the lack of historical specificity or contextualization in the film. He refers to the anti-miscegenation laws of 1920s Louisiana as well as the film's failure to acknowledge just exactly what period of the Jazz Age it reflects, asking whether it is "before or after the Mississippi River flood of 1927 that burst Louisiana's infamous levees and stranded hundreds of thousands of blacks in refuge camps?"[32] While no one expects a children's film to address such issues as miscegenation, his reading of the film stands in stark contrast to the message of the film that evokes a colorblind reading. This criticism, and his evocation of the obvious parallels to the devastation wreaked both by Katrina and the lackadaisical response to the crisis, can be read as a direct reply to those who want to read the film and Disney's choice to locate it in New Orleans as a sign of New Orleans' rebirth. This is made evident in the lyrics of the film's opening song in the lines that refer to the dreams of both rich and poor people, dreams that reach fruition in New Orleans. Anika Noni Rose, the voice of Tiana, explains the choice of New Orleans as the perfect setting because of the devastation: "Where else do [African-American] children need to see themselves as progressive and strong and having the ability to make their dreams come true?"[33] Sergio A. Mims, writing for *EbonyJet*, seemingly in response to oppositional readings such as Foundas, extols his readers to "remember, however, that we're talking about a Disney cartoon aimed at children, not a Michael Moore documentary or a Spike Lee film. What Disney cartoon [he asks], or live action film for that matter, has ever dealt with real social or political concerns?"[34] An oppositional reading would respond with the question why not then locate the film in contemporary America, in the age of Obamerica,[35] moving it out of the "big house" of Charlotte's father Eli "Big Daddy" La Bouff, and away from the age of Jim Crow laws that place Tiana and her mother literally at the back of the streetcar? Disney's 2007 Cinderella story *Enchanted*, with its white princess played by Amy Adams, takes place in 21st century New York City; the classic yet contemporary Cinderella story, a mix of animation and live action, appealed to audiences who made it number one at the box office its opening weekend and ultimately earning over $340 million worldwide.[36]

In film and television studies, representation is defined as being either mimetic or simulacral, the former referring to representations that reflect a cultural or social reality (i.e., life as it is) and the latter referring to representations that create an inaccurate portrayal that can be seen to effect change or improve conditions but can also be seen as having the ability to displace the actual reality. While it is true that Tiana as an aspiring and ultimately actual business owner does reflect the social reality of black entrepreneurs and a black middle class, her character's success becomes more complex and potentially problematic when read as one point on a spectrum of black depictions that also includes *The Blind Side* and *Precious*, both also released in 2009.[37] This is not to suggest that her capitalistic aspirations are in any way problematic or inaccurate; rather, when viewed through the lens of a color-blind ideology, her success works to further disenfranchise other minorities who have yet to attain that success because that ideology posits that hard work allows everyone to access the American Dream while ignoring social, economic, educational, or political inequities that might actually limit that access. So, according to a color-blind ideology, race has nothing to do with success or failure; those who fail to succeed do so at the level of the individual, thus exonerating the hegemonic culture. The happy Disney ending of *The Princess and the Frog* is thus both mimetic and simulacral: Tiana represents middle-class black America while also suggesting that this is a universally attainable position. In the end, Tiana and Naveen defeat the villain, return to human form, marry and open her restaurant. How is that anything but a positive message? But, is she too Black or not Black enough?

The Princess and the Frog was one of five films nominated in the animation category at the 82nd Annual Academy Awards, while two other "race" films also received nominations this year: *The Blind Side* and *Precious*, both of which garnered Oscars for either the lead or supporting female. However, what is intriguing is not the nomination for *The Princess and the Frog* itself but the mode of its introduction to the Oscars' vast viewing audience. While each of the other four films in the animation category had its respective lead character appear in a brief monologue, the producers of the Academy Awards chose to have Prince Naveen and the jazz-playing alligator Louis be the spokespeople for the film. So, while audiences were either introduced to or reminded of Mr. Fox from the film *Fantastic Mr. Fox* (voiced by George Clooney), the epony-mous *Coraline* (with the voice talents of Dakota Fanning), the curmudgeonly Carl Fredricksen and his talking dog Dug from *Up* (voiced by Ed Asner and Robert Peterson), and the fairy Aisling from *The Secret of Kells* (voiced by Christen Mooney), Princess Tiana was visibly absent and silenced, replaced instead by the frog form of Naveen and the minstrel-like Louis (voiced by Brazilian Bruno Campos and Michael-Leon Wooley), who "inadvertently" sits on Naveen, thus providing comedic relief while erasing the racialized aspect of the film. Given the money and time invested in the creation of this film, and Disney's desire to "get it right," Tiana's absence becomes even more com-plex.

Clearly aware of the body of criticism addressing Disney's reliance on racial tropes and racist representations in both classic Disney films and more recent attempts to create films that incorporate diversity (see Giroux et al), the producers of this film sought to create a new heroine, one who does not embody either literally or figuratively the previous princesses of color. In a study of Disney's previous multi-cultural princesses, Pocahontas (1995), Ariel from *The Little Mermaid* (1985), Esmeralda from *The Hunchback of Notre Dame* (1996), and Jasmine from *Aladdin* (1993), Celeste Lacroix points out that "there appears here ... to be an increasing focus on the body in the characters of color. Whereas the costuming of these characters reflects stereotypical images of each woman's ethnicity, the overall effect, taken with the increasing volup-tuousness of the characters, works to ... [associate] the women of color with the exotic and the sexual."[38] Lacroix's reading of these princesses foregrounds the problems and criticisms leveled against Disney's earlier women of color; their bodies, costumes, hair, and facial features are indicative of difference and Otherness. Princess Tiana marks a break from this normalizing sense of white-ness in that she is the embodiment of both intellect and a conservative phys-icality, as made evident in both bodies—waitress and frog. Never does Tiana appear in midriff baring or off-the-shoulder clothing, nor is her physicality displayed through the cliff diving of Pocahontas or the gypsy dancing of Esmer-alda. She is neither exoticized nor overtly sexualized; instead, she is, according to Manohla Dargis, "something of a drudge and a bore [who doesn't] have time for dancing."[39] However, the *New Republic*'s advance for the film claims that "Disney gets it right—Black American-ness has rarely been captured in animation in worthy fashion ... this [publicity] still reveals one of the deftest, most soulfully accurate renditions of a Black American in the history of animation."[40] *Essence* magazine's Demetria Lucas happily proclaimed "Disney's much-anticipated *The Princess and the Frog* is finally here and our Black Princess doesn't disappoint—in fact, she exceeds our expectation."[41]

Classic Disney clearly imagined an audience that was white and that shared the ideologies of the hegemonic culture; *Jungle Book*, *The Lion King*, *Song of the South*, and *Aladdin*, for example, all illustrate Disney's recognition of the social and racial positioning of its audience, a positioning that would recognize tropes of blackness or racial representation but that would not problematize the use of those tropes in any way. However, more recent Disney films and television shows have attempted to widen that audience base, but in such a way as to not alienate the core audience that is white. Juxtaposing readings such as Dargis and the *New Republic*'s, a "drudge and a bore" versus "soulfully accurate," underscores the complexity of Disney's project to incorporate diversity in twenty-first century America. If, as Robert Gooding-Williams argues, "American culture lives and breathes by racial representations, relentlessly relying on them to make sense of American history, society, and politics,"[42] then Disney is not going to seriously challenge those tropes of blackness, regardless of their recognition that "every little girl, no matter her color, represents a new marketing opportunity."[43] And yet, consumers are buying into Princess Tiana in record numbers; Disney launched its line of movie-related products months before the actual debut of the film in theatres and these items have been "fly[ing] off the shelves."[44] According to *Variety*'s Marc Graser, *The Princess and the Frog* merchandise, including Princess Tiana dresses and bedding, is "outselling other Disney-branded items ... more than 45,000 [Princess Tiana] character dolls have sold in less than a month."[45]

Cultural critic David Roediger uses the term "racial inbetweenness" to describe the collapsing of racial categories that both embraced recent European immigrants as "white" and kept them separate because of their perceived and constructed differences.[46] Such inbetweenness creates a racial middleground, a portrayal of color that is "safe and sanitized"—these racial representations thus both appeal to a minority audience while at the same time retain a white viewership that is able to identify with the middleground these characters occupy. This inclusivity or middleground status appeals to a larger viewership; rather that creating a culturally or country-specific character and therefore demographic, Disney conflates cultures and customs in such a way as to demonstrate a commitment to diversity without loss of viewers. In *The Princess and the Frog*, Prince Naveen occupies this middleground position. He is from the fictional country of Maldonia, is voiced by Brazilian actor Bruno Campos, and is "not Black, but he's not White either."[47] Indeed, Disney's John Lasseter refers to the "wavy-haired, tan-skinned prince as a 'person of color'"[48] in a way that both locates Naveen outside racial discourses of black and white and works to exclude race through his very depiction as a racialized character.[49]

Despite Disney's intent to redress a wrong, namely the absence of black princesses, theories of encoding and decoding illustrate the malleability of the message on the part of the viewer whose perspective is either one of negotiated or oppositional meaning: "in many ways [the film is] a can't win situation. An African American lead character will be seen by some as an extension of Obama-style progress, and by others as catering to a racial targeting strategy that is no longer relevant because of Obama. For some it will be too Black, for others not Black enough."[50] It is this very question of blackness, whether too much or not enough, that locates this film in this complex cultural moment. While race does resonate in the film, it is sublimated, not foregrounded; adherents of a politics of colorblindness would argue that this sublimation is good, that culturally, we are in a moment "beyond" race, but it is this very sense of being "beyond" race that is so problematic. With a black man in the White House and a black princess on the silver [read white] screen, viewers might be lulled (or led) into an inflated sense of black progress; indeed, the 2010 *Pew Report* finds that "economic measures have shown that black households, after steady income gains in previous decades, have lost ground to whites after 2000."

While Disney is at least addressing the need for inclusivity in its representational strategies, the complexities that surround discourses of race in this country guarantee that whatever message Disney desired to encode will be read through multiple lenses and ideological perspectives.[51] In 1951, W.E.B. DuBois explained that "[p]ictures of colored people were an innovation," ... at that time it was the rule of most white papers never to publish a picture of a colored person except as a criminal."[52] Six decades later, in an era when audiences have a black president as a reference point, seemingly, it is a question of representation again. If in fact there has been a paucity of positive representation of blackness, then is this somewhat historically accurate portrayal a positive step? Good hair notwithstanding, in an era when animals, toys and aliens seem to be the fodder of children's entertainment, with this film Disney is at least engaging with the complex nature of race in 21st century America.

Notes

1. Disney's "Princess line brings in $4 billion a year on sales of everything from *Sleeping Beauty* pajamas to Cinderella's glass slippers," NPR *Marketplace*, 28 October 2008.
2. Stuart Hall, "Encoding and Decoding in the Television Discourse," in *Channeling Blackness: Studies on Television and Race in America*, Darnell M. Hunt, ed. (New York: Oxford University Press, 2005), 46–59.
3. *Ibid.*, 46–47.
4. *Ibid.*, 48–49.

5. Interview with Jeff Kurtti, "Inside the Art of *The Princess and the Frog*: The Making of an American Fairy Tale," *The Wall Street Journal*, November 25, 2009.

6. Brooks Barnes, "Her Prince Has Come. Critics, Too," *The New York Times*, May 31, 2009, Fashion. Brooks refers to an Internet rumor that claimed Maddy, short for Madeline and sounding too much like Mammy, was originally cast as a "chambermaid for a white woman." Bobbi Misick discusses these changes as well in "Controversy Over *The Princess and the Frog*,' *Essence*, November 30, 2009, Entertainment.

7. Caroline White, "Why *The Princess and the Frog* Is Making History While Looking to the Past," *Times Online*, January 7, 2010.

8. Sergio A. Mims, "*The Princess and the Frog* Review," EbonyJet.com, December 8, 2009, http://www.ebonyjet.com/entertainment/movies/index.aspx?id=15520.

9. Roger Ebert, "*The Princess and the Frog*," *Chicago Sun-Times*, Movie Reviews, December 9, 2009, http://rogerebert.suntimes.com/apps/pbcs.dll/article?AID=/20091209/REVIEWS/912 099996/1023

10. Box Office Mojo. *The Princess and the Frog*, February 28, 2010, http://boxofficemojo.com/movies/?id=princessandthe frog.htm.

11. CNN.com, December 13, 2009, http://www.cnn.com/2009/SHOWBIZ/Movies/12/13/boxoffice.ew/index.html; *The New York Times*, December 14, 2009, Movies.

12. Angharad N. Valdivia, "Mixed Race on the Disney Channel: From *Johnny Tsunami* through *Lizzie McGuire* and Ending with *The Cheetah Girls*," in *Mixed Race Hollywood*, eds. Mary Beltrán and Camila Fojas (New York: New York University Press, 2008), 286.

13. Eduardo Bonilla-Silva, "The Linguistics of Color Blind Racism: How to Talk Nasty About Blacks Without Sounding 'Racist,'" *Critical Sociology* Volume 28, Issue 1–2 (2002): 42.

14. Eduardo Bonilla-Silva, *Racism Without Racists: Color-Blind Racism & Racial Inequality in Contemporary America*, 3d. ed. New York: Rowman & Littlefield, 2010, 2–3.

15. Shotgun style homes in New Orleans (and throughout the south) were originally narrow, twelve-foot wide, one story homes built on small lots, very close to the sidewalk or street. The houses themselves had one door and window at the front and another door and window at the rear; inside, the four or five rooms ran in a straight line from the front of the house to the back with no hallways and often no indoor plumbing. They were built in large numbers to accommodate the influx of working class blacks, and the name is thought to come from the fact that a shotgun could be fired from the front door to the back although that explanation could be apocryphal.

16. Manohla Dargis, "That Old Bayou Magic: Kiss and Ribbit (and Sing)," *The New York Times*, November 25, 2009, Movies.

17. Utilizing the voice of iconic Oprah re-assures viewers that this vision of blackness is safe in the same way that she is safe and sanitized. See Janice Perry as well as Beretta E. Smith-Shomade for an analysis of Oprah as a "de-raced" figure.

18. *The Princess and the Frog*, (2009) DVD, directed by John Musker and Ron Clements (Burbank, CA: Buena Vista Home Entertainment Inc., 2010). Audio Commentary by Filmmakers.

19. Lori Baker-Sperry and Liz Grauerholz, "The Pervasiveness and Persistence of the Feminine Beauty Ideal in Children's Fairy Tales," *Gender and Society* Vol. 17, No. 5 (Oct. 2003): pp. 711–726.

20. In 1932, Walt Disney signed an exclusive publishing contract with Western Printing and Lithographing Company, the largest "lithographic company and publisher of children's books in the world" (Baker-Sperry & Grauerholz, 715).

21. *Ibid.*, 719.

22. Jeff Kurtti, *The Art of The Princess and the Frog*, San Francisco: Chronicle Books, 2009, 8.

23. *Ibid.*, 90.

24. *Ibid.*, 90.

25. *Ibid.*, 32, 35.

26. *Ibid.*, 130.

27. *Ibid.*, 26.

28. DeNeen L. Brown, "After Decades of Snowy Whites, Black 'Princess' a True Dream," *The Washington Post*, December 11, 2009, Style.

29. Scott Foundas, "Disney's *Princess and the Frog* Can't Escape the Ghetto," *Village Voice*, November 24, 2009.

30. Patricia Hill Collins explores this question of representation in her 2004 *Black Sexual Politics*.

31. Stuart Hall, 48–49.

32. Foundas, "Ghetto."

33. Rachel Bertsche, "Someday My Princess Will Come," Oprah.com, November 18, 2009.

34. Sergio A. Mims, "*The Princess and the Frog*: Review," EbonyJet.com, December 8, 2009, http://www.ebonyjet.com/entertainment/movies/index.aspx?id=15520.

35. Eduardo Bonilla-Silva, *Racism Without Racists: Color-Blind Racism and Racial Inequality in Contemporary America* 3rd Edition, New York: Rowman & Littlefield, 2010, 207.

36. Box Office Mojo, *Enchanted*, March 13, 2008, http://www.boxofficemojo.com/movies/?id =enchanted.htm

37. *Precious*, based on the 1996 novel *Push* by Sapphire and set in the 1980s, tells the story of overweight, illiterate, abused, HIV positive sixteen-year-old black Precious Jones, pregnant for the second time with her father's baby. *The Blind Side* tells the real life story of black Michael Oher, a foster child without a home who is adopted by a wealthy white family. Their influence and affluence enable him to finish high school, attract the attention of college football scouts, and ultimately win a full scholarship to university, which leads to his NFL career. While clearly a rags to riches story, *The Blind Side* suggests that black success is only through white patronage and association; the other black characters in the film remain mired in lives of violence, drugs, and death. *The Blind Side* has earned more than $200 million, and was nominated for two Academy Awards; Sandra Bullock, cast as the devout Christian mother, won an Academy Award, a Golden Globe Award, a Screen Actors Guild award and a People's Choice award for her role.

38. Celeste Lacroix, "Images of Animated Others: The Orientalization of Disney's Cartoon Heroines from The Little Mermaid to The Hunchback of Notre Dame," *Popular Communications*, 2(4) (2004): 213–299.

39. Dargis, "That Old Bayou Magic."

40. John McWhorter, "Disney Gets It Right," *The New Republic*, June 5, 2009.

41. Demetria Lucas, "It Ain't Easy Being Green: *Princess and the Frog*," Essence.com, November 25, 2009, http://www.essence.com/entertainment/film/it_aint_easy_being_green_princess_and_ the.php

42. Robert Gooding-Williams, *Look, A Negro: Philosophical Essays on Race, Culture and Politics* (New York: Routledge, 2006), 7.

43. Dargis, "That Old Bayou Magic."

44. NPR, November 24, 2009

45. Marc Graser, "Pulling Her Weight," *Variety*, November 23–29, 2009.

46. David Roediger, *Working Toward Whiteness: How America's Immigrants Became White: The Strange Journey from Ellis Island to the Suburbs* (New York: Basic Books, 2005).

47. Adrienne Samuel Gibbs, "Disney's Princess Tiana: A Brown-Skinned Beauty Finally Gets Her Prince," *Ebony*, December 2009/January 2010, Features, 62. Interestingly, in addition to referring to Tiana as a "brown-skinned beauty," Demetria Lucas points out that Naveen's levels of melanin seemed to change and increase between early trailers and the actual release of the film ("It Ain't Easy Being Green.").

48. Samuel Gibbs, "Disney's Princess Tiana."

49. In her study of Nickelodeon, Sarah Banet-Weiser argues that the "inclusion of explicitly racial images on Nickelodeon programming coincides with the exclusion of a specifically racial agenda, so that inclusion functions as a kind of exclusion" (171).

50. Eric Easter, "Disney Begins the Push on a Risky Gamble," EbonyJet.com, May 13, 2009, http://www.ebonyjet.com/entertainment/movies/index.aspx?id=12978.

51. Betsy Sharkey, film critic for the *Los Angeles Times*, exemplifies the difficult nature of Disney's project: "whether it's a worry about offending African Americans with 'cartoonish' exaggerations, or a desire to make the film palatable for white audiences, or both, the animators have been very careful with their pens when it comes to drawing black characters on the page. Just about everyone here has 'good hair,' and Tiana could be Halle Berry's kissing cousin." "Our Wish Come True; 'Princess' Grants Us a Return to Disney's Song-filled Fantasy," *Los Angeles Times*, November 25 2009, Calendar.

52. Quoted in Anne Elizabeth Carroll, *Word, Image, and the New Negro: Representation and Identity in the Harlem Renaissance* (Bloomington: Indiana University Press, 2005), 232.

Bibliography

Baker-Sperry, Lori, and Liz Grauerholz. "The Pervasiveness and Persistence of the Feminine Beauty Ideal in Children's Fairy Tales," *Gender and Society* 17, no. 5 (Oct. 2003): 711–726.

Banet-Weiser, Sarah. *Kids Rule: Nickelodeon and Consumer Citizenship.* Durham: Duke University Press, 2007.

Barnes, Brooks. "Her Prince Has Come. Critics, Too." *The New York Times*, May 31, 2009, Fashion.

Bertsche, Rachel. "Someday My Princess Will Come." *Oprah.com*, November 18, 2009

Bonilla-Silva, Eduardo. "The Linguistics of Color Blind Racism: How to Talk Nasty About Blacks Without Sounding 'Racist.'" *Critical Sociology* Volume 28, Issue 1–2 (2002): 42.

_____. *Racism Without Racists: Color-Blind Racism and Racial Inequality in Contemporary America*, 3d Ed. New York: Rowman & Littlefield, 2010.

Box Office Mojo. *Enchanted*, March 13, 2008, http://www.boxofficemojo.com/movies /?id=enchanted.htm

Box Office Mojo. *The Princess and the Frog*, February 28, 2010, http://boxofficemojo. com/movies/?id=princessandthe frog.htm.

CNN.com, December 13, 2009, http://www.cnn.com/2009/SHOWBIZ/Movies/12/ 13/boxoffice.ew/index.html

Collins, Patricia Hill. *Black Sexual Politics: African Americans, Gender, and the New Racism.* New York: Routledge, 2004.

Cortés, Carlos E. *The Children Are Watching: How the Media Teach About Diversity.* New York: Teacher's College Press, 2004.

Dargis, Manohla. "That Old Bayou Magic: Kiss and Ribbit (and Sing)." *The New York Times*, November 25, 2009, Movies.

Davis, Amy. *Good Girls and Wicked Witches: Women in Disney's Feature Animation.* New Barnet, England: John Libbey Publishing Ltd., 2006.

Diawara, Manthia. "Black Spectatorship: Problems of Identification and Resistance" in *Film Theory, and Criticism,* 5th ed., Leo Braudy and Marshall Cohen, eds. New York: Oxford University Press, 1999.

Foundas, Scott. "Disney's *Princess and the Frog* Can't Escape the Ghetto." *Village Voice*, November 24, 2009.

Giroux, Henry. "Mouse Power: Public Pedagogy, Cultural Studies, and the Challenge of Disney," in *The Giroux Reader*, Christopher G. Robbins, ed. Boulder CO: Paradigm, 2006.

_____. *The Mouse That Roared: Disney and the End of Innocence.* Lanham MD: Rowman & Littlefield, 1999.

Gubar, Susan. *Racechanges: White Skin, Black Face in American Culture.* New York: Oxford University Press, 1997.

Gooding-Williams, Robert. *Look, A Negro: Philosophical Essays on Race, Culture and Politics.* New York: Routledge, 2006.

Hall, Stuart. "Encoding and Decoding in the Television Discourse," in *Channeling Blackness: Studies on Television and Race in America*, Darnell M. Hunt, ed. New York: Oxford University Press, 2005: 46–59.

Harris, Anita. *All About the Girl: Culture, Power and Identity.* New York: Routledge, 2004.

King, C. Richard, Carmen R. Lugo-Lugo, and Mary K. Bloodsworth-Lugo. *Animating Difference: Race, Gender, and Sexuality in Contemporary Films for Children.* New York: Rowman & Littlefield, 2010.

Lacroix, Celeste. "Images of Animated Others: The Orientalization of Disney's Cartoon Heroines From The Little Mermaid to The Hunchback of Notre Dame." *Popular Communications* 2(4) (2004).

McWhorter, John. "Disney Gets It Right," *The New Republic*, June 5, 2009.

Mims, Sergio A. "*The Princess and The Frog* Review," *EbonyJet.com*, December 8, 2009, http://www.ebonyjet.com/entertainment/movies/index.aspx?id=15520.

Mitchell, Vince. "Disney Cashes in on Obama Era with Black Princess Tiana," *The Times* (London), November 30, 2009, Features, 48.

The New York Times, December 14, 2009, Movies.

Newsinger, John, "Me Disney, You Tarzan." Race & Class, 42(1) (2000): 78–81.

NPR. "Despite Black Princess, Disney's Race Record Mixed." January 1, 2010.

Real, Michael R. *Mass-Mediated Culture*. Englewood Cliffs, NJ: Prentice-Hall, 1977.

Roediger, David. *Working Toward Whiteness: How America's Immigrants Became White: The Strange Journey from Ellis Islands to the Suburbs*. New York: Basic Books, 2005.

Samuels Gibbs, Adrienne. "Disney's Princess Tiana." *Ebony*, December 2009/January 2010, Features, 62.

Seiter, Elaine, and Vicki Mayer. "Diversifying Representation in Children's TV: Nickelodeon's Model" in *Nickelodeon Nation* Heather Hendershot, ed. New York: New York University Press 2004.

Sharkey, Betsy. "Our Wish Come True; 'Princess' Grants Us a Return to Disney's Song-filled Fantasy." *Los Angeles Times*, November 25, 2009, Calendar.

Smith-Shomade, Beretta E. "You Better Recognize: Oprah the Iconic and Television Talk," *Shaded Lives: African American Women and Television*. New Brunswick, NJ: Rutgers University Press, 2002.

Valdivia, Angharad N. "Mixed Race on the Disney Channel: From *Johnny Tsunami* through *Lizzie McGuire* and Ending with *The Cheetah Girls*," in *Mixed Race Hollywood*, by Mary Beltrán and Camila Fojas, eds. New York: New York University Press, 2008.

Wasko, Janet. *Understanding Disney: The Manufacture of Fantasy*. Malden, MA: Polity/Blackwell Publishers, 2001.

Wells, Paul. *The Animated Bestiary: Animals, Cartoons, and Culture*. New Jersey: Rutgers University Press, 2009.

White, Caroline. "Why *The Princess and the Frog* Is Making History While Looking to the Past," *Times Online*, January 7, 2010.

Willis, Susan. *A Primer for Daily Life*. New York: Routledge, 1991.

Zook, Krystal Brent. *Color by Fox: The Fox Network and the Revolution in Black Television*. New York: Oxford University Press, 1999.

SECTION II—TRADITIONS AND TRANSFORMATIONS: ESSAYS ON GENDER AND SEXUALITY

Fighting the Cold War with Pinocchio, Bambi *and* Dumbo

DANIELLE GLASSMEYER

As Stanley Kubrick's *Full Metal Jacket* (1987) ends, Joker and his comrades, fresh from what Animal Mother has called "a slaughter," sing the theme song from *The Mickey Mouse Club*. The Marines walk through a 1968 field with weapons at the ready, returned from quelling a sniper, and the first discernible lines of their song ironically celebrate scenes just transpired.

They have worked hard, played fair, and have reached harmony, perhaps regrettably. In the scene prior, Joker had removed the final barrier of difference between him and his fellows when in cold blood he shot—"wasted," in the film's parlance—the female sniper who had killed three of their number. Ostensibly, it was a desire to play fair that motivated Joker's action—he didn't want to leave her to the "mother-loving rats," as did Animal Mother. Without doubt what they did—moving forward through a hostile bombed-out city—to come face to face with the sniper was hard work. Most significantly, shooting the sniper has made Joker "hard-core," earning him membership in the killing club to which his helmet declares he was born. Now in harmony with his fellows, he sings the *Mickey Mouse Club* theme song, while in voice-over he daydreams about "Mary Jane Rottencrotch," a fantasy woman created by Sgt. Hartmann earlier in the film. When the Sergeant's vocabulary becomes Joker's, viewers know that, finally, his training has worked. Singing *The Mickey Mouse Club* theme with his fellow Marines, Joker is no longer resistant, or dissident, but whole-heartedly a Marine.

I suppose one could read this song differently. It could be read as the singers' or filmmaker's self-irony: the song might beg the question how these boys went from daydreaming of Doreen, Darlene and Annette to becoming hardcore killers. Or the song may be read in a realist mode as a psychotic break—traumatized young men retreating into the safe place of childhood security. Read in light of one critic's efforts to demonstrate Disney productions as the root of all positive impulses of the 1960s counter-culture, the shared anthem might even be construed as a sign that these Marines have miraculously resisted all the training and values that brought them to the dehumanized state that typifies the last third of Kubrick's film.[1] The interpretation that I find most provocative, however, is as an antecedent script: Kubrick's choice, I suggest, entices viewers to consider *The Mickey Mouse Club* as productive of these hardcore men.

As testimony to the show's power to shape a generation, Stephen Watt records the reminiscence of a former *Mickey Mouse Club* cast member. As she toured in Vietnam, Doreen Tracy "reported that without fail a soldier in the audience would stand and request that she lead them in singing the show's theme song. Thousands of battle-hardened American troops would voluntarily rise to their feet and raise their voices in unison, bellowing out the lyrics."[2] As in Kubrick's iteration, their motive for taking up the song may remain, ultimately, undecidable: we can never know what these troops felt or thought as they sang this "anthem." We can be sure, however, that these soldiers, in a very real way, saw themselves within a discursive world shaped by Disney productions, including the *The Mickey Mouse Club*.[3] Seen daily by millions of fans, it was a kid-hosted variety show that combined song and dance, with skits, newsreels, travelogues and cartoons.[4] Hardly the kind of material that elicits bloodlust. But the concern of *Full Metal Jacket* is not the killing *per se*. The film suggests that these former living room Mouseketeers would do almost anything to conform to the ethos they imbided from Disney.

Kubrick's implicit suggestion that this iconic Disney production played a formative role in shaping the masculinity of the Vietnam generation may be reformulated to query an earlier generation: what Disney scripts contributed to the formation of the boys who became the Cold Warriors of the late 1950s? To answer this question, I turn to three of Disney's "golden age"[5] films: *Pinocchio* (1940), *Dumbo* (1941), and *Bambi* (1942). The differences between the films' narratives are significant and noteworthy, but for the moment I will stress the commonalities. All three title characters are "born" on-screen and enjoy an apparently nurturing early home life; yet soon all three ambiguously gendered, under-mothered or motherless babies,[6] bereft of family, are forced to make their own ways in the world. Each of these unlikely subjects reveals hidden qualities that fit him to be a leader. They don't do so independently, as might be expected from the American instance of the *bildungsroman*—the autonomous individualism of the self-made man narrative within which Walt Disney's own rise to fame is often read[7]—but with the help of others. That help, in all three cases, comes not from their "kind," but from another species. The centrality of this mentoring relationship, no less than the fact that the relationship is construed across boundaries of species difference that would otherwise be thought to be unbridgeable, is the point on which my analysis turns.

The argument I would like to make about these three films is that the narrative they portray, sketched here, readied a small, but extremely influential portion of the Cold War American generation to embrace a new masculine identity on the global stage: that of mentor to emergent Asian nations. Members of the Vietnam Lobby, notably John Kennedy, Tom Dooley, and Mike Mansfield, with proponents of Eisenhower's People-to-People program, and influential Cold War pundits like *Ugly American* authors William Lederer and Eugene Burdick, conjointly and singly eschewed a continuation of America's role as authoritarian "world's policemen" that some of them had so heartily enacted a half-generation earlier as veterans of World War II. These men who came to prominence in the Cold War saw themselves as potential nurturers of other men and, I would like to argue, the Disney films they saw just before shipping out to fight the good war provided the scripts that eventually helped them to see themselves this way—as, if you will, surrogate mothers to those demarcated as different by means of "racial" markers. I would like to make this argument, but I can't, at least not in the space this essay affords. For one thing the time line is a little off (for instance, John Kennedy would have been near 20 when *Pinocchio* was released—folks of all ages saw Disney movies, but still...). For another, arguments about cultural impact of films on real viewers are infamously hard to prove.

What I can prove is that Tom Dooley, who would be celebrated as an exemplary American for his ideas and actions from 1955–1962,[8] in the late-1950s found in Disney's Golden Age films an ideal medium for demonstrating to Southeast Asians the meaning of America. I can also articulate how these films demonstrate a vision of a relationship between a fledgling entity and an experienced mentor that resonated with Dooley's vision for the relationship between Southeast Asia and America. I'll first briefly analyze the coherence of Dooley's mission to Asia with his comments about Disney films and how he hopes to influence America's consciousness about Asia, and Asia's about America, through movies. I will close with a sustained reading of *Pinocchio* and how its text encourages pre-war and post-war readings that shift from a focus on creating a model American child, to articulating a role for Americans in relationship to "children" of other nations.

Bambi Conquers Laos

Thomas Anthony Dooley, Jr., would have been about 13 when *Pinocchio* was released in 1940. By 1956 (the time Dr. Tom Dooley shot into American consciousness with the publication of his first memoir, *Deliver Us from Evil*), *Pinocchio*, *Dumbo*, and *Bambi* would have been well into their teens, if any of them succeeded in becoming "real boys." The world Dooley writes about couldn't have appeared further from the worlds of these three Disney creations. *Deliver* details his experiences as a Navy physician and refugee camp director during the 1954 evacuation of Vietnamese refugees from North to South Vietnam just before the partition of that country into communist and "free" halves in compliance with the Geneva Agreement.

The Navy doctor's memoir, along with good looks and charm, captured American imaginations; for many readers, Dooley put Southeast Asia, a region better known at the time by its French colonial designation, Indochina, on the map. His goal in part was to make the strife in Vietnam, and throughout Southeast Asia, a reality to readers; singly and cumulatively, Dooley's memoirs sought to make these countries targets for US concern by styling them as worthy recipients of American aid and affection. Aside from American involvement in the region for the twenty years that followed, sales and publicity of the volumes suggest that Dooley succeeded in his aims. *Deliver*, like his two subsequent memoirs, sold well and was picked up for publication in *Reader's Digest*, and over the next 6 years, Dooley became a media darling, regionally, in the Catholic press, and across the nation, and his 1961 death from malignant melanoma at age 32 would only add to his fame and influence.[9] He had parted from the Navy under ambiguous circumstances,[10] but the exposure around *Deliver* and its media tour secured Dooley a platform from which to launch Medico, an international benevolence organization focused on bringing modern medicine and medical practice to Southeast Asia. His Navy sanctioned memoir was followed by *The Edge of Tomorrow* in 1958 and *The Night They Burned the Mountain* in 1960. An astute fundraiser, Dooley used the sales of the books to fund further missions to Asia.[11]

The Edge of Tomorrow details Dooley's first Medico mission to Laos. The goal of that mission, Dooley explains, was to bring average Americans into contact on a person-to-person level with average Asians—in this case mountain Laos who perch precariously on the verge between Laos and communist China. Although there have been suggestions that Dooley's mission may have been a cover for CIA activity,[12] Dooley phrases the mission in the simplest of terms: his goal is to show "American face to a lot of Asians who had been told that American white-men didn't give a damn."[13] The idea that white men did not give a damn, Dooley explicates, comes largely from the administrative practices of former colonial powers that governed Asia, who failed to recognize the inherent value of Asian natives and thus used them for their own gain. In his mission and in his memoirs, Dooley insistently shows how his ideal Americans differ from their colonial predecessors.

That difference is articulated through two main tenets. The first is that Americans are willing to meet Asians face-to-face—on a person-to-person basis that levels the relationship.[14] In contrast to the colonialists that Dooley depicts, who are always on "platforms" and "pedestals" wearing "nice white suits" and looking down upon Asians, his Americans are always down "in the mud" pushing right alongside their Asian counterparts.[15] The second tenet is that Americans will love and nurture Asians, who are constructed in his memoirs as children, out of the cultural immaturity that makes them susceptible to an array of vices, including superstitions, ignorance, and communism. While the preponderance of his mission focuses on showing Asians that American white-men do "give a damn" by giving medical care, training for native nurses, instruction in sanitation practices, and approaching the Asians without superiority, an equally significant task lies in modeling Americanness, and exposing Asians to American ideas. Through these methods, Dooley suggests, Americans will cultivate an American essence he feels is hidden within Asians.

Elsewhere I've written about Dooley's sentimentalization of Southeast Asians and his rhetorical construction of these lands as bereft of adequate mothering, yet filled with children eager to love and be loved by Americans.[16] Dooley assures readers that, like all children, Asian children respond with love when they are shown kindness: on the basis of affection, education will proceed and, later, international political bonds will be forged. Thus tales of American sailors' kindness to refugee children and reciprocal love from the children dominate *Deliver Us from Evil*. Stories about adult refugees often lack the emotional wallop with which Dooley invests his recounting of the relationship between his "boys," the sailors, and fortuitously orphaned children of Vietnam. When *The Night They Burned the Mountain* is published in *Reader's Digest* in 1960, Dooley's focus on Asian children has become a fixation on Asians *as* children. There, a photo caption informs readers that Laos is the "wonderful Kingdom of Kids"[17]; the rest of the photo spread is curiously deficient in images of adult Lao. If any Asian ever counted as an adult to Dooley, after five years of selling them to his U.S. audience, Dooley has emptied his textual Asia of its adult population. Indeed, as Teresa Gallagher and the Dooley fan club assemble "Dooley kits," Gallagher's audience comes to understand the Asia that Dooley's readers envision. She describes a Dooley kit as "a small cloth draw-string bag, [which] contains a bar of soap, a face-cloth, a comb, a tube of toothpaste, some tissue, a balloon, a small light toy, a lollypop and some socks."[18] Americans like Gallagher imagine Dooley, and themselves by Dooley's proxy, as a nurturing force caring for a continent filled with needy children.

Thus to Dooley, choosing from an array of strategies for reaching out to Asian charges and demonstrating Americanness to them, it seems quite natural to show Disney movies. Dooley lists the movies he has brought with him to Laos: "*Bambi, Snow White, Fantasia, Popeye* [*sic*] [and] *Dumbo*."[19] Given that the rest of Disney's Golden Age films are present here, *Popeye* is more likely a mistake for *Pinocchio* than an interloper among the Disney canon, especially in light of the Dooley Foundation's later mania for Disney productions. As Dooley and, after his death, the Dooley Foundation spread their efforts throughout Asia: "vehicles are named after Disney characters 'Lady' and 'Tramp.' The x-ray unit in Pakse is 'Pluto' and the pick-up truck in Khong is

'Dopey' ... 'Pinocchio' was shipped for An Lac, Saigon, and our jeep in India is 'Mickey Mouse.'"[20] For Dooley and his supporters, Disney is a perfect fit with Medico's function as an American organization in Asia.

In 1958, Dooley celebrates Walt Disney cartoons as the ideal medium for teaching Asians about America while gathering knowledge about Asia to share with America. Having cajoled Walt Disney into donating a projector, generator, soundtrack and twenty films to his mission, Dooley shows the movies to his Lao audience. He comments to Teresa Gallagher, "When the sun sets on whatever village we are in, we show a movie."[21]

Dooley's commitment to nightly showings of Disney movies is not really comprehensible to me, even as I write these paragraphs.[22] While creating a screen is done simply enough by hanging a sheet, the projector must be powered, which means that a fifty pound generator and fuel accompany them on every journey, many of which must be completed on foot. Already burdened with medical and personal supplies, carrying heavy film projection equipment up mountains and down valleys seems either folly or reflective of a belief in some intensely deeper value of the films. Yet that deeper value is not *directly* communicated to the Lao who see the films. As hundreds of Lao gather to see these Disney films, Dooley comments: "I remember how we had once considered dubbing in a Lao sound-track on these movies, and then abandoned the scheme as too costly. Now I was glad we had left them as they were. Walt Disney's creations have a universal language of their own."[23]

As they are available to many interpretations, Disney films are far from "universal"; nor do they fully elude interpretation by speaking "their own" special language; nor are they in any sense a pure medium.[24] Thus, it is worth pausing to consider what message Dooley imagines *Bambi* might relay to the Lao, especially since Dooley speaks of the film not in terms of persuasion or entertainment, but in terms of conquest. He comments as an aside in a letter sent back home: "Needless to say, *Bambi* has conquered Laos."[25] On first glance, *Bambi* is about coming of age in a patriarchal society: Bambi leaves his mother's world and joins his father, overseeing his people from a proud distance. Yet, *Bambi* may be a parable meant to promise American men at America's entry into World War II that they, like Bambi, will prevail against enemies threatening their home. Yet again, it may be an ecological critique, for all disturbances to Bambi's idyllic youth have one source: his mother is shot, and the dogs and fire that terrorize Bambi's sweetheart are set by "man."[26] Reading *Bambi* allegorically, the deer could be taken to symbolize any native people, and "man" more specifically might be read as "white man"; this could be a story about white colonizers encroaching on native populations. If so, then Dooley, via Disney, threatens that "man" will kill Lao mothers and young natives will have to turn to a male figure, as Bambi turns to Thumper, to continue the nurturing education interrupted by their mothers' deaths. Dooley's endorsement of *Bambi*'s efficacy in Asia highlights the film's narrative coincidences with Dooley's intervention. Both *Bambi* and Dooley empty their narratives of embodied maternity to supplant it with nurturance practiced by a male figure of another "species."

Bambi's meditations on maternity are more disturbing in context with other Disney films shown by Dooley.[27] When *Dumbo*'s (1941) mother, Mrs. Jumbo, is enraged when others mock her child's appearance, she is locked away and Dumbo learns skills far beyond those of other elephants and becomes a great success in the care of Timothy Mouse. *Pinocchio* lives in a world where the only women are fairies, fish or puppets and with a cricket for a conscience. What's more, in all three films, the innocence of the young protagonists invites the exploitive impulses of those around them. Thus, when the people of Laos are "conquered" by Disney, they internalize a threat to biological motherhood, an awareness of exploitive forces always ready to strike, and the promise of an alternative, masculine, nurturing presence that will ultimately be the source of rescue.

Disney Prepares Southeast Asians to Accept Dooley's Mission

The Disney movies also reveal an inner truth about Asians to Dooley, which he shares with his readers. As the villagers gather in the yard facing the screen, Dooley studies their faces and reflects,

> No matter how you try to point out to Americans that Asians cry and love, fear and hate, and react to the same stimuli the same way we do, you still hear the comments, "Well, the Asiatics can take it, they've always had poverty," or "The yellow horde can take more pain than white men," or "They are inscrutable, colder, more calculating," or "You can't trust a yellow man."[28]

Dooley does not note that, quite possibly, Americans had learned some of these stereotypes from watching Disney short cartoons produced during World II: cartoons like *Commando Duck* (1944) show the Japanese enemy as alternately foolish and treacherous.[29] Rather, watching the Lao villagers watch Disney, "I thought: How many times had I been told that the Lao were lazy people, ignorant, backward, indifferent to their own betterment?.... Here in Vang Vieng I had living proof of its falsity. Never have I seen people respond so readily to encouragement, or to make so much from so little help."[30] The Lao audience is enriched through bearing witness to the inner life of wooden boys, big-eared elephants, and deer; so, too, Dooley's viewing of the Lao audience enables him to enrich his readers' awareness of these others' inner lives.[31]

One could say that, acting after Disney and counterintuitive as it may seem, Dooley anthropomorphizes Asians. Disney encourages viewers to see an inner "human essence" that lies within creatures that appear to be radically different from themselves. As the animals of the forest speak tendernesses and wisdoms to each other, as Timothy Mouse encourages Dumbo, and Jumbo and Dumbo speak love beyond measure through their intertwining trunks, so too even a block of wood can have feelings. Perhaps Dooley's efforts parallel Disney's as he attempts to show an inner humanity that his contemporary audience disbelieved. He explains, "Living in a village with them, being completely saturated with their life, their religion, their aches and pains, and joys and simple happinesses, yet still being Irish American at heart and in my reasoning, I am thrust in a peculiar position. I have to explain some of the churlish world to my Asians, and when I return I am going to try to explain something of Nam Tha to America."[32] Dooley envisions "ordinary people doing an extraordinary job in Asia."[33] Those ordinary people are distinctly American and are instrumental in bringing racial others to maturity, just in the way the script was written by Disney.

Progressive Era Protagonists; Cold War Mentors

In his study *Babes in Tomorrowland: Walt Disney and the Making of the American Child, 1930–1960*, Nicholas Sammond traces the emergence and development of the Disney canon against the changing backdrop of child-rearing theory and practice that coincides with Disney's rise to prominence, Disney's celebration by child-care experts as positive media, and the company's changing ethos in cold war America. Sammond's charge is to trace how the early-century critique of the movies as potentially denigrating to children's characters makes the obverse possible: one can also argue that movies can contribute to children's moral growth. Disney, he demonstrates, built upon this possibility. Once identified as a positive influence, the company consciously cultivates that image.

Sammond's second major focus is related to that cultivation. Sammond argues that Walt Disney himself—his past, his work ethic, and his status as a self-made man—is best understood as a prototype for the ideal "generic child," the goal to which training of children attained in the late 30s and early 40s. Not only are Disney films lauded for their positive influence; Disney's characters are assumed to embody Disney's characteristics. Thus, the theory went, children who see Disney films imbibed the qualities that made Disney who he was.

The 1930s progressive scripts for reforming childcare practices, Sammond argues, stressed conformity, and parental regulation of needs and drives: supported by intense scrutiny of the child, these scripts promised eventual internalization of these privileged values. On the one hand were texts that stress fears of children unsupervised and improperly trained, and on the other were texts that exemplify positive outcomes when the child was properly raised. Sammond cautions, however, that norms by which such judgments were measured had been derived from white middle class children. Thus the normal child that cultural texts prized, sought and attempted to form was a white middle class child. As Sammond makes clear, for a 1940s audience primed on child-studies of the '30s, the preoccupation of *Pinocchio, Bambi,* and *Dumbo* with regulating and normalizing children would be these films' most significant theme.[34]

For Sammond, Pinocchio is the manifestation of that "normal" generic child and the social hopes and worries invested in him. Sammond argues that the values that the Blue Fairy charges Pinocchio with demonstrating—goodness, bravery and truth—are values of the white middle class, and the trials are also class-focused. Drawn to the stage, then lying about how he landed in Stromboli's cage, Pinocchio is barely recovered when he falls prey to new temptations. During the trip to Pleasure Island, Pinocchio enjoys drink, tobacco, pool-playing and vandalism in the company of Landwick, a Bowery-accented wastrel who needn't work too hard to seduce Pinocchio away from his unmarked accent and clean habits. The film threatens these boys, transformed into jackasses, with a life of hard labor, convincingly demonstrating Sammond's theory. He argues that Depression-era parents and children learned that "indulgence in the pleasures of the working class ... led to a life as a beast of burden. Ultimately, one was either a manager or managed, and the choices one made determined the outcome."[35]

The same audience that would focus on these points in *Pinocchio* would likely focus upon Dumbo's quest for a function within the circus economy that will render him, not fame, but simple dignity and acceptance for who he really is, a real identity that is finally revealed when he learns he can fly, and upon the tests that Bambi endures before he can assume his place next to the Great Prince. "Becoming real" for Dumbo and Bambi resonates with gaining autonomous selfhood and Sammond explains that the 1940s audience would code this cultural pinnacle of maturation as "self-management." These films, Sammond indicates, are shaped by 1930s cultural emphasis on the need to develop autonomy and self-management among a population enervated and made hopeless by the Depression. Sammond demonstrates that Disney's films disseminated these values to a widespread cultural audience, acting as, if you will, surrogate training manuals for parents to use to measure the success of their child-rearing.

Sammond's presentation of the issues and discourses through which 1940s viewers would watch Disney films convinces me that those viewers would focus upon the film's representation of the fetishized "normal" child, even though, he allows, the films did not suggest they had to do it alone. For instance, Jiminy Cricket's presence, Sammond posits, suggested to parents that they "needed help, a conscience to whisper to the child ... someone to steer him past the wrong pleasures" and towards "the rewards of hard work, deferred gratification, and self-control."[36] I suggest that figures like Dooley may be more interested in golden age films for the sake of mentor characters than for their discourse on the child—and perhaps that interest in mentors is justified by the Disney Company's production choices and its subsequent marketing practices that increasingly focus upon the mentor characters.

I turn to *Dumbo* first; because it is wholly a Disney creation, without the source texts that inspired *Bambi* and *Pinocchio*, its production choices highlight the adaptive choices made in the other two. In particular, the film's flirtation with a potential critique of class and race is contained through association with animal species that re-directs the narrative to its mentoring story. For example, the gossiping, affected tones of the female elephants starkly contrasts Timothy's class-marked American accent, which in turn contrasts the African American accented hipster discourse of the crows. The accents help predict the narrative arc. One might expect that the female elephants would care for the baby elephant. Yet they are focused wholly on external beauty, and disturbingly aligned with a discourse of racial supremacy. They are, in the words of one of the elephants, a "proud race" and Dumbo's ears alone are enough to make him a "disgrace" to that race. Dumbo is marginalized and then exiled from his kind. Having already earned him the moniker "Dumbo," his ears cause him to bungle the "pyramid of pachyderms" and so to injure the others, and drive him to his desperate demeaning turn as a clown, from which Timothy, with the eventual help of the crows, rescues him. Thus the characters' alignment with species and their class and race-marked accents underscore a story of dysfunction of racial affinity and underscore the need for cross-race mentoring.

Timothy Mouse is this film's answer to Jiminy Cricket, with a similar worldly-wise exterior and a tender heart. Tiny in stature, dressed finely in a ringmaster's hat and tailcoat, draped in gold braid, he's as proud of his appearance as Jiminy, and a stark contrast to his mentee in how he is drawn. Timothy walks on two feet, in contrast to Dumbo's four, and his characteristics are human; in contrast, silent Dumbo wears only a hat and acts like an elephant—most notably, Dumbo sways when standing still, and grasps Timothy tail in his trunk to follow him. Timothy initially seeks revenge upon the female elephants by scaring them on Dumbo's behalf, but otherwise is content to help Dumbo find possible niches in the circus, and to comfort the little elephant when he is dejected. Indeed, the film is careful to echo Jumbo's care for Dumbo in a reprise of the bath scene in which Timothy scrubs the clown makeup from Dumbo's face, and dries his tears. Timothy Mouse, anathema to elephants, and feared by Dumbo on first contact, is the figure who truly cares for little Dumbo, helps him to make his way in the world, and helps him discover his hidden talents.

Disney's *Bambi* reveals its focus on mentoring most strongly in its contrast to its source text. Where the film shows an Edenic commingling of forest life, Felix Salten's 1928 novel is a dark story of a young deer growing up in a world of deer. Salten's *Bambi* is set in a violent world in which animals fear each other. Bambi's strong shaping influences are his extended family: his aunt's children, some young bucks who eventually become Bambi's rivals, and, occasionally, the Great Prince. Characters like Friend Owl and Thumper are based, if at all, upon the idea of an idea of an animal: Salten barely develops a nameless screech owl and one Mr. Hare who is violently killed by a fox. Thus it seems clearly a Disney innovation when Thumper physically manipulates Bambi's form and shares words of wisdom about kindness and proper vegetable consumption.

Disney's *Pinocchio* is created without a mother at all, of course—the child of Gepetto's carving and painting skill—in a home where all generativity is man's purview. The film lingers on Gepetto's creations—clockworks constructed on a cricket's scale, with tiny humanized dramas played out on the hour or at the turn of a key. In a sequence that moves from the natural world to violence, we see first clockwork ducks and birds, and soon a hunter shooting a bird, a drunkard lolling out a window, and finally a mother spanking her child. Shown following Gepetto's song "Little Wooden Head," this small survey of the darker human impulses seems a fitting counterpoint to the disturbing between-ness of the manipulated puppet, who alternately strokes and kicks Figaro; seen through the side of Cleo's bowl, the puppet is revealed in its dissonant and distorted essence. Later, when Gepetto is awakened by Pinocchio, now alive but not yet human, falling from the work table, these clockworks are re-animated by Gepetto's gunshot, but soon replaced by clockworks selected by Gepetto and Pinocchio with more positive scenarios—an angelic herald, a mother bird feeding her young, a stately couple dancing. There is something wrong with these creations, Pinocchio among them—a shallowness, a manipulability that is highlighted by a reprise of Gepetto's puppetry when he controls the now-living Pinocchio by manipulating his suspenders—but of course that is story's point: even the least malleable of creations can be manipulated by others unless they develop bravery, truthfulness and unselfishness sufficient to become "real."

Pinocchio seems allegorical, of course, when his liederhosen and Bavarian hat, and Gepetto's German accent are considered, of the dawning totalitarian commitment of both the Germany his clothes echo, and the Italy from whence his name comes. Those countries, to the American press, seemed to be little more than marionettes being operated at their leaders' wills. Where, the press asked later, when faced with the Nuremberg defense, were their consciences? Perhaps, like Pinocchio's they could fit inside the brain of a cricket.

Disney's innovations in *Pinocchio* are most revealing of the ethos that may power the Cold War rereading of Disney's Golden Age. For instance, in Collodi's tale, Gepetto wants a child because his wife died, but she is never mentioned in Disney. But Collodi's cricket is changed even more dramatically.[37] Originally, Disney had envisioned a film without the cricket, but early in production, the staff worried that Pinocchio seemed cold and heartless. The cricket was added to house Pinocchio's other half—the conscience that he would eventually internalize. Early story meetings dealt with the difficulty of drawing Jiminy—apparently crickets are pretty frightening in extreme close-up. Yet the commitment to retaining the character was firm. As sketching and scripting moved forward, Disney reputedly predicted "If only I could find someone who could see Jiminy the way he should be. If we can just get him right, he'll become as immortal as Mickey Mouse."[38] Indeed. The film might better be called Jiminy Cricket when its final structure is considered.

If Pinocchio is still a wooden head—a *tabula rasa*—a complete vacuum, but with powers of locomotion and with the ability to choose but no moral or experiential register against which to measure his choices, we could be relieved to know that a conscience has been provided to him. Yet, we should, as viewers, be deeply worried about Pinocchio's lack of preparation for his world, as should Gepetto when he blithely sends the puppet-boy to school. Jiminy Cricket's value as Pinocchio's conscience is preemptively undermined as he agrees to be a conscience because of attraction to the Blue Fairy. Preening over his own transformed appearance from vagabond to "Sir Jiminy Cricket," Jiminy unsurprisingly "almost forgot about" "ol' Pinocch." Indeed, his instructions to "give a little whistle" when Pinocchio needs help are about the height of his effectiveness as conscience. Drawn as a womanizer and a scamming opportunist, for all the good he does Pinocchio one could almost wish for a reprise of Collodi's choice in the original tale: there, the Cricket gets squashed.[39]

Yet, the film is given to Jiminy as the focalizing character. Through him we witness the story. The film opens on him, and purports to recount how he learned the lesson that, "When You Wish Upon a Star," a person's—or cricket's—dreams may be realized. In the opening sequence, the camera even replicates his perspective, mimicking his hopping toward Gepetto's house, and it closes on his thanks to the Blue Fairy and shows him rewarded with his badge. Structurally, we are privy to Gepetto and Pinocchio's story only because Jiminy enters Gepetto's home. While whole scenes do happen outside his vision, the film is consistent enough to be read as being told through his eyes. What's more, Jiminy's character is clearly an American type within an easily traced tradition of the tough-guy with a tender heart.[40] He is streetsmart, wisecracking, an improviser, world-wise yet quick to sympathize with the innocent and weak and just as quick to defend them. His American-ness is underscored in the context of those characters that tempt and exploit Pinocchio. Stromboli, Honest John and the Coachman, in practice and accent, are bastions of the old country and palpable threats to Pinocchio, and Jiminy is his only protection.

Just as the film insists on Jiminy's centrality to the story, the importance of Jiminy to Disney as a corporation is also clear. His song, "When You Wish Upon a Star" is more endemic than "It's a Small World": "When You Wish Upon a Star" is played under the company logo at the start and finish of every Disney film, and sampled in most commercials for Disney products and theme parks even today. What's more, in the 1950s Jiminy Cricket appeared regularly on the *Mickey Mouse Club* as the narrator of two segments that purported to teach children about their bodies and good behavior.[41] For Disney, as for American audiences in the late 1950s, the significant character in these coming of age classics is not the innocent and naïve child, but the American mentor who guides him.

These three films, in their original moment, certainly lent themselves to a reading that meditates on the meaning of childhood in 1940s America, and on social concerns with producing children who are "brave, good and true." Read against the backdrop of 1955–60, incipient meanings in the old scripts surface and the role of singular Americans reaching across race difference, recoded as species' boundaries, to help weaker "species" seems more emphatic. Neither reading may be definitively attributed to Walt Disney productions as a final or fixed meaning; rather, perhaps, what surfaces in a reading of a text changes to serve its cultural moment.

Notes

1. See Brode's *From Walt to Woodstock.*
2. Stephen Watt, *The Magic Kingdom: Walt Disney and the American Way of Life* (Boston: Houghton Mifflin, 1997), 335.
3. This classic Disney television program appeared for one hour every weekday afternoon from October 3, 1955 to September 1959, and ran in syndication as a half hour program from 1962–5 (Watt, 335).
4. Sammond provides reference to 1958 Nielsen numbers that reported the show was seen in over 7 million homes and by 21 million viewers (348). Commenting on what he calls the show's "oddly martial format," Sammond notes that the series struck a balance between conformity and individualism "by placing that individualism in the service of the club as a whole, channeling innate personal talent and drive into collective projects" (346).
5. So named by Stephen Watt and Christopher Finch among texts I've reviewed.
6. Lynda Haas details the dark fates of many mothers in Disney films in her essay, "Eighty-six the Mother: Murder, Matricide and Good Mothers."
7. Sammond comments explicitly on the fashioning of Walt Disney's life story to fit within this American trope on pages 74–5, and implicitly throughout his study.
8. For a catalogue of the many encomiums piled upon Dooley, see James Fisher's cultural biography. Among those he highlights: "A Splendid American," a "Non-Ugly American," "Doctor America" and, predictably, an "American Hero."
9. Dooley was a native of St. Louis, a graduate of Notre Dame University and a Catholic, so regional and religious media picked up his story eagerly. He also gained national attention. His doings were regularly reported in national magazines and newspapers, and he was of sufficient celebrity to merit an appearance on *What's My Line?* and *This Is Your Life.* He would eventually be suggested for sainthood. James Fisher records this media coverage in detail, and I viewed some of the extensive holdings on Dooley at the Western Manuscript Archive at University of Missouri at St. Louis.
10. Fisher suggests that Dooley was accused of active homosexuality while in uniform.
11. Fisher captures Dooley's adept blending of business acumen with benevolence when he dubs him a "Madison Avenue Schweitzer."
12. In *Dr. America*, James Fisher considers thoroughly this suggestion, which was originally posited by Diane Shaw in an *LA Times Magazine* article in 1991.
13. Dooley, *Edge*, 13.
14. Dooley does not explicitly reference then-President Eisenhower's "People-to-People" pro-

gram, but his fan club leader/secretary, Theresa Gallagher does, explaining that, like the People-to-People program, Medico promoted individual action as "the key to international friendship and world peace" (Gallagher, 22, 32). Eisenhower mentions inaugurating this program in September 1956, but does not refer to it again in *The White House Years: Waging Peace, 1956–1961* (410).

15. Dooley's use of the "platform" image is recounted in James Monahan's *Before I Sleep: The Last Day of Dr. Tom Dooley* (New York: Farrar, Straus and Cudahy, 1961). The other images are recounted in Lawrence Elliot's *The Legacy of Tom Dooley* (New York: The World Publishing Company, 1969).

16. I have developed these themes in my essay "Tom Dooley and the Cold War Revision of 'Indochina'" in *Sinographies: Writing China*.

17. Dooley, *Night*, 300.

18. Gallagher, 8.

19. Gallagher, 35.

20. Gallagher, 7.

21. Gallagher, 19.

22. And yet, his practice seems to be more typical of American practices than not. Similarly, writing of USIS interventions in Formosa in the late forties, George Kerr describes how that agency sent "mobile units" consisting of sound trucks and projectors) into the hinterlands of that Island to show American films as part of their mission to "tell the people about democracy" (147).

23. Dooley, *Edge*, 53.

24. Uelman notes, "Mickey and his gang undoubtedly portrayed the 'American ideals' Disney hoped to preserve" (10). Disney's ideals include sexual conservatism and staunch anticommunism (Ostman, 82); Disney crushed union activity at his studio and testified as a friendly witness in 1940s Congressional hearings (Smoodin, 3, 20). Disney's films are at least as ideological as any other cultural product.

25. Gallagher, 19.

26. A.W. Hastings's essay "*Bambi* and the Hunting Ethos" traces the film's reputation as anti-hunting propaganda that indicts villainous man's aggressions against innocent nature.

27. Linda Haas notes that often "a mother appeared in the original text, but was excised in the Disney revision" (196).

28. Gallagher, 28.

29. In some measure, Dooley was disabusing his American audience of ideas that had been inculcated by Disney during the war. In several short cartoons produced between 1942 and 1945, caricatures of Japanese appear. Hirohito, along with Hitler and Mussolini, is mocked in "Der Fuehrer's Face" (1943), which won an Academy Award that year. The depiction of Hirohito as bucktoothed and bespectacled became the Disney standard when Japan and the Japanese were to be portrayed. Soon, in "How to Be a Sailor" (1944) Goofy torpedoes a series of bucktoothed and spectacled vessels arrayed before a rising sun. The 1944 "Commando Duck" darkens the caricature considerably. First, a scene shows two Japanese soldiers disguised as a rock and a tree bungle a chance to shoot Donald due to exaggerated rituals of politeness. The next scene shows an array of rifles leveling on Donald; while one putatively Japanese-accented voice eagerly anticipates the shot, another such voice urges the first to hold his fire for a moment because "Japanese custom say, always shooting a man in the back please."

30. Dooley, *Edge*, 53.

31. The passages cited here focus on Dooley's mission to Vietnam and Laos, and, indeed, as his missions progress, Dooley shows increasing sensitivity to the uniqueness and particularity of Asian cultures. Still, his focus on particular nations must be read within the context of Cold War American foreign policy in which the "domino theory" encouraged a rhetoric of interchangeability. The domino theory stressed that if any Asian nation fell to Communism, all would fall—it didn't matter which fell first. Dooley and other Asia Firsters seem to have held the obverse to be true as well: that intervention in any Asian nation was a good thing. For an overview of the development of the domino theory, consult Olson and Roberts, *Where the Domino Fell: America and Vietnam, 1945–1990*.

32. Gallagher, 28. Fisher argues that Dooley's Irishness was often "invoked to reaffirm his stature as the quintessentially 'regular' American" (*Dr. America*, 73).

33. Gallagher, 42.

34. After World War II, Sammond notes a sea-change in child study presumptions that retreat from regulation and regimentation of childhood, and embrace a "natural child" in response to the threatening outcome of totalitarian regimes' training of children into docile masses. In reaction, US child care theory moved toward a more child-centered approach. In exemplifying the ways that Disney echoes and voices the concerns of the two eras, Sammond turns to different film texts. He considers the proliferation of Disney nature films in the post-war years, and focuses largely on *Pinocchio* to examine the prescriptions of the earlier era.

35. Sammond, 78.

36. Sammond, 78. Similarly to Sammond, Watt groups *Dumbo, Bambi,* and *Pinocchio* as Disney's "populist" feature films, and the three heroes as epitomes of Depression-era American concerns. Watt asserts that Dumbo is "the virtuous, defenseless underdog who struggles against arbitrary forces, bucks up his courage, finds his way to productive work, and ultimately joins with other marginalized figures to overcome their oppressors. His story was a social and political allegory for Depression-era America" (90).

37. According to Claudia Card, in Collodi's tale, Pinocchio squashes the cricket when it annoys him; later, when he is in distress, he calls upon the cricket, who appears to him as a ghost (63).

38. Mosley, 181.

39. It seems that even as production started a rendition vey true to Collodi's tale was planned. Collodi stresses the heartlessness of the wooden boy and so did Disney. But, looking at the storyboards one day, Ham Luske commented that "'We've made him into an unfeeling little monster instead of a human being. Walt, what this kid needs is a conscience." So compelling was Luske's insight that, according to Mosley, "Walt called production to a halt while the character of Jiminy Cricket was developed" (179).

40. The tradition of the "man of feeling"—who is all the more manly for his feeling reaction to the pain and distress of others—is very long indeed (one need only think of all the weeping men of 19th century fiction who are applauded by male and female novelist alike for their "manly show of emotion"). In its post–World War II American permutation, the wisecracking, cynical, American man who is celebrated for his ability to feel quite often feels for—and takes care of—children. I have in mind novel heroes like Bellow's *Henderson, the Rain King* who redeems himself by adopting an African child, and Salinger's Holden Caulfield who dreams only of protecting children. In addition, films include *The Geisha Boy* in which Jerry Lewis protects a young Japanese orphan, and *Hell to Eternity* (1960) and *Dondi* (1961) in which David Janssen similarly protects orphaned children of Asian and Italian (respectively) descent; famously, although not produced until 1968, in *The Green Berets*, John Wayne assures a Vietnamese orphan that the child is the reason Americans are in Vietnam. Each text rings changes on the tender-hearted-tough-guy, as well as on the American-mentor-to-child-from-another-nation theme.

41. Sammond reproduces an advertising page directed at teachers alerting them to Jiminy's segments on the show (359).

Bibliography

Bellow, Saul. *Henderson, the Rain King.* New York: Viking, 1959.

Brode, *From Walt to Woodstock: How Disney Created the Counterculture.* Austin: University of Texas Press, 2004.

Card, Claudia. "Pinocchio," *From Mouse to Mermaid: the Politics of Film, Gender, and Culture.* Eds. Elizabeth Bell, Lynda Haas, and Laura Sells. Bloomington: Indiana University Press, 1995, 62–71.

Dooley, Thomas A., M.D. *Deliver Us from Evil: The Story of Viet Nam's Flight to Freedom.* New York: Farrar, Straus and Cudahy, 1956.

_____. *The Edge of Tomorrow.* New York: Farrar, Straus and Cudahy, 1958.

_____. *The Night They Burned the Mountain.* New York: Farrar, Straus and Cudahy, 1960.

_____. "The Night They Burned the Mountain," *Reader's Digest* 76 (May 1960): 93–99+.

Eisenhower, Dwight D. *The White House Years: Waging Peace, 1956 1961.* Garden City, NY: Doubleday, 1965.

Elliott, Lawrence. *The Legacy of Tom Dooley.* New York: The World Publishing Company, 1969

Finch, Christopher. *Walt Disney's America.* New York: Abbeville Press, 1978.

Fisher, James. *Dr. America: The Lives of Thomas A. Dooley, 1927–1961.* Amherst: University of Massachusetts Press, 1997.

Gallagher, Teresa. *Give Joy to My Youth: A Memoir of Dr. Tom Dooley.* New York: Farrar, Straus and Giroux, 1965.

Glassmeyer, Danielle. "Tom Dooley and the Cold War Revision of 'Indochina'" in *Sinographies: Writing China.* Eds. Eric Hayot, Haun Saussy, and Steve Yao. Minneapolis: University of Minnesota Press, 2007.

Haas, Lynda. "Eighty-six the Mother: Murder, Matricide and Good Mothers," *From Mouse to Mermaid.* Eds. Elizabeth Bell, Lynda Haas, Laura Sells. Bloomington: Indiana University Press, 1995, 193–211.

Hastings, A. W. "*Bambi* and the Hunting Ethos." *Journal of Popular Film and Television* 24, no. 2 (1996): 53–59.

Kerr, George F. *Formosa Betrayed.* Boston: Houghton Mifflin Company. 1965.

Monahan, James. *Before I Sleep: The Last Days of Dr. Tom Dooley.* New York: Farrar, Straus and Cudahy, 1961.

Mosley, Leonard. *Disney's World.* New York: Stein and Day, 1985.

Olson, James, and Roberts, Randy. *Where the Domino Fell: America and Vietnam, 1945–1990.* New York: St. Martin's Press, 1991.

Ostman, Ronald E. "Disney and Its Conservative Critics." *Journal of Popular Film and Television* 24, no. 2 (Summer 1996): 82–89.

Salinger, J. D. *Catcher in the Rye.* New York, Boston: Little, Brown, 1951.

Salten, Felix. *Bambi: A Life in the Woods.* Trans. Whitaker Chambers. New York: Grossett and Dunlap, 1929.

Sammond, Nicholas. *Babes in Tomorrowland: Walt Disney and the Making of the American Child, 1930–1960.* Durham: Duke University Press, 2005.

Shaw, Diana. "The Temptation of Tom Dooley." *Los Angeles Times Magazine,* 15 December 1991: 43+.

Smoodin, Eric. "Introduction: How to Read Walt Disney," *Disney Discourse: Producing the Magic Kingdom.* Ed. Eric Smoodin. New York: Routledge, 1994, 1–20.

Uelman, Amelia J. *Seeing the U.S.A.: The Landscapes of Walt Disney.* Washington, DC: Georgetown University Press, 1991.

Watt, Stephen. *The Magic Kingdom: Walt Disney and the American Way of Life.* Boston: Houghton Mifflin, 1997.

"*You the Man, Well, Sorta*": *Gender Binaries and Liminality in* Mulan

Gwendolyn Limbach

Introduction

Disney's *Mulan*, released in 1998, is one in a sequence of animated feature films from the company that proffer outspoken, seemingly rebellious, female characters: Disney's New Woman. In *Mulan*, as in the Chinese folktale of Hua Mulan[1] upon which it is based, the young heroine impersonates a man to join the army in her ailing father's stead. Though adapted from this well-established legend, the Disney version retains certain "distinctive Chinese cultural traits and historical facts to construct a 'Chinese' flavour" while organizing the film around an Americanized cultural pathos.[2] Whereas in the poem Mulan cross-dresses with the aid and approbation of her parents, in the film Mulan runs away from home, breaking away from her family to find her identity. Thus in this translation, Disney not only puts an American teen spin on the story of Mulan but also reorganizes it around the typical Western fairy-tale ideals, ones which privilege masculinity over femininity.

Indicative of the film's motif of crossing boundaries, *Mulan* begins with the Huns crossing the Great Wall into China. In response, the emperor issues a conscription notice and drafts one man from every family into the imperial army. Believing that her father will be killed if he fights, Mulan steals his armor and sword, running away to join the army to save him. At first glance, the story of a daughter becoming a warrior "woman" to defend family and country seems to espouse a progressive, feminist message to its viewers. However, Mulan's transgression supports patriarchal[3] power structures rather than disputes established gender roles. Cross-dressing challenges commonly held

115

notions of binarism, questioning gender categories and what exactly is "female" and "male," whether these are considered essential and biological or cultural and constructed. Transvestism poses the question, if one relies on sartorial artifacts to designate gender (girls wear pink, boys wear blue), how does one "read" gender when those designations are changed? While it appears that the film celebrates its protagonist as a liminal character and sets up gender as culturally fabricated, these constructions are in fact based on essentialist notions of biological sex. Rather than blurring the boundaries between genders, Disney's *Mulan* continually differentiates men and women through "axiomatic" concepts of what is female and what is male.

The film illustrates continual boundary-crossings: The Huns invade China, Mulan crosses genders, and Li Shang's troops cross from novices in training camp to heroes on the battle field.[4] Yet only those crossings that reaffirm the established masculine order are allowed to remain; whereas the victorious soldiers maintain their lauded position, the Huns are defeated, and Mulan becomes an obedient daughter and future bride. Although narratives of cross-dressing often subvert the predominant social discourse surrounding gender, Disney's *Mulan* contains the disruption that arises when a woman becomes a man to reinforce the gender binary and deny any agency that occurs when these boundaries are crossed.

Honor Through Heterosexuality

Two of the ostensible themes of the film are established through the first song, "Honor to Us All": in particular, that honor is the most precious commodity an individual can provide the community; and that fulfilling societal imperatives, fitting in to one's (gender) role, is difficult but necessary for survival. In order to gain the former one must succeed in the latter. As Mulan prepares to meet the matchmaker, who holds the girls' place in society in the balance, she copies notes onto her arm as if about to take a test she's ill-equipped to pass. The necessities for impressing the matchmaker do not reside within Mulan but must be placed on her as visible indicators: "quiet, demure, graceful, polite, delicate, refined, poised, punctual."[5] These characteristics are not innate and do not come from within Mulan; rather, they are to be learned and reiterated, to be placed on the body, just as the make-up and fancy dress, in order to designate her as female.

Both visually and lyrically the scene demonstrates that Mulan (and, by extension, all other girls), must submit to a feminizing process. Mulan, before the intervention of society's restrictive gender requirements, is not made of the right materials to be formed into a proper woman, which in this context is equivalent to a proper bride. She is substandard in the eyes of the women who mark—and make—girls who bring honor to their families. Nevertheless, because every girl must become a bride (read: truly female), Mulan undergoes the transformative process through which she will be created. As her mother and grandmother take Mulan from shop to shop, we learn exactly what is required to be a girl and thus bring "honor to us all." Each proprietor of femininity lists the extensive qualities that make a bride, and each lesson for becoming female is both oral and visual: Mulan is told what she must be and then made into that model. Rather than adhering to the demands of her family role, Mulan continually resists her transformation. She is pushed and pulled by hairdressers and costumers, always looking pained and uncomfortable in her own body. Every characteristic, even a tiny waist, is fabricated rather than natural, and none are essentially linked to the biological "fact" of Mulan's sex. Like the make-up painted on her face, the above qualities are culturally constructed markers of femininity that one assumes as a rite of passage into womanhood.

But one cannot pass through this rite without finally meeting the local matchmaker and earning her approval. She will determine a girl's future position in relation to society, and the girls recognize the consequences when they equate her with an undertaker. The power this woman yields, more frightening than death itself, emphasizes the necessity of heterosexual approbation in order to secure a place in society. Mulan stumbles through the marketplace, trying to catch up and—literally and figuratively—fall in line with the other potential brides. While they smile and repeat the hope of bringing honor, each girl looking nearly identical, Mulan stares ahead in disbelief that she must be like them in appearance and action. Their transformation culminates through finding husbands and integrating them fully into the heterosexual matrix by which they will be recognized as women. Thus a woman is delineated by her appearance only in that it leads to heterosexuality. The song and scenes make clear that a daughter can only bring honor to herself and her family by becoming a bride. Without fulfilling her assigned gender role through marriage she and her family merit no honor, nor can she honor the Emperor by bearing sons. In this world Mulan has no other options than wife and mother, they "are presented as the ultimate goal" for all girls, "suggesting that there are no 'female' alternatives in relationships."[6]

Reflecting on the Self

After the matchmaker declares, "You may look like a bride, but you will never bring your family honor!" Mulan returns home, and, upon seeing her father's hopeful face, turns away to reflect (literally) on her position.[7] In Mulan's mind (and within society), the terms "bride" and "daughter" are conflated, and following the matchmaker's chastisement, Mulan questions exactly what part she is meant to play. The film takes the notion of the perfomativity of gender a step further and creates a literal metaphor for Mulan's identity questions in the form of theatrical roles. As Judith Butler indicates, "Performativity is thus not a singular 'act,' for it is always a reiteration of a norm or set of norms, and to the extent that it acquires an act-like status in the present, it conceals or dissimulates the conventions of which it is a repetition ... its apparent theatricality is produced to the extent that its historicity remains dissimulated."[8] The preparations for meeting the matchmaker reduce the perfomativity—the repetition and citation of gender norms—to a set of acts that one exhibits in the moment, as if that perfomativity were a conscious choice; thus the dressing and making-up process conceals the historical actuality of required and unconscious reiterations of gender norms.

Indeed, to the extent that one declares "It's a girl!" at birth, the naming of the girl "initiates the process by which a certain 'girling' is compelled, the term ... governs the formation of a corporeally enacted femininity that never fully approximates the norm.... Femininity is thus not the product of a choice, but the forcible citation of a norm."[9] Once Mulan realizes that she cannot approximate or properly cite the feminine norm, she questions only herself and her "performance" rather than the norm itself. Yet, as Garber notes, "Gender roles and categories are most vulnerable to critique when they are most valorized, when their rules, codes, and expectations are most ardently coveted and admired."[10] Though Disney impugns the extravagant means through which a girl conforms to gender expectations, it never challenges the expectation itself. Rather than critiquing the institution that requires a proper wife to be only silent and beautiful, the film instead focuses on the crisis an individual experiences when she does not meet the requirement. The paternal edict "I know my place, it is time you learned yours"[11] commands Mulan to assimilate a preconceived gender role rather than rebel and form a new one.

Asking who she sees in her reflection underscores the importance of the physical manifestations of one's gender role in Mulan's world. When she looks at herself Mulan shows only sadness at what appears before her. The reflection of what should be the perfect bride and daughter does not touch the reality of what is underneath the female facade. Both of Mulan's reflections—the painted and unpainted faces—are conveyed on the temple stones of her family shrine. Placed there to honor the Fa family ancestors, the stones represent both the duty Mulan owes her father and her inability to fulfill that duty in her current form. She realizes that "only by changing her outer appearance can [she] reflect her inner identity."[12] That Mulan does not recognize the *girl* in her reflection, that she reflects her inner identity via cross-dressing, raises the question of whom (and what gender) Mulan wishes to enact. Although "[t]hematically this song functions as a monologue through which the heroine expresses her longing for an accredited individuality," that accredited individuality is inextricable from a condoned gender role.[13] Disney reinforces the cultural constraint that one's identity is dependent on the successful realization of one's gender imperatives through Mulan's personal crisis after she fails to earn the matchmaker's approbation.

Mulan sees her identity as wrapped up in the artifice of sartorial markers so that, when she does not receive the designation of woman in her female clothes and make-up, she begins to doubt what kind of identity she is to have/perform. She seems unaware of the implications of this mode of gender construction, yet when Mulan passes as male by employing the right clothes, she demonstrates that both her feminine clothes and her armor are costumes that do not actually correspond to the gender of the person whom they cover. Thus, as Garber notes, "Transvestism, deployed strategically as disguise, uncovers as it covers, reveals the masquerade that is already in place."[14] Mulan may be biologically identified as female, but, as the matchmaker scene and the ensuing song "Reflection" attest, she does not fulfill the gender roles required of her. Trying to be the "perfect" bride or the "perfect" daughter is a masquerade already in place and literalized via the white face paint she wears at the bride selection. When she decides to run away, trying to "learn her place" as her father admonished, Mulan trades one mask for another, and the success she experiences with the male disguise only emphasizes her previous failure with the female one.

Making a Man

If "Honor to Us All" functions as an account of the constructedness of female gender, then its counterpart "I'll Make a Man Out of You," which plays over the montage of the soldier's training, both juxtaposes and makes explicit the contention that gender is a cultural product. Mulan's transformative toilette is a "subconscious recognition that 'woman' in patriarchal society is conceived of as an artifact—and that the logical next step is the recognition that 'man' is likewise not fact but artifact, himself constructed."[15] The film exploits this recognition in both senses via the subsequent scenes at the training camp. Rather than copying crib notes onto her arm to pass as a proper daughter and bride, Mulan—now dressed in male clothing and named Ping—carries Mushu, a small dragon guardian, through the camp, listening to his whispered guidance on how to "act like a man." Thus the Wu Shu camp functions on two levels: training new recruits to be soldiers as well as training Mulan to be a man. If "wife" is the cultural artifact of woman in the film, then "soldier" is the cultural artifact of man. It is much more common to speak of "making a man" out of some (male) candidate; some martial or sexual exercise will "'make a man' of the hapless boy.... To 'make' a man is to test him."[16] Becoming a man is an active process, requiring some physical or sexual prowess on the part of the subject. Becoming a woman, in contrast, is a passive process, to be enacted upon a silent object. Though Shang takes the rhetorically active place within the song (he is the one "making" a man of others), Ping and the other soldiers equally participate in the process of their making; they learn hand-to-hand combat, archery, rocket launching, and a plethora of physical activities to become their own agents of achieving manhood.

However, qualifiers of manhood are not as distinct as those for woman-hood. Whereas the women in town tell Mulan exactly how she must look to be female, descriptions of being a man are cloaked in simile. The comparisons to elements of nature attempt to frame manliness as part of the natural world and thus not constructed by conventional society. The use of similes also func-tions to obscure the delineation of exactly *what does* make a "man"; perhaps what lies behind this lyrical vagueness is, according to Garber, a "sneaking feeling that it should not be so easy to 'construct' a 'man.'"[17] For in these lines there are no step-by-step directions for the process of becoming, only the repeated, baritone-voices of the chorus commanding each soldier to "Be a man." The montage sequencing of these scenes provides only evidence of the change the soldier make into men, not *how* such a change came about—what the characters did to become men. In "Honor to Us All," Mulan receives instructions accompanied by their actions: the woman painting Mulan's face sings about being pale at the same moment she applies the white paint. In contrast to Captain Li's dictates to be a man, the process of becoming a woman is given as an instruction manual and made accessible to any who wishes to learn and mimic it.

Also juxtaposed to the feminine transformation, the male experience is one of physicality and awareness of the body. Mulan is taught that the female body is not for her own use, that its value is only measurable by its attractiveness to future husbands. Her male façade Ping, on the other hand, is shown that the masculine body is essential to male self-definition, that it must be fully integrated with the psyche to establish gender. Recall that Mushu's first lesson to Mulan in passing is imitating a "man walk" into the training camp. Mushu can tell her what to do to walk like a man, but without knowledge of her capa-bilities Mulan cannot pass in the eyes of other men. Her near failure to become a man results from her body's inability to attain physical goals despite her emotional and intellectual desire to do so.

Though the film attempts to place male and female genders on opposing sides of an intractable boundary, by relying on a binary structure to support its definition of these genders it in fact exposes a contradiction. As Eve Sedg-wick observes in her analysis of binaries, valorized terms are nonetheless dependent upon subordinate terms for meaning.[18] The film emphasizes that women are not considered equal to men—indeed, even after Mulan defeats Shan-Yu, the emperor's counselor refutes the claim that "she's a hero" with the rejoinder "she's a woman."[19] Furthermore, as Shang and the other soldiers reveal, manhood is not only an active process of making a man but also defined in opposition to woman/girlhood ("Be a man.... Don't be such a girl"). Thus manhood is not an entity unto itself, separate from womanhood; rather, it depends on the latter for its constitution.

As in the confrontation with the matchmaker, Mulan nearly fails to become a fully realized participant in the heterosexual matrix. Neither man nor woman, she would be unmarked, non-existent within her community and within discourse. Shang tells Ping to go home asking, disbelieving that he can make a man out of the novice. Mulan disobeys the command and works on her own to prove her manhood. She must scale the high wooden pole, phallic in its near impossibility of being conquered, with weights that represent strength and discipline to retrieve an arrow at the top. Though Ping has gone through military training and followed Shang's orders, helped (and more often hindered) by Mushu, she has not attempted anything alone. Now, with her family's honor and her own existence being threatened, Mulan must rely only on herself to become a man. She must transition from passive object upon which gender is written and become the subject-agent that claims a gender and a role in the community. Thus in answer to Shang's question of how he could make a man out of Ping, Mulan demonstrates that *he* cannot; as the cross-dressed figure it is up to Mulan to make herself a man, to move from passive object to active subject. The most important step here is the claiming of her bodily power and integrating physical and mental strength to "make it" to the top, to "make herself a man." Because she is able to scale the pole when the other men cannot, it appears that her "power inheres in her blurred gender, in the fact of her crossing-dressing, and not—despite the stereotypical romantic ending—in *either* of her gendered identities."[20]

The Agency of Liminality

For one positioned as a woman warrior, Mulan spends relatively little time cross-dressed in her military garb, let along actually fighting. In the Chinese poem, Mulan spends 12 years in the army and fights hundreds of battles before she returns home,[21] yet Disney's version reduces her time cross-dressing (and thus between genders) into a span of a few weeks. In both narratives we are not meant to pay an inordinate amount of attention to her male facade; Disney especially desires "to appropriate the cross-dresser 'as' one of the two sexes ... to look away from the transvestite as transvestite, not to see cross-dressing except as male or female manqué, whether motivated by social, cultural, or aesthetic designs."[22] Though Garber calls this tendency an "*under-estimation* of the object," it would be more apropos in the case of Disney to name it a proper estimation of the object's—transvestism's—power. On the one hand, adapting the story of a cross-dressing girl "seems to desire women's liberation by showcasing a Chinese female warrior to accentuate the image of strong women: girls can be soldiers."[23] On the other, focusing and celebrating too much the cross-dressed figure might resemble too closely supporting an outright challenge to dominant gender norms. As Sam Abel notes, Disney "cannot critique traditional gender roles because [it] buy[s] into them."[24]

Instead, the film normalizes the story of the transvestite through a progress narrative: Mulan always has a reason to explain (or explain away) her transvestism, whether to keep her father from being killed or "to prove [she] could do things right. So when [she] looked in the mirror [she'd] see someone worthwhile."[25] There must be a reason so that "any discomfort felt by ... the audience ... is smoothed over and narrativized by a story that recuperates social and sexual norms, not only reinstating the binary (male/female) but also retaining, and encoding, a progress narrative: s/he did this in order to (a) get a job, (b) find a place in a man's world, and (c) realize or fulfill some deep but acceptable need in terms of personal destiny."[26] Hence Mulan does not cross-dress in order to usurp cultural power denied her because she is female, nor does she cross-dress for personal or sexual fulfillment. Rather, her transgression is reinscribed as, at first, filial piety and later as journey to realize her place in society.

To reinforce that Mulan does not truly desire to be a man she is never shown to particularly enjoy manhood, nor does she seem to understand the cultural power she now possesses as Ping; she is made a man at training camp and subsequently her first desire is to ensure that "just because [she] look[s] like a man doesn't mean [she has] to smell like one."[27] Being a man is depicted as a physically unappealing prospect: the men in the camp are rowdy, violent, and mean to Ping, and Mulan describes them as "disgusting." Conversely, the soldiers treat femaleness as equally unwanted: Li Shang starts training the new recruits by shaming them, asking if they're daughters rather than sons. Fellow soldier Yao offhandedly insults Ping, Chien-Po, and Ling by calling them girls; when Ping does not want to play-fight with Yao Ling tells her "Don't be such a girl."[28] Clearly, being a girl is inferior, but men are gross and *real* girls would not want to be (like) them. For the gender binary and patriarchal power structures to remain intact gender crossing cannot be an attractive option for women, and it is implied that if not for filial piety Mulan would never cross-dress.

Whether she derives any pleasure from passing as a man, the film does not hint at (and more often denies it); Mulan's mission is to bring honor to her family through military accomplishment, and she finds that opportunity in the aptly named Tung Shao Pass. Vastly out-numbered and under-equipped, Shang's troops encounter the entire Hun army on the mountain pass that leads to the emperor's palace. After an unsuccessful volley, Shang commands the soldiers to aim the last rocket at the Hun leader, Shan-Yu, and prepare to fight to the death. Thinking quickly, Mulan sheaths her sword and grabs the remaining rocket, running into the open space between the troops. By firing the rocket into a snow embankment and causing an avalanche, Mulan defeats the entire Hun army by herself in one fell swoop. To reiterate Garber: her "power inheres in her blurred gender, in the fact of her crossing-dressing"; when Mulan is at her most powerful she is between genders. That this triumph occurs on the Tung Shao Pass—the path *between* mountain peaks, the mountain itself as a *border between* two lands (rural China and Imperial City)—and that she does so by running into the *No Man's* Land *between* the two armies further affirms the power of crossing.

After defeating the Hun army, as well as rescuing Shang from the avalanche, Mulan is lauded as "the bravest of us all" and "king of the mountain."[29] But following these pronouncements of full acceptance as a man she faints from a sword injury and is literally uncovered as female. Her greatest victory is immediately undercut by the revelation of her gender. Whereas the Mulan of the original poem unmasks herself after the war, Disney's Mulan has no choice in the matter. In the poem, after Mulan triumphantly returns home, she chooses to dress as a woman again and reveal herself to her fellow soldiers, who accept her wartime cross-dressing without question. Her exposure in the film, however, functions as punishment for her liminal behavior, and after her "true" gender is discovered, Mulan does not try to pass again. Whereas narratives of cross-dressing are often meant to open possibilities of alternative power structures, the film denies this possibility by consistently delineating between male and female; while Mulan can pass in the eyes of her comrades (for a time), she is constantly redesignated as female to the audience. Once she recrosses the gender boundary back to femaleness there is apparently no return; she earns accolades from the emperor, returns home to her family, and gains a fiancé—now that she is a "real" woman there is no reason to cross-dress.

While Mulan earns heroic admiration as Ping when she defeats the Hun army, her "true" heroism is later enacted when she is dressed as a woman. Though she has been abandoned by the troops, indeed almost killed for high treason, when Mulan learns that a few Huns have survived the avalanche and infiltrated the Imperial City she continues in her soldier's role, if not her soldier's garb. After Shan-Yu and his remaining soldiers barricade themselves in the palace with the emperor, Shang, Yao, Ling, and Chien-Po attempt unsuccessfully to penetrate the palace doors with a stone statue. Using her already established strategic thinking, Mulan formulates a plan: She and the three soldiers impersonate concubines to give Shang an opportunity to rescue the emperor. Hoi F. Cheu calls this "the most unconvincing scene," in which the cross-dressed soldiers "save China from the dishonourable terrorists with their femininity."[30] Cheu continues: "This cross-dressing scene is certainly designed to make girls feel good about being 'women' by evoking a sense of poetic justice after what the men have done to Mulan for her transgression."[31] It is tempting to view Mulan cross-dressing her male comrades in the same manner that she was to meet the matchmaker, but in this scene the men are not figures of power but figures of parody. The three "concubines" are revealed in harsh lighting and strike bold, masculine poses despite their clothing. Their change is a spectacle meant to elicit audience laughs rather than challenge their so-called innate maleness. Whereas Mulan must viably pass as a man to uphold family honor and not be killed for treason, the men do not attempt to truly pass as women; they remain only men in women's clothes.[32] Nor do their lives and honor depend on successfully cross-dressing; it is treated almost as a lark. With the reprise of "Make a Man Out of You" in the background, the scene renders Mulan's previous transgression a joke rather than a powerful statement. And as Cheu's particular word choice asserts, the cross-dressing is "poetic justice" for abandoning Mulan—the soldiers are feminized as punishment. In this moment the message is clear: femininity is ridiculous and should be mocked when men exhibit it.

Once Shang, the only one who fully retains his masculine appearance, stops Shan-Yu from striking the emperor down and the other men take the emperor to safety, the Hun leader focuses his ire on the young captain. Seeing Shang unconscious on the ground, Mulan goes to his aid as he begins to wake up. Shan-Yu attacks Shang, slapping him and grabbing him by the collar as he yells, "You took away my victory!" Before he can go further Mulan hits him with her shoe and states, "No! I did!" as she pulls her hair back to resemble her former self.[33] Shan-Yu remembers her as "the soldier from the mountain," refusing to place her in either gender and thus maintaining her liminal status even when she is sartorially female. Immediately he pursues Mulan without paying heed to her gender. Shan-Yu is the only character who does not reference Mulan's gender in their interactions, nor is he concerned with her crossing; he does not rein in his attacks or taunt her because she is female. Rather, he treats Mulan as an equal opponent who stands in the way of his victory.[34]

When he corners her on the roof of the palace, Mulan's only weapon is her fan, the oft-used symbol of femininity, against Shan-Yu's sword, an obvious phallic reference. As his sword penetrates the fan's paper, Mulan closes the fan and twists the sword out of Shan-Yu's grasp, grabbing it from the air and turning the weapon upon its owner. While Mulan's resourcefulness is vital to her victories against this enemy, the winning strategy here, in Disney's approximation, is to rely on feminine accoutrements rather than masculine war munitions. In addition, rather than defeating Shan-Yu on her own, Mulan relies on outside help. Once she has the sword, she calls to Mushu, who fires a rocket[35] at Shan-Yu that hits and propels him to the fireworks tower, which explodes and leaves no doubt of his defeat. Importantly, Mulan uses his sword against Shan-Yu by pinning him directly in the rocket's path; however, because she finally defeats the Hun leader as a woman when she was unsuccessful as a man, and because Shan-Yu's death is what ultimately saves China, the power of the liminal figure is diminished. It is neither Mulan-the-man who defeats the enemy nor Mulan-the-liminal: rather, it is only when Mulan employs her femininity, represented by the fan, that she succeeds—she must emerge from liminality into the fully feminine. Disney exploits the girl-power pathos of the moment at the expense of the truly powerful actions of the cross-dresser.

Thus the girl who returns to her daughter/future bride role is celebrated while the ungendered, rebellious person is marginalized.

When Mulan meets the emperor, she is prepared to accept his seeming condemnation as he lists her recent deeds in a denouncing tone, but is surprised to, in fact, receive praise. The emperor bows to Mulan, saying, "You have saved us all,"[36] and the people assembled around the palace bow as well. The emperor further commends her by making Mulan a member of his council, recognizing not simply her military prowess but her intelligent strategizing. Though a council position elevates Mulan well above other jobs available to women and effectively marks her as equal to the other men on the council, the emperor offers little change to the social position of women in general. Mulan may transcend certain gender roles, but the roles themselves remain the same. As she does in the original poem, Mulan refuses the council offer in favor of returning home to her family, thus willingly returning to previous gender roles that have not changed since she left. Instead of employment, the emperor now offers his pendant, "so your family will know what you have done for me," and the sword of Shan-Yu, "so the world will know what you have done for China."[37] Both the imperial crest and the weapon function as indicators of Mulan's social status, but neither marks her as a woman.[38] In fact, the conferral of her enemy's sword effectively bestows upon Mulan an officially condoned phallus, marking her instead as male.

Regendering and Conclusions

However, rather than allowing Mulan to complete her journey with her gender left "in-between" (a woman who possesses the phallus) and thus challenging the accepted gender binary, the film negates the agency of transgression at the moment she reaches the apex of her social power. The yearning for home nullifies Mulan's self-sufficiency and rebellion against the gender norms that home represents. Moreover, immediately upon returning to her family, Mulan relinquishes these gifts, her social and gender markers, to her father as signs that "honor the Fa family,"[39] placing herself fully under the dominion of patriarchal power. Fa Zhou ignores these abdicated symbols and only then embraces Mulan as his daughter, approving her return to her familial role and "proper" gender.

As this and the previous scenes illustrate, "The good, strong woman always returns to the man's world. When Mulan defeats the Huns her emperor recovers his power; when she returns home her father retakes the order of the house."[40] The desire for home, the forsaking of her sword to her father, and, finally, the arrival of Shang to fulfill the role of Prince Charming all function to displace any liminal agency and re-designate Mulan as fully female. Thus, the pinnacle of her development, according to Disney, is not when she holds the sword of her enemy and the Emperor bows to her, but rather when Shang comes to "stay for dinner."[41] Mulan's story begins with transgression to enact filial piety and "concludes with her fulfillment of these values. In the final scene, Mulan represents a reconciliation of the conflicts incurred by her boundary-crossing action and a restoration of the social norms."[42] Once these norms and her gender are firmly reestablished, the film can end with the obligatory happily ever after of the Western fairy tales it imitates.

Though Sui Leung Li claims, "The woman warrior is one of the most threatening unconventional female figures to the patriarchal imagination," in both the original legend and the Disney version Mulan's subversive power is suppressed and she happily returns to her social and familial position, suggesting little room for cultural transformation.[43] In the Chinese poem, Mulan arrives home with her comrades, still dressed as a man. When she changes into her feminine clothing and applies make-up, Mulan reveals her female gender to the soldiers, who are shocked but accept her because they fought so long together. In dialogue that is unattributed, the speaker (who most assume is Mulan) says, "The he-hare's feet go hop and skip,/ The she-hare's eyes are muddled and fuddled./ The two hares running side by side close to the ground,/ How can they tell if I am he or she?"[44] The poem's comic ending revels in the confusion of gender conventions at the same time it returns Mulan to her gender role within the domestic realm. Because the Disney version predicates Mulan's development on her transgression against patriarchal norms, when she returns to her former domestic role that violation is negated. The film adaptation may halfheartedly question how gender roles are traditionally fulfilled, but it never impugns the roles themselves: Mulan may not behave like American society's version of a bride, but that does not mean she should not fulfill the role. The path is different but the destination is the same in Disney's world. Because *Mulan* is a "retelling based on the use of elements typical of a fairy tale," the traditional narrative must find its completion through the arrival of Shang and the implied courtship and marriage that will follow.[45] This ending marks her acquiescence to the social order she rebelled against by running away from home. Thus, even though the film seems to celebrate Mulan's liminality and the agency she gains because of her boundary crossing, Disney in fact contains the truly progressive significance of her actions in order to instill its own message of traditional gender roles.

Notes

1. Dates back to the Northern Wei Dynasty (386–534). The original tale never professes any progressive aims in Mulan's cross-dressing—indeed, by dressing like a boy and taking her father's place in the army Hua Mulan's actions are not rebellion but rather approved and supported by her father as a sign of family duty.

2. For more detailed analyses of the racial issues raised in *Mulan* see Jun Tang and Sheng-mei Ma. Quotation from Jun Tang, "A Cross-Cultural Perspective on Production and Reception of Disney's Mulan Through its Chinese Subtitles," *European Journal of English Studies* 12.2 (2008): 152.

3. Patriarchy, as I use it throughout the essay, refers to the social order in which fathers, and by extension all men, claim a broad and disproportionate share of power and authority. Masculinity will refer to qualities and characteristics traditionally associated with the male sex. Here masculine gender is not biologically determined whereas male sex is.

4. Notably this occurs on the Tung Shao Pass the road through the mountains that border the Imperial City

5. *Mulan*, directed by Tony Bancroft and Barry Cook (1998, The Disney Corporation).

6. Tanner et. al, "Images of Couples and Families in Disney Feature-Length Animated Films." *American Journal of Family Therapy* 31.5 (2003): 369, 365.

7. *Mulan* (1998).

8. Judith Butler. *Bodies that Matter: On the Discursive Limits of "Sex."* (New York: Routledge, 1993): 12.

9. Ibid, 232.

10. Marjorie Garber. *Vested Interests: Cross-dressing and Cultural Anxiety.* (New York: Routledge, 1997): 51.

11. *Mulan*, directed by Tony Bancroft and Barry Cook (1998).

12. Lisa Brocklebank, "Disney's *Mulan*—the "True" Deconstructed Heroine?" *Marvels & Tales: Journal of Fairy-Tale Studies* 14. 2 (2000): 275.

13. Lan Dong, "Writing Chinese America Into Words and Images: Storytelling and Retelling of The Song of Mu Lan," *The Lion and the Unicorn* 30.2 (2006).

14. Marjorie Garber, *Vested Interests*: 282.

15. Ibid, 249.

16. Ibid, 93.

17. Marjorie Garber, *Vested Interests*: 102.

18. Sedgwick, *Epistemology of the Closet*: 9–10.

19. *Mulan* (1998).

20. Marjorie Garber, *Vested Interests*: 6. Though Garber is discussing Dorothy in the 1982 film *Tootsie*, the description is still apt. Mulan exhibits the most agency when dressed as Ping

21. Han H. Frankel, *The Flowering Plum and the Palace Lady: Interpretations of Chinese Poetry*, (New Haven: Yale University Press, 1976): 68–72.

22. Ibid, 10.

23. Hoi F. Cheu, *Cinematic Howling* (Vancouver: University of British Columbia Press, 2008): 3–4.

24. Sam Abel, "The Rabbit in Drag: Camp and Gender Construction in the American Animated Cartoon" *Journal of Popular Culture* 29.3 (1995): 188.

25. *Mulan* (1998).

26. Marjorie Garber, *Vested Interests*: 69.

27. *Mulan* (1998).

28. *Ibid.*

29. *Ibid.*

30. Hoi F. Cheu, *Cinematic Howling*: 2–3.

31. *Ibid.*

32. Indeed, Yao's beard is not covered with white make-up and clearly visible.

33. This emphasizes hair, especially within the film, as the pivotal marker of gender. Recall that before Mulan even puts on her father's armor she first cuts off and ties back her hair. All quotations from *Mulan* (1998).

34. As both are Others in Chinese society, both outsiders from the social order, perhaps Shan-Yu sees Mulan as an equal in her own right.

35. This rocket is simply a large firework, whereas the rocket Mulan used on the mountain was a military weapon.

36. *Mulan* (1998).

37. *Ibid.*

38. Indeed, while observing Mulan and Fa Zhou's reunion, Mulan's grandmother quips "Huh. She brings home a sword. If you ask me she should've brought home a man!" For the women in her life, Mulan's "masculine" accomplishments don't mean as much as the societal demands that Mulan marry—thus truly become a woman.

39. *Ibid.*

40. Hoi F. Cheu, *Cinematic Howling*: 7.
41. *Mulan* (1998).
42. Lan Dong, "Writing Chinese America..." (2006).
43. Siu Leung Li, *Cross-Dressing in Chinese Opera* (Hong Kong: Hong Kong University Press, 2007): 83.
44. Han H. Frankel, *The Flowering Plum and the Palace Lady: Interpretations of Chinese Poetry* (New Haven: Yale University Press, 1976).
45. Jun Tang, "A Cross-Cultural Perspective on Production...": 150.

Bibliography

Abel, Sam. "The Rabbit in Drag: Camp and Gender Construction in the American Animated Cartoon." *Journal of Popular Culture* 29, no. 3 (Winter 1995): 183–202.

Brocklebank, Lisa. "Disney's *Mulan*—the "'True' Deconstructed Heroine?" *Marvels & Tales: Journal of Fairy-Tale Studies* 14, no. 2 (2000): 268–283.

Butler, Judith. *Bodies that Matter: On the Discursive Limits of "Sex."* New York: Routledge, 1993.

Cheu, Hoi F. *Cinematic Howling: Women's Films, Women's Film Theories.* Vancouver: University of British Columbia Press, 2008.

Dong, Lan. "Writing Chinese America Into Words and Images: Storytelling and Retelling of The Song of Mu Lan." *The Lion and the Unicorn* 30, no. 2 (2006): 218–233.

Frankel, Han H. *The Flowering Plum and the Palace Lady: Interpretations of Chinese Poetry.* New Haven: Yale University Press, 1976, 68–72.

Garber, Marjorie. *Vested Interests: Cross-Dressing and Cultural Anxiety.* New York: Routledge, 1997.

Li, Siu Leung. *Cross-Dressing in Chinese Opera.* Hong Kong: Hong Kong University Press, 2007.

Ma, Sheng-mei. *The Deathly Embrace: Orientalism and Asian American Identity.* Minneapolis: University of Minnesota Press, 2000.

Sedgwick, Eve Kosofsky. *The Epistemology of the Closet*, 2d. ed. Berkeley: University of California Press, 2008.

Tang, Jun. "A Cross-Cultural Perspective on Production and Reception of Disney's *Mulan* Through Its Chinese Subtitles." *European Journal of English Studies* 12, no. 2 (Aug. 2008): 149–162.

Tanner, Litsa Renée, et al. "Images of Couples and Families in Disney Feature-Length Animated Films." *American Journal of Family Therapy* 31, no. 5 (Oct. 2003): 355–3.

Youngs, Gillian. "The Ghost of Snow White." *International Feminist Journal of Politics* 1, no. 2 (Sep. 1999).

"What Do You Want Me to Do? Dress in Drag and Do the Hula?" Timon and Pumbaa's Alternative Lifestyle Dilemma in The Lion King

GAEL SWEENEY

On the Savannah: Elsinore Versus Broadway

Near the dramatic climax of *The Lion King,* a battle between Prince Simba and Pretender Uncle Scar, Simba suggests that sidekicks Timon the Meerkat and Pumbaa the Warthog create a diversion to lure away Scar's hyena cohorts. The cheeky Timon cocks his head and demands, "What do you want me to do? Dress in drag and do the hula?" An instant later—after a cry of "Luau!"—he's doing just that, tricked out in grass skirt, lei, and hot pink hibiscus over his left ear, with his "bestest best friend," the pig-like Pumbaa, as the main course. Their musical drag diversion, done as a Broadway-style 11:00 p.m. showstopper, buys Simba the time to defeat his nemesis and become the sole Lion King of the Pride Lands. This moment of high camp at the climax of Disney's animated rewrite of *Hamlet* with lions[1] may seem incongruous, but I have a stuffed Timon-in-drag doll, as well as a collectible "Luau" figurine, and signed print, all from the Disney Store, all immortalizing this now iconic image. Because as much as Simba, Mufasa, Nala, and the other lions are the heart of *The Lion King,* the characters who steal every scene are this film's versions of Rosenkrantz and Guildenstern,[2] Timon and Pumbaa, those long-time companions whose overtly queer sensibility problematizes and ultimately subverts the film and its themes with what I will call—with a bow to the deeply ingrained heteronormativity[3] of the Disney Organization—their Alternative Lifestyle Dilemma.

129

Disney Under Siege

The Lion King attracted controversy from its release in June 1994. While there has always been criticism of Disney from the Left for perceived corporatization of popular culture and racism and sexism in portrayals of minorities and women, in the 1990s, the organization which virtually invented the term "family-friendly" increasingly became the target of boycotts by conservative religious and "family values" interest groups. As the post–"Uncle Walt" entertainment giant branched out into more adult fare, buying Miramax Films and the ABC television network, as well as initiating more progressive internal policies, such as same-sex partner benefits, these moves were viewed suspiciously by conservatives, who began speaking out against the formerly revered company. Roman Catholic Cardinal John O'Connor blasted Disney for releasing the controversial British film *Priest* through Miramax, while the anti-abortion American Life League accused the company of purposely planting subliminal sexual imagery in their animated features. Rev. Jerry Falwell, who famously outed purple, purse-carrying Tinky Winky of the children's show *The Teletubbies,* called for his Baptist followers to boycott Disney products and theme parks, while the American Family Association claimed that under CEO Michael Eisner Disney had become "one of the leading promoters of the homosexual lifestyle, as well as the homosexual political and social agenda in America today."[4] Their leader, Rev. Donald Wildmon, became the most vociferous critic of the company, railing against its insidious "homosexual agenda" and labeling two beloved animated characters as "the first homosexual Disney characters ever to come to the screen."[5] Liberal commentators found much to mock in the Religious Right's earnest search for "proof"—the word "sex" hidden in a swirl of dust, a phallic turret on a cartoon castle, an animated minister with an erection, ABC allowing Ellen DeGeneres to come out on her sitcom—of the Disney Evil Empire's campaign to corrupt Christian youth and promote a perverse homosexual lifestyle. It's easy to poke fun at people like Wildmon, hysterically seeing things that aren't really there.

Except ... when there IS something there. Something delightfully subversive[6] and supremely popular. Because Rev. Wildmon's bête noire, *The Lion King,* celebrates Timon the Meerkat and Pumbaa the Warthog, who are certainly the first openly gay animated characters in the Disney canon. And that poses a series of dilemmas for viewers attempting to sort out the contradictory messages of *The Lion King.*

Performing Meerkat and Warthog

Timon and Pumbaa are the "lovable" (Disney's characterization) comic sidekicks of Simba, the would-be Lion King. Timon and Pumbaa are in the mode of what Steve Seidman calls "comedian comedy," like the Marx Brothers,

Martin and Lewis, Eddie Cantor, and Bob Hope and Bing Crosby: they are personas more than actors, addressing the audience directly, interpolating song-and-dance routines into the action and playing on their extra-cinematic selves with references to "showbiz" outside the diegetic universe of the film. This brings forth our first dilemma: Timon and Pumbaa subvert the "realistic" (in so far as animated characters can be realistic) performance style of the film. In general, animals in *The Lion King* behave like animals (albeit Disney animals): they walk on all fours, hunt (and kill) their prey, and are drawn in a fairly realistic style—with two important exceptions. They may wear the guise of meerkat and warthog, but Timon and Pumbaa have nothing to do with Africa. Said Nathan Lane: "My character, Timon, is more like a used-car salesman. Pumbaa and Timon are the low comedians. Kinda like two guys from Brooklyn who stop in the desert and became lovable cohorts."[7] The two guys from Brooklyn who show up in exotic locations and get into comic adventures are the mainstay of the road picture, best exemplified by Hope and Crosby, but also Laurel and Hardy, Martin and Lewis, and other comedy duos. Rather than realistic-acting animals performing a morality play set in pre-lapsarian Africa, Timon and Pumbaa are a classic comic duo dropped into a cartoon version of *Hamlet*. Timon is the crooning, egotistical wit, relying on verbal humor, puns, double entendres, wry looks, and double takes, while Pumbaa is the physical comedian, full of farts, belches, pratfalls, and visual gags centering on his ample belly and prominent rump.

Eric Smoodin points out that during the age of the classic cartoons, the 1930s and 1940s, animation stretched the boundaries of the Production Code because they were able to get away with double meanings and the kind of rude physical humor live actors would never be permitted to say or perform: "While cartoon sexuality was controlled by Hollywood's Production Code, animation also stretched the code or openly battled with it, in part for reasons related to studio competition, audience demographics, and historical context."[8] Many "adult" characterizations and pieces of business were put into cartoons covertly, especially by mavericks at the Warners Studio and independents like Max Fleischer, while studio execs assumed they'd to go over audience heads.[9] Many of the best animators, marginalized by their parent studios, made shorts that reflected their own concerns and sensibilities, creating cartoons that are often startlingly political, bawdy, and satiric, much in the manner of a certain flamboyant meerkat and flatulent warthog.

Critics have noted the similarities between Timon and Bugs Bunny in design, attitude, and language. Both are wisecrackers (Bugs' catchphrase is "I'm a little stinker, ain't I?") and tricksters, and both are fluid in sexuality, regularly donning drag, singing show tunes, ragging on notions of love and romance, and undermining relationships between other characters. But Timon, unlike the solitary Bugs, has a loyal "significant other": Pumbaa, his "bestest best friend." These two characters are obviously a same-sex couple—something singular in the Disney canon. They live together, they work together, and, long after their relationship has been affirmed, they raise a child together—a lion cub named Simba. Both characters are outcasts from their respective societies—Timon from the meerkat tunnels because, according to his "Diary," he broke into song while on guard-duty, and Pumbaa from his sounder due to excessive odor—but they find happiness together in their Oasis "dream home," a place isolated from the Pride Lands. Like many traditional film couples, they demonstrate that opposites certainly attract. Whereas Timon is a skeptic (perhaps mirroring his Shakespearean namesake, *Timon of Athens*), Pumbaa is sentimental and romantic. Pumbaa wants to adopt lion cub Simba because he's cute and helpless, ignoring that the cub will grow up to view his mentors as prey, while Timon only agrees for purely selfish reasons—"Maybe he'll be on OUR side!"—but together they become loving and devoted "foster parents."[10] When the adolescent Simba attempts to confront his destiny, the pair advise "You gotta put your behind in the past" (i.e., put your past behind you): it's the present that matters, not who you once were, but who you are now. The question of whether your identity and responsibility is to yourself or to your family is a universal dilemma, but one especially relevant to gay people, who have often been rejected by their families and found new "families" among like-minded friends. Obviously, the ultimate point of *The Lion King* is that Simba must realize where his true destiny lies and return to the Pride Lands and his responsibilities as king, but that message isn't "problem-free."

"Hakuna Matata": A Problem-Free Philosophy?

Which brings the next dilemma: Pumbaa and Timon's Oasis paradise is a site of major contradiction and conflict between that intended message of *The Lion King* ("Remember who you are") and the "problem-free philosophy" of "Hakuna Matata." (defined as "no worries, no responsibilities"). The utopian pleasures of their in sectarian enclave contrasts starkly with the deadly desert from which they rescue Simba, the Elephant's Graveyard of the hyenas, and Pride Rock itself, both before and after the reign of Mufasa: these are places Darwinian survival, of kill or be killed, of jealousy, greed, and Machiavellian plots. In their safe and secure Oasis, Timon and Pumbaa become surrogates for the murdered Mufasa and raise Simba to adulthood. With their humor, their charisma[11] and their marketability, Timon and Pumbaa take on an importance not in keeping with their peripheral status to the plot, and begin to overwhelm the "official" message of the film, offering a subversive alternate reading. Pumbaa and Timon can be read as gay-identified characters, living the closest thing to an "alternative lifestyle" to be found in the Disney universe, and making that lifestyle a true option to the family values- heavy "moral" of the story. Timon and Pumbaa embody the sensualist philosophy of "Hakuna Matata" and persist as self-proclaimed "outcasts" in direct contrast to the Machiavellian family intrigues of the Pride Lands. This contradiction comes across strongly in the narrative, but also in the characterizations and marketing strategies of the film and later the television series, leaving the viewer (both child and adult alike) with a contradictory message about whether your responsibility is to your family and tradition, or to yourself and pleasure.

Obviously, as the plot plays out, Simba (and by implication the viewers of the film) is meant to reject "Hakuna Matata" and return to his obligations as the king of the Pride Lands. Timon and Pumbaa aren't the most likely parental figures, but they can't have done such a bad job with their foster son: Simba is able to defeat Scar and claim his birthright. The real dilemma is that "no worries, no responsibilities" and "remember your responsibilities" are mutually exclusive concepts, yet the film wants to have it both ways. King Mufasa (the resonant James Earl Jones) may be an authoritative voice from heaven, but Timon and Pumbaa and the philosophy they represent are presented as more appealing, more fun, and much more marketable than the heavy-handed and ultimately violent path of Pride Rock.

Show Tunes and Insect Brunches: How to Be Gay in Disney

The alternative lifestyle of Timon and Pumbaa elicits the next dilemma of *The Lion King*. Do cartoon characters, especially those in traditional G-rated, child-centered animated features, have sexual identities? And if they do, how are those identities portrayed without actually suggesting sex acts? Sex is taboo in animated features (discounting underground films such as *Fritz the Cat*), especially at Disney, where the tradition of "family entertainment" is practically a fetish. So what do we make of Timon and Pumbaa? British gay cultural critic Mark Simpson, writing about Laurel and Hardy, another comedian comedy duo beloved by children and adults equally and famous for their "harmless" and clean comedy style, states that in dealing with the non-erotic, almost pre-sexual relationship between Stan and Ollie, one must say that "Laurel and Hardy are not 'gay.' But they are not 'straight' either."[12] Instead they exist in opposition to and in critique of heteronormative masculinity, and their confrontations with the adult world of regulation and repression are the basis of much of their comedy and our enjoyment of them. The skinny meerkat and the fat warthog partners function in much the same way as Stan Laurel and Oliver Hardy and extend a similar transgressive pleasure.

The very presence of Timon and Pumbaa in a children's animated feature offers a subversive reading within what is otherwise an determinedly conservative text. In the imagery and narrative (drag, camp mannerisms, two males raising a child together), in the songs they sing (by gay superstar Elton John), in their vocal characterizations (by gay Broadway star Nathan Lane, one of Terrence McNally's stock company players and the star of *The Birdcage,* Mike

Nichols' film version of French drag comedy *La Cage Aux Folles,* and Lane's frequent co-star, straight comic actor Ernie Sabella), and even in the marketing of products and a spin-off television series (Christmas ornaments of Timon in grass skirt and lei, Pumbaa's huge rump foregrounded on pillowcases), Timon and Pumbaa are decidedly queer characters. Their performance style, especially compared to that of the Pride Rock lions, is pure camp.[13] They also display many of the stereotypical markers of "gayness" in American popular culture. They read as white and New York (at least when compared to supporting character like the hyenas, voiced by Whoopi Goldberg and Cheech Marin, who read as urban and "Ghetto" and barrio!), are exaggerated in gesture and attitude, arch in expression and double entendre, overly emotional, and have an affinity for Broadway show tunes unusual in animals born and raised on the plains of Africa. As *New Yorker* reviewer Terrence Rafferty notes of Timon's "showstopper" performance: "The meerkat wisecracks constantly ... and tends to get carried away when he sings and dances."[14] In other words, Timon isn't just a drama queen, he's a theater queen!

As stated previously, Timon and Pumbaa are outcasts from their respective families (in a film where family is the key to one's identity), their social groups (meerkat tunnel and warthog sounder), and their species expectations (meerkat and warthog is not a pairing to be found in the "natural" order of things). In a world where mating and creating a family is primary, Timon and Pumbaa are content in their all-male enclave, complete with hot tub-like pool and insect buffet brunches. They also display a pronounced antipathy to heterosexual romance, as they prove when their adoptee, Simba, shows an interest in female interloper Nala, who, interestingly, can beat him up! And then there's Timon's famous hula drag. In the film, Timon puts on a grass shirt and lei, with a red hibiscus over his left ear, in order to distract the attacking hyenas, but the truth is that both Timon and Pumbaa revel in drag. In episodes of their television series *The Lion King's Timon and Pumbaa,* Timon donned a sarong, a pink waitress uniform, and another grass skirt and hibiscus, but this time with a string of pearls. Another continuing bit centered on Timon's various turns as a waiter ("My name is Timon; I'll be your waiter"), a modern updating of the old gay hairdresser stereotype. Pumbaa also appeared in drag during the series, most notably posing as Timon's wife to fool his mother so she won't realize that her son is living with his male warthog partner. Then there are statements made by Lane and Sabella during *The Lion King* publicity blitz, which range from sly innuendoes about their characters to forthright outing, including their joint interview with *The New York Times* and Lane's hilarious *Tonight Show* turn about gay, Jewish meerkats performing show tunes on the "Borscht veldt."[15]

The characters of Timon and Pumbaa are also unusual for Disney in that they were created from the actors' Broadway personas, rather than being cast to fit preconceived characters. Phil Harris in *The Jungle Book* and Robin

Williams in *Aladdin* were two of only a handful of actors other than Nathan Lane and Ernie Sabella to ad lib many of their lines—and Lane and Sabella were unique in being allowed to record their lines together rather than singularly, as did the other voice actors. In this way Lane and Sabella put their individual stamps on the characterizations. Timon and Pumbaa were only created after Lane and Sabella, performing in the same musical on Broadway, arrived together to audition for the hyenas and began to joke around in the attitudes of their *Guys and Dolls* characters, which partly explains the stylistic anomaly of these streetwise, New Yorkese creatures. Improvised dialogue inspired whole comic bits, such as Timon's hula, and even bodily functions were incorporated into the narrative. One day Lane encouraged Sabella to make a rude noise into the microphone: "'We never thought they'd use it,' Mr. Sabella says, but the warthog's flatulence is now a running gag in the finished movie. 'They stole everything,' he says."[16] The characters were then animated (Timon by Mike Surrey and Pumbaa by Tony Bancroft) from videos of Lane and Sabella acting out their lines together, capturing their distinctive features, such as Sabella's fat, blustery cheeks, and Lane's eloquent eyebrows and anguished shoulder shrugs. Characters voiced by actors with distinctive vocal styles and personalities, such as Timon and Pumbaa, Robin Williams' Genie, Phil Harris' Baloo, or Pat Carroll's Ursula, have often become the most memorable and beloved.[17] Disney products are usually kitschy instead of campy, but it's interesting that the popular Cruella DeVil, Genie, and Ursula are all extremely camp creations, while Lane's Timon is the campiest of all, whether in drag, doing show tunes a la Jolson, or demonstrating the most flamboyant hand gestures since Jack Benny. Lane, who was still publicly closeted at the time, but whose sexuality was widely known in New York theater circles, told the *New York Times* that "Timon is really me.... It's essentially me talking." When asked what specific aspects of his character the animators used, he replied, archly, "Oh, you know, staggering sensuality. Sexual danger."[18] This is not what most Disney voice artists would be touting, but it's typical of the comments Lane and Sabella made in support of the film.

If Lane and Sabella's campy interpretations influenced the development of their characters, then openly gay composer Elton John certainly impacted the way his music was used in the film, but to a different effect. The Academy Award winning ballad "Can You Feel the Love Tonight?" was originally a comic parody of soft-focus movie interludes sung by Lane and Sabella. But John objected to the way *The Lion King* team had conceptualized his song as a satire. Said co-director Rob Minkoff: "Elton really felt it was part of the Disney tradition to keep the love song romantic,"[19] and the number was taken away from Timon and Pumbaa (except for the intro and tag ending) and given to Simba and Nala, revamped from a pointed satire to the kind of gushy ballad it been had intended to mock. The song is thus heteronormalized by playing it "straight," turning a comic critique of traditional Disney romance into an idyll of heterosexual awakening. It's possible that John, whose stock-in-trade is love songs for mainstream audiences, was uncomfortable with Lane and Sabella's camp send-up of his song (and by implication, his entire catalog) and therefore squelched their version. It's also possible that he recognized the power of Timon and Pumbaa's appeal, realizing that if the pair successfully undermine Nala, then Simba has no reason to question life at the oasis, let alone decide to reject it.

"Carnivores! Oy!": Disney and the Jewish Question

Timon the Meerkat is not only gay-identified, but also New York and Jewish-identified: "Timon has a recognizable ethnicity.... 'Sure, he's Jewish,' says Mr. Lane. 'Didn't you see him kiss the mezuza on the little tree?'"[20] Nathan Lane, an Irish Catholic from New Jersey, instilled in his portrayal of Timon an amalgam of elements: his assertive stage persona as Nathan Detroit in *Guys and Dolls*, his gay leads in Terrence McNally comedic dramas *Love! Valour! Compassion!* and *The Lisbon Traviata*, the gay sidekicks and neighbors he played in films such as *Frankie & Johnny*. But he also stirred in more than a hint of New York Jewish humor. Lane delighted in ad-libbing phrases such as "Carnivores! Oy!" "So ... Where ya from?" and the deathless "What do you want me to do? Dress in drag and do the hula?" in a voice with more than just a touch of Flatbush Avenue. Walt Disney himself was known to be anti-semitic in his personal life, if not in his business. Joked Lane of the traditionally conservative attitude at Disney: "I heard Walt wasn't very fond of the Jewish people. I'm sure he's spinning around in a refrigerator somewhere."[21] So how much was Lane (in consort with Sabella) consciously subverting Disney norms? I would argue a lot, and that the writers and animators gleefully encouraged and nurtured his over-the-top interpretation of the role. Lane openly twitted Disney Producer Jeffrey Katzenberg, proclaiming Timon and Pumbaa's alternative sexuality on television and in print, and aligning the duo with various minority groups—Jews, gays, meerkats, people who sing out loud in public places—not usually associated with Disney product (but very often in Disney production and business!):

> "Timon's a feisty little cheerful fellow," says Mr. Lane. "He has a very nice life. He and Pumbaa seem to have a very nice arrangement—though I couldn't say what the extent of their relationship is." The suggestion is obvious. Mr. Lane's grin is devilish. "I know what Nathan says about them," says Mr. Sabella, laughing. "'These are the first homosexual Disney characters to come to the screen.' Now that ought to get Jeffrey Katzenberg's attention. Hello!"[22]

Katzenberg's response to the actors' teasing was reportedly, "I love it when you guys make fun of me"[23]—but he didn't deny the possible validity of their remarks. The irony of all this banter is that one of the attack points of the Religious Right in their campaign against *The Lion King* and Disney outlined earlier, is that the company and its products were part of a conscious "assault against Christianity"[24] by Jewish CEO Michael Eisner and his minions, who had distorted the American, Christian, and family-oriented fare served by "Uncle Walt" and replaced it with "Zionist sentiments" that not only denigrated Christian values, but in film such as *The Lion King* and *Pocahontas,* "distort(ed) European-American history and disparag(ed) white America's racial-cultural heritage."[25] During a mid–1990s debate about Hollywood "family values," Billy Crystal offered that, "When people say 'Hollywood Elite' what I really hear is 'Jew.'"[26] So perhaps it's to be expected that beyond the initial criticisms from the Left of the film as racist (the hyenas as Black and Hispanic stereotypes), sexist (the father and son relationship that marginalizes Sarabi and Nala), homophobic (Scar[27]), were overshadowed by Right-wing Fundamentalist harangues against Disney itself. *The Lion King* a cog in a larger campaign of overtly sexual and homosexual propaganda linked to the release of the British independent film *Priest* in the spring of 1995 by Disney subsidiary Miramax, and was part of an on-going "Hollywood versus American Family Values" diatribe that called for the boycotting of all Disney products. As stated earlier, anti-abortion group The American Life League railed against "subliminal messages" hidden in Disney animated films, claiming that Disney cartoon features are full of erotic content and accus(ing) the head of the multimedia giant of peddling off-color products in the guise of family entertainment.... "I have no idea what (Disney CEO) Michael Eisner thinks he's doing. I have no way of knowing what their plan is for our kids. But they're making a fortune and these cartoons are filled with sexual imagery."[28]

Judie Brown, president of the group, called for all Disney products to be removed from stores—a request Eisner and the Disney organization simply ignored. As *The Lion King* was released to video and DVD, spawned two sequels and a television series, and as *Pocahontas* (1995) continued Disney's animated feature success, the threatened boycott had little effect.[29] But perhaps the greatest impact these campaigns had was less on business and more on the artistic process, where the creators seemed to delight in tweaking their critics. In the Timon and Pumbaa television series, as well as the second DVD sequel, *The Lion King 1½,* the characters were made even more subversive to "Christian" norms. Timon, still voiced by Nathan Lane, was gayer than ever and unmistakably Jewish, gaining a last name, Berkowitz, a stereotypical Jewish mother who calls him a *"meshugener,"* and an Uncle Max who wants him to go into the family business.

"Home Is Where Your Rump Rests": Funny Uncles on Pride Rock

While Pumbaa and Timon were created around actors Nathan Lane and Ernie Sabella, their addition solved a major plot dilemma: what to do with

Simba during his adolescence. The original storyboards showed Simba brooding ineffectually on Pride Rock like a leonine Hamlet, while Scar and his hyenas ran rampant. Exiling Simba gave him an alternative to the Pride Lands, as well as much-needed comic relief after the trauma of Mufasa's violent death. Simba's Oasis interlude allows him to grow up in safety, but it also exposes him to a philosophy completely at odds with the law of Mufasa. Which brings us to the ultimate dilemma of *The Lion King*. In order to be true to its moral, Timon and Pumbaa should be rejected in favor of privileging the dominant social order of the Pride Lands. But is that what actually happens? Who and what, in the end, is Simba? Is he only a reflection of his father, the rightful heir to Mufasa's authority? Or is he a true product of the "no worries, no responsibilities" lifestyle of his unconventional foster fathers? At the Oasis, Timon and Pumbaa, with Simba, are a selfcontained unit, a created family bound not by blood-ties, but by friendship and love. Although Timon's mother, Ma Berkowitz, appears in the television series (leading directly to Pumbaa dressing in drag), and also appears with Uncle Max in the made-for-DVD sequel, *The Lion King 1½*, both Timon and Pumbaa are adamant in their songs and dialogue that they have rejected family and species because they were themselves rejected. In a film overtly about fatherhood, Timon and Pumbaa are fatherless, yet they offer a different model of parenthood to Simba, one that privileges pleasure and care of the self. And of that other possible father— it's problematic. Is "Uncle Scar" also a father? In *The Lion King II: Simba's Pride*, we learn that he is, but the plot, dealing with the redemption of his black sheep son, is pure soap opera with little of the original film's charm. And do we really know who is Nala's father? This point was hotly debated at the time on *Lion King* internet groups such as alt.fan.lion-king. Is she Simba's half-sister, or Scar's daughter? Either solution brings up uncomfortable possibilities. But Scar is more an anti-father figure, the antithesis of Mufasa: under Scar's sterile regime the Pride Lands wither, the herds move on, there are seemingly no cubs and a lot of frustrated lionesses.[30] In contrast, Timon and Pumbaa's Oasis is lush and abundant, and if there's no overt sex there, there is also no overt death.

Timon and Pumbaa have a refreshing disdain for the tangled family drama of the Pride Rock lions, even when they are quick to aid their foster son. But as they help Simba, these "funny uncles" (as contrasted to Scar's "evil uncle") continue to flaunt convention, social regulation, and the prevailing ideology. Their pleasure is not in the serious work of hunting, but in eating bugs, wallowing in mud, breaking wind, and breaking rules, triumphing as low-comedians and rebels against authority. In this Timon and Pumbaa are true carnivalesque characters. Pumbaa's disorderly body, flatulence, belches ("Pumbaa, with you everything is gas!"), malapropisms, and dimwittedness (his name means "foolish one" in Swahili) hide a sweet, sympathetic nature and idiot savant insight, but he can also fight back when the chips are down: "They call me MR. PIG!" he bellows at the hyenas before he charges. Timon, the "brains of the outfit," uses his uncontrollable speech (Disney promotional material refers to him as a "motormouth") and camp wit to cut through much of the narrative angst, speaking honest truths. When he first views the destroyed Pride Lands, he grimaces, seeing not a magic kingdom but a morally corrupt and ravaged wasteland. Says Timon in disbelief: "We're going to fight your uncle for this? Talk about your fixer-upper!" These characteristics get the pair into trouble, but also get them out. Doing the hula isn't simply transgressive, it demonstrates the value of thinking outside of the box, something the pragmatic lions can't seem to manage.

Timon and Pumbaa immediately recognize the danger in the appearance of Nala at the Oasis. For Pumbaa, the danger is actual—the lioness attempts to kill the warthog for food, introducing death and the reality of the "food chain" into their insectarian Eden. But for Timon, Nala is a different kind of threat: the romantic ballad "Can You Feel the Love Tonight?" underlines Nala's function in bringing Simba back to his main "theme"—and back to heteronormativity. Simba's discovery of his sexuality is simultaneous with remembering who he really is: the Lion King. Simba and his pals live in a preadolescent fantasy of no parents, no school, no girls—until Nala appears. Timon understands exactly how Nala will break up their happy menage: "With all this romantic atmosphere, Disaster's in the air!" "Our trio's down to two!" he sobs, "In short, our pal is doomed!" As Simba tells the dubious Nala, "Pumbaa and Timon: You learn to love 'em." Timon equates the appearance of Nala at the Oasis with The Fall: it's the end of their stint in Paradise. Nala is a voice of moral choice (along with Rafiki), but also a sexual object, a dangerous carnivore ("OY!"), and the ultimate fatal female (Pumbaa should be Simba's prey, as Timon so correctly points out). These values are all equated with Pride Rock and the survival-of-the-fittest ethos (of which mating is equal to eating). Scar not really an anomaly there, but the logical result of it: power to the strongest is the Law of the Jungle (the original name of *The Lion King* was *King of the Jungle*). Simba must fight: even as he says, "I'm not like you, Scar," he becomes like Scar, and like Mufasa and all the Lion Kings before him, ruling by strength. However, Simba's foster fathers have also taught him ways that Mufasa never dreamed of: how to use his wits, how to make a joke, and how to sell a show tune.

In the final scene, Pumbaa and Timon "rest their rumps" on top of Pride Rock next to Simba and Nala; Timon, characteristically, shakes his fists over his head in a gesture of victory. But can Pumbaa and Timon be integrated into the Pride Rock ideology when they stand so contrary to it, having always placed themselves outside the Circle of Life, refusing its kill or be killed ideology and rigid hierarchy?[31] Both "Hakuna Matata" and the deleted song "Warthog Rhapsody" (written by Elton John and Tim Rice and included on the *Rhythm of the Pride Lands* CD) celebrate their freedom from the dictates of society, the work ethic, and the regulation of the body, while glorifying living for the moment and reveling in natural functions, the latter song offering the laid-back Pumbaa as the role model for this blissful lifestyle, but only if you stay upwind of him! Characteristically, one of Timon's first acts in the Pride Lands is to dress in drag. Timon's drag turns in the films and television series are always in the name of helping someone, but the carnivalesque pleasure he takes in dressing up is obvious, as the virgin sacrifice scene the "Boara Boara" episode demonstrates. This is not an act which the humorless Mufasa (who lost his song, "To Be King" for just that reason) would have approved, but which the Oasis-raised Simba not only tolerates, but encourages.

Around the World with Timon and Pumbaa

The Lion King swiftly became the most successful animated film in up to that time. In its first weekend in general release, June 1994, it took in an estimated $42 million (twice that of Disney's previous hit, *Aladdin*), making for the third largest opening weekend up to that time, after *Jurassic Park* and *Batman Returns*. Unlike earlier Disney features, which had to wait years for re-release, film was given a second wind in the same year as its initial run: withdrawn in September 1994 and released again at Thanksgiving, it took advantage of both the summer and Christmas movie-going seasons, generating over $740 million at the box office worldwide. In its first month on sale, March 1995, the video cassette sold 20 million units, becoming the new number one video seller and earning over $1 billion in retail merchandising sales in toy stores, retail outlets like Walmart, and Disney Stores. The characters of Timon and Pumbaa soon became ubiquitous, available as stuffed animals, cards, collectible figurines, limited edition prints, games, nightshirts, bath toys, and Halloween costumes, to name a few. Many of these products featured the most subversive moment in the film, the "Luau" scene; you have to wonder at thousands of children playing with a stuffed meerkat in drag—not something Uncle Walt would have envisioned!

As the most recognizable, and therefore saleable, characters in the film, they were the logical choice to be spun off into their own television cartoon series, *The Lion King's Timon and Pumbaa* (a.k.a. *Around the World with Pumbaa and Timon*), as well as featuring in the 1998 Tony Award-winning Broadway version and a straight-to-DVD sequel, *The Lion King II: Simba's Pride*, and starring in their own straight-to-DVD feature, the extremely meta *The Lion King 1½*. The television show, first on CBS, then on the Toon Disney cable outlet, made no attempt to tone down Pumbaa and Timon's colorful personalities. If anything, both characters appear in drag numerous times and Timon especially is more flamboyant than ever. The question of how Timon and Pumbaa are ultimately integrated into the Pride Lands is avoided by setting many of their adventures before *The Lion King*. In "Doubt of Africa" they befriend a tigress and anticipate the reasoning they will use in adopting Simba: "What if she's on OUR side?" In another episode, "Never Everglades," they raise a baby alligator, Pumbaa, Jr., who hatched underneath the warthog's ample rump. Pumbaa is happy to be a mother, but "Uncle Timon" mourns for their carefree "Hakuna Matata" days when they didn't have such a responsibility. Other episodes focus on the pair far away from Africa: on a cruise ship, in the Old West, the South Seas, Russia, Paris, and, of course, on Broadway, leading Nathan Lane to refer to the show as "Timon and Pumbaa Go to Las Vegas."[32]

More than fifteen years after its initial release, Timon and Pumbaa continue to be the "faces" of *The Lion King.* Whether in film or DVD, on Broadway or television, the inimitable warthog and meerkat long-time companions are still singular representatives of the philosophy of "Hakuna Matata"—and subversive forces in the monolithic Disney universe. Every Christmas I look forward to hanging my Disney-sanctioned ornaments of Timon in a grass skirt and Pumbaa with an apple in his wide mouth among the traditional Santas, elves, and angels. It's a small rebellion, perhaps, but one I'm certainly not alone in performing, like the boys themselves belting out another show tune on the Serengeti, with great satisfaction.

Notes

1. When television writer Jeffrey Stepakoff began working in the Disney Feature Animation department in 1994, he was given some ideas to develop that summed up the Disney storytelling philosophy. One note read "King Lear/Joseph with Bears." Out of such a note, *The Lion King* was born.

2. From the insert booklet for *The Lion King 1½* DVD release, which reiterates the original film as a retelling of *Hamlet*, while also suggesting that this sequel owes more to Tom Stoppard than William Shakespeare.

3. Heteronormativity, the idea that culture always privileges heterosexuality and therefore always marginalizes homosexuality and queerness, is well accepted in the gay community, but what constitutes "normal" is still a contentious issue. Some queer theorists hold that any attempt to "normalize" gay people, with gay marriage, desire for acceptance by the straight community, etc., further labels homosexuality as "abnormal." See Michael Warner's *The Trouble with Normal* for a deeper discussion.

4. Quoted in Mark Weber, "Subverting the Disney Legacy," *Journal of Historical Review* (September–October 1998).

5. Quoted in James R. Peterson, "The Ridiculous Right," *The Playboy Forum*, December 1995.

6. By "subversive" I mean anything that undermines the status quo. But when dealing with Disney specifically, I mean anything that is presented as "naturally" innocent and meant for children, such as cartoon characters, animals, and fairy tales, but is undermined by overtones of sexuality or queerness. Because Disney's reputation is almost ridiculously white bread, such "subversive" elements bring a thrill of the forbidden to what can otherwise be a very flat and conventional text. Timon and Pumbaa certainly bring that unexpected frisson, which is why I believe they are so popular.

7. "Real Roar of *The Lion King*," *Disney Adventures*, July 1994. Online interviews.

8. Eric Smoodin, *Animating Culture* (New York: Routledge, 1993), 3.

9. That animators in the past often peppered their cartoons with subversive and even X-rated imagery gives credence to the fears of the Family Values crowd, but rather than being intentionally

provocative, such inside jokes were never intended to be seen by an audience. Only with the advent of video and the pause button did they come into general notice.

10. The "Diary" is included in the *Exclusive Mini-Storybook* insert in the DVD release of *The Lion King 1½*.

11. As critic Richard Dyer calls the marker of true film stardom.

12. Mark Simpson, *Male Impersonation: Men Performing Masculinity* (New York: Routledge, 1994), 274.

13. "Camp" is another one of those terms, like "normal," that seem to have a different meaning depending on the context or even the era (see Susan Sontag, Esther Newton, and Andrew Ross for examples), but I see it in the context of Timon and Pumbaa as a style of performance that is pointedly ironic, over-the-top, sexually suggestive, broadly comic, and leans heavily on cross-dressing and reference to performers from the past who also fit this criteria. For instance, Timon's drag turn harkens back to kitschy Fifties Hawaiian imagery, while Bugs Bunny prefers Forties musicals, Carmen Miranda, and Grand Opera divas.

14. Terrence Rafferty, "No Pussycat," *New Yorker*, June 20, 1994, 87.

15. Jess Cagle, "No Mere Kat," *Entertainment Weekly*, July 8, 1994, 24.

16. DeNicolo, "A Pair of Runyon Guys Roam the Serengeti," *New York Times*, June 12, 1994, 15.

17. Compare Lane's tour de force as Timon or Carroll's delightfully evil Ursula to Mel Gibson's wooden Captain John Smith: he's the more famous star, but as a voice and animated persona his character has little screen impact.

18. DeNicolo, 15.

19. Ari Posner, "The Mane Event," *Premiere*, July 1994.

20. DeNicolo, 18.

21. *Ibid.*

22. DeNicolo, 15.

23. *Ibid.*

24. Weber.

25. *Ibid.*

26. Quoted in Frank Rich, "Dole's True Lies," *New York Times*, June 4, 1995.

27. Scar, the voice of Jeremy Irons in his best George Sanders drawl, seems more in line with the Brit-as-villain trend in recent American films, rather than homosexual-as-villain. There is also more than a trace of Irons' portrayal of Claus von Bulow in *Reversal of Fortune*, especially when he says to Simba, "You have no idea," von Bulow's famous catch-phrase. Of course, many Americans seem to agree with Archie Bunker and read a British accent, especially upper class "RP" speech, as innately "faggy." But Scar's Britishness and affectedness is matched and contrasted with that of Zazu the Hornbill (Rowan Atkinson), a prissy character done more in the manner of Clifton Webb or Eric Blore—haughty but ultimately sympathetic.

28. Aly Sujo, "Sex in Disney Toons? 'Ridiculous' Says Company," *Reuters New Service*, September 1, 1995.

29. Wildmon's American Family Association didn't officially call off the boycott until Eisner stepped down as Disney Chairman/CEO in 2005. It will be interesting to see if these groups reignite their campaign with the October 2009 appointment of a gay head of Disney Studios, Rich Ross (the first openly gay head of any Hollywood studio), as well as a gay president of Disneyland Resorts, George Kalogridis, the former chief of Disney's Paris theme park. Since the toleration of the popular, but unsanctioned, "Gay Days" at all the Disney parks has been a flashpoint with conservative Christian groups in the past, Kalogridis' new job may well bring increased attention to the event. Ironically, Ross, former head of the Disney Channel, had been praised by a number of conservative groups for his family oriented programming—but that was before his sexuality was widely known by the general public.

30. A scene in which Scar propositions Nala, causing her to flee the Pride Lands, was rejected before the animation process began.

31. *The Lion King 1½* offers an alternate ending to the narrative: Timon and Pumbaa lead Ma, Uncle Max, and the rest of the meerkats back to the Oasis to live, apparently on permanent vacation.

32. Anne E. Kornblut, "Q and A: *Lion King* and Broadway Star Nathan Lane," *New York Daily News*, March 12, 1995, Sunday Extra section, 8.

Bibliography

Ansen, David. "Gay Films Are a Drag: For Hollywood, Laughs Are the Safest Sex." *Newsweek*, March 18, 1996, 71.

Ascher-Walsh, Rebecca. "Does Hollywood Have a Jewish Problem?" *Entertainment Weekly*, 291, August 18, 1995.

Auletta, Ken. "Awesome: Michael Eisner's Comeback." *New Yorker*, August 14, 1995, 24, 26–32.

Bakhtin, Mikhail. *Rabeleis and His World*, trans. Helene Iswolsky. Bloomington: Indiana University Press, 1984.

Bell, Elizabeth, Lynda Haas, Laura Sells, eds. *From Mouse to Mermaid: The Politics of Film, Gender, and Culture*. Bloomington: Indiana University Press, 1995.

Biskind, Peter. "Win, Lose—But Draw." *Premiere* 8:11, July 1995, 80–6, 108.

Brode, Doug. *Multiculturalism and the Mouse: Race and Sex in Disney Entertainment*. Austin: University of Texas Press. 2006.

Cagle, Jess. "No Mere Kat: As the Voice of Simba's Pal Timon, Nathan Lane Makes Africa the Borscht Veldt." *Entertainment Weekly*, 230, July 8, 1994.

_____. "Special Report: The Gay 90s." *Entertainment Weekly* 291, September 8, 1995.

Chethik, Neil. "The Men's Column: *Lion King* Reinforces Stereotypes." *Cleveland Plain Dealer*, July 10, 1994.

_____. "The Men's Column: *Lion King* Type Bares His Fangs." *Cleveland Plain Dealer*, July 24, 1994.

Connors, Joanna. "Kid-appeal Rules Making of *Lion King*." *Cleveland Plain Dealer*, June 24, 1994.

_____. "Out of the Closet? Hollywood Opens Its Door to Gay Themes." *Cleveland Plain Dealer*, September 17 1995, Sunday Arts section.

_____. "*Pocahontas* Rewrites HERstory." *Cleveland Plain Dealer*, June 23, 1995.

Corliss, Richard. "The Mouse Roars." *Time*, June 20, 1994.

Cotter, Bill. "Chapter 36: *The Lion King's Timon & Pumbaa* Television Episode Guide," *The Wonderful World of Disney Television*. New York: Hyperion Books, 1997.

Creekmur, Corey K., and Alexander Doty, eds. *Out in Culture: Gay, Lesbian, and Queer Essays on Popular Culture*. Durham: Duke University Press, 1995.

Daly, Steve. "Mane Attraction." *Entertainment Weekly* 230, July 8, 1994).

DeCordova, Richard. "The Mickey in Macy's Window: Childhood, Consumerism, and Disney Animation," *Disney Discourse*, ed. Smoodin: 203–13.

Delfiner, Rita. "O'Connor Blasts *Priest* & Disney." *New York Post*, April 7, 1995.

Denby, David. "Beastly Boys: Reviews of *Wolf* and *The Lion King*." *New York Magazine*, June 22, 1994, 77–79.

DeNicolo, David. "A Pair of Runyon Guys Roam the Serengeti." *New York Times*, June 12, 1994, Sunday Arts section, 15, 18.

"Disney's Ross First Openly Gay Studio Chief." *Disney News: Contact Music*, October 7, 2009. http://www.contactmusic.com/news.nsf/story/disneys-ross-first-openly-gay-studio chief_1118387

Doty, Alexander. *Making Things Perfectly Queer: Interpreting Mass Culture*. Minneapolis, MN: University of Minnesota Press, 1993.

Dutka, Elaine. "*The Lion King* Has Largest Disney Movie Opening Ever." *Los Angeles Times*, June 29, 1994.

Dyer, Richard. Heavenly Bodies: Film Stars and Society. New York: St. Martin's Press, 1986.

_____. *Stars*. London: British Film Institute, 1979.

Eisner, Jane R. "*Lion King* Sends Kids a Bad Message About Dependency." *Cleveland Plain Dealer,* July 7, 1994.

Eliot, Marc. *Walt Disney: Hollywood's Dark Prince.* New York: Harper Collins, 1994.

Erb, Cynthia. "Another World or the World of an Other? The Space of Romance in Recent Versions of *Beauty and the Beast.*" *Cinema Journal* 34: 4, Summer 1995.

Foster, David. "Critics Seek to Dethrone *Lion King.*" *Lake County Ohio News-Herald,* July 26, 1994.

French, Janet Beighle. "Disney Cashes in Again: *Lion King* Motif Saturates Market." *Cleveland Plain Dealer,* June 24, 1994.

_____. "*Lion King, Flintstones* Toys Tested." *Cleveland Plain Dealer,* June 24, 1994.

Goldstein, Patrick. "The Big Picture: Disney's Rich Ross: Hollywood's First Openly Gay Studio Chairman." *Los Angeles Times,* October 6, 2009.

Griffin, Sean. *Tinker Belles and Evil Queens: The Walt Disney Company from the Inside Out.* New York: New York University Press, 2000.

Hartinger, Brent. "Ask the Flying Monkey!" *AfterElton.com,* October 19, 2009, http://www.afterelton.com/askmonkey/10–19–2009 (accessed October 20, 2009).

Hofmeister, Sallie. "Disney to Put *Lion King* Into Early Hibernation." *New York Times,* August 13, 1994.

Horn, John. "Box Office Stuffing Makes New Movies' Profits Larger Than Life." *Cleveland PlainDealer,* July 21 1994, Associated Press story.

_____. "Can You See the Cash Tonight?" *Lake County Ohio News-Herald,* July 17, 1994, Associated Press story.

Keets, Heather. "Warthogging the Spotlight: Ernie Sabella, the Voice of Pumbaa." *Entertainment Weekly,* August 12, 1994.

Klass, Perri. "A *Bambi* for the '90s, Via Shakespeare." *New York Times,* June 19, 1994, Sunday Arts section.

Kornblut, Anne E. "Q and A: *Lion King* & Broadway Star Nathan Lane." *New York Daily News,* March 12, 1995, Sunday Extra section.

Lileks, James. "The Cartoon Police Are After Disney Again." *Lake County News-Herald,* June 23, 1995, Distributed by Universal Press.

The Lion King: Original Motion Picture Soundtrack. Walt Disney Records, 1994.

"*Lion King* Becomes Disney's All-time Money King, Too." *Cleveland Plain Dealer,* August 3, 1994, Bloomberg News Service.

The Lion King's Timon & Pumbaa (a.k.a. *Around the World With Timon & Pumbaa*). Television Series 1995–1998. CBS and Toon Disney. Not available on DVD.

Lipson, Eden Ross. "A Better Reason to Fear *The Lion King*: The Latest Blockbuster Movie Tells Audiences to Face Up to Life. Egad!" *New York Times,* July 10, 1994.

Maltin, Leonard . "Funny Bunny: Bugs at Fifty." *Bugs Bunny Magazine Special Issue,* 1990, 18–23.

_____. *Of Mice and Magic: A History of American Animated Cartoons.* New York: Plume, 1980.

Margheret, Frank, and Allan Parrish. "Disney Flick Wake-up Call for 'Lion Sleeps Tonight.'" *Lake County Ohio News-Herald,* August 12, 1994, TGIF section.

Martin, Hugo. "Company Town: George Kalogridis Named President of Disneyland Resort." *Los Angeles Times,* October 13, 2009.

Maslin, Janet. "The Hero Within the Child Within." *New York Times,* June 15, 1994.

Nichols, Peter M. "Some See 'Sex' in the Clouds of *The Lion King,*" *New York Times,* September 2, 1995.

Persons, Dan. "Disney TV Gets Edgy with Shnookums & Meat." *Visions: The Magazine of TV, Home Video & New Media* 1, no. 1, Autumn 1995.

_____. "Disney's *The Lion King* Goes Interactive." *Visions: The Magazine of TV, Home Video & New Media* 1, no. 1, Autumn 1995.

Petersen, James R. "The Ridiculous Right (Say It Ain't So, Barney)." *The Playboy Forum,* December 1995. Archived in "The Cartoon Mentality of the Religious Right: Positive Atheism." http://www.positiveatheism.org/wrt/antijerry.htm (accessed March 26, 2009.

Posner, Ari. "The Mane Event." *Premiere* 7:11, July 1994.

"Problems with Movies: The Truth About the Disney Company." Mission Islam. http://www.missionislam.com/family/disney.htm (accessed March 26, 2009).

"The Project on Disney," *Inside the Mouse: Work and Play at Disney World.* Durham: Duke University Press, 1995.

Rafferty, Terrence. "No Pussycat: *Lion King* Review." *New Yorker,* June 20, 1994, 86–7.

"Real Roar of *The Lion King,*" *Disney Adventures,* July 8, 1994, America Online (accessed September 4, 1995).

Rhythm of the Pride Lands: Music Inspired by The Lion King. Walk Disney Records, 1995.

Rich, Frank. "Dole's True Lies. *New York Times,* June 4, 1995, Editorial page.

Rubenstein, Caren. "Tips on Surviving a Safari to the Animated Jungle." *New York Times,* July 14, 1994.

"Rumors Fly Like *Aladdin*: Allegations of Illicit Messages in Three Children's Videos." *Wall Street Journal*, October 25, 1995.

Sandstrom, Karen. "*Lion King* Soundtrack Set to Roar." *Cleveland Plain Dealer,* June 19, 1994.

Scapperotti, Dan. "40 Years of Disney Television." *Visions: The Magazine of TV, Home Video & New Media* 1, no. 1 (Autumn 1995).

Schickel, Richard. *The Disney Version: The Life, Times, Art, and Commerce of Walt Disney.* New York: Simon & Schuster, 1968.

Seidman, Steve. *Comedian Comedy: A Tradition in Hollywood Film.* Ann Arbor: UMI Research, 1981.

Sheehan, Henry. "*The Lion King* Positioned for Holiday Re-release." *Orange County CA Register,* August 16, 1994.

Simpson, Mark. *Male Impersonation: Men Performing Masculinity.* New York: Routledge, 1994.

Smoodin, Eric. *Animating Culture: Hollywood Cartoons from the Sound Era.* New Brunswick, NJ: Rutgers University Press, 1993.

_____, ed. *Disney Discourse: Producing the Magic Kingdom.* New York: Routledge, 1994.

Snow, Tony. "Culture Warriors Smite *Lion King.*" *Cleveland Plain Dealer,* August 2, 1994.

Stallybass, Peter. *The Politics and Poetics of Transgression.* Ithaca, NY: Cornell University Press, 1986.

Steinback, Robert L. "Boycott of Disney Won't Promote Family Values." *Cleveland Plain Dealer,* November 30, 1995, Knight-Ridder Service.

Stepakoff, Jeffrey. *Billion-Dollar Kiss: The Kiss That Saved Dawson's Creek and Other Adventures in TV Writing.* New York: Gotham Books, 2008.

Strode, Tom. "Disney Sponsored Homosexual Benefit Before Eisner Denied 'Any Agenda.'" *Baptist Press News,* December 9, 1997. http://www.bpnews.net/bpnews.asp?id=4565 (accessed March 26, 2009).

Sujo, Aly. "Sex in Disney Toons? 'Ridiculous' Says Company." *Reuters News Service,* September 1, 1995.

Svetkey, Benjamin. "Disney Catches Hell: Gay Day and 'Subliminal' Messages at

Mickey & Co. Bring on the Religious Right's Wrath." *Entertainment Weekly* 305, December 15, 1995, 42–43.

Sweeney, Gael. "The King of White Trash Culture: Elvis Presley and the Aesthetics of Excess," *White Trash: Race and Class in America*, Annalee Newitz and Matt Wray, eds. New York: Routledge, 1996.

Terzian, Philip. "Subliminal Images in Disney Films?" *Providence RI Journal Bulletin,* November 27, 1995.

Twitchell, James B. *Carnival Culture: The Trashing of Taste in America.* New York: Columbia University Press, 1992.

Warner, Michael. *The Trouble with Normal: Sex, Politics, and the Ethics of Queer Life.* Cambridge, MA: Harvard University Press, 1999.

Weber, Mark. "'Culture War' Profile: Subverting the Disney Legacy: How Michael Eisner Has Transformed the 'Magic Kingdom.'" *Journal of Historical Review* 17, no. 5 (September-October 1998): 10–13.

Zoglin, Richard. "Nathan Lane—Uncaged." *Time,* March 25, 1996, 70.

Mean Ladies: Transgendered Villains in Disney Films

Amanda Putnam

"I want to watch one without a mean lady."

That's what my three-year-old daughter said to me last spring, hoping I'd be able to find a Disney film for her to watch that didn't have a scary female character in it. Skeptically, already considering the overwhelming common knowledge of evil stepmothers in fairy tales, I investigated the ever-growing children's DVD pile in our home, setting aside film after film after film with yet another nasty antagonist in it. But as I considered each Disney villain, especially in regard to his or her gendered characteristics, what I discovered truly gave me pause.

As we already know, most of the heroes and heroines of the beloved Disney film franchise are hyper-heterosexual—they fall in love, get married, and, as we understand it, live happily every after, often singing, dancing, and acting googley-eyed right off into the sunset.[1] Indeed, the primary characters reveal heterosexual goals by offering stereotypical and exaggerated portrayals of a traditionally gendered appearance (which then attracts an equally stereotypical character of the other sex). Later, these primary characters reinforce that identification through conventional behavior within their romantic relationships, as well as through their stated marital goals. These static identifications carefully craft a unified portrayal of happy heterosexism, which is clearly marked as the path to contentment and goodness.

But what I didn't realize until I fruitlessly examined that pile of DVDs was that the villains of Disney films also offer a distinct pattern via appearance and behavior—one that is quite disparate from the hyper-heterosexual heroes and heroines, and one that is disturbingly problematic. In contrast to the heterosexist leads, many of the villains display transgendered attributes—depicted as women with either strong masculine qualities or as strangely de-feminized, while the male bad guys are portrayed as effeminate, often complete with stereotypical limp-wristed affectation. These repeated motifs become even more disconcerting when they are coupled with the evil machinations for which, well, villains are known. In other words, animated characters that offered transgendered characteristics that were positive or even simply neutral might be worth noticing to determine how or why that character related to others, especially the heterosexist leads; however, when gender-bending traits are assigned strictly to villains, then tension arises in terms of determining what, exactly, Disney is preaching so heartily and so frequently to its preschool choir.

The boundary-crossing of gender roles occurs in many Disney films, most notably in the Princess series, but also in animal-themed films as well. Specifically, several villainous female characters are masculinized in distinct ways, for example the stepmother and stepsisters in the *Cinderella* series and Ursula in *The Little Mermaid*.[2] These females are certainly the "mean ladies" my daughter wanted to avoid. However, the gender-bending traits appear within male villains as well, as they are given overt (and even garish) feminine traits— some bordering on an implicit homosexual characterization. Specifically *The Lion King*'s Scar, *Aladdin*'s Jafar, and *Pocahontas*'s Ratcliffe also become transgendered villains, and eventually, my daughter grouped these characters as "mean ladies" too.

But Disney creating transgendered characters, of course, is not the issue, as doing so simply reflects society at large in a broader, more inclusive manner. As the organization Parents, Families, and Friends of Lesbians and Gays (PFLAG) indicates, "transgendered people are individuals of any age or sex who manifest characteristics, behaviors or self-expression, which in their own or someone else's perception, is typical of or commonly associated with persons of another gender." Thus, transgendered characteristics are those in which the sex of a person is not entirely congruent with their gender identity or actions. In other words, those who cross boundaries of traditional and/or stereotypical gender identities may appear to be subtly, or even flamboyantly, transgendered.

However, when transgendered qualities are marked as only apparent in evil characters, then a stigmatized standard of normative behavior is being created and promoted. Meredith Li-Vollmer and Mark E. LaPointe indicate in their article "Gender Transgression and Villainy in Animated Film," that "Gender is established and sustained by socially required identificatory displays; through interaction, gender is continually exhibited or portrayed, and thus comes to be seen as 'natural.'"[3] Likewise, when gender is exhibited in ways that have been identified socially as "unnatural," social stigmas or prejudicial evaluations may be incited. Li-Vollmer and LaPoint continue, stating, "By performing gender outside of normative expectations, individuals may therefore draw into question much more than their gender: In a culture with firmly naturalized constructions of gender, gender transgression may also cast doubt on a person's competence, social acceptability, and morality."[4] In many of Disney's films, the villains portrayed are not only the bad guys in terms of their nefarious choices and desires, but also due to their so-called deviant behaviors via their gender performance. By creating only wicked characters as transgendered, Disney constructs an implicit evaluation of transgenderism, unequivocally associating it with cruelty, selfishness, brutality, and greed.

Obviously, their complex gender identities are not what make these Disney villains wicked though. All of the villains act despicably: some bully and torment, while others are power-hungry or obsessive. As noted in *The Disney Villain*, "their behavior is aberrant, they are seemingly more colorful than the average person and they cause intense things to happen."[5] In fact, "the character with evil intent supplies the strongest of contests throughout the performance."[6] Their villainy creates the situation from which the hero and heroine must escape—and from whom the heroes are most clearly defined. In other words, "we need evil to locate our good."[7] The villains create the storyline— they have the plan, the methods, and the personality to problematize the situation—and typically that storyline also "disrupt[s] and frustrate[s] heterosexuality's dominance" by antagonizing the happily-ever-after of the heroes and heroines.[8] The princesses and their princes simply react to those plans, allowing their "goodness" to be shown via their reactions to the bad guys. And yet, these evil actions or desires have very little to do with their gender-bending portrayals—in fact they are superfluous from them. However, it is the noxious combination of transgendered characteristics with these characters' evil plots and exploits that makes this spicy blend so unpalatable once clearly recognized—and yet, that combination goes unrealized by most viewers, whether child or adult—accepted without examination, reinforcing the heterosexism of current contemporary culture.

To best understand the villains' complicated gender identities, it's first important to examine the high profiles of the main characters to which they are contrasted. The dominant heterosexuality of the heroes and heroines is significant because it helps display the stark dissimilarity of the villains' transgendered depiction. For many of the leading male and female characters, their heterosexuality is illustrated first through their appearance. Strong, commanding princes and other handsome male leads are coupled with young beautiful women, many with long hair and most in flowing attire, which emphasizes their hour-glass figures.

Disney princesses are most frequently shown wearing one main outfit, which was created to reinforce their heterosexuality. All of their clothes are form-fitting, with a few of them also revealing cleavage.[9] Sleeping Beauty, Belle, and Tiana all bare the tops of their breasts via ballroom gowns with low necklines. Similarly, Cinderella wears low, scoop-necked dresses that emphasize a small waist and rounded bust. In *Pocahontas*, the lead character wears a one-shouldered mini-dress, which exposes both ample cleavage and long legs. Jasmine wears an off-the-shoulder bra with flowing, transparent harem pants, which linger several inches below her navel, and Ariel wears only shells on her breasts, while the top of her mermaid tail similarly dips intriguingly low beneath her belly button. In making each heroine's outfit form-fitting, especially around her breasts, waist, and hips, Disney accentuates the ideal heterosexual female figure to viewers: curvy breasts and hips, an unrealistically small waist—and tight apparel to show it all off.

In fact, critiquing Pocahontas's appearance in more depth suggests a concerted effort to make her hyper-heterosexual. While Nakoma, Pocahontas's best friend, wears a revealing mini-dress too, the difference in their appearance is considerable. Both women have tiny waists; however, Pocahontas has extremely large breasts in comparison to Nakoma's more modest bosom, emphasizing Pocahontas as the female lead. Discussing the dubious historical accuracy of transforming Pocahontas into a clearly much older (and sexier) woman than the actual Powhatan princess of American lore, Mark I. Pinsky indicates that "the transformation of a preteen ... to a nubile babe in off-the-shoulder buckskin, with pouty, collagen lips"[10] should not be overlooked. In fact, supervising animator Glen Keane explained "Jeffrey Katzenberg (then the chairman of Walt Disney Studios) said he wanted her to be the most idealized and finest woman ever made."[11] Clearly, like others in the Disney Princess series, Pocahontas's appearance heavily markets the heterosexual feminine vision.

A proliferation of stereotypically female behaviors, such as standard finishing school traits, pre-occupations with domestic work, as well as an affinity for animals also mark many of the princess characters as ultra-feminine, at least as Disney defines it. Even with no apparent dancing lessons, Sleeping Beauty, Cinderella, Belle, and Tiana are light on their feet as they dance with their respective Princes. Of course, all of the princesses sing well since each Disney film is a musical, but Ariel also has the lead singing role in the production which starts the film. Both Cinderella and Tiana show amazing grace and poise, with Cinderella being able to balance three tea trays (one on her head!) while going upstairs to serve her stepfamily, and Tiana similarly balancing a variety of plates and trays while waitressing. Snow White, Cinderella, and Sleeping Beauty clean houses while smiling, seemingly enjoying the work. Likewise Tiana demonstrates a strong work ethic to clean and renovate an abandoned building so as to become a chef for her new restaurant. The princesses also have numerous animal friendships, which they nurture maternally. Snow White, Cinderella, and Sleeping Beauty befriend forest animals and house mice, while Ariel befriends fish, crabs, and a crane. Likewise, Jasmine's "only friend" before she leaves the palace is her huge pet tiger. Tiana actually becomes a frog, and is then happily assisted by numerous swamp bugs and creatures. While Belle is primarily friendly with the people of the castle who were transformed into furniture and household goods, these characters act in similar ways to the animal friends of other princesses. These traditional female behaviors, used as standardized Disney tropes of femininity, signal to viewers that the princesses are all heterosexual, maintaining goals of marriage, domestic life, and family.

Disney heroes typically play a smaller part than their princess; however they too embody heterosexual characteristics in their appearance and behavior, thus providing male balance to the film. Taller than each respective princess, broad-shouldered, square-jawed, and muscular, their attributes become standardized heterosexual male physical characteristics. They also participate in "manly" activities, such as horseback riding, hunting, sailing, sword-fighting, and even hand-to-hand combat, when necessary. Additionally, they share two crucial characteristics: they fall in love with the heroine immediately,[12] and they rescue her when needed.[13] For example, Cinderella and her Prince sing, "So This Is Love" as they dance for the first time, while Ariel falls in love with Prince Eric upon seeing him from afar on his boat. Thus, the appearance and behavior of the male-female leads emphasize their heterosexuality, and that flirtation is rewarded: most of the princesses marry their prince at the end of the film,[14] underscoring the goals of heterosexual attraction, love, marriage, and eventually, family.

Even Disney's animal royalty depict hyper-heterosexuality in similar ways as their human counterparts. In *The Lion King*, King Mufasa and his mate, Sarabi, are happily married, with their newborn cub Simba introduced at the beginning of the film. The lion couple adheres to traditional gender roles in raising their son: Mufasa shares his wisdom with Simba about their ancestors and Simba's place as the future king, while Sarabi ensures Simba is clean, fed, and obedient. Soon, viewers find out Simba and his childhood friend, Nala, are betrothed, asserting another standard heterosexual goal of marriage even though they are only young cubs. When the two lions meet again as young adults, they immediately fall in love, reassuring viewers that they will willingly marry each other to fulfill the heterosexual agenda. Clearly, Disney's royalty, whether human or animal, portray a safely traditional heterosexual view of the world, which offers a clear contrast to the complexity of the transgendered villains who are introduced slightly later in each film.

Dramatic and daring, the villains often outperform their heterosexual rivals, setting up a transparent comparison between "normative" and "deviant" gendered behaviors, but also connecting the villains' transgenderism with sarcasm, selfishness, cruelty, greed, and brutality. Many of the female Disney villains are subtly masculine—their faces, body shape, and behavior lend "mannish" traits to their characters.[15] In portraying them this way, the villains contrast sharply with the ultra-feminine princesses. This allows my daughter, one of Disney's intended audience, to recognize more easily who is "good" in these films—and who is not. But it also gives a bewildering message regarding difference, suggesting that real transgendered people are extremely dangerous and to be avoided at all costs.

Lady Tremaine, the stepmother in the *Cinderella* series, and her two daughters, Drizella and Anastasia, are *supposed* to be mean—viewers already know this from the Grimms' fairy tale on which Disney's film is based. Likewise, various versions of the tale exclaim their ugliness.[16] But the way Disney portrays their villainy via transgendered characteristics is what is fascinating—and disturbing.

In contrast to the lithe feminine figure of Cinderella, both stepsisters are decidedly masculine. Neither stepsister has breasts as both girls are flat-chested, appearing, in fact, square-bodied, with no difference in width between their chest and their waist. The complete absence of their breasts makes them appear both mannish and non-reproductive, contrasting strongly with Cinderella and other princess figures, with their heterosexual reproductive agendas. Likewise, instead of the gently scooped or deep necklines of the princesses, Drizella and Anastasia head off to the ball wearing squared-off necklines, which accentuates their flat chests. Likewise, their dresses both have extremely large bustles, emphasizing their lack of a female figure and awkwardness.[17]

Additionally, the stepsisters' faces are boyish and considered unfeminine by most others. With scowling brows, large round eyes (and even rounder noses), plus a jowly lower jaw and neck, their faces are reminiscent of Disney's Pinocchio or the Lost Boys of *Peter Pan*.[18] As he watches the stepsisters awkwardly engaging his son, the King negatively shakes his head and hands vigorously, saying, "I give up. Even I could not expect the boy to...," implying that both stepsisters are just too ugly to even contemplate his son marrying them. Even before they are allowed to try the glass slipper on, the Duke winces at the sight of them.[19] Bell, Haas and Sells argue that that the two stepsisters cross the gender line completely, appearing male: "with their flat chests, huge bustles, and awkward curtsies, [the stepsisters] could as well be read as comic drag acts in this balletic fantasy."[20] Clearly, their ugliness is really maleness costumed as female.

Both stepsisters, and Anastasia in particular, are further associated with masculinity via their large feet, which contributes to their extreme clumsiness, ensuring a safe distance from princess poise. Throughout the original film, the stepsisters' feet are shown to be at least three times as large as Cinderella's, sometimes taking up the entire screen.[21] Whether lying in bed, curtsying to the prince, or being fitted for the slipper, the stepsisters' feet are massive and fleshy. In contrast, the Grand Duke shows just how tiny the glass slipper is that fits Cinderella—it fits inside his palm with the toe of the shoe as small as his fingers. In the first *Cinderella* film, Anastasia tries on Cinderella's tiny glass slipper, but manages only to get her big toe inside. In the third *Cinderella* film, her fleshy foot actually fits (much to the visible dismay of the Grand Duke), via Lady Tremaine's evil use of the Fairy Godmother's wand. Astonished and thrilled, Anastasia immediately undermines this feminine quality by displaying ungainliness: Anastasia crashes around the room, twirling the cat while screeching, "It fits!" Lady Tremaine even catches her daughter's legs mid-cartwheel, allowing Anastasia's dress to fall over her head, revealing her bloomers, before Anastasia collapses with her rump in the air. In effect, this scene ensures that preschool viewers understand Anastasia as the bumbling, awkward impostor that she is: although the shoe fits, she is *not* a true princess.

Further, the stepsisters exhibit a range of behaviors that mark them as masculine. When waiting to be introduced to the Prince, the girls are gawky in their presentation, Drizella also making the mistake of bowing, instead of curtsying to the Prince. The mistake makes her appear even more mannish, as she chooses a traditionally male form of presentation, bolstering the concept that she is not *really* a girl at all. Likewise, both stepsisters are clumsy and awkward, tripping over themselves and others constantly—Anastasia even humiliates herself by stepping on the Prince's feet a record seven times when they dance in *Cinderella III*.[22] The sisters also physically fight with each other, emphasizing their boyishness by participating in still more traditionally male behavior. Cinderella's ever-present gracefulness contrasts their lack of femininity at every awkward sashay and piercing melody (in fact, Cinderella even giggles demurely about their lack of singing talent).

Finally, both stepsisters participate in a physical assault that solidifies a hidden masculinity. Cinderella is dressed for the ball in a pink gown that her animal friends helped transform, while she finished the many chores expected of her by her stepfamily. Realizing that the beautiful Cinderella will easily outshine her daughters, the music heightens ominously as Lady Tremaine helps her daughters notice that Cinderella's dress incorporated an abandoned sash and necklace, recently discarded from their closets. In what is arguably a pseudo-rape scene,[23] Drizella first grabs and breaks Cinderella's necklace, while Anastasia pulls at Cinderella's dress. The stepsisters tear at the other girl's clothing, ripping it from her body while Cinderella attempts to shield herself, covering her neck, face, and body with her hands. Walt Disney described what he intended with the scene as "they rip the hell out of her.... As they're pulling the poor girl to pieces, the stepmother watches coldly with a little smile on her face."[24] The dress is left as a one-shouldered rag, torn and ruined, and thus Cinderella cannot attend the ball. The stepsisters' angry, cruel faces loom large in the screen during the attack as their monstrous behavior confirms their lack of femininity.

In contrast to her flat-chested boyish daughters, Disney's Lady Tremaine manages to keep a vaguely female shape, but her facial features and behaviors mark her as both unfeminine as well as unmotherly, even to her own daughters. Her face is sharp-edged, with large eyes and a pointy chin, a clear divergence from Cinderella's softened cheeks, nose, and lips. Her nose is crooked and large for her face, more reminiscent of *101 Dalmatians* male villains Horace and Jasper, rather than typical Disney female features. Her over-plucked, arched eyebrows characterize her expressions as surprised and menacing, while the coloring of her face, which transforms from gray and tan to dark green depending on her mood and actions, reveals the evilness associated with her. "There was hardly a moment when the Stepmother was not running something through her mind, constantly scheming, which made her such a menace. Her piercing, penetrating eyes gave a look of intense concentration as she watched Cinderella."[25] With these physical characteristics ala Disney, Lady Tremaine is distanced from femininity.

But it is her behavior to her daughters and stepdaughter that un-sexes her, as she dominates them thoroughly and harshly. While the tale always had her showing only cruelty to Cinderella, for no apparent reason, Disney's version takes the original and escalates it. Lady Tremaine trips the footman carrying the glass slipper in the original film—even though her own daughters' feet have already failed to fit it—so that Cinderella won't even have the opportunity to escape her tyranny. In *Cinderella III*, intent on gaining wealth and power, Lady Tremaine changes her own daughter's appearance into a copy of Cinderella via the magic wand so that Anastasia can marry the Prince. In perhaps the penultimate evil mother decision, she eventually attempts to kill Anastasia when the girl defies her mother.[26] In a film series where ultra-feminine Cinderella sings even while doing an immense amount of unpleasant, never-ending chores, this vindictive villain's behavior pushes Lady Tremaine completely outside the realm of what Disney defines as feminine or motherly.[27]

Ursula, the Sea Witch in *The Little Mermaid*, also retains some female qualities, but like Lady Tremaine, overwhelming communicates a transgendered presence. Ursula is a huge black and purple octopus, with styled white hair standing straight up, large eyes with deeply painted lids of blue and gray, and incredibly arched eyebrows. Her huge lips and nails are painted bright red, and she has a "beauty mark" mole on her right cheek. Her makeup, saggy jowls and large breasts create a vaguely female, voluptuous figure; however the exaggeration of those features, combined with her deep voice and overtly sexualized body movements suggests something much more masculinized. *The Disney Villain* remarks that "when we first see her in the film, we are appalled at her appearance, and realize that here is someone to be reckoned with."[28] Of course, the reason "we are appalled" is not just because this villain is scary (after all, the villains are supposed to be scary!). Instead audience members love (and hate) Ursula because she crosses gender boundaries and becomes a comic pseudo-female villain.

> Physically, the sea-witch is drawn as a queer predatory monster with a grotesque overwhelming body that occupies the whole screen.... Moreover, Ursula's queerness subverts gender categories thus turning this female witch into an ironic positive figure; "a multiple cross-dresser," who destabilises gender through her excess and theatricality.[29]

When Ursula suggestively tells Ariel to use "body language" to attract Prince Eric, Ursula's overweight body and tentacles, her deep voice, and the excessive, sexualized shimmies are reminiscent of a drag queen on stage, overly made up and singing deeply, appearing both female and male simultaneously.

Some critics have argued that Ursula was always supposed to be transgendered; in fact, Pinsky notes Ursula "was modeled on the modern drag queen Divine, according to the film's directing animator, Reuben Acquino."[30] Clearly with her white blond hair, overwhelming size, deepened voice, and accentuated eyebrows, the resemblance to Divine is uncanny.[31] As well, many of her mannerisms and language choices also remind viewers of Divine. Complaining of her expulsion from King Triton's kingdom, Ursula exposes fleshy, wiggling upper arms, large rounded breasts over an excessive stomach, along with her sagging jowels, then says, "And now look at me—wasted away to practically nothing—banished and exiled and practically starving." The scene ends with her long black thick tentacles curling around the screen, until only her eyes are still apparent. Obviously this obese, overindulgent octopus is nowhere near malnourished, but the dramatic phrasing and movement coupled with her enormous size presents Ursula as overly theatrical and campy. Her exaggerated characteristics begin to read more and more like a flamboyant drag queen, than that of a real exile concerned with starvation.

In these ways, female villains become more and more separated from their dainty heroines, and their carefully-crafted creepiness depends on a distinct division from traditionally feminized characteristics (and the overtly heterosexual heroines mentioned earlier). As well, it's understandable that Disney would want the villains to appear distinctly different—their audience members are as young as one or two years old, and Disney wants the youngsters to identify with the heroes and heroines, clamoring for Disney Princess products after seeing each film. They need them to understand easily who is good and who is not—and they *do*, as shown by my daughter's comments and inclinations. But when Disney creates female villains primarily as transgendered characters—and transgendered characters as the primary evil characters in their storylines, then it crosses a line of attempting to show the polarity of good and evil to its youngsters, and becomes a disjointed misinformation telling young children that difference is *not* okay—in fact, that those who are transgendered are evil and to be avoided at all cost. These gross exaggerations and profiling create a disturbing message that is repeated ad nauseam to our youngest movie-watchers, who watch these films incessantly in our homes.

Similarly fascinating (and equally problematic) is the way in which Disney's male villains are crafted to avoid heterosexual competition with the heroes. By feminizing the male villain, even bordering on overtly homosexual characterizations, *The Lion King*'s Scar, *Aladdin*'s Jafar, and *Pocahontas*'s Ratcliffe also become "mean ladies"—the stuff of which my daughter was wholly terrified. But while they may be evil, they definitely *aren't* masculine.

While lion Scar looks only vaguely feminine in his appearance,[32] his lack of physical prowess, his language choices, and the lack of a female mate mark his character as crossing into transgendered territory. Unlike the other two male lions (Mufasa and the adult Simba), Scar willingly admits he has little physical aptitude, connecting him strangely with Disney's typical portrayal of female characters.[33] In one scene, Mufasa believes Scar has challenged him. Quickly denying being insolent to the much-fiercer Mufasa, Scar continues "Well, as far as brains go, I got the lion's share. But, when it comes to brute strength ... I'm afraid I'm at the shallow end of the gene pool." Sean Griffin states in *Tinker Belles and Evil Queens: The Walt Disney Company from the Inside Out* that Scar "makes up for his lack of strength with catty remarks and invidious plotting ... fairly swish[ing] ... in his attempt to usurp the throne."[34] Scar uses his body and his tone, much like Ursula did, to carefully craft his transgenderism.

Later, another sarcastic reply again promotes the idea of Scar as transgendered. Noticing Scar's continued lack of respect for the future ascension, Mufasa points out his son Simba will be king. Scar's sardonic "I'll practice my curtsy" reiterates his acerbic personality, but also adds a transgendered effect as it locates Scar again in the female role, curtsying instead of bowing to the future king. Like Drizella's bow to the Prince, the gendered behavior reversal draws the attention of the viewer, categorizing Scar as gender-bending.[35]

Scar also has no mate, even when he becomes King.[36] Unlike Mufasa, who mated with Sarabi, and Simba who is betrothed to Nala, Scar chooses no lioness as his queen, and thus, has no heir. He depends on Sarabi for her food gathering skills, even though they share no romantic interest. In fact, Scar's main friends are outside the pride as he bullies and rules the hyena pack, marking him as living far outside the heterosexist lion culture.[37] Feminized and powerless, Scar cannot compete with his brother or nephew, even though he targets them as rivals. Just as when preschool viewers knew that Anastasia wasn't a true princess (even though the shoe fit), they likewise realize that Scar isn't the true king—his covert homosexual status helps them know he's the bad guy.

Jafar, as the male villain in *Aladdin*, also crosses gender boundaries via appearance and behavior. Tall and thin, Jafar's posture and bearing accentuates his difference from other male characters. As Li-Vollmer and LaPointe note, "Jafar ... wears a long gown with a nipped waist and sleeves that billow above the elbow and fit closely along the forearm to reveal his very slender lower arms and wrists. The pronounced ornamentation on the shoulders of his gown only direct more attention to the artifice of broad shoulders, not the true broad physique of a real man. All the other men, including the Sultan and other high-ranking characters, wear pants."[38] Likewise, Jafar is the only male in the film to wear eye make-up, typically a female preoccupation. Again, Li-Vollmer and LaPointe observe "These cosmetic forms of gender transgression are most noticeable in the context of other male characters, whose facial features are not highlighted with animators' cosmetics."[39] Subtly differentiating male villains from the male heroes via makeup and costume, the bad guys are increasingly associated with femaleness. Li-Vollmer and LaPoint also observe that several male Disney villains "have ... tall, willowy frames with gracefully slender limbs and slim waists,"[40] which are strangely close to our original "mean ladies"—the evil queen in *Snow White* and Maleficent in *Sleeping Beauty*.[41]

Additionally, Jafar's behavior is feminized. He is prissy and preening, unwilling to explore The Cave of Wonders for the magic lantern himself (unlike the heroes and heroines who eagerly head into adventurous escapades, even if they are dangerous). Sean Griffin also shares that lead animator Andreas Deja "admits to conceiving of the [Jafar] character as a gay man 'to give him his theatrical quality, his elegance.'"[42] Griffin continues, arguing it is easy to find the "'gay-tinged' villainy in Disney ... by watching how Jafar arches his eyebrows in disdain, or in the sneer that curls Scar's mouth as he endures the heterosexual patriarchy in which he finds himself."[43]

Like Scar, Jafar's lack of interest in a female partner also suggests his transgenderism. Jafar shows no romantic or sexual interest in the beautiful Jasmine until his male sidekick, Iago, suggests marrying Jasmine in order to become Sultan; and when Jafar does force Jasmine to obey him (wishing the Genie to compel her to fall in love with him), the wish is not motivated by lust, but rather by his obsession for more power. Thus, Jafar's only incentive to pursue a heterosexual relationship is to humiliate Jasmine and anger Aladdin.

However, the male villain in *Pocahontas* exhibits the most flamboyantly transgendered characteristics of all male Disney villains. Governor John Ratcliffe first appears on screen dressed in pink and purple clothes, sporting pigtails tied with pink bows,[44] and carrying a small lapdog. He puts his pinky finger up to drink his tea and dances effeminately, wearing a pink feathered boa. David Ogden Stiers affects a lisp in the voice for Ratcliffe, contributing to the stereotypical homosexual model. Ratcliffe's associates are also affected by his transgendered depiction: his pug is shown with a bouffant hairdo in a bubble bath, while Ratcliffe's male manservant, Wiggins, speaks with a high-pitched voice, cuts topiary into animal shapes, and desires to create gift baskets for the Indians.[45] Clearly, Ratcliffe is not the masculinized hero like John Smith, nor the serious Indian warrior, Koucom. Instead he is the unlikable villain, who is yet another "mean lady": effete, if not outright homosexual.

By reinforcing the gender-bending identity of Ratcliffe in contrast to the heterosexual male characters, Ratcliffe becomes more unpleasant, more untouchable, and more remote. Sassafras Lowrey adds that Ratcliffe

> does not partake in the physical work of "digging up Virginia" ... he dresse[s] flamboyantly and sings "I'll glitter," positioning him far outside of the norms of acceptable heterosexual masculinity. This is particularly true as men who are performing physical labor, thus displaying stereotypical heterosexual actions[,] surround him.[46]

In fact, *The Disney Villain* states clearly that the animators "preferred to depict our examples of vileness through a strong design which eliminated realism and kept the audience from getting too close to the character."[47] While this statement refers to the "safe distance" kept between the devil via his screen positioning, for example, in *Fantasia*, and viewers, it can also refer to the distance created via villains who appear different from the preschool viewer. In other words, child viewers understand that not only is Ratcliffe the villain, but he is the *gay* villain who is clearly different from almost every other male character in the film. By making him grossly flamboyant and disparate from all other men, while associating him with greed, violence, and ignorance, child viewers disassociate completely from his character, glad that he ends up in the brig on the way home. This breeds blatant prejudices among children viewers regarding any difference, but especially those which are associated with transgenderism.

Disney films are often regarded as harmless family entertainment—one in which members of all ages are welcome to enjoy the thrills and spills of their favorite animated character. As such, they have been overlooked until recently as content in need of analysis. The transgendered villains and their hyper-heterosexual heroes and heroines offer an interesting contrast to each other worth exploring more deeply, as do the problematic message about gender and difference that is being sent consistently to Disney's child viewers.

While there are no Disney characters that actively announce their homosexuality or transgenderism, there is considerable evidence that Disney's gender-bending characters are flourishing. Fascinatingly, some of these transgendered characters are among the most popular. Ursula and Scar consistently rank highly, not just among villains, but also among all Disney characters.[48] So then, if some of these transgendered characters still manage to gain a following, why is it significant to note this strangely fascinating pattern?

Obviously Disney is a powerhouse media outlet, watched by millions of children all over the world, and "the Disney Princess films comprise five of the six top revenue-generating Disney films of all time."[49] It has been argued by H. A. Giroux that Disney films influence children as much as other cultural influences, such as school, church, and family, as their videos are repetitively watched via home DVDs.[50] Thus, the characterization of transgendered villains marks gender-bending characters (and eventually real people) as "evil" simply through the ongoing establishment of the pattern; i.e., if the "mean ladies" are consistently transgendered, it implies a larger statement is being made about what kind of people cross traditional gender boundaries in behavior and appearance—and that larger statement is one soaked in prejudice and disparagement.

Finally, creating only villains as transgendered people also suggests something about the consumerism of these films—i.e., that Disney willingly plays into stereotypes and fears about homophobia as well as accepts the crushing dominance of heterosexism within the larger community. In other words, if all of the villains are gay or have complicated gender-bending identities, it suggests that viewers find homosexuality or untraditional gender behavior and appearance unsettling, at best, and thus, that it's okay to treat people who are different from the heterosexual norm as dangerous or disgusting because they *will* hurt you; after all, they are villains. At worst, viewers may feel they can be openly hostile to those who are different via transgendered appearance and behavior—and our preschool set is especially vulnerable to this message. As Li-Vollmer and LaPointe argue,

> By drawing on information gleaned from their real-life encounters and their viewing of media images, children organize information about gender roles and gender performances into their schemata about what it is to be male or female (Fiske & Taylor, 1991); therefore, media viewing is both a source and a location of children's gender schema development (Durkin, 1984). Children's gender schemata, like all schemata, are less developed than those of adults, and are, therefore, more susceptible to influence from new sources and experiences, including media; as young people's gender schemata develop over time, they become more resilient to change (Fiske & Taylor, 1991).[51]

So, when my daughter asks me at the grocery store if the cashier is a boy or a girl, because he has a ponytail, I have to realize that she's responding to the abundance of traditional gendered stereotypes in our culture, including confusing signals from Disney films—and she's right, most boys *don't* wear ponytails; longer hair and ponytails *can* be characteristics that are associated with girls. However, since some boys wear ponytails (and some girls don short-clipped hair), it's also important to explain that the gendered difference she's noting on the outside is only part of the picture, and it may have little to do with behavior or intent. The ponytail-wearing man is not *evil* simply because he challenges a gendered stereotype. Thus, while the Disney villains *are* mean, cruel, and petty, often out to rule the world in despicable ways, it's not because they are girly men or tomboys.

Notes

1. Litsa Renée Tanner et al explains this via the results of their study, "Marriage/children as the expected course for [Disney] couples [is] most often illustrated by the characters getting married shortly after meeting or falling in love (often in the very next scene), and at times having children soon afterward." Litsa Renée Tanner, et al, "Images of Couples and Families in Disney Feature-Length Animated Films," *American Journal of Family Therapy* 31.5 (2003): 360, Academic Search Premier.

2. Cruella De Vil in *101 Dalmatians* also portrays many physical and verbal transgendered characteristics and is worthy of more analysis. Likewise, Sean Griffin argues that both the "vengeful Queen in *Snow White* and the evil sorceress Maleficent in *Sleeping Beauty* ... look like drag queens" due to their facial features and theatrical behavior. Sean Griffin, *Tinker Belles and Evil Queens: The Walt Disney Company from the Inside Out* (New York University Press: New York, 2000), 73.

3. Li-Vollmer, Meredith and LaPointe, Mark E., "Gender Transgression and Villainy in Animated Film," *Popular Communication* 1: 2 (2003): 90.

4. *Ibid.*, 91.

5. Ollie Johnston and Frank Thomas. *The Disney Villain* (Hyperion: New York, 1993), 15.

6. *Ibid.*, 11.

7. *Ibid.*

8. Griffin, *Tinker Belles and Evil Queens*, 75.

9. Only Snow White, the very first princess, is known for a dress that does not emphasize her body, although she still has a lithe figure. This can be most clearly associated with the time of that picture's release (1937).

10. Mark I. Pinsky, *The Gospel According to Disney: Faith, Trust, and Pixie Dust* (Louisville: Westminster John Knox Press, 2004), 165.

11. Debra Bradley, "Disney Gives Pocahontas Sexiest Cartoon Image Ever," *Dallas Morning News, The Free-Lance Star*, June 23, 1995, http://news.google.com/newspapersnid=1298&dat= 19950623&id=uy0zAAAAIBAJ &sjid=wQcGAAAAIBAJ&pg=3630,4507147

12. In 78.3% of Disney films, "it took a matter of minutes for couples to fall in love." Litsa Renée Tanner, et al, "Images of Couples and Families in Disney Feature-Length Animated Films," 364.

13. England and Descartes note in their study, "While the princes have less screen time overall, they perform a relatively high number of rescues, suggesting that princes see more action comparatively." Dawn England and Lara Descartes, "Gender Role Portrayal and the Disney Princesses," University of Connecticut, April 19, 2008, Honors Thesis Poster Presentation.

14. Only Pocahontas does not marry the lead male, which notably would have contradicted history to have her do so.

15. While outside the realm of this essay, voice inflection and language choices for all the villains offer interesting material for transgendered analysis too.

16. Interestingly, the stepsisters are not described as ugly in the Grimms' version, instead as "beautiful, with fair faces, but evil and dark hearts." D. L. Ashliman, "Cinderella," Grimm Brothers' Home Page, 2009, Original by Jacob and Wilhelm Grimm, 1857, http://www.pitt.edu/~dash/grimm021.html.

17. Interestingly, in *Cinderella II*, Anastasia's figure changes in significant ways: her waist is defined, showing a noticeable difference between the size of her chest and waist. This change is likely connected to Anastasia's more prominent role in *Cinderella II*, and as someone who, with Cinderella's help, asserts herself against her own (evil) mother.

18. Again, in *Cinderella II*, Anastasia's appearance also changes—her long hair is brushed out in soft curls (versus the ringlet sausages of the first film), her face is more slender, and her nose is less bulbous. These modifications—along with her larger role of securing her own heterosexual relationship with the baker's son, reinforce an alignment of feminine features with heterosexuality and marital goals.

19. In contrast, the Duke smiles broadly when he views Cinderella's small legs and feet through his monocle as she runs down the stairs after being trapped in her room.

20. E. Bell, L. Haas, and L. Sells, *From Mouse to Mermaid: The Politics of Film, Gender, and Culture* (Bloomington: Indiana University Press, 1995), 112.

21. Similarly, *Beauty and the Beast*'s Gaston emphasizes his hyper-masculinity via similar large-screen shots of his feet.

22. Once again, this too changes in *Cinderella II*, where Anastasia dances gracefully around her room with her cat, Lucifer.

23. Rape is not a male trait obviously, but it is much more commonly associated with male perpetrators than female. In fact, per RAINN's website, most rape statistics in the United States focus on male attacker–female victim implicitly. Finding statistics on female perpetrators is quite challenging.

24. Johnson and Thomas, *The Disney Villain*, 100.

25. *Ibid.*, 99.

26. In *Cinderella II*, Lady Tremaine abandons Anastasia when the girl defies her to be with the baker's son (who is absent in *Cinderella III*).

27. Lady Tremaine's behavior is consistent with Grimms' description of her, where she suggests to both her daughters to cut off their toe or heel to fit the slipper—and supplies the knife for the deed.

28. Johnson and Thomas, *The Disney Villain*, 186–191.

29. Libe Garcia Zarranz, "Diswomen Strike Back? The Evolution of Disney's Femmes in the 1990s," *Atenea*, (2007): 57, Academic Search Premier.

30. Pinsky, *From Mouse to Mermaid: The Gospel According to Disney*, 140.

31. Interestingly, when Ursula becomes Vanessa, the young woman that looks like Ariel, she sings: "What a lovely little bride I'll make / my dear, I look divine...," perhaps a nod to Ursula's model.
32. Li-Vollmer and LaPointe suggest that Scar's "slim face and pointed chin" give his face a more "delicate" face than Mufasa or Simba. Li-Vollmer and LaPointe, "Gender Transgression and Villainy in Animated Film," 97.
33. England and Descartes's study of Disney films indicated that physical strength was a characteristic least likely to be observed in the main female leads. England and Descartes, "Gender Role Portrayal and the Disney Princesses."
34. Griffin. *Tinker Belles and Evil Queens*, 211.
35. A later comment by Scar to Simba that he "has no idea" just how "weird" Scar is stretches into a latent "queer" reference as well. See Griffin's text for more explicit analysis.
36. In later straight-to-DVD sequels and Broadway productions, Scar's female mate issues are more thoroughly investigated as he is grouped with several lionesses and even attempts to seduce Nala unsuccessfully.
37. Griffin goes further with this point, noting that Scar is also associated with Nazism and drought, two disturbing connections at best, but especially with his transgendered characteristics. Griffin, *Tinker Belles and Evil Queens*, 212.
38. Li-Vollmer and LaPointe, "Gender Transgression and Villainy in Animated Film," 99–100.
39. *Ibid.*, 98.
40. *Ibid.*, 98.
41. Two directors of animation, Ron Clements and John Musker, even told Andreas Deja, the lead animator of *Jafar*, to "look at Maleficent" in regards to Jafar's movement. Johnson and Thomas, *The Disney Villain*, 213.
42. Griffin. *Tinker Belles and Evil Queens*, 141.
43. *Ibid.*, 142.
44. While the hairstyle is of the time period, no other male character in the film wears his hair like it, especially not with pink ribbons.
45. Lowrey also suggests that Wiggins and Ratcliffe are implied homosexual lovers. Sassafras Lowrey, "I'll Glitter," *Fuchsia Focus: A Queer Critique of the Media*, 10 July 2007, http://fuchsiafo-cus.blogspot.com/2007/07/ill-glitter.html
46. Lowrey, "I'll Glitter."
47. Johnson and Thomas, *The Disney Villain*, 18.
48. *Disney Villains*, 2010, http://www.disneyvillains.net/
49. Karen E. Wohlwend, "Damsels in Discourse: Girls Consuming and Producing Identity Texts Through Disney Princess Play," *Reading Research Quarterly* 44.1 (Jan–March 2009): 57 (27). Expanded Academic ASAP. Gale.
50. Giroux, H. A. "Animating Youth: The Disneyfication of Children's Culture," *Socialist Review*: 23–55. Quoted in Lauren Dundes, "Disney's Modern Heroine Pocahontas: Revealing Age-Old Gender Stereotypes and Role Discontinuity Under a Façade of Liberation," *Social Science Journal* 38 (2001): 353–365. Academic Search Premier. EBSCO.
51. Li-Vollmer and LaPointe, "Gender Transgression and Villainy in Animated Film," 93.

Bibliography

Ashliman, D. L., "Cinderella." Grimm Brothers' Home Page. 2009. Original by Jacob and Wilhelm Grimm, 1857. *http://www.pitt.edu/~dash/grimm021.html.*

Bell, E., Haas, L., and Sells, L. "Introduction: Walt's in the Movies." *From Mouse to Mermaid: The Politics of Film, Gender, and Culture.* Bloomington: Indiana University Press, 1995, 1–20.

Bradley, Debra. "Disney Gives Pocahontas Sexiest Cartoon Image Ever." *Dallas Morning News, The Free-Lance Star*, June 23, 1995, *http://news.google.com/newspapers?nid=1 298&dat=19950623&id=uy0zAAAAIBAJ&sjid=wQcGAAAAIBAJ&pg=3630,4507147*

Disney Villains. 2010. *http://www.disneyvillains.net/*

162   SECTION II: TRADITIONS AND TRANSFORMATIONS

Dundes, Lauren, and Alan Dundes. "Young Hero Simba Defeats Old Villain Scar: Oedipus Wrecks the Lyin' King." *Social Science Journal* 43.3 (2006): 479–485. *Academic Search Premier.* EBSCO.
England, Dawn, and Lara Descartes. "Gender Role Portrayal and the Disney Princesses." University of Connecticut. April 19, 2008. Honors Thesis Poster Presentation. 12 January 2010. *http://www.familystudies.uconn.edu/undergraduate/honors /posters/Dawn%20England%20poster.pdf*
Giroux, H. A. "Animating Youth: The Disneyfication of Children's Culture." *Socialist Review*: 23–55. Quoted in Lauren Dundes, "Disney's Modern Heroine Pocahontas: Revealing Age-Old Gender Stereotypes and Role Discontinuity Under a Façade of Liberation." *Social Science Journal* 38 (2001): 353–365. *Academic Search Premier.* EBSCO.
Griffin, Sean. *Tinker Belles and Evil Queens. Tinker Belles and Evil Queens: The Walt Disney Company from the Inside Out.* New York University Press: New York. 2000.
Hill, Jim. Jim Hill Media, "Why (For) Pat Carroll Wasn't Actually Disney's First Choice to Voice Ursula in 'The Little Mermaid,'" 15 June 2007. *http://jimhillmedia. com/blogs/jim_hill/archive/2007/06/15/why-for-pat-carroll-wasn-t-actually-disney-s-first-choice-to-voice-ursula-in-the-little-mermaid.aspx*
Johnston, Ollie, and Frank Thomas. *The Disney Villain.* Hyperion: New York. 1993.
Li-Vollmer, Meredith and LaPointe, Mark E. "Gender Transgression and Villainy in Animated Film." *Popular Communication* 1: 2 (2003), 89–109.
Lowrey, Sassafras. "I'll Glitter." *Fuchsia Focus: A Queer Critique of the Media.* 10 July 2007 *http://fuchsiafocus.blogspot.com/2007/07/ill-glitter.html*
PFLAG: Parents, Families, and Friends of Lesbians and Gays. "About Our Transgendered Children." *Out of the Closet Into Our Hearts.* February 25, 2007. *http://www.crit-path.org/pflag-talk/tgkidfaq.htm*
Pinsky, Mark I. *The Gospel According to Disney: Faith, Trust, and Pixie Dust.* Louisville: Westminster John Knox Press, 2004.
RAINN: Rape, Abuse, and Incest National Network. "Statistics." 2009. *http://www. rainn.org/statistics*
Tanner, Litsa Renée, et al. "Images of Couples and Families in Disney Feature-Length Animated Films." *American Journal of Family Therapy* 31.5 (2003): 355. *Academic Search Premier.* EBSCO.
Towbin, Mia Adessa, et al. "Images of Gender, Race, Age, and Sexual Orientation in Disney Feature-Length Animated Films." *Journal of Feminist Family Therapy* 15.4 (2003): 19–44. *Academic Search Premier.* EBSCO.
"Voicing 'Scar' in *The Lion King*—Jeremy Irons." June 05, 2009. *http://www.youtube.com/ watch?v=apJxdRYI32Y*
Willman, Chris. "You Can't Hide His Lion Eyes." Originally in *Los Angeles Times.* Reprinted in *Irons Ink: Press Archive.* 15 May 1994. *http://www.jeremy-irons.com /press/archive/18.html*
Zarranz, Libe Garcia. "Diswomen Strike Back? The Evolution of Disney's Femmes in the 1990s." *Atenea* (2007) 55–67: *Academic Search Premier.* EBSCO.

SECTION III—OF BEASTS AND INNOCENTS: ESSAYS ON DISABILITY

"You're a Surprise from Every Angle": Disability, Identity, and Otherness *in* The Hunchback of Notre Dame

MARTIN F. NORDEN

In 1994, the Walt Disney company created a stir in the entertainment industry when it announced its intention to produce two movies based on Victor Hugo's 1831 novel, *Notre-Dame de Paris*: a live-action film and an animated musical. Though the company soon abandoned the idea of a live-action feature,[1] it did follow through with its plan to create an animated film. Originally proposed in 1993 by Disney creative development executive David Stainton, who had been inspired by a *Classics Illustrated* comic-book retelling of Hugo's story,[2] the production was greenlighted by production executive Jeffrey Katzenberg, produced by Don Hahn, and co-directed by Gary Trousdale and Kirk Wise.[3] The company gave it a unique premiere on June 19, 1996, by presenting it on six giant screens in the Superdome in New Orleans shortly after an elaborate parade led by Disney corporate executives Michael Eisner and Roy Disney had wound its way through the city's French Quarter. With much fanfare, the studio released the film nationwide two days later and around the world in the months that followed. Like most of its predecessors adapted from Hugo's novel, the film bore the patently offensive title *The Hunchback of Notre Dame*.[4]

Since so much of this film centers on yet another moving-image rendering of one of literature's most famous disabled characters, I propose to examine the representation of its pivotal figure of Quasimodo, his corporeality (his "gnarled envelope,"[5] to borrow Hugo's translated phrase), and his world from the general perspective of a relatively new field of scholarly inquiry: disability studies (DS), about which a few words need to be said. Akin to feminist studies

163

and queer studies in its emphasis on the body as the locus of frequently conflict-
ing discourses, disability studies has among its aims the deconstruction of disability representations in order to lay bare their underlying assumptions and
strategies. DS scholars reject the two paradigms that have long governed the
contextualization of disability: the Moral model, which equates disability with
evil and/or punishment from a divine source; and the Medical model, which
treats disability mainly in pathological, "problem-to-be-overcome" terms while
privileging practitioners in the medical and rehabilitative fields. Disability
studies scholars have instead championed a third paradigm: the Social model,
which posits that a person's disabled status is a social and cultural construction.
Far from regarding people with disabilities (PWDs) as simplistic emblems of
evil or divine retribution, or as hard-luck, embittered individuals forever
dependent on well-meaning, able-bodied "experts," advocates of the Social
model argue instead that PWDs are a significant minority group that, like
other minorities and women, has been subjected to alternating rounds of bigotry, paternalism, and indifference. Unlike the earlier paradigms, the Social
model has a pronounced reflexivity (DS scholars are quite aware that it and
the other models are socio-cultural constructions, too), and that quality helps
make it a powerful tool for prying open cultural expressions that might otherwise go unnoticed and unquestioned. For example, a DS person might highlight a seemingly innocent utterance in a Disney press release—that Quasimodo
is "an angel in a devil's body"[6]—to underscore the point that remnants of the
ages-old Moral model still permeate our culture.[7]

    This chapter explores a number of intertwined concerns: identity issues,
the longstanding stereotypes that inform the Quasimodo character, and the
ways that other characters and indeed the filmmakers themselves objectify him.
Of particular interest are the ways that other characters define Quasimodo and
how he defines himself, the latter process of which is often revealed through
his imaginary conversations and songs with three Notre Dame gargoyles. As
much a study of filmmakerly attitudes as it is of the film itself, this chapter will
show that the film seems to preach acceptance of society's Others but is in fact
an embodiment of bogus "political correctness." Though the film seemingly
argues on behalf of inclusiveness—as when the townspeople happily carry Quasimodo on their shoulders at the film's conclusion, for example—he is still very
much an isolated Other. For the vast majority of the film's duration, there is no
community for him of any sort except for his imaginary gargoyle friends. The
movie appears to critique the view that "different" people should be kept separate
and isolated, yet it simultaneously perpetuates it and, worse, wallows in it.

* * *

    The Disney film's considerable variances from Hugo's novel are reasonably
well known and require no detailed accounting here.[8] I begin the analysis
instead with a discussion of the challenges facing the Disney production team,

its responses to those challenges, and the bearing of the team's solutions on the development of the film's disabled character.

As numerous commentators have pointed out, Hugo's dense, powerfully tragic novel—best remembered for its deafened, severely disabled bell ringer and his unrequited love for a Roma woman—hardly seemed suitable subject matter for a typical Disney animated musical. Disney has long been known for appropriating centuries-old source material, but almost always that material had taken the form of folk and fairy tales. Now, however, Disney had selected an exceptionally dark piece of classic adult literature with the daunting task of making it child-friendly.

The filmmakers themselves were quite mindful of the difficulties ahead. "We knew it would be a challenge to stay true to the material, while still giving it the requisite amount of fantasy and fun most people would expect from a Disney animated feature," said co-director Kirk Wise. "We were not going to end it the way the book ended, with everybody dead." Producer Don Hahn expressed a similar sentiment. "On its surface, 'The Hunchback of Notre Dame' as a Disney musical/action/adventure/comedy doesn't exactly relate," said he, adding that "we knew that there were many pitfalls: characters with disabilities, bigotry, gypsies and the Catholic Church." Their general solution for taking care of the disabled character and the other so-termed "pitfalls" was unsettlingly simple, however; they elected to turn their film's narrative into a variation on the *Beauty and the Beast* storyline.[9]

In retrospect, such a decision should not be surprising to anyone familiar with the filmmakers' track record. The same producer-director-director triumvirate responsible for the Disney *Hunchback*—Hahn, Trousdale, and Wise— played identical roles in the creation of the multiple award-winning Disney animated feature *Beauty and the Beast* in 1991, and they doubtless believed that what worked well for them once would work well for them again.

Hahn readily acknowledged the similarity. "'Beauty' is the rural equivalent of 'Hunchback,'" he said. "This is very much the urban Parisian story. We always joked that we should just do 'Cyrano' and get it over with. To complete the misshapen heroes of France stories."[10] The filmmakers anticipated critics' and audiences' perception of a kinship among the two films (indeed, a headline writer for the *Los Angeles Times* ungraciously referred to the new production as *Beauty and the 'Back*)[11] and introduced some superficial changes to create distance between the productions. The films' narrative and thematic resemblance, however, is unmistakable. As *Los Angeles Times* reporter John Clark put it, Disney's *Hunchback* was very similar to *Beauty* in that it "was an animated musical that took place in France and featured a misshapen hero and a beautiful heroine. In both films, beauty is only skin-deep."[12]

In the commentary track on the *Hunchback* DVD, Wise and Trousdale engaged in an exchange that sheds further light on their approach to the Hugo novel:

WISE: Gary and I realized that there are aspects of the story that were so archetypal, if you will, that it read almost like a fairy-tale.
TROUSDALE: When you strip the story down to its bare bones, you've got a
monster who lives in a tower.
WISE: Yeah, locked in a tower by his evil stepfather.
TROUSDALE: A beautiful dancer and a knight on a horse. And just great—
great kind of fairy-tale elements that were put together.

By reducing the Hugo narrative to a *Beauty and the Beast* level, the filmmakers thus fell back on one of the most enduring beliefs about "good" PWDs:
that they possess an inner beauty that compensates for their less-than-perfect
exteriors. Though presumably well-intentioned, such a simplistic belief represents stereotyped thinking at its most insidious precisely because it appears
to be well-intentioned and therefore typically goes unquestioned. Films guided
by this perspective almost always package the other characters' eventual recognition of that inner beauty as facile and brief "feel-good" moments during the
waning moments of the narrative. Such moments do little to ameliorate the
damaging message often conveyed throughout the rest of the story: that PWDs
are freakish if not animalistic entities that deserve to be shunned, feared, or
humiliated.[13]

Such is the case with Disney's *Hunchback*. Unlike the far more complex
Quasimodos who inhabit the numerous live-action renderings of Hugo's novel,
Quasi (to use the film's childlike diminutive) is clearly inscribed by the filmmakers as a good and worthy PWD. Like the other Quasimodos, however, he
is frequently contextualized in beast-like terms.

This latter point is reflected in some subtle and not-so-subtle ways in the
film. For example, the filmmakers wanted to suggest that Quasi has an active
fantasy life inside the bell tower and had him create a tabletop miniature of
the Notre Dame courtyard replete with figurines he modeled after actual people. The toy figure he created of himself is quite telling; it shows him down
on all fours, as if he were an animal. Since Quasi is the creator of the figurine,
the film thus implies that this is how he sees himself. Indeed, he confirms the
point later in the film when he gazes at the beast-like figurine of himself and
says very matter-of-factly "I am a monster" to his stepfather Frollo, who has
conditioned him to think of himself in subhuman terms. Though Quasi certainly has his pro-social side, the filmmakers were quick to acknowledge that
the character posed a special challenge; he lacked what Trousdale referred to
as the "teddy-bear factor," a quality that Hahn, Trousdale, and Wise had
bestowed on *Beauty*'s Beast in abundance. They had to find a way of making
Quasi, for lack of a better word, cuddlier.[14]

Having chosen a storyline that could not help but define its lead character
in brutish terms, the production team was now charged with the task of developing a visual design for Quasimodo that rendered him reasonably sympathetic.
In what should have been a sign of problems to come, the studio had enormous

difficulty coming up with that general "look." *Entertainment Weekly* writers Anne Thompson and David Karger reported that the animation team took nearly eight agonizing months to design what they termed a "kid-friendly" version of the film's central figure.[15] In a revealing comment, the film's supervising animator, James Baxter, said that Quasimodo "had to be grotesque, downtrodden, and appealing at the same time"—a highly problematic combination of attributes, to be sure. Baxter went through a veritable mountain of preliminary sketches to little avail, a point confirmed by Kirk Wise. "We had a zillion different designs for Quasi," said the film's co-director. "There were some designs where he looked like a teenage guy with bad posture. There were other designs where he looked like one of the Seven Dwarfs."[16]

The difficulties extended to the type of vocalization that Tom Hulce, the actor hired to give voice to Quasi, could provide for the character. Since the film was to be a musical with ample singing and dancing, its creators decided early on to efface several important identity factors in Hugo's bell ringer: his profound deafness, brought on by a half-dozen years of bell-tolling, and his self-imposed uncommunicativeness. They wanted their Quasi to hear, speak, and sing perfectly well but could offer precious little guidance to Hulce about the character, at least, early on. With no clear sense of the direction that Quasimodo's visualization and indeed his general concept were taking, the discouraged actor harbored thoughts of resigning from the production. "My job was to find all the parts of the character and let them live," Hulce said. "I thought about suggesting that maybe we weren't going to find it. But it finally fell into place. There was a sense of relief that maybe we weren't going to have that conversation."[17]

The production team eventually settled on a look and a vocal strategy that together emphasized the bell ringer's youth. On its surface, such a decision might appear to have been inspired by a point made in *Notre-Dame de Paris*; Hugo identified Quasimodo's age as about twenty, and so does the movie.[18] The fact that the two Quasimodos share the same chronological age, however, tells only a small part of the story; it says nothing about the characters' levels of maturity, the differences among which are vast. Hugo bluntly noted that Quasimodo, who had begun his bell-ringing duties at the age of fourteen, was already "grown up" by the start of the story; though an adult young in years, he had prematurely aged after having weathered more than his share of life's travails.[19] Disney's Quasi, on the other hand, comes across as not much more than an awkward child with major self-esteem problems. Indeed, Charles Kimbrough, an actor who voiced one of Quasi's gargoyle friends, likened him to a pimply teenager:

> The Hunchback, without losing any of his power or creepiness, is almost like an adolescent, a young boy. Kids connect with that insecurity, particularly if you're a little shy, if your acne is a little heavy, or you're self-conscious or embarrassed

to go out. The whole gist of the film is trying to get Quasimodo to get to the Feast of Fools, to get out, you know, and enjoy himself and really have a life. I think that hits kids where they live.[20]

The creation of a character who does not think highly of him- or herself is not especially unusual for Disney; in fact, the studio's "exploration of the outcast, the person who has self-esteem problems," to cite Disney animation head Peter Schneider, is rather commonplace. "If you look at all of the films over the last eight years, they all deal with that issue, whether it's Ariel or the Beast or Simba," said Schneider, concluding that "the goal is to find a place where you belong." What makes it more of a DS issue, however, is the Disney team's use of disability imagery to suggest those concerns. In other words, the filmmakers used Quasimodo's physicality to imply that he is emotionally stunted. As supervising animator James Baxter put it, Quasi's "being bent over was a metaphor for his wanting to hide." The symbolic and metaphoric dimension of disability, which has had a long and inglorious history in literature and film, had found its way into another major cultural expression yet again.[21]

The film represents Quasi's arrested development in other ways, most famously via his relationship with three animated gargoyles named Victor, Hugo, and Laverne. They are his only community for much of the movie, and that is not saying much; they are split-off chunks of his own imagination and represent his conscience, fantasies, etc., in a Calvin-and-Hobbes fashion. He is the only person to whom they speak (when other people are in the scene, the gargoyles are stone). When they therefore exclaim "You're a surprise from every angle" and compare the shape his body to that of a croissant—to cite several of their more tasteless actions—they represent things that he thinks about himself. The gargoyles' explicit and implied messages are troubling, to say the least, and go a long way toward undercutting whatever sympathies the filmmakers had created for its disabled character.

Film critics and media watchdog groups were quick to pick up on the film's trivialization of disability issues and Quasi's inability to sustain mature relationships. For example, *Los Angeles Times* chief film critic Kenneth Turan labeled Disney's construction of Quasi "a problem," elaborating that Hugo's "great grotesque ... has been turned by Disney's team of five writers (Tab Murphy, Irene Mecchi, Bob Tzudiker & Noni White and Jonathan Roberts) into a Sensitive New Age Guy, cuddly enough to be called Quasi by his intimates, burdened not by severe deformity or deafness but by that curse of modern times, lack of self-esteem." In the U.K., the film had the dubious distinction of winning the "One in Eight" group's Raspberry Ripple award for worst feature-film portrayal of a person with a disability, principally because it portrayed its PWD as a social outcast incapable of maintaining adult relationships.[22]

The Disney team's decision to emphasize Quasi's youthfulness also reflects a larger issue that has long haunted movie representations of disability: the

infantilization of PWDs. When Patt Morrison of the *Los Angeles Times* suggested that the film turned "the tragically disfigured Quasimodo into just a
funny-looking kid you might see on a telethon,"[23] she was doubtless alluding,
however crudely and obliquely, to the annual MDA Labor Day telethon long
associated with Jerry Lewis. With its "Jerry's Kids" imagery prominently on
display, the MDA telethon has been the most conspicuous example of mainstream society's tendency to contextualize PWDs, regardless of age, as children
in need of nurturing and protection by able-bodied adults. Disney's *Hunchback*
is yet another example of that way of thinking.

The film's dominant figure of Quasi is rooted in an exceptionally longstanding disability-related stereotype: the "Sweet Innocent," a figure that
embodies the deep-seated belief that PWDs must rely on mainstream society
for everything. Often designed as a child or a maiden who is "perfect" in every
respect except for an impairment, the Sweet Innocent typically, and effortlessly,
brings out the protectiveness of most able-bodied people in his or her orbit.
As I have noted elsewhere, adjectives that readily define the figure include
humble, gentle, respectful, passive, cheerful, spiritual, virginal, pure, and
pitiable.[24] The literary world's most famous example is Tiny Tim, and when
Disney created Quasi it added a most unlikely figure to that stereotype collection.

The Sweet Innocent is only one—albeit the most prominent one—of a
virtual pantheon of negative images that informs the characterization of Quasi.
In many respects, he is a multi-faceted character, but each facet reflects some
aspect of a longstanding disability stereotype. In other words, he is an uneasy
amalgamation of problematic disability-related imagery. He has a bit of the
"Comic Misadventurer" (a person who causes allegedly humorous problems,
self-directed or otherwise, because of his/her disabled status) about him, and
he also bears some resemblance to perhaps the most odious of disability stereotypes, the "Obsessive Avenger." The Obsessive Avenger, typically an Ahab-
like male who relentlessly seeks revenge on those he holds responsible for his
disabling circumstances or other moral-code violations, was the principal
stereotype that undergirded Lon Chaney's representation of Quasimodo in
the 1923 live-action version of *The Hunchback of Notre Dame.*[25] In a sense, this
stereotype anchors one end of the disability-stereotype spectrum while the
Sweet Innocent holds down the other. In a move virtually unprecedented in
the history of movie representations of disability, the Disney company in
essence swapped the diametrically opposed images of the Avenger and the
Innocent in the creation of its animated bell ringer.

Of course, it is not as simple as that. For starters, Disney's Quasi is not
cured of his impairments (a standard conclusion for most Sweet Innocent narratives, such as *Orphans of the Storm, City Lights*, and the numerous movie versions of *A Christmas Carol*), and he retains vestiges of the Obsessive Avenger
image. With bulging forearms that would make Popeye envious, Quasi is

endowed with an uncanny bestial strength often associated with the Avenger. He delivers several powerful kicks to Phoebus while hiding his unconscious rival under a table, for instance, and later, in a surge of preternatural strength, he bursts the chains that have been binding him to several pillars. Quasi also bears some resemblance to the larger-than-life "Supercrip" image, particularly in his spectacular rescue of Esmeralda and what *Variety* film critic Jeremy Gerard referred to as "his positively arachnoid agility on the walls and parapets of Notre Dame." Indeed, Disney animation head Peter Schneider claimed the film "is about how we all want to be heroic. It's that whole Superman idea that we all secretly harbor to save the day, no matter what we look like or who we are," adding that "in this case, it's a little problematic guy to society who gets that shot." Nevertheless, the Sweet Innocent is Quasi's dominant defining image.[26]

The *Hunchback* team hammered the point of Quasi's childlike qualities from the very beginning, even down to the way that the film reveals the bell ringer's background information: via a puppet show offered to a gathering of Parisian children. The puppet show quickly transforms into a flashback that transports the audience to a time twenty years earlier. Quasi is introduced as a literal infant, though ironically he is not visualized beyond the level of an anonymous bundle wrapped in swaddling clothes. The audience can only assume certain things about his appearance based on the horrified reaction and utterances of his soon-to-be stepfather, Frollo. He calls the infant "a monster," and when the Notre Dame Archdeacon stops him from dropping the child down a well, he replies: "This is an unholy demon. I'm sending it back to hell where it belongs." This prelude—a powerful piece of animation that features the death of the Roma woman who had been caring for the infant—haunts the remainder of the film.

When the film finally shows Quasi, he has reached the age of twenty. He lives alone high up in the Notre Dame bell tower, with only three stone gargoyles for companions. The film initially shows him engaged in a tender act; he encourages a baby pigeon, which has refused to leave its nest, to fly with the other pigeons. He gently handles it and asks it if today will be the day that it flies. The baby bird appears quite nervous until a flock of pigeons has flown by. It then perks up quite a bit. "Go on," Quasi says to it. "Nobody wants to be cooped up here forever." The pigeon happily flies off and joins the other birds, just as Quasi, to whom one of his imaginary gargoyle pals utters the same line later on, joins the "flock" of Parisian townspeople on their way out of the courtyard at the end of the film. An isolated creature—and, pointedly, a baby—the pigeon quickly comes to symbolize Quasi and his own dilemmas.

Consciously or not, the film's production team accentuated Quasi's youthful side by tempering its *Beauty and the Beast* storyline with a variation on the Oedipal scenario. Analysts taking a Freudian psychoanalytic perspective could easily argue that the emotionally-stunted Quasi has developed an attraction toward the maternal and unobtainable Esmeralda while simultaneously engaging in an intense rivalry with a paternal figure split into two halves: "good father" Phoebus and "bad father" Frollo. When Quasi clasps his hands over those of Phoebus and Esmeralda near the end of the film, he is doing more than simply giving them his blessing; he is also signifying that he has resolved his Oedipal crisis. From such a perspective, there is little wonder why Quasi cannot have a mature relationship with Esmeralda; he is, despite his years, just a kid.

Film critics had no trouble picking up on Quasi's childlike dimensions. John Horn of the Associated Press noted that "Hulce, who toyed around with several Quasimodo voices, finally settled on a form of speech that makes the character sound like a bashful young man." The *New York Daily News*'s Jami Bernard, who raved about the film, suggested that Quasi was "the lonely kid who sticks out like a sore thumb." The lines he speaks—"I am deformed ... and I am ugly"—are, in Bernard's words, "the lament of a child no one will play with." Bernard also noted that "To make the creature [sic] just this side of adorable, the animators have drawn him as a virtual child, with a toddler's awkward gait, a baby's smushed nose, his fang like a first tooth coming in."[27]

The people who created Quasimodo likewise saw him as an outcast child. Kirk Wise sagely observed that "I think everybody at some time in their life has felt like Quasimodo. Children are keenly aware of what it's like to be left out. So kids immediately warm up to him." As a press release makes plain, the Disney publicity machinery shared this perspective: "Quasi is a bit like a child who just wants to go to the party but is having a real problem with his parents. Clearly, he's someone who's had a very limited experience of life. And even though he's had to deal with lots of abuse, he has an indomitable spirit and refuses to be put down."[28]

Given the utterances and actions of the people responsible for the film, it should come as no surprise that *Hunchback*'s imagery is, to put it mildly, problem-fraught. On the one hand, the *Hunchback* team leaders gave lip service to a number of generalities that implied that theirs was an enlightened film on issues of difference, tolerance, and inclusion. "I think it's wrong for us to say that the only hero you can see in a Disney film is a handsome or beautiful hero," said Hahn. "Sitting here in 1996, you can have a hero that unconventional, and Quasi falls into that category." Added Wise: "This film promotes positive values. Compassion, understanding of people different than yourself. It has an anti-hypocrisy message. Everyone sometime has felt like Quasi for one reason or another."[29] On the other hand, the Disney studio did itself and its audiences a major disservice by refusing to work with disability consultants during the film's development despite multiple requests. The company had set a precedent not long before when it agreed to consult with Native American experts on its 1995 film *Pocahontas* following complaints about its stereotyping of Arabs in *Aladdin* (1992). In the case of *Hunchback*, however, the company vigorously rejected proposals to collaborate with disability experts. In perhaps a reflection of the outdated Medical-model view that disabled people are a bunch of hard-luck individuals and not a cultural minority, it insisted there was no need for such consultants.

Before the movie opened, an executive at rival Universal Studios predicted potential difficulties. "This could be a tough one. Basically you have a child held captive. Then there's that whole handicap, societal misfit aspect," said the executive. "But you know Disney, if there's a way to sell it, they'll figure it out. They've certainly tread this path many times before ... and quite successfully." Disney executive Peter Schneider was just as sanguine. "We know that someone will always take issue with something," he said. "But we just deal with that when it comes along. We never grapple over whether someone will take issue with something or not. It's all about telling the tale."[30] Or, perhaps more accurately, it's all about the Disney juggernaut making money.

In response to Disney's announcement that it would produce an animated film based on Hugo's novel, Paul Spudich, a San Franciscan with kyphoscoliosis, organized a letter-writing campaign to protest Disney's decision and specifically asked the company to change the film's title. "Absolutely not," replied Disney spokesman Howard Green, who went on to note that "we will do something that is very sensitive to the concerns of handicapped people, or the physically challenged, or whatever the correct term is these days." The directors themselves clearly had no intention of changing the title. "There were questions asked by unnamed people about whether we should call it 'The Hunchback of Notre Dame' because 'hunchback' is a hurtful word," said Trousdale, who left little doubt about his perspective after posing a follow-up rhetorical question: "You're going to call it 'The Differently Abled Bell Ringer'?" Trousdale's colleague Wise likewise failed to recognize the hurtfulness of the term: "I think most people eventually understood that you call more attention to it by changing it than you would by not changing it."[31] As though that's a bad thing.

A Disney executive who directly responded to Spudich was Sanford Litvack, the company's Executive Vice President in charge of Law and Human Resources. "Far from depicting the central character as loathsome or unlovable," he wrote in a letter to Spudich, "our draft screenplay tracks the story of a person who at first feels and is made to feel he is deformed, but learns that he has great value as a human being. Although he is shown at the outset as being treated wrongly and cruelly by the world, he demonstrates that he is noble, a hero, as he and the world learns [sic] that it is who you are inside, not what you look like, that matters."[32]

Unsatisfied with Litvack's response, Spudich wrote back and asked to examine the script. This time, Litvack stonewalled him. "I want to assure you that it is not the intention of this company—and never was—to hurt people with disabilities," he wrote. "We are not, however, in a position to share with people outside the company advance previews of our stories or screenplays since, as I am sure you can appreciate, the entertainment business is fiercely competitive." In light of the film's musical number "A Guy Like You" (which, among other things, shows Quasi looking into a mirror that immediately shatters and the gargoyles, representing his imagination, holding a wienie roast while Paris burns), Litvack's concluding statement was ludicrous: "We are confident that our adaptation of the French classic work will treat the characters and issues in a dignified manner."[33]

* * *

Why all this concern about a movie and its representations, one might ask? After all, aren't we simply talking about, as Alfred Hitchcock once said, only a movie?

Yes, it's a movie, but it's so much more than that; for disabled people, movies such as *The Hunchback of Notre Dame* are harmful and divisive expressions that reinforce negative beliefs that can lead to further discrimination. "Deformity, whether it be a hunched back or less disfiguring handicaps, is hardly a topic for Disney's 'fun and games' approach to reality," wrote Carole Henkoff, a New Jersey woman with multiple sclerosis. Other PWDs elaborated on this general point. "The portrayals put forward by Disney contribute to the attitudinal barriers that keep many disabled people from being accepted into communities," wrote Alana Theriault, a Berkeley-based woman with scoliosis. "What does this movie say about those of us with disabilities?" queried Kathi Wolfe, a Falls Church, Virginia, freelance writer who is legally blind. "It says our only friends are stone gargoyles, that we are never ordinary people but only monsters or superheroes; that no matter how heroic we are, we will never have a loving, romantic relationship." She added "I and others with disabilities fear that the release of this film and Disney's accompanying marketing blitz will increase the ridicule encountered by both disabled children and adults." The late Paul Longmore, a San Francisco State University professor who had a curved spine and paralyzed arms as a result of a bout with childhood polio, said, "I have had children recoil from me because they have seen movies that taught them to fear or pity anyone who looked like me. Unfortunately, Disney's *Hunchback* may increase these negative attitudes."[34]

Sadly, the concerns of Henkoff, Theriault, Wolfe, Longmore, and other PWDs about Disney's *Hunchback* turned out to be justified. Particularly troubling was a British Film Institute report that the term "hunchback," which had largely fallen out of use in the United Kingdom, made an unwelcome comeback in the six months following the release of Disney's film in that country; people with kyphosis or scoliosis were now having that disparaging term flung at them again. Worse, the U.K. witnessed an upsurge in physical attacks on PWDs. The British Scoliosis Society complained to Nicholas Scott, the Minister of Disabled People, that people with scoliosis had been the targets of more than one hundred assaults in the months following the release of the Disney film, whereas none had occurred in the six months prior.[35] There seems little question that the film helped fan the flames of prejudice and discrimination.

As I hope this essay has shown, the animated *Hunchback* is politically correct cinema at its worst. It seems to preach tolerance of society's Others while criticizing attempts to segregate and isolate them, yet it relies on age-old stereotypes and other forms of outdated thinking about PWDs to propel its narrative. I very much agree with Annalee Ward's remarks about the significant dissonance that exists between the film's surface story and its subtext:

> The overt messages of the film are strong: "It is what's inside that matters," but the subtext does not always support this idea. It is that conflict between the overt and the subtle that makes for a confusing and morally ineffective film; the subtext obfuscates the main theme by making it more complex and, in some instances, working against it. For example, the message that Quasi has character where it counts—inside—is countered by the message that people are afraid of him and cheer when he is pilloried and subjected to cruel tauntings and being pelted with rotten vegetables. The film thus illustrates, right or wrong, that looks do matter—at least initially.[36]

If there is anything resembling a "happy ending" or a saving grace to the rather dismal scenario surrounding Disney's *Hunchback of Notre Dame*, it comes from an unlikely source: the film's direct-to-video sequel, *The Hunchback of Notre Dame II* (2002). Produced by Disney's TV animation division, the unit responsible for the inexpensive, lower-quality productions geared toward the 4-to-8-year-old crowd, *Hunchback II* was released simultaneously with the DVD edition of the first Disney *Hunchback* film. Clocking in at a mere 68 minutes and featuring rather flat songs, a cut-rate villain, and a timeworn story about a crooked traveling circus, the film nevertheless accomplishes something that hardly ever occurs in Hollywood disability-themed films; it raises the very distinct possibility that its disabled character might have a fulfilling romantic life. Quasi meets Madellaine, a young woman who dreams of becoming a famous tightrope walker but has been forced into servitude by the corrupt owner of a circus. She is initially repulsed by Quasi's appearance, but after she sees that he has a way with children (he and Zephyr—the young son of Esmeralda and Phoebus—are fast friends) she finds him more appealing. After the requisite number of misunderstandings and moments of jeopardy, and much to Disney's credit, *Hunchback II* concludes by creating the strong impression that its disabled character is not doomed to a life of isolation. The only thing pitiable about the film from a DS perspective is that it was directed only toward very young children. Nevertheless, the kids who saw it got the message that disabled people can indeed lead lives full of acceptance and love—and not just platonic love—and that's an important start.

Notes

1. Disney's plan to produce two films based on the Hugo novel is noted in Kirk Honeycutt, "Disney Double for 'Hunchback,'" *Hollywood Reporter*, 19–21 Aug. 1994, 41. Disney may have dropped the live-action project because competing companies TNT and Todd-AO/TAE Productions had announced similar productions.

2. Published in 1944, the *Classics Illustrated* comic book based on the Hugo novel went through numerous printings and featured a variety of cover designs. Number 18 in the CI series, it was adapted by Howard Hendrix and illustrated by R. Crandall and George Evans.

3. With any Disney film, there is always a question of authorship beyond the general level of the studio itself. It is widely acknowledged that Disney production executive Jeffrey Katzenberg exerted enormous influence during the studio's animation "rebirth" in the late 1980s and gained notoriety for micromanaging productions during his tenure. At the time of Hunchback's development, however, Katzenberg was involved in a very messy split with Disney and went on to help form a rival company, DreamWorks SKG. His departure left a significant void in executive oversight, and as a result Hahn, Trousdale, and Wise enjoyed an unusual degree of autonomy while making their film. As Wise noted at the time of the film's release: "We actually got to make a lot of huge creative leaps with very little executive attention, which was kind of fun." It is therefore reasonable to assume that Hunchback is far more the product of its producer-director team than were the Katzenberg-era Disney films that preceded it. For more information on the Katzenberg departure and its ramifications for the Hunchback team, see John Clark, "With Katzenberg Gone, It's a Whole New World," *Los Angeles Times*, 16 June 1996, 86.

4. In Japan, where the term "hunchback" had been banned from television for years because of its offensiveness, the film's title was changed to *The Bells of Notre Dame*. However, Disney used the closest approximations of "hunchback" in the titles of the versions marketed to French- and Spanish-speaking audiences: *Le Bossu de Notre Dame* and *El Jorobado de Notre Dame*, respectively.

5. Victor Hugo, *The Hunchback of Notre-Dame*, trans. Catherine Liu (New York: Modern Library, 2004), 148.

6. Disney's *Hunchback of Notre Dame* Press Kit, 29, as cited in Annalee R. Ward, *Mouse Morality: The Rhetoric of Disney Animated Film* (Austin: University of Texas Press, 2002), 69.

7. For a sampling of the many scholarly works that have addressed the various models noted in the text, see Lennard J. Davis, ed., *The Disability Studies Reader*, 3d ed. (New York: Routledge, 2010); Tobin Siebers, *Disability Theory* (Ann Arbor: University of Michigan Press, 2008); Rosemarie Garland Thomson, *Extraordinary Bodies* (New York: Columbia University Press, 1996); Ann Pointon and Chris Davies, eds., *Framed: Interrogating Disability in the Media* (London: British Film Institute, 1997); Hector Avalos, Sarah J. Melcher, and Jeremy Schipper, eds., *This Abled Body: Rethinking Disabilities in Biblical Studies* (Atlanta: Society of Biblical Literature, 2007); and Mike Oliver, *Understanding Disability: From Theory to Practice* (New York: St. Martin's Press, 1996).

8. See http://www.statemaster.com/encyclopedia/The-Hunchback-of-Notre-Dame-(film) for an accounting of key details. See also Ward, 58–61.

9. Wise cited in Anne Thompson and David Karger, "Playing a Hunch," *Entertainment Weekly*, 21 June 1996 http://www.ew.com/ew/article/0,,293046,00.html; Hahn cited in Todd Camp, "'Hunchback' Shows a Different Side of Disney," *Fort Worth Star-Telegram*, n.d., n.p., reprinted in http://www.frollozone.org/interviews.html.

10. Hahn cited in John Clark, "A Quasi Original," *Los Angeles Times*, 16 June 1996, 6.

11. See the subtitle for Clark, "Quasi," 6.

12. Clark, "Quasi," 6.

13. For more information on the visibly different person—the "freak"—in popular culture, see Rosemary Garland Thomson, ed., *Freakery: Cultural Spectacles of the Extraordinary Body* (New York: New York University Press, 1996); Robert Bogdan, *Freak Show: Presenting Human Oddities for Amusement and Profit* (Chicago: University of Chicago Press, 1988); and Rachel Adams, *Sideshow U.S.A.: Freaks and the American Cultural Imagination* (Chicago: University of Chicago Press, 2001).

14. Trousdale cited in Clark, "Quasi," 6.

15. Thompson and Karger.

16. Baxter cited in Thompson and Karger; Wise cited in Clark, "Quasi," 6.

17. Hulce cited in John Horn, "Will Disney's '*Hunchback of Notre Dame*' Scare Young Children?"

Associated Press, as published in *Lawrence Journal-World*, 20 June 1996, D-6. Hulce's relief upon seeing the final Quasi designs says something about his expectations; he found the animation to be "much less monstrous—I was surprised how tame he was."

18. The Disney version is one of the exceedingly few adaptations to follow Hugo's lead on this point. The principal actors who have played Quasimodo in live-action films—Lon Chaney, Charles Laughton, Anthony Quinn, Anthony Hopkins, Mandy Patinkin—were all forty or older when they did so.

19. Hugo, 146.

20. Kimbrough cited in Jeanne Wolf, "Taken for Granite," *TV Guide*, 6 July 1996, 36.

21. Schneider cited in Clark, "Quasi," 6; Baxter cited in John Cutter, "Hunchback Quasimodo Has a Real-Life Disease," *St. Petersburg Times*, 9 July 1996, D-1.

22. Kenneth Turan, "Quasi-Adult Quasimodo," *Los Angeles Times*, 21 June 1996, entertainment sect., 1. For more information on the Raspberry Ripple awards and the "One in Eight Group" that bestows them, see http://www.prnewswire.co.uk/cgi/news/release?id=24074.

23. Patt Morrison, "These Stories Are Classics for a Reason," *Los Angeles Times*, 21 June 1996, F-10.

24. Martin F. Norden, "Tiny Tim on Screen: A Disability Studies Perspective," in *Dickens on Screen*, ed. John Glavin (Cambridge: Cambridge University Press, 2003), 196.

25. For a brief study of the Chaney film, see Martin F. Norden, *The Cinema of Isolation: A History of Physical Disability in the Movies* (New Brunswick, NJ: Rutgers University Press, 1994), 89–92. Further discussions of the general disability stereotypes noted in this essay occur throughout the Norden text. Laurie E. Harnick provided a useful tracing of Quasimodo's cinematic evolution in her "Lost and Found in Translation: The Changing Face of Disability in the Film Adaptations of Hugo's Notre Dame de Paris: 1482," in *Screening Disability: Essays on Cinema and Disability*, ed. Christopher R. Smit and Anthony Enns (Lanham, MD: University Press of America, 2001), 87–95.

26. Jeremy Gerard, rev. of *The Hunchback of Notre Dame*, *Variety*, 17 June 1996, n.p.; Schneider cited in Judy Brennan, "Disney Defense Dept.: A 'Hunch' There May Be Criticism," *Los Angeles Times*, 2 June 1996, 22. As questionable as Quasimodo's representation is—the beastly connotations, the Sweet Innocent quality, etc.—it could have been much worse. Floyd Norman, a Hunchback animator, noted a number of scenes that had been dropped from the final film. They included, in his words, "Brenda Chapman's wonderful introduction to the mysterious Quasimodo lurking in the shadows. Children in the streets of Paris tell scary stories of the 'monster' in the bell tower, and the audience eagerly anticipates the first appearance of the Hunchback." Norman also noted that he "storyboarded a wacky pub sequence where Quasimodo, disguised as an 'ugly woman' is hit on by a drunken patron. Eventually, the hunchback reveals himself and the drunk swears off booze forever." Norman cited in "Toon Tuesday: Looking Back on Disney's *The Hunchback of Notre Dame*—Part Deux" jimhillmedia.com/blogs/floyd_norman/archive/2008/11/18/toon-tuesday-looking-back-on-disney-s-the-hunchback-of-notre-dame-part-deux.aspx.

27. Horn, D-6; Jami Bernard, "This 'Hunchback' Is a Hump Dinger!" *New York Daily News*, 21 June 1996, n.p.

28. Wise cited in Horn, D-6; for the publicity quote, see disney.go.com/vault/archives/characters/quasimodo/quasimodo.html. Wise's final sentence is of course open to debate. In this same article, Horn notes that Quasi's appearance and public humiliation scenes "sent some tearful 4-year-olds bolting for the lobby" during early screenings. As for the press release, I can't help but wonder if its author was using the phrase "put down" to imply that Quasi was comparable to a sickly or troublesome animal about to be "put down" by a veterinarian.

29. Hahn cited in Camp; Wise cited in Thompson and Karger.

30. Schneider and the unnamed Universal executive cited in Brennan, 22.

31. Green cited in "Disney Says No to Disability Consultants," *One Step Ahead*, 16 Jan. 1995, 4; Trousdale and Wise cited in Clark, "Quasi," 6.

32. Sanford M. Litvack, letter to Paul Spudich, 6 Oct. 1994.

33. Sanford M. Litvack, letter to Paul Spudich, 8 Dec. 1994.

34. Carole Henkoff, "Disney's 'Hunchback'; Not Quite Fun and Games," *New York Times*, 28 July 1996, 2–31; Alana Theriault, "Don't Need Your Pity," *San Francisco Chronicle*, 1 July 1996, n.p.; Kathi Wolfe, "Disney's Feel-Good 'Hunchback' Offends Disabled," *Milwaukee Journal Sentinel*, 7 July 1996, n.p.; Longmore cited in Wolfe.

35. "Distorted Images?" http://www.bfi.org.uk/education/teaching/disability/introduction/ distortedimages.html.
36. Ward, 77.

Bibliography

Adams, Rachel. *Sideshow U.S.A.: Freaks and the American Cultural Imagination.* Chicago: University of Chicago Press, 2001.
Avalos, Hector, Sarah J. Melcher, and Jeremy Schipper, eds. *This Abled Body: Rethinking Disabilities in Biblical Studies.* Atlanta: Society of Biblical Literature, 2007.
Bernard, Jami. "This 'Hunchback' Is a Hump Dinger!" *New York Daily News,* 21 June 1996, n.p.
Bogdan, Robert. *Freak Show: Presenting Human Oddities for Amusement and Profit.* Chicago: University of Chicago Press, 1988.
Brennan, Judy. "Disney Defense Dept.: A 'Hunch' There May Be Criticism." *Los Angeles Times,* 2 June 1996, p. 22.
Camp, Todd. "'Hunchback' Shows a Different Side of Disney." *Fort Worth Star-Telegram,* n.d., n.p., reprinted in http://www.frollozone.org/interviews.html.
Clark, John. "With Katzenberg Gone, It's a Whole New World." *Los Angeles Times,* 16 June 1996, p. 86.
_____. "A Quasi Original." *Los Angeles Times,* 16 June 1996, p. 6.
Cutter, John. "Hunchback Quasimodo Has a Real-Life Disease." *St. Petersburg Times,* 9 July 1996, sect. D, p. 1.
Davis, Lennard J., ed. *The Disability Studies Reader.* 3rd ed. New York: Routledge, 2010.
"Disney Says No to Disability Consultants." *One Step Ahead,* 16 Jan. 1995, p. 4.
"Distorted Images?" http://www.bfi.org.uk/education/teaching/disability/introduction/ distortedimages.html.
Gerard, Jeremy. Rev. of *The Hunchback of Notre Dame, Variety,* 17 June 1996, p. 16.
Harnick, Laurie E. "Lost and Found in Translation: The Changing Face of Disability in the Film Adaptations of Hugo's *Notre Dame de Paris: 1482.*" In *Screening Disability: Essays on Cinema and Disability,* edited by Christopher R. Smit and Anthony Enns, 87–95. Lanham, MD: University Press of America, 2001.
Henkoff, Carole. "Disney's 'Hunchback'; Not Quite Fun and Games." *New York Times,* 28 July 1996, sect. 2, p. 31.
Honeycutt, Kirk. "Disney Double for 'Hunchback.'" *Hollywood Reporter,* 19–21 Aug. 1994, p. 41.
Horn, John. "Will Disney's *Hunchback of Notre Dame* Scare Young Children?" *Associated Press,* as published in *Lawrence Journal-World,* 20 June 1996, p. 6D.
Hugo, Victor. *The Hunchback of Notre-Dame.* Translated by Catherine Liu. New York: Modern Library, 2004.
"*The Hunchback of Notre Dame.*" http://www.statemaster.com/encyclopedia/The-Hunchback-of-Notre-Dame-(film).
Morrison, Patt. "These Stories Are Classics for a Reason." *Los Angeles Times,* 21 June 1996, p. F10.
Norden, Martin F. *The Cinema of Isolation: A History of Physical Disability in the Movies.* New Brunswick, NJ: Rutgers University Press, 1994.
_____. "Tiny Tim on Screen: A Disability Studies Perspective." In *Dickens on Screen,* edited by John Glavin, 188–198. Cambridge: Cambridge University Press, 2003.
Oliver, Mike. *Understanding Disability: From Theory to Practice.* New York: St. Martin's Press, 1996.

Pointon, Ann, and Chris Davies, eds. *Framed: Interrogating Disability in the Media.* London: British Film Institute, 1997.

"Quasimodo." disney.go.com/vault/archives/characters/quasimodo/quasimodo.html.

Siebers, Tobin. *Disability Theory.* Ann Arbor: University of Michigan Press, 2008.

Theriault, Alana. "Don't Need Your Pity." *San Francisco Chronicle*, 1 July 1996, n.p.

Thompson, Anne, and David Karger. "Playing a Hunch." *Entertainment Weekly*, 21 June 1996 http://www.ew.com/ew/article/0,,293046,00.html.

Thomson, Rosemarie Garland. *Extraordinary Bodies: Figuring Physical Disability in American Culture and Literature.* New York: Columbia University Press, 1997.

_____, ed. *Freakery: Cultural Spectacles of the Extraordinary Body.* New York: New York University Press, 1996.

"Toon Tuesday: Looking Back on Disney's *The Hunchback of Notre Dame*—Part Deux" //jimhillmedia.com/blogs/floyd_norman/archive/2008/11/18/toon-tuesday-looking-back-on-disney-s-the-hunchback-of-notre-dame-part-deux.aspx.

Turan, Kenneth. "Quasi-Adult Quasimodo." *Los Angeles Times*, 21 June 1996, entertainment sect., p. 1.

Ward, Annalee R. *Mouse Morality: The Rhetoric of Disney Animated Film.* Austin: University of Texas Press, 2002.

Wolf, Jeanne. "Taken for Granite." *TV Guide*, 6 July 1996, p. 36.

Wolfe, Kathi. "Disney's Feel-Good 'Hunchback' Offends Disabled." *Milwaukee Journal Sentinel*, 7 July 1996, n.p.

Dopey's Legacy: Stereotypical Portrayals of Intellectual Disability in the Classic Animated Films

Karen Schwartz, Zana Marie Lutfiyya and Nancy Hansen

Disney's first animated film, *Snow White and the Seven Dwarfs*,[1] was based upon the Grimm brothers' fairy tale, *Little Snow-White*.[2] The original story included seven dwarfs but did not individualize them.[3] In the Disney version, the dwarfs have names, personalities and distinct features and characteristics. The seventh dwarf, Dopey, is characterized as an "idiot,"[4] "mentally retarded,"[5] and with "Down's syndrome-like features,"[6] and was entirely a Disney fabrication. The purpose of this chapter is to critically explore the character of Dopey in the context of stereotypical portrayals and imaging of people with intellectual disabilities.

Although Dopey will serve as our frame of reference, we will also consider two other Disney characters: Gus, the mouse in the 1950s film *Cinderella*[7] and Gaston's sidekick, LeFou in the 1991 version of *Beauty and the Beast*.[8] We have chosen these characters for several reasons. First, they all have a large enough role in their respective films to allow for a proper analysis. Second, these characters span a period of over seventy years, from 1937 to 2007. Third, some of these characters either re-appear in sequels or the original film is re-released, thus reinforcing continuity over the decades. And finally, all of the characters we have chosen were envisioned and created in a unique way by Disney which differed from the original text in a significant way. Dopey, Gus and Le Fou are all characters who, beneath the surface of their seemingly benign presence, foster and perpetuate largely negative messages about intellectual disability[9] that are harmful and damaging to the individuals so labelled.

For over 70 years, Disney has played an integral role in North American popular culture by creating full-length animated feature films that have been enjoyed "intergenerationally" and are "quite likely a part of most children's lives in the U.S."[10] However, these films are so much more than simply entertaining. As Giroux explains, they "possess at least as much cultural authority and legitimacy for teaching roles, values, and ideals as more traditional sites of learning."[11] For our purposes, examining Disney films allows us to "scrutinize" their "cultural and social messages"[12] to get a better understanding of how society perceives and responds to people who are different.

In their examination of race, racialization, and sexuality in films by Disney, Pixar and Dreamworks, Lugo-Lugo and Bloodsworth-Lugo suggest that film narratives serve to reinforce ideologies, thus creating stories which are "powerful agents of socialization" and also "provide children with the necessary tools to reinforce expectations about normalized racial and sexual dynamics."[13] We propose to extend this analysis to considerations of intellectual disability. We think it is important to examine how certain portrayals in Disney movies stress the need to conform to normalized, typical or even stereotypical expectations of intelligence and intellectual ability, by creating characters with intellectual disabilities who we both laugh at and distance ourselves from.

Devaluation, Stigma and Devalued Social Roles

In societies, we generally have a tendency to evaluate people, often characterizing others in either positive or negative ways.[14] In understanding how people evaluate and form judgements about others, it is important to remember that what we actually observe about someone is only part of the process.[15] Two other important factors that play a role in how we judge people include a) any past experiences we might have had either with the person we are actually observing or with a group with whom we associate that person; and b) our social environment.[16] The social environment means the "values, expectations, norms [and] conventions" our society holds about certain people or groups of people.[17] We argue that film portrayals are important in this context because past experience may, in fact, be influenced by exposure to certain movie characters. Movies are also crucial to the creation and perpetuation of our social environment.

When we evaluate someone negatively, we are devaluing that individual. In making these kinds of judgements, we tend to devalue the people who have characteristics that we find to be undesirable.[18] A negative characteristic can also be referred to as a "stigma" or "an attribute that is deeply discrediting."[19] The significance of being branded in this way means that "we believe the person with a stigma is not quite human. On this assumption we exercise varieties of discrimination, through which we effectively, if often unthinkingly, reduce [the perceived's] life chances,"[20] or the opportunities available during the course of one's life. In the context of people with intellectual disabilities, to be stigmatized or devalued as such "is to have one's moral worth and human value called into question."[21]

How is a person's humanness and worth challenged? Wolfensberger suggests that people with intellectual disabilities, as devalued people, have historically tended to be cast in a number of "negative social roles."[22] We will look at several of these roles[23] to see how they are described and how these roles are historically linked to ways in which people with intellectual disabilities were treated. We will then use this framework or iconography to analyze the Disney characters.

The first role we discuss is that of the non-human or sub-human animal and that of the "other."[24] This characterization leads to the perception of devalued people as "having primitive, animalistic feelings and behaviors."[25] The notion of whether or not people with intellectual disabilities were truly human can be traced as far back as Plato and Aristotle, who considered the ability to reason a key to being human, and called into question the humanness of those who could not.[26]

Although these ideas may seem antiquated, consider the following description of institutional life in the 1800s. Residents were

> more frequently than not either naked or covered in rags, placed in narrow, dark, damp cells ... with no bedding except a little straw ... without fresh air, without light, without water ... and chained in caves which would not have been thought good enough for wild beasts.[27]

Equally dismal descriptions were exposed in the United States in the second half of the twentieth century.[28]

Wolfensberger also notes the prevalence of the role of object of ridicule where people with intellectual disabilities are "made the butt of jokes, laughed at, teased and tormented for other people's amusement."[29] Historically, such people were commonly known as fools[30] or village idiots. Winzer notes that, as long ago as ancient Rome, people with intellectual disabilities were sometimes kept "as a fool for the amusement of the household and its guests."[31] This practice continued through the Middle Ages and Renaissance when such individuals were "procured for amusement or other home purposes."[32] In the later part of the 19th century and into the twentieth, freak shows stressed the role of object of ridicule by emphasizing characteristics who were "exaggerated into caricatures of the grotesque."[33]

The final role that we will focus on is that of the "eternal child" who "never matures into adult status and competence, and whose behaviors, interests, capabilities, etc., will always remain at a childish level."[34] The characterization of people with intellectual disabilities as children also has a long history. For example, in England in the 13th century people with intellectual disabilities were defined as individuals of "retarded intellectual development whose mental capacities never progressed beyond that of a child."[35] Such thinking continues today where references to adults with intellectual disabilities as having the "mental age" of a baby or child are common.[36] In fact, many parent narratives have reinforced the "eternal child" role.

Iconography of Intellectual Disability

For many people who have no direct knowledge of or experience with disability, popular films become "a major information source on the very nature of disabilities."[37] If the portrayals of intellectual disability in film reinforce many negative stereotypes, the prejudicial assumptions that are imbedded in the movie become harmful to the individuals so labelled. This perpetuation means that people come to misunderstand and even fear individuals with disabilities, resulting in "their systematic, intentional exclusion from society."[38]

A few authors have written about different film characters who have had intellectual disabilities, and the ones we sample here are not meant to be an exhaustive list. Lennie, in the film *Of Mice and Men*, has been described by Devlieger, Baz & Drazen as an animal and as a child.[39] Several other portrayals have also included the role of the child, such as Karl in *Sling Blade*, Dominick in *Dominick and Eugene*, Salomon in *The Hand That Rocks the Cradle*[40] and Forrest in *Forrest Gump*.[41]

Images or iconography signal to the viewer that the character has an intellectual disability, without such a statement ever needing to be expressly made. In an examination of recent film characters, Kimpton-Nye illustrates this concept. Forrest Gump has a "seriously short haircut," a shirt "uncomfortably buttoned up at the neck, white socks with coloured hoops and a pair of bedraggled training shoes."[42] When Forrest speaks, he has a "'stupid-sounding' drawl" and his overall presentation is the portrayal of "a man-child, a loveable fool, an incorruptible 'simpleton.'"[43] Even the name "Gump" means "a foolish person, a dolt."[44]

The two main characters in the film *Dumb and Dumber*, Lloyd and Harry, are also carefully described. One has a "nerdy" haircut, a goofy smile exposing a chipped front tooth, and runs with "his legs sticking out sideways." The other has a "dishevelled mop of hair, scuffed black shoes, white socks, scruffy track suit bottoms, a T-shirt and a dirty hooded sweatshirt." He walks hunched over and with a shuffle. "Both Lloyd and Harry come across to the viewer as awkward, stupid schoolboys."[45]

Kimpton-Nye has also described Lennie in a newer version of *Of Mice and Men*. He wears

> a large, floppy cloth cap, a scruffy denim jacket and, most importantly, massive baggy dungarees ... he has a quizzical look on his face. His mouth is always open in "dumb" amazement. His eyes dart back and forth, always struggling to comprehend what is going on.[46]

We will now turn our attention to the iconography of intellectual disability using the classic animated Disney characters of Dopey, Gus and Le Fou to illustrate our points.

The Characters

Snow White's Dopey

In the Grimms' tale, *Little Snow-White*, the dwarfs are not described or named and nothing distinguishes the seventh dwarf from the other six. In the Disney version of the fairy tale, the seventh dwarf, Dopey, is significantly different than the other dwarfs. He was the most challenging dwarf to create because Disney felt he was the character they were "depending upon to carry most of the belly laughs."[47] In creating Dopey, Walt Disney commented that animators "tried to make him too much of an imbecile, which was not what we had in mind."[48] Gabler suggests that Walt Disney himself "contributed to this notion" by describing Dopey as "slow at figuring things out.... Dopey can't even get the spoon right."[49] The character was also described in the creation process as having "a kid personality with small nose and eyes fairly large with a little outward slant to make them elfish" and as "sort of childish."[50] In the end, the creators had a "breakthrough" when they began to think of Dopey "not as an elf or as an innocent or as a child but as a 'human with dog mannerisms and intellect.'"[51] Although Walt Disney used the name Dopey to suggest the character was "a little off-beat,"[52] according to the Oxford English Dictionary, "dopey" means stupid or dumb.[53]

Notwithstanding Walt Disney's assertion, when watching *Snow White* it becomes clear that Dopey is an amalgamation of all of these conceptualizations and bears resemblance to several of Wolfensberger's devalued roles, including the sub-human animal and Other, the object of ridicule and the eternal child. In fact, all of these roles are alluded to in Disney's various discussions about Dopey. His animal-like characteristics include a tongue that protrudes like a dog, drooling, panting, moving on all fours, large ears that wiggle, and an ability to make noises but not speech. As Happy explains to Snow White, "he don't talk none ... he don't know, he never tried." In one scene, Dopey has a chain of pots stuck to his rear end, swinging like a tail when he walks. When he gets wet, he shakes the water off like a dog. Later he chases an elusive bar of soap, getting down on all fours, with his behind in the air like an animal waiting to pounce.

Dopey is also depicted as being "other." When the dwarfs march in step, Dopey is never in step with them. He carries his hoe on the opposite shoulder and often lags behind the group, running to catch up. When the dwarfs huddle to discuss things, Dopey is not part of the group. He is the last dwarf to do everything, except when he is pushed to the front to be first at the undesirable or dangerous tasks. When the dwarfs decide someone needs to go upstairs to see who is in their cottage, Dopey is grabbed and shoved forward to investigate, proving he is the most dispensable in the group. When the dwarfs run out of the cottage thinking a monster is chasing them, they slam the door on Dopey before he has a chance to escape with them. He gets flung back into the pots and pans and emerges covered in them, looking like a monster. He is also physically the Other. While six of the dwarfs have brown eyes, Dopey's eyes are blue. Interestingly, Faulkner's "idiot" in *The Kingdom of God* and his character Benjy in *The Sound and the Fury*, both had eyes that are described as cornflower blue.[54] Peavy argues that blue eyes are symbolic of innocence, naïveté and simple mindedness, all characteristics shared by Dopey.[55] In her analysis of Disney cartoon characters and eye colour, Arcus also notes that "blue-eyed characters tend to portray vulnerability."[56]

Many scenes show Dopey as an object of ridicule. When the dwarfs are in the mine, Dopey puts gems in his eyes, sticks out his tongue, wiggles his ears and grins, which make him look stupid. In response, Doc shows his disapproval by hitting Dopey on the head. Dopey's eyes roll around in their sockets and appear crossed on a number of occasions. He is the "punching bag" for the other dwarfs, as he is repeatedly stepped on when others climb over him. At one point he gets beat up by the other dwarfs who think he is a monster. Later he ends up with a pot stuck on his foot, giving him a ridiculous gait when he walks. Even without the pot, when he walks, he often trips, making his gait seem much different than the other dwarfs. He also gets his head stuck in the railing, falls down the stairs and skips and pirouettes, making him look silly. When he smiles, his big grin is clearly "dopey."

Of all the dwarfs, Dopey is the most child-like. He looks like a baby, with no beard, only a few short hairs springing from his head, and a lone top tooth. He often has a dreamy look in his eyes, as if he is not paying attention. His actions are also very child-like. When he gets tangled up with Doc, he ends up in Doc's lap, with his arms around Doc's neck, grinning broadly. He cries on Doc's shoulder as Snow White lies sleeping under the witch's spell and later wipes his mouth on his sleeve, as many young children do. In the scene after Snow White and the dwarfs sing and dance, Dopey lies curled up, asleep like a baby. His oversized clothing adds to the overall image of a bunting bag, with a flowing coat and sleeves that are too long and hang over his hands.

Western society often equates intellectual disability with incompetence.[57] Dopey is shown to be incompetent in many ways throughout the film. When he has a job to do, he often has trouble carrying out even simple tasks. His job in the mines involves the menial task of sweeping up. After a day's work, Dopey tosses not only his bag into the vault, but also himself. He then forgets to leave the vault key on its hook. When the dwarfs return home and notice something amiss in their cottage, they tiptoe inside, only to have Dopey loudly bang the door shut. The others "shush" him, and he then turns and "shushes" the door. When the dwarfs are washing up before dinner, Dopey has trouble holding the soap, as it keeps slipping from his grasp. He ends up swallowing it and hiccupping bubbles, unaware of what has transpired. The idea of Dopey's incompetence hits home most clearly during this scene. He gets dunked in the water and when he tries to expel the water by putting a finger in his mouth, the water shoots out of both ears. When he swallows the bar of soap, his head disappears and a giant bubble emerges in its place. Both images imply nothing but an empty head.

The movie itself was a huge success, with critics lavishing praise and audiences of over 20 million people.[58] In his discussion of the film, Maltin specifically mentions "Dopey's marvellous expressions, tongue protruding from the side of his mouth ... eyes rolling in carefree abandon."[59] Halliwell says that Dopey is occasionally "pushed beyond the role of comic foil" when he is "transformed" into Snow White's dancing partner and when he twice receives a kiss goodbye from Snow White.[60] He claims that Dopey's role "is ambiguous and far from easy to classify."[61] We disagree with both of these analyses, arguing that this portrayal and others like it, have had and continue to have a significantly negative impact on the lives of those people living with an intellectual disability.

Cinderella's Gus (Octavius)

In 1950, thirteen years after *Snow White*, Disney released *Cinderella*, another full length classic feature film, based on Charles Perrault's tale *Cinderella or The Little Glass Slipper*.[62] In the original work, animals do not play a central role. Mice are featured only briefly as the creatures who are transformed into Cinderella's horses. In the Disney version, mice and birds are major characters and appear as Cinderella's friends. One of those mice is Octavius, who is given the nickname Gus, or "Gus Gus" as he is often called. Gus is different from the other mice in the film, and nowhere is this more evident than his juxtaposition against his friend and protector, Jaq. Gus is separated out from the rest of the mice as "other," portrayed largely in the role of the child, and clearly stands out as someone who is incompetent.

Like Dopey, Gus is presented as the "other." He is a chubby mouse, whose t-shirt fails to cover his belly, whereas the other mice are lean and wear clothing that fits. He speaks in a low register which differs from the high squeaky voices of the other mice, stutters when he talks and is the most difficult mouse character to understand. When the mice are in groups, Gus is often standing apart, trying to peek around others and, like Dopey, his place is last in line.

Gus was created with several mannerisms that make him appear very child-like. He is often seen putting his finger to his mouth; he sticks out his tongue and giggles; he tends to repeat words and phrases, including the oft-spoken "duh"; and in many scenes, he is waving and clapping his hands together, which comes across as childish. Because he often shouts things out at inappropriate times, Jaq and the others are always "shushing" him. It is clear throughout the film that Jaq looks after Gus, sometimes leading him by the hand, at other times pushing or pulling him along and often stepping in to rescue him.

Gus' childish mannerisms are reinforced by his actions in the film. Two detailed scenes focus on Gus in the role of the child. In one scene near the beginning of the film, Cinderella has announced breakfast time. The mice gather to head for the courtyard to eat. When they see the cat blocking their way outside, they turn back and run into the mouse hole for cover. Gus presses on, clearly not understanding the danger, although he has been warned about the cat. The other mice grab him and pull him to safety, pushing him to the end of the line. Through a "drawing of straws" using tails, Jaq is chosen to distract the cat. When Jaq realizes he has drawn the "short tail," he looks worried. Gus misunderstands what has happened and shakes Jaq's hand enthusiastically, congratulating him as if Jaq has won a prize. This clearly distinguishes him from the other mice, who take off their hats and hold them to their chests, bow their heads and look scared while ominous music plays in the background. The reaction of the other mice, coupled with the music, reinforce the inappropriateness of Gus' reaction to the situation.

After the danger with the cat has passed, Gus and three other mice go to collect their corn pieces. One young mouse collects two pieces of corn, drops one in a scramble to escape the cat and leaves it to run for safety. Gus, who has collected many pieces of corn, drops his as well, as he is carrying too many. Rather than leave them, as the other young mouse has done, he tries repeatedly to pick up all his pieces, notwithstanding the danger of the cat's presence. Although the young mouse learned his lesson quickly, Gus does not. He continues to struggle to get every piece, relying on Jaq's cunning to distract the cat for as long as possible. This scene implies that Gus simply cannot learn from his mistakes and will forever be stuck in this child-like role, requiring others to look out for him and to rescue him from danger.

In another scene, the birds and mice have worked hard to re-create Cinderella's gown for her so she can attend the ball. When she is finally finished all of her chores, she tiredly climbs the stairs to her attic room. As she opens the door, she is greeted by the birds and mice. The birds open the wardrobe to reveal the completed dress while the mice yell "surprise!" Gus, in his excitement, misunderstands the occasion and yells "happy birthday!" This confused utterance again shows the difficulty Gus has in appropriately responding to common social situations. In reaction to Gus, Jaq turns to him with a stern and annoyed look, waves his arms and says crossly, "No, no, no, no!"

Another major characterization of Gus is as an incompetent. In one scene, Jaq signals to Gus and other mice who are about to play a prank on Lucifer. While the other mice react by nodding and laughing silently, Gus looks puzzled. He finally gets the joke and laughs loudly, for which he is scolded by his friends. When the mice are out in the yard getting breakfast, all the mice grab their corn but Gus cannot manage to get any food until Cinderella shoos away all the other animals and leaves a pile of corn only for him. In the scene where Jaq and Gus the steal a ribbon and necklace, Gus manages to bungle his job and ends up breaking the necklace, scattering the beads everywhere. Later on, as the Fairy Godmother turns the pumpkin into a coach, all the mice flee except Gus, who gets tangled in its vines. And finally, at the end of the film, when the mice throw rice at Cinderella's wedding, Gus decides to eats his instead, revealing yet another social miscue. All of these examples clearly reinforce the portrayal of Gus, not only as someone who is not competent, but as someone who will never fit in or be able to learn.

Beauty and the Beast's Lefou

In the classic abridged version of *Beauty and Beast* written by Jeanne-Marie Leprince de Beaumont in the 1700s, the main characters are Beauty, her unnamed father, brothers and sisters, and the Beast.[63] This is in stark contrast to the Disney film version, which features a host of characters including Gaston, Belle's potential suitor, and his sidekick, LeFou. In French, *fou* means mad or fool[64] and LeFou certainly lives up to his name. In the film, he is portrayed as an animal, an object of ridicule, a child-like figure and as incompetent.

LeFou is given several non-human-like characteristics. When he moves, he scampers like a small animal and waddles like a penguin. His nose is pink, round and pig-like. This is emphasized in a scene where Gaston flings him into a muddy pond and he emerges, covered in dirty water, next to a pig. As the pig and LeFou turn to each other, their similarities are strikingly reinforced. LeFou is often seen with his tongue hanging out and Gaston constantly carries him around as one would carry an animal.

His role as "other" is emphasized in several scenes. Near the beginning of the film, Gaston hits LeFou on the head. This makes is a very hollow sound, implying that LeFou's head is empty of thought and reason. In another scene, Gaston and LeFou are paying Belle a surprise visit so that Gaston can propose to her. As they hide in the bushes, Gaston holds back the branch of a tree to get a better look at her cottage. When he lets go of the branch, it flings back, hitting LeFou in the face. As a result, his mouth is filled with the leaves from the branch, suggesting that he has nothing relevant or worthwhile to say. In yet another example outside Belle's cottage, Gaston orders LeFou to wait outside in a snow bank until Belle and her father return. When they finally arrive home, LeFou is posing as a snowman and has frozen in the cold. This image of a blue-faced LeFou leaves the viewer with the feeling that he does not have the sense to come in from the cold, and also that it is acceptable to sacrifice him to the freezing elements because he has no real value or worth as a human being.

LeFou's most significant characterization is that of the object of ridicule. He is very short, has big gaps between his teeth, talks with a high, squeaky voice and giggles. In the first scene alone he is carried by his neck, dropped to the ground, has a rifle bounced on his head, and is squirted with a jet of water from a pump by a group of young women who do not even notice his presence. In a scene with Gaston and the townsmen in a tavern, LeFou is repeatedly hit, punched and thrown about the room. Chairs, benches and pots all get thrown at him. He pirouettes on his toes around the room, with eyes crossed and rolling in their sockets. At the end of the scene, he is squashed under Gaston's huge chair, where he remains pinned. In other scenes, he has a beer stein stuck on his face and winds up with a tuba stuck on his head.

The role of the child is also evident in the character of LeFou. For example, there are several times in film when LeFou is carrying steins of beer, with the intention of bringing one to Gaston and having one for himself. However, he never actually manages to actually drink his beer. As soon as he tries to take a sip, it either gets grabbed by another character or spilled, implying that LeFou is too young to be drinking. Also in the tavern scene, Gaston is shown juggling eggs and then popping them into his mouth. When LeFou tries to imitate Gaston, he throws his eggs up in the air and they all splatter onto his upturned face, making LeFou appear as an inept child compared to Gaston's feats of manliness. In the scene when Gaston tries to convince the villagers to join him in going after the Beast, LeFou gets scared by Gaston's words and hides behind a woman's apron. Once the mob reaches the Beast's castle, Gaston and several of the village men use a large tree trunk as a battering ram to break down the castle door. While they fight to gain entrance, LeFou stands beside them, reinforcing the image that he is not really a man, as they are, but a child who does not have the strength to do a man's job.

LeFou's incompetence is also illustrated throughout the film. At the beginning of the movie, he fails to catch a goose shot down by Gaston. Rather than catching the dead bird in his bag, it falls to ground. In the tavern, he flings a glass of beer in Gaston's face by mistake. For this he gets smacked by Gaston and is sent flying across the room. He ends up with a pot on his head which he cannot remove, much like Dopey. After Gaston's proposal to Belle, LeFou strikes up his band at the most inappropriate time, showing he lacks the common sense to think before he acts. He is a character who does not learn or succeed in any way, and clearly lacks competence to do even the simplest of tasks.

A Continuing Legacy

The dwarf characters in *Snow White* live on through DVDs, stuffed figures and other merchandise. Dopey himself remains Disney's most "loveable" dwarf.[65] The dwarfs were also used as a template for the Weasel Gang in the

1988 Disney film *Who Framed Roger Rabbit?*[66] In the film's audio commentary, screenwriter Peter Seaman describes the gang as a "mutant version of the Disney dwarfs."[67] One of the Weasel members, Stupid, was modelled after Dopey. He wears a striped t-shirt that is several sizes too small and a beanie cap with a propeller on top. His teeth stick out, as does his tongue. He has his finger in his mouth and wears sneakers whose laces are untied. Disney is releasing a high definition version of *Snow White* in 2009.

Cinderella is nearing its 60th anniversary. It has been released for home audiences as new generations continue to watch it. The film has been the impetus for two sequels, *Cinderella II: Dreams Come True*[68] and *Cinderella III: A Twist in Time.*[69] Both of these movies feature Gus, who appears unchanged. He continues to be led about and watched over by Jaq. In the opening scene of *Cinderella II* alone, Gus scampers after Jaq, drops his hat, crashes into Jaq and is "shushed" for talking too loudly. In both films he is portrayed as an incompetent child. He needs rescuing, falls behind, gets stuck, is chastised, and always struggles to catch up.

Beauty and Beast was such a successful film that it was nominated for an Academy Award for best picture, the first for an animated film. Disney re-released the movie in 2002 with additional footage. In 2010 a high definition version will be available.

Our analysis of Dopey, Gus and LeFou has revealed the creation and perpetuation of an audio-visual "language" or iconography of intellectual disability in animated Disney characters. As Wolfensberger's work suggests and our analysis demonstrates, this language is established in five ways, including (a) the language used about the character, (b) the physical appearance of the character, (c) the way the character is presented vis-à-vis other characters, (d) the role into which the character has been cast, and (e) the character's competencies (or lack thereof).

The language used is primarily focused on the names the characters are given, although this is not applicable to Gus. However, one need only consider the words "dope" and "fool" to realize what these particular characters are going to be like and the role they are going to play in the story.

The physical appearance of Dopey, Gus and LeFou are very telling. Facial expressions reveal few or oddly spaced teeth, rolling and crossed eyes, large ears, and protruding tongues. Speech and language is either not present, difficult to understand, or uttered in high, squeaky voices that do not resemble those of adults. In the case of Dopey and Gus, their clothing is ill-fitting. We wish to point out that a character's physical appearance includes his or her body, mannerisms and clothing. Often clothing and costumes are used as way of extending a character's portrayal. While actual body characteristics and clothing are two different elements to a character's appearance, both potentially carry information about who that character is. When combined, these elements serve to reinforce each other.

Both the language used and the physical appearance of these characters reinforces the perception that they are set apart from the other characters in the film. This status is also revealed in the ways they are physically distanced from other in group scenes: Dopey is often left out of conversations and planning with other dwarfs, Gus is not included in the group of mice when they make plans and LeFou is not part of the other patrons in the tavern scene. However, physical distance is only part of the story. All three characters are used as punching bags, teased and exposed to danger, suggesting subtly that these are acceptable ways in which to interact with individuals with intellectual disabilities.

Dopey, Gus and LeFou have simultaneously been cast into the roles of animal/other, child, object of ridicule and incompetent. The presentation of an adult character as having the characteristic of child-like naïveté reinforces the notion that the adult lacks intelligence. This kind of presentation serves to call into question the status of character as an adult and is one of the ways in which intellectual disability is portrayed in these films. In this essay, we have separated the role of the child from the role of the incompetent. However, the two roles are at times conflated because children are "typically considered as at least less competent than adults."[70] Competence refers more specifically to "the capacity or potential for adequate functioning-in-context as a socialized human."[71] This conflation is most apparent in the Gus character, although both roles are evident in all three films. Used together, the role of the child and the role of the incompetent convey and reinforce the imagery of intellectual disability.

If, as Safran argues, film portrayals of disability can serve to inform a naïve public about people with disabilities, then inaccurate portrayals can potentially create misunderstandings and foster prejudicial attitudes toward these individuals.[72] The children watching these films may not be able to distinguish between the apparently acceptable ways in which these characters are treated in the movies and ways in which classmates with intellectual disabilities are to be treated in school. Families watching Dopey, Gus and LeFou may not understand that people with intellectual disabilities can and do develop significant competencies in many areas of life.

The stereotypical portrayals Disney has created reinforce the historical patterns of treatment to which people with intellectual disabilities have been subjected. In recalling Walt Disney's protestations that Dopey was not supposed to be portrayed as an "imbecile," we argue that portrayals such as those described here are even more damning because the character need not be expressly described as having an intellectual disability. This message is clearly revealed by the characters' inherent traits which are so inexorably linked to intellectual disability in people's minds that direct reference is unnecessary as it is simply assumed. It is this likelihood that has the potential to cause the greatest damage.

Conclusion

Societal assumptions of incompetence lead to the development of policies and programs for people with intellectual disabilities that are segregationist and disabling. These perceptions foster misconceptions and rob people with intellectual disabilities of the chance to experience the depth and texture of life. We suggest that it is very dangerous to accept these kinds of portrayals without questioning why they exist and what purpose they serve. Therefore, the rationale of critical analysis is to encourage people to think about these issues and challenge stereotypical portrayals as a way of creating greater acceptance of and respect for difference in our society.

Acknowledgments

The authors wish to thank Ryan and Rebecca Sherbo for their contributions to this essay.

Notes

1. *Snow White and the Seven Dwarfs* (1937), DVD. Directed by David Hand (Burbank, CA: Walt Disney Home Entertainment, 2001).
2. Helen M. Arnold, "Snow White and the Seven Dwarfs: A Symbolic Account of Human Development," *Perspectives in Psychiatric Care* 17 (1979): 219.
3. Bruno Bettelheim, *The Uses of Enchantment: The Meaning and Importance of Fairy Tales* (New York: Alfred A. Knopf, 1976), 210.
4. Martin Halliwell, *Images of Idiocy: The Idiot Figure in Modern Fiction and Film* (Burlington, VT: Ashgate, 2004), 219.
5. Paul K. Longmore, "Screening Stereotypes: Images of Disabled People," *Social Policy* 16 (1985): 31.
6. Robert Bogdan and Douglas Biklen, "Handicapism," Social Policy 7 (1977): 16.
7. *Cinderella* (1950), DVD. Directed by Clyde Geronimi, Wilfred Jackson and Hamilton Luske (Burbank, CA: Walt Disney Home Entertainment, 2005).
8. *Beauty and the Beast* (1991), DVD. Directed by Gary Trousdale and Kirk Wise (Burbank, CA: Walt Disney Home Entertainment, 2002).
9. We use the term intellectual disability to refer to those individuals previously labelled over the course of history as fools, idiots, morons, imbeciles, mental defectives and the feeble-minded. The term most familiar to readers might be "mental retardation." Although this term is still in limited use, it is considered highly derogatory by the people so labelled and is being replaced by the term "intellectual disability." More information on terminology can be found on the American Association on Intellectual and Developmental Disabilities (AAIDD) website at: http://aaidd. org/content_104.cfm. More information on the elimination of the "r-word" can be found at: http://www.r-word.org/.
10. Mia A. Towbin et al., "Images of Gender, Race, Age, and Sexual Orientation in Disney Feature-Length Animated Films," *Journal of Feminist Family Therapy* 15 (2003): 24.
11. Henry A. Giroux, *The Mouse that Roared* (Lanham, MD: Rowman & Littlefield, 1999), 84.
12. *Ibid.*, 85.
13. Carmen R. Lugo-Lugo and Mary K. Bloodsworth-Lugo, "Race, Racialization, and Sexuality in Four Children's Animated Films by Disney, Pixar, and DreamWorks," *Cultural Studies Critical Methodologies* 9 (2009): 167–168.
14. Wolf Wolfensberger, *A Brief Introduction to Social Role Valorization: A High-Order Concept for Addressing the Plight of Societally Devalued People, and for Structuring Human Services* (Syracuse, NY: Training Institute for Human Service Planning, Leadership and Change Agentry, 1998), 3.
15. *Ibid.*, 34–37.

16. *Ibid.*, 35.
17. *Ibid.*, 35.
18. *Ibid.*, 7.
19. Erving Goffman, *Stigma: Notes on the Management of Spoiled Identity* (Englewood Cliffs, NJ: Prentice-Hall, 1963), 3.
20. *Ibid.*, 5.
21. Robert Bogdan and Steven Taylor, *The Social Meaning of Mental Retardation: Two Life Stories* (New
   York: Teachers College Press, 1994), 14.
22. Wolf Wolfensberger, "A Brief Overview of Social Role Valorization," *Mental Retardation* 38 (2000): 107.
23. Wolfensberger also discusses other aspects of devaluation, which we will not describe here.
24. Wolfensberger, *A Brief Introduction to Social Role Valorization*, 14.
25. *Ibid.*, 14–15.
26. Tim Stainton, "Reason and Value: The Thought of Plato and Aristotle and the Construction of Intellectual Disability," *Mental Retardation* 39 (2001): 452.
27. Richard C. Scheerenberger, *A History of Mental Retardation* (Baltimore: Brooks Publishing, 1983), 67–68.
28. Burton Blatt and Fred Kaplan, *Christmas in Purgatory: A Photographic Essay on Mental Retardation* (Syracuse, NY: Human Policy Press, 1974).
29. Wolfensberger, *A Brief Introduction to Social Role Valorization*, 15.
30. There are other conceptualizations of the fool as one who is able to speak the truth to power, which we will not consider in any depth here.
31. Margaret A. Winzer, "Disability and Society before the Eighteenth Century," in *The Disability Studies Reader*, ed. Lennard J. Davis (New York: Routledge, 1997), 83.
32. Scheerenberger, 33.
33. Braddock and Parish, 37. See also Robert Bogdan, *Freak Show: Presenting Human Oddities for Amusement and Profit* (Chicago: University of Chicago Press, 1988), 119–146.
34. Wolfensberger, *A Brief Introduction to Social Role Valorization*, 14–16.
35. Richard Neugebauer, "Mental Handicap in Medieval and Early Modern England: Criteria, Measurement and Care," in *From Idiocy to Mental Deficiency: Historical Perspectives on People with Learning Disabilities*, eds. David Wright and Anne Digby (London: Routledge, 1996), 25.
36. Bogdan and Biklen, 17.
37. Stephen P. Safran, "Disability Portrayal in Film: Reflecting the Past, Directing the Future," *Exceptional Children* 64 (1998): 227.
38. Bogdan et al., 32.
39. Devlieger, Baz and Drazen, 8.
40. *Ibid.*
41. Andy Kimpton-Nye, "Gump and Co.," in *Framed: Interrogating Disability in the Media*, eds. Chris Davies and Ann Pointon (London: British Film Institute, 1997), 32.
42. *Ibid.*, 31–32.
43. *Ibid.*, 32.
44. *Oxford English Dictionary*, s.v. "gump."
45. Kimpton-Nye, 33.
46. *Ibid.*
47. Gabler, 251.
48. Hollis and Sibley, 15.
49. *Ibid.*, 252.
50. *Ibid.*, 251–252.
51. *Ibid.*, 252.
52. Hollis and Sibley, 15.
53. *Oxford English Dictionary*, s.v. "dopey."
54. Charles D. Peavy, "The Eyes of Innocence: Falkner's 'Kingdom of God,'" *Papers on Language and Literature* 2 (1966).
55. *Ibid.*
56. Doreen Arcus, "Vulnerability and Eye Color in Disney Cartoon Characters," in *Perspectives on Behavioral Inhibition*, ed. J. Steven Reznick (Chicago: University of Chicago Press, 1989), 295.

57. Michael V. Angrosino, "Mental Disability in the United States: An Interactionist Perspective," in *Questions of Competence*, ed. Richard Jenkins (Cambridge: Cambridge University Press, 1998), 25.
58. Marc Eliot, *Walt Disney: Hollywood's Dark Prince* (New York: Birch Lane Press, 1993), 102.
59. Leonard Maltin, *The Disney Films* (New York: Crown Publishers Inc., 1973), 31.
60. Halliwell, 219.
61. *Ibid.*, 219.
62. Charles Perrault, *Perrault's Complete Fairy Tales*, trans. W. Heath Robinson (New York: Dodd, Mead and Company, 1961).
63. Jeanne-Marie LePrince de Beaumont, *Beauty and the Beast*. Available from: http://www.fullbooks.com/Beauty-and-the-Beast.html (accessed July 5, 2009).
64. The ARTFL Project, s.v. "fou," http://machaut.uchicago.edu/?resource=frengdict&action=search&english=&french=fou&root=&pos=%25 (accessed June 24, 2010).
65. Hollis and Sibley, 15.
66. *Who Framed Roger Rabbit?* (1988), DVD. Directed by Robert Zemeckis, (Burbank, CA: Touchstone Pictures, 2003).
67. *Ibid.*
68. *Cinderella II: Dreams Come True* (2002), DVD. Directed by John Kafka (Burbank, CA: Walt Disney Home Entertainment, 2002).
69. *Cinderella III: A Twist in Time* (2007), DVD. Directed by Frank Nissen (Burbank, CA: Walt Disney Home Entertainment, 2007).
70. Richard Jenkins, "Culture, Classification and (In)competence," in *Questions of Competence*, ed. Richard Jenkins (Cambridge: Cambridge University Press, 1998), 3.
71. *Ibid.*, 1.
72. Safran, 227.

Bibliography

Angrosino, Michael, V. "Mental Disability in the United States: An Interactionist Perspective." In *Questions of Competence*, edited by Richard Jenkins, 25–53. Cambridge: Cambridge University Press, 1998.

Arcus, Doreen. "Vulnerability and Eye Color in Disney Cartoon Characters." In *Perspectives on Behavioral Inhibition*, edited by J. Steven Reznick, 291–297. Chicago: University of Chicago Press, 1989.

Arnold, Helen, M. "Snow White and the Seven Dwarfs. A Symbolic Account of Human Development." *Perspectives in Psychiatric Care* 17 (1979): 218–222, 226.

Bettelheim, Bruno. *The Uses of Enchantment: The Meaning and Importance of Fairy Tales*. New York: Alfred A. Knopf, 1976.

Blatt, Burton and Fred Kaplan. *Christmas in Purgatory: A Photographic Essay on Mental Retardation*. Syracuse: Human Policy Press, 1974.

Bogdan, Robert. *Freak Show: Presenting Human Oddities for Amusement and Profit*. Chicago: University of Chicago Press, 1988.

_____, and Douglas Biklen. "Handicapism." *Social Policy* 7 (1977): 14–19.

_____, Douglas Biklen, Arthur Shapiro, and Spelkoman David. "The Disabled: Media's Monster." *Social Policy* 13 (1982): 32–35.

_____, and Steven Taylor. *The Social Meaning of Mental Retardation: Two Life Stories*. New York: Teachers College Press, 1994.

Braddock, David L., and Susan L. Parish. "An Institutional History of Disability." In *Handbook of Disability Studies*, edited by Gary L. Albrecht, Katherine D. Seelman, and Michael Bury, 11–68. Thousand Oaks, CA: Sage Publications, 2001.

Devlieger, Patrick J., Tal Baz and Carlos Drazen. "Mental Retardation in American Film: A Semiotic Analysis." *Semiotica* 129 (2000): 1–28.

Eliot, Marc. *Walt Disney: Hollywood's Dark Prince*. New York: Birch Lane Press, 1993.

Gabler, Neal. *Walt Disney: The Triumph of the American Imagination.* New York: Alfred A. Knopf, 2006.

Giroux, Henry A. *The Mouse That Roared: Disney and the End of Innocence.* Lanham, MD: Rowman & Littlefield, 1999.

Goffman, Erving. *Stigma: Notes on the Management of Spoiled Identity.* Englewood Cliffs, NJ: Prentice-Hall, 1963.

Halliwell, Martin. *Images of Idiocy: The Idiot Figure in Modern Fiction and Film.* Burlington, VT: Ashgate, 2004.

Hollis, Richard and Brian Sibley. *Walt Disney's Snow White and the Seven Dwarfs and the Making of the Classic Film.* New York: Hyperion, 1994.

Jenkins, Richard. "Culture, Classification and (In)competence." In *Questions of Competence,* edited by Richard Jenkins, 1–24. Cambridge: Cambridge University Press, 1998.

Kimpton-Nye, Andy. "Gump and Co." In *Framed: Interrogating Disability in the Media,* edited by Ann Pointon and Chris Davies, 31–35. London: British Film Institute, 1997.

Leprince de Beaumont, Jeanne-Marie. *Beauty and the Beast.* 1756. Available from: http://www.fullbooks.com/Beauty-and-the-Beast.html (accessed July 15, 2009).

Longmore, Paul K. "Screening Stereotypes: Images of Disabled People." *Social Policy* 16 (1985):31–37.

Lugo-Lugo, Carmen R. and Mary K. Bloodsworth-Lugo. "'Look Out New World, Here We Come'? Race, Racialization, and Sexuality in Four Children's Animated Films by Disney, Pixar, and DreamWorks." *Cultural Studies Critical Methodologies* 9 (2009): 166–178.

Maltin, Leonard. *The Disney Films.* New York: Crown Publishers Inc, 1973.

Neugebauer, Richard. "Mental Handicap in Medieval and Early Modern England: Criteria, Measurement and Care." In *From Idiocy to Mental Deficiency: Historical Perspectives on People with Learning Disabilities,* edited by David Wright and Anne Digby, 22–43. London: Routledge, 1996.

Peavy, Charles D. "The Eyes of Innocence: Falkner's "The Kingdom of God." *Papers on Language and Literature* 2 (1966).

Perrault, Charles. *Perrault's Complete Fairy Tales.* Translated by W. Heath Robinson. New York: Dodd, Mead and Company, 1961.

Safran, Stephen P. "Disability Portrayal in Film: Reflecting the Past, Directing the Future." *Exceptional Children* 64 (1998): 227–238.

Scheerenberger, Richard C. *A History of Mental Retardation.* Baltimore: Brookes Publishing, 1983.

Stainton, Tim. "Reason and Value: The Thought of Plato and Aristotle and the Construction of Intellectual Disability." *Mental Retardation* 39 (2001): 452–460.

Towbin, Mia A., Shelley A. Haddock, Toni S. Zimmerman, Lori K. Lund and Litsa R. Tanner. "Images of Gender, Race, Age, and Sexual Orientation in Disney Feature-Length Animated Films." *Journal of Feminist Family Therapy* 15 (2003): 19–44.

Winzer, Margaret A. "Disability and Society before the Eighteenth Century." In *The Disability Studies Reader* edited by Lennard J. Davis, 75–109. New York: Routledge, 1997

Wolfensberger, Wolf. *A Brief Introduction to Social Role Valorization: A High-Order Concept for Addressing the Plight of Societally Devalued People, and for Structuring Human Services,* 3d. ed. Syracuse, NY: Training Institute for Human Service Planning, Leadership and Change Agentry (Syracuse University), 1998.

_____. "A Brief Overview of Social Role Valorization." *Mental Retardation* 38 (2000):105–123.

A Place at the Table:
On Being Human in the
Beauty and the Beast *Tradition*

TAMMY BERBERI and VIKTOR BERBERI

One finds versions of the beauty and the beast tale as early as Ancient Greece and in cultures spanning the globe, from India to Africa, France, and Italy. Its universal appeal is certainly due to its archetypal nature, in the juxtaposition and proximity of two fundamental categories of human existence: beauty and repulsion. Lennard Davis, author of *Enforcing Normalcy*, describes the role of such stories in explaining human impulses in this way:

> Myths of beauty and ugliness have laid the foundations for normalcy. In particular, the Venus myth is one that is dialectically linked to another. This embodiment of beauty and desire is tied to the story of the embodiment of ugliness and repulsion. So the appropriate mythological character to compare the armless Venus with is Medusa.[1]

This chapter examines this dialectic in three versions of the tale that are inspired by the French tradition. The best known of these was written by Jeanne-Marie Leprince de Beaumont and published in France in 1756.[2] It clearly served as the basis for Jean Cocteau's 1945 film, *La Belle et la bête*, the script of which reproduces verbatim much of Leprince de Beaumont's tale. In contrast, Disney's 1991 animated film represents an extensive revision of the classic tale that nonetheless remains faithful to the objectives of the traditional fairy tale genre. As Jack Zipes points out, these aims were "part and parcel of the class struggles in the discourses of that period."[3] Zipes goes on to cite Armstrong and Tennenhouse on such struggles for hegemony: "A class of people cannot produce themselves as a ruling class without setting themselves off against certain Others. Their hegemony entails possession of the key cultural terms determining what are the right and wrong ways to be a human being."[4]

Over the past thirty years, disability theory has been pivotal in redefining the "the right and wrong ways to be a human being." It may seem a bit of a stretch to use disability theory to discuss Cocteau's rather homely beast or Disney's buffalo with a fiery temper. Yet, as Paul Wells points out in the introduction to *The Animated Bestiary*, such characters are "able to carry a diversity of representational positions. At one and the same time, such characters can be beasts and humans, or neither; can prompt issues about gender, race, and ethnicity, generation and identity, or not; and can operate innocently or subversively, or as something else entirely."[5] In short, once you put a buffalo in breeches, anything goes.

The extent to which each version challenges notions of the Other can be explained in part by authorial intention and the starkly different creative visions of Cocteau and the Disney production team. Working on his film at the end of World War II, Cocteau clearly meant for his aesthetic choices to resist not only the conventions of contemporary cinema (and the public's taste for films of a certain kind), but those of the fairy tale, as well: "To realism, I would oppose the simplified, formalized behavior of characters out of Molière (at the beginning of the film). To fairyland as people usually see it, I would bring a kind of realism to banish the vague and misty nonsense now so completely worn out."[6] Indeed, in creating his vision of the classic fairy tale, he intended to shatter its mold:

> My story would concern itself mainly with the unconscious obstinacy with which women pursue the same type of man, and expose the naiveté of the old fairy tales that would have us believe that this type reaches its ideal in conventional good looks. My aim would be to make the beast so human, so sympathetic, so superior to men, that his transformation into Prince Charming would come as a terrible blow to Beauty, condemning her to a humdrum marriage and a future that is summed up in that last sentence of all fairy tales, "And they had many children."[7]

Thus in the final frames of the film, a transformed Prince remarks, "What's wrong, Belle? It's almost as if you miss my ugliness," and continues, "Are you disappointed that I look like your brother's friend?" "Yes," she replies, and then revises, "No." For the Prince, she is an "odd little girl," dazed and bewildered, as though anesthetized by the Beast's metamorphosis. When the Prince asks, "Are you happy?" she offers a tentative smile, answering, "I'll have to get used to it." Hereafter she becomes increasingly girlish in her replies. The Prince seems to prop her up, the camera angle making her appear much smaller than he. She offers meekly, "I like to be afraid ... when I'm with you" and looks up at him to ask, "Is it far?" the kind of simplified question a little girl might ask about a fairytale kingdom. And off they fly, literally, on some sort of zipcord, into a slate gray sky, their ridiculous feet reeling behind them.[8]

Writing in 1968, Richard Schickel characterizes Walt Disney's perspective in these terms:

> Disney, the man who could never bear to look upon animals in zoos or prisoners in jail or other "unpleasant things," was truly incapable of seeing his material in anything but reductive terms. [Walt Disney] came always as a conqueror, never as a servant. It is a trait, as many have observed, that many Americans share when they venture into foreign lands hoping to do good but equipped only with knowhow instead of sympathy and respect for alien traditions.[9]

The Disney version of *Beauty and the Beast* was taken up in the late 1980s by Walt Disney's nephew, Roy C. Disney. Interestingly, Walt Disney had explored the project in 1937, after the success of the animated full-length feature *Snow White and the Seven Dwarfs*, and again in the 1950s. On both occasions he struggled with some of the more daunting aspects of the project: the fact of there being only two main characters and the challenge of creating a beast that was at once "beastly" enough and sympathetic. Ultimately, he shelved the project in favor of others. It took another generation of animators to develop the storyline as it appears in the 1991 version, arguably the most successful feature Disney has ever produced. It won three Golden Globe Awards and was the first animated feature in the history of the Academy Awards to be nominated for Best Picture.[10]

The film had no shortage of commercial appeal but, for many critics, fell far short of capturing the magic of the original tale. In recasting the Beast as an appealing, humanized character, Disney's film allows for no real transformation. Long before Disney produced *Beauty and the Beast*, Schickel had pointed out Walt Disney's failure to answer "in imaginative intensity and depth of feeling" the original fairy tales he had remade, attributing it to a desire to overlook their more horrific aspects.

The beast's appearance is a *leitmotiv* in all three versions. In the 1756 version of the tale, the beast is "monstrous," and "horrible," so "hideous" that Belle nearly faints the first time she looks upon it. When the beast asks Belle whether she finds him ugly, she replies, "You are very kind. I must confess that your goodness pleases me, and when I come to think of it, you no longer seem so ugly." Thus it is conversations about its appearance that reveal the beast's humility and kindness as well as Belle's virtue, propelling the tale to its happy conclusion when the beast is transformed into a human prince as a reward for Belle's purity of heart: "You have preferred virtue to beauty and wit," declares the lady of Belle's dream.[11] Conversations such as these, present in both Leprince de Beaumont's version and Disney, invoke the Victorian correlation between an unsightly appearance and a blemished soul and its corollary, beauty and goodness. The cultural impact of this correlation—a refurbished iteration of the Venus/Medusa archetype—was tremendous, shaping the reception of Darwin's *The Origin of the Species* in the mid-nineteenth century and culminating in Cesare Lombroso's early theories of criminal profiling a few decades later.

Cocteau presents a hideous Beast, as well, and addresses directly by means of several aesthetic choices an issue that is less salient in the original: what exactly is the nature of a beast who walks, talks, and articulates a full range of human emotions? Is it human or an animal? Cocteau and actor Jean Marais went to great lengths in creating a realistic—that is, animal—beast, and it is one: it has coarse fur and long teeth, drinks from the river rather than a cup, hunts deer in the woods, and appears regularly bathed in the blood of wild prey. Indeed, the Beast is only human enough to suffer shame at these many indignities of being an animal in Belle's presence. As if to reiterate their different species, Cocteau films Belle walking through a hall filled with classical statues, while the Beast roams the garden among statues of dogs and deer. The Beast pines for Belle in her absence by stroking her white fur shawl; she wears a silly tiara with its silver garland sprigs that suggest an animal's antlers. At the precise moment that Belle openly challenges its repeated marriage proposals, admonishing, "Let's be friends. Don't ask me for anything more," the Beast is distracted by a deer running past through the woods. These many details in the film and Belle's accoutrements serve to underscore the authenticity of the Beast *as animal.*

Cocteau's emphasis on their different species is countered by Belle's skepticism as she describes the Beast to her father. To his supposition, "So this monster has a soul?" she replies, "He suffers, father. One half of him struggles with the other. He is crueler to himself than he is to other human beings." This characterization of the Beast clearly invokes Cartesianism in the father's assumption that an animal would not have a soul. Belle's reply challenges Cartesian logic, describing a struggle between two "halves" of itself: the animal who is absolutely in his element tracking deer in the woods and cleaning his paws, and the human who longs for love. This exchange is unique to the Cocteau version and important in understanding his aims: the Victorian analogy between appearance and morality is present in Belle's depiction, but not in the Beast's. In fact, for Cocteau, the divergence of character and appearance is essential to setting up the "humdrum life" that Cocteau imagines for Belle, and serves as the linchpin for his condemnation of normative values pertaining not only to gender roles, but to notions of normal embodiment.

At the end of Leprince de Beaumont's story, as the Beast lies dying next to the riverbed, Belle sprinkles water on its forehead in an attempt to revive it. This clear allusion to baptism precipitates the Beast's metamorphosis, as if to confirm the presence of a soul. Surely inspired by this detail in the original tale, Cocteau gives the Beast a magic glove, which Belle places on its right hand. The glove introduces thematically the central conflict of Lancelot legend:

Lancelot's quest for Guinevere's heart has been read as an allegory for man's quest for salvation and Christ's quest for a human soul. On the other hand, the love between Lancelot and Guinevere is adulterous, so its realization precludes Lancelot's salvation. In a similar catch-22, the Beast's love for Belle is also forbidden—they are different species—and yet its transformation completely undermines its purity of intention: Belle must resign herself to a fairy tale fate.

In contrast, Disney's Beast hardly seems animal at all. With its broad shoulders, silky fur, and rich, molasses voice, it is anything but horrible in its appearance. Nonetheless, when Belle's father arrives in the castle, the Beast's reaction on seeing him—"What are you staring at? [....] So, you've come to stare at the Beast, have you?"—suggests that this film, too, means to address the monstrous nature of the Beast's body, as well as its freakish appeal.[12] The Beast's question confirms that it understands itself as spectacle and challenges the audience to wonder about its own role in perpetuating such tales. Yet an insistent focus on the Beast's fiery temper prompts us to look past the uniqueness of the Beast's body and its predicament in favor of the human moral failure that predominates in its depiction. Its status is further mitigated by the fact that animals as well as everyday objects—teapots, candelabras, ottomans, and clocks—are anthropomorphized in a way that both trivializes and universalizes difference. This Beast's metamorphosis invokes Christian motifs, but in rather hyperbolic terms: the Disney Beast, already so humanized, undergoes a sort of apotheosis, becoming a suffering *pietà* cradled by the Beast's swirling pelt and then a man (in the classical Western image of Christ) with rays of light shooting from his fingertips.

Disney's reticence to engage with "unpleasant things" explains in part why its beast is only animal in a figurative sense, able to reflect the negative human qualities of anger and impatience. Indeed, the beast we encounter in Disney is resolutely human, depicted neither as sufficiently abject visually nor as truly conflicted as to his true, fundamentally human, nature. By glossing over any real encounter with the Other, Disney avoids calling into question assumptions regarding the nature of what it means to be human. Patrick Murphy relates such consolatory notions of the human in part to the absence in the Disney films of "wild nature," something that, as Other, might challenge these static notions:

> Disney's full-length animated films reveal a consistent, although incoherent, worldview on nature and women that is escapist and androcentric. The escapism is based on denying wild nature as an integral part of the biosphere at the world level and as a part of individual character as the personal level. The denial of *wild* nature serves the fabrication of a timeless, universal, and unchanging order articulated in part by means of cultural values and generalizations.[13]

In Leprince de Beaumont and Cocteau, instead, the way in which the visual encounter between Belle and the Beast is depicted underscores their different natures, asking us to question the very categories of human and animal as they are constructed one against the other. In *Staring: How We Look*, Rosemarie Garland Thomson reminds us that faces are "the first territory our eyes inhabit when we encounter one another, and goes on to describe Levinas's "ethics of the face," according to which "the face is an expression of the person and a moral signifier."[14] The encounter with the face of the Other not only asks us "not to let him die alone," but puts us in a position "to be unable to kill."[15] Levinas is among those thinkers who have engaged in a deep reflection on the relationship between humans and animals and the ethical implications of this relationship. The brief essay "The Name of a Dog, or Natural Rights" describes his own experience in a Nazi prison camp at the end of the Second World War and, in particular, the extraordinary episode of a lost dog who finds his way into the camp. The dog, given the name Bobby by the prisoners, is referred to by Levinas as "the last Kantian in Nazi Germany" for its apparent ability to recognize the humanity of these individuals who have been reduced by their captors to the status of animals. The looks exchanged between Levinas and Bobby, however, are complicated by the fact that, in the end, the animal can only respond to the human gaze to the extent to which the observer projects the animal as human.[16]

Both Levinas's essay and Cocteau's *La Belle et la bête* belong to the same historical moment—no doubt Cocteau had begun making preparations for the film while Levinas was still a prisoner of war—and, indeed, both works stand out as anomalous, yet distinct, responses to the tragedy of the war. If Levinas's initial discussion of the ethical problem of killing and eating animals strikes one as inappropriate given the immediate context of the slaughter and brutalization of human beings, Cocteau's reelaboration of the beauty and the beast tale was on its release similarly jarring. Betsy Hearne notes: "At the time it came out [Cocteau's film] shocked a population devastated by World War II with its focus on what seemed of slight importance—a fairly tale—compared to the harsh realities of survival."[17] Both texts, however, acknowledge the danger of speaking in fables, which of course is also the danger of recourse to figurative uses of the other. Twice in the course of his essay Levinas interrupts the flow of his thought as his language threatens to descend into the purely figurative. At one point, he exclaims: "But enough of allegories! We have read too many fables and we are still taking the name of a dog in the figurative sense."[18]

Cocteau goes so far as to suggest that his film is accessible only to those capable of a particular relationship with animals: "The poet Paul Eluard says that to understand my film version of *Beauty and the Beast*, you must love your dog more than your car."[19] In the film, when Belle, having asked the beast to allow her to visit her sick father, strokes his head, he comments: "You coax me as though I were an animal." Her reply makes clear her surprise that he would imply otherwise: "But you are an animal." Like Levinas's biblical text—

"troubled by parables"—Cocteau "challenges the metaphor" of the beast by asking us to dwell on literal meanings rather than hastily reproduce codified figurative associations projected onto difference. And as Levinas will always be, Cocteau, too, is invested here in maintaining a kind of integrity of the Other. In this sense, just as Levinas's Bobby proves ultimately to be, Cocteau's beast is also *"trop bête."*[20] The ability continually to define and redefine notions of the human in a way that allows for a kind of *coming into being* requires that one avoids imagining the Other in figurative terms. If Disney seems unable to allow the other to challenge our understanding of what it means to be human, it is perhaps more than anything a result of a habit of thought that appeals to static anthropomorphism of animal and object become the human other. Mickey will forever be the "man who doesn't know he's a mouse."[21]

The stark difference in aesthetic priorities is also apparent in the portrayal of the servants in both films. In Cocteau, their limbs jut from walls and slither out of tables to serve a guest's every whim, yet spectators are offered no explanation. Are their bodies perhaps trapped within its walls? Cocteau devotes considerable energy to capturing Belle's father's reaction as they slither in and out of his visual field, their oily gray tone often blending with the dark walls of the castle. They are somewhat familiar and awfully accommodating, yet at the same time terrifyingly strange. Spectators watch him, wondering at, and learning from, his quietly startled response to them. One cannot help but wonder whether these specific aesthetic choices are symbolic of the dehumanization of prisoners of war in Nazi camps, and Belle's father's tentative reaction symbolic of that of the French, who were unaware of the real goings on in the camps until the liberation in 1944 but may have understood on a subconscious level the real implications of their existence.

In contrast to these uncanny limbs, Disney brings a whole staff of cheery accoutrements to life. When resurrecting *Beauty and the Beast* for the third time in the mid-eighties, creators had to figure out how to sustain spectator interest in only two characters. The addition of anthropomorphized household objects solved that challenge but introduced new ones. Animators struggled with how, in specific terms, to humanize a candelabra or a teapot. Ultimately, Lumière, who does not have legs, manages to dance the cancan thanks to animators creating the impression of movement through blurring; Mrs. Potts, only a head, is able to express a full range of emotions and movement. In essence, while Cocteau made the creative choice to dwell upon fragmentation of the human form, Disney strove to maintain the illusion of wholeness and a complete range of abilities.[22]

Despite the stark differences in aesthetic projects, all of these peripheral figures relate to meals and eating, the central trope that best establishes a tradition. In each of the three versions, strangers enter the castle to find an elaborate table, so that the scene is a first indication of the Beast's social class and the thematic introduction of class difference. In Leprince de Beaumont and

Cocteau, scenes of eating serve the double function of reinforcing exclusionary notions of propriety related to class and community: in both versions, after her father loses his fortune, Belle is forced to take up duties as a servant. In Cocteau, during her visit home, Belle's royal appearance and diamond teardrops heighten an already singular thematic focus on issues of class. In one key scene, as Belle serves dinner, Félicie remarks, "She misses her luxuries and our commonness disgusts her ... Mademoiselle surely thinks she is too good to wait on us now."

Equally important in both versions is the Beast's request to watch Belle as she eats. These scenes associate the theme of looking at/seeing/understanding the Other with the site of the display of human propriety from which the Beast is ultimately excluded. In Leprince de Beaumont's tale, the magnificent table that Belle and her father find waiting for them prompts her to speculate on the Beast's intentions:

> The horse went of its own accord to the stable, and the good man entered the great hall with his daughter. There they found a table, magnificently dressed and laid with two places. The merchant had no desire to eat, but Beauty, forcing herself to appear calm, sat down at the table and served her father; then she said to herself: "The Beast gives me such food because he wants to fatten me before eating me."

Subsequently, the beast's pleasure in watching her eat would seem to confirm Belle's initial suspicion:

> At noon she found the table laid, and while she ate the meal she heard an exquisite concert, although she could not see anyone. In the evening, as she was about to sit down at the table, she heard again the noise the Beast made, and in spite of herself she shivered with terror. "Beauty," said the monster, "are you willing to let me watch you sup?"

Such scenes find their culmination in the tale's conclusion, when the beast's attempted suicide takes the form of a repression of his natural desire to eat as an animal, which is compensated by a kind of scopic pleasure: "The Beast opened his eyes and said to Beauty: 'You forgot your promise, and my sorrow at losing you made me want to die of hunger; but I die content since I have the pleasure of seeing you again.'"[23]

In *Powers of Horror: An Essay on Abjection*, Julia Kristeva develops the notion of the abject as something that, situated outside of the symbolic order, "disturbs identity, system, order" and "does not respect borders, positions, rules."[24] The encounter with the abject, often embodied in the marginalized individual, is characterized by a sense of repulsion and is experienced by the subject as a traumatic event. Our sense of the abject is at times triggered by the experience of eating. Kristeva writes, "Food loathing is perhaps the most elementary and most archaic form of abjection."[25] She goes on to discuss dietary restrictions in *Leviticus*.[26] In Cocteau's film, in which depictions of voyeurism and eating repeatedly coincide, it is during the various representations of meals and eating that the repulsive nature of the beast as Other becomes most apparent, and where he stands outside of the Biblical prohibitions regulating the human consumption of flesh.[27] In one scene where the Beast is caught having feasted on wild prey, the stage directions in the film's screenplay underscore the power of the gaze in forcing an internalization of the experience of abjection:

BEAUTY: My God! You're covered in blood!
She starts back in horror.
THE BEAST: Forgive me...
BEAUTY: For what?
THE BEAST (*almost groveling*): For being a beast, forgive me.
BEAUTY (*firmly*): It doesn't become you to talk in that way. Aren't you ashamed of yourself? Go and clean yourself and go to sleep.
She stands there looking at him in all her innocence and purity. The Beast is overcome with shame and self-disgust.
THE BEAST (*in despair*): Close the door! Close the door! (*She doesn't move.*)
Quick ... quick, close the door. Your look is burning me, I can't bear it.[28]

Here, as in Leprince de Beaumont, short of death, there is no question of the Beast's inability to forsake his animal nature to join Belle at the table. In contrast, Disney's Beast invites Belle to dinner and sits down to dine across from him. This Beast is not so much an animal as an extremely awkward, ill-mannered human being; its clumsy manner and slurping will be remediated with practice as part of an overall grooming process undertaken by the castle's lively band of accoutrements. In order to win the girl, the Beast must temper his anger, hide his fangs, stand up straight, and learn to use a knife and fork. Of course, the stakes are high for all involved, for if Belle can learn to love the Beast by midnight on the eve of its twenty-first birthday, household accoutrements will also undergo metamorphosis, returning to a life as cheerful (human) servants. A rousing choral number, "Human Again," apparently cut from the original script because its lyrics destabilized the temporal frame of the rest of the storyline, was rewritten and included in the 10th Anniversary DVD edition. It includes a scene of Belle and the Beast reading (*Romeo and Juliet*). Belle is cast as a tutor, which both underscores the Beast's blossoming humility and clarifies her role as conveyor of cultural norms. Spectators are to deduce from the scene that the Beast, having softened (and taken up Shakespeare), is increasingly human, transformed by love as well as learning. Significantly, an alternative version of the lyrics of "Human Again," widely cited on the Internet, reveals Belle and Beast reading about Guinevere's grief after King Arthur's death: the shift to *Romeo and Juliet* for its publication on the 10th Anniversary DVD serves not only to remedy the potential obscurity of medieval legend but removes the prohibition on their relationship and places it on par with a timeless love story.[29]

The Disney acculturation process follows the same trajectory as what Paul Longmore terms a "drama of adjustment," the stock depiction *par excellence* among stereotypical portrayals of disability.[30] In a drama of adjustment, a central character copes with anger and resentment about his impairment. Nondisabled characters in the film condemn a "bad attitude" and encourage his emotional adjustment and self-acceptance, proffering advice as if they understand better than he the issues at hand. Such dramas culminate with an angry confrontation, at the end of which the central character acquiesces. As Longmore points out, dramas of adjustment never engage issues of prejudice or social injustice; the responsibility for conformity to prevailing discourses about ability and disability falls squarely on the shoulders of the individual. Thus in Disney's version, Mrs. Potts and her entourage groom the Beast, coach him in the use of good manners, and even hand him a spoon at the dinner table. One of the film's most memorable moments, the song "Be Our Guest" (sung by the servants who welcome Belle to a formal dinner with the Beast), calls up a range of ideas associated with the high-brow world of French culinary pomp, its choral nature invoking a sense of community and demonstrating by association the complete acculturation of the beast into the human world.

Paul Darke adds to Longmore his formulation of the "normality genre" and the notion that an "impaired" present time frame is typically juxtaposed to an idealized, normal past.[31] For Darke, impairment must be contained and / or normalized in order to uphold social norms relating to both beauty and ability. In the film, the Beast isolates himself from others, having internalized the stigma of its difference. The Beast's idealized past is symbolized by the slashed portrait of the prince and literally kept under lock and key in the west wing of the castle that Belle is forbidden to visit. Her transgression and discovery of this ideal is a necessary step in the exposition of the film that culminates in their courtship and in the Beast's acculturation process: his sudden ability to dress the part of a suitor and waltz Belle around the ballroom floor.

Yet, at the same time, Disney juxtaposes an alternative narrative that highlights the complexities of stigma and social prejudice. The film opens with "Belle," a rousing *hommage* to 19th-century cultural norms that depicts petty mercantilism and the rise of capitalism in a provincial village. In contrast, the Beast withdraws into the solitude of his dark castle, so ashamed is he of his new, unsightly appearance. Yet rather than casting withdrawal as a "natural" response to the Beast's appearance, the movie on the whole suggests the importance of learned responses. As such, Gaston leads the charge to "Kill the Beast!" drawing upon all sorts of lore to rally the crowd and insisting, "If you're not with us you're against us!" While Gaston's reaction capitalizes upon fears of (Belle's father's) supposed madness, spectators are left to consider Disney's depiction of mass hysteria, which is far too over-determined to be taken at face value, and which itself alludes to the titillating appeal of such universal narratives of difference: "It's a nightmare but it's one exciting ride." The film thus draws upon a host of tropes central to understanding the perception and categorization of difference, particularly as the bourgeoisie gained ascendancy and as its identity as a class solidified.[32]

Moreover, the figure of the wayward mendicant, an original addition to the Disney frame story, ties into cultural iterations of difference in the 19th-century. In *The Ugly Laws*, Susan M. Schweik studies a series of local ordinances that were passed in cities across the country from the mid-nineteenth century to the beginning of World War I in what she describes as a kind of "civic contagion" prohibiting the exposure of disease for the purposes of begging. As late as 1974, a few such ordinances remained on the books. Chicago's city ordinance, passed in 1881, reads,

> Any person who is diseased, maimed, mutilated, or in any way deformed so as to be an unsightly or disgusting object, or an improper person to be allowed in or on the streets, highways, thoroughfares, or public places in this city, shall not therein or thereon, expose himself to public view, under the penalty of a fine of $1 for each offense.[33]

In *Claiming Disability*, Simi Linton offers a modern update to the nineteenth-century ugly laws, citing a pair of letters to Ann Landers in 1987:

> I have the right to go out and I pay good money for a meal to enjoy it. The sight of a woman in a wheelchair with food running down her chin would make me throw up. I believe my rights should be respected as much as the rights of the person in the wheelchair ... maybe even more so, because I am normal and she is not.
>
> In my opinion, restaurants should have a special section for handicapped people, partially hidden by palms or other greenery, so they are not seen by other guests.[34]

Conjuring the same scopic fascination and repulsion that is so prevalent in the three versions and so closely associated with food, the letters are evidence that the impulse to sequester physical difference was still part of the American imaginary surrounding issues of physical difference while the Disney film was in production. Indeed, the late eighties was a period of sweeping change in the history of the disability rights movement, and a few other details in the film lend themselves to parallels in this realm. President Bush signed into law the Americans with Disabilities Act (ADA) in July of 1990, legislation that acknowledged that a whole population of people with disabilities who had grown up benefiting from the protections afforded by Section 504 of the Rehabilitation Act were now poised to graduate from college and expected to participate fully in the benefits and opportunities of adulthood, as employees as well as consumers. One of the most original provisions of the ADA was the role that stigma, or the perception of a person's abilities or disabilities, might play in shaping a person's opportunities, and the legislation sought to guarantee access as well as attempting to prevent discrimination in the workplace.[35]

This history seems to lend significance to the specific details of the film's exposition, making contemporary the emphasis on capitalist productivity in the film's opening sequence. Historical context might also explain the visual exposition of "Human Again," wherein the servants associate their return to human form with the physical labor of cleaning the castle after such a long period in disrepair. Its idealization of a full range of physical abilities is remarkable, for not only are they to clean, they are to clean while waltzing in rhythmic and graceful unison with dozens of their peers. Cogsworth's dream of a peaceful and prosperous retirement suggests the opportunities that the ADA seeks to guarantee. Likewise, the prologue seems to parallel the intent of the legislation, as in order to break the spell, the Beast must be alluring enough to make Belle love him before he reaches legal adulthood, the demographic the ADA drafters had in mind. In the meantime, Belle is forbidden to visit the "west wing" of the castle. Here, the magic rose, with its last petal dangling, is kept under glass and Belle (who transgresses the prohibition) gets a glimpse of the prince's former beauty and, by extension, of an idealized, "normal" past. The west wing of the castle, "off-limits," may of course be read as the West Wing of the White House, itself a loaded metaphor for the full participation in civic life that so many activists felt had been denied them.

In essence, this reading of the implications of physical difference in three versions of the beauty and the beast tale has come full circle, beginning with an exploration of the beast as fundamentally Other, especially in Cocteau. In contrast, Disney apparently sought to mitigate the Beast's absolute difference by humanizing it and indeed, making it an *ideal* suitor. This depiction, less transgressive than its predecessor, nonetheless incorporates elements that seem to acknowledge progressive historical developments, making way for alternative readings of disability and a place for the Beast at the table.

Notes

1. Lennard Davis, *Enforcing Normalcy, Disability, Deafness, and the Body* (New York: Verso, 1995) 131.

2. Jeanne-Marie Leprince de Beaumont. *La Belle et la bête*, Trans. Francis Steegmuller, in *The Criterion Collection notes for Jean Cocteau, La Belle et la bête.*

3. Jack Zipes, "Breaking the Disney Spell," *From Mouse to Mermaid: The Politics of Film, Gender, and Culture*, eds. Elizabeth Bell, Lynda Haas and Laura Sells (Bloomington: Indiana University Press, 1995, 21–42) 24.

4. Cited in Zipes, 24.

5. Paul Wells, *The Animated Bestiary: Animals, Cartoons, and Culture* (New Brunswick, NJ: Rutgers University Press, 2009) 3.

6. *Jean Cocteau: Beauty and the Beast* (Criterion Collection Notes, 2003, n.d.).

7. Criterion Collection Notes.

8. *La Belle et la bête* (1946), Dir. Jean Cocteau, perf. Jean Marais, Josette Day (The Criterion Collection, 2003, DVD).

9. Richard Schickel, *The Disney Version: The Life, Times, Art and Commerce of Walt Disney* (New York: Simon & Schuster, 1968) 226.

10. *The Making of Beauty and the Beast* (1991) Disney Classic, Buena Vista Home Entertainment, 21 April 2010 youtube.com.

11. Leprince de Beaumont.

12. *Beauty and the Beast, 10th Anniversary DVD*, Kirk Wise and Gary Trousdale, 1989.

13. Patrick Murphy, "'The Whole Wide World Was Scrubbed Clean': The Androcentric Animation of Denatured Disney," in *From Mouse to Mermaid: The Politics of Film, Gender, and Culture*, eds. Elizabeth Bell, Lynda Haas and Laura Sells (Bloomington: Indiana University Press, 1995, 125–136) 125.

14. Rosemarie Garland Thomson, *Staring: How We Look* (Oxford: Oxford University Press, 2009) 95.

15. Qtd. in Thomson, 100.

16. Emmanuel Levinas, "The Name of a Dog, or Natural Rights," *Difficult Freedom: Essays on Judaism*, trans. Seán Hand (Baltimore: Johns Hopkins University Press, 1990, 151–153).

17. Betsy Hearne. *Beauty and the Beast: Visions and Revisions of an Old Tale* (Chicago: University of Chicago Press, 1989) 79–80.

18. Levinas.

19. Criterion Collection Notes.

20. David Clark, "On Being 'The Last Kantian in Nazi Germany': Dwelling with Animals After Levinas," in *Animal Acts: Configuring the Human in Western History*, eds. Jennifer Ham and Matthew Senior (New York: Routledge, 1997, 165–98) 188.

21. See Andrea Dini, "Calvino e Walt Disney: Iconografia della bestia" (Quaderni del '900, II, 2002, 35–50) for a discussion of anthropomorphism in Walt Disney's essay that appeared in the Italian journal *Il Politecnico* in 1946 (no. 20, Feb 9) with the title "La mia officina."

22. *The Making of Beauty and the Beast.*

23. Leprince de Beaumont.

24. Julia Kristeva, *Powers of Horror: An Essay on Abjection*, trans. Leon Roudiez (New York: Columbia University Press, 1982) 4.

25. Kristeva, 2. See especially the chapter "Approaching Abjection," 1–31.

26. Kristeva. See the chapter "Semiotics of Biblical Abomination," 90–112.

27. "You shall be men consecrated to me; therefore you shall not eat any flesh that is torn by beasts in the field; you shall cast it to the dogs" (Exodus 22:31).

28. Jean Cocteau, *Three Screenplays: L'Eternel Retour, Orphée, La Belle et la Bête*, trans. Carol Martin-Sperry (New York: Grossman, 1972) 224.

29. Alan Mencken and Howard Ashman, "Human Again," Metro Lyrics, 24 May 2010 http://www.metrolyrics.com/human-again-lyrics-alan-menken.html.

30. Paul K. Longmore, "Screening Stereotypes: Images of Disabled People," in *Screening Disability: Essays on Cinema and Disability*, eds. Anthony Enns and Christopher R. Smit (Boston: University Press of America, 2001).

31. Paul Darke, "Understanding Cinematic Representations of Disability," in *The Disability Reader: Social Science Perspectives*, ed. Tom Shakespeare (New York: Continuum, 1998) 181–200.

32. Lennard J. Davis's foundational essay, "Constructing Normalcy," originally published in *Enforcing Normalcy, Disability, Deafness, and the Body* (pp. 23–49), focuses on the rise of embodied norms as part and parcel of the development of the bourgeoisie in nineteenth-century France.

33. Susan M. Schweik, *The Ugly Laws* (New York: New York University Press, 2009) 2.

34. Excerpts from Ann Landers column, spring 1987, cited in Simi Linton, *Claiming Disability: Knowledge and Identity* (New York: New York University Press, 1998) 34.

35. For a concise overview of the bill's drafting and passage, see Joseph P. Shapiro, *No Pity: Americans with Disabilities Forging a New Civil Rights Movement* (New York: Three Rivers Press, 1994), especially chapter four.

Bibliography

Bell, Elizabeth, Lynda Haas and Laura Sells, eds. *From Mouse to Mermaid: The Politics of Film, Gender, and Culture.* Bloomington: Indiana University Press, 1995.

Clark, David. "On Being 'The Last Kantian in Nazi Germany': Dwelling with Animals after Levinas," in *Animal Acts: Configuring the Human in Western History*, eds. Jennifer Ham and Matthew Senior. New York: Routledge, 1997, 165–98.

Cocteau, Jean. *Beauty and the Beast: Diary of a Film.* New York: Dover, 1972.

_____. *Three Screenplays: L'Eternel Retour, Orphée, La Belle et la Bête*, trans. Carol Martin-Sperry. New York: Grossman, 1972.

Darke, Paul. "Understanding Cinematic Representations of Disability." In *The Disability Reader: Social Science Perspectives.* Ed. Tom Shakespeare. London/ New York: Continuum, 1998.

Davis, Lennard. *Enforcing Normalcy: Disability, Deafness, and the Body.* New York: Verso, 1995.

Dini, Andrea. "Calvino e Walt Disney: Iconografia della bestia." *Quaderni del '900*, II, 2002, 35–50.

Hearne, Betsy. *Beauty and the Beast: Visions and Revisions of an Old Tale.* Chicago: University of Chicago Press, 1989.

Jean Cocteau: Beauty and the Beast. Criterion Collection Notes, 2003.

Kristeva, Julia. *Powers of Horror: An Essay on Abjection*, trans Leon Roudiez. New York: Columbia University Press, 1982.

Leprince de Beaumont, Jeanne-Marie. *La Belle et la bête.* Trans. Francis Steegmuller. In The Criterion Collection for Cocteau, Jean. *La Belle et la bête.*

Levinas, Emmanuel. "The Name of a Dog, or Natural Rights," in *Difficult Freedom: Essays on Judaism*, trans. Seán Hand. Baltimore: Johns Hopkins University Press, 1990, 151–153.

Linton, Simi. *Claiming Disability: Knowledge and Identity.* New York: New York University Press, 1998.

Longmore, Paul K. "Screening Stereotypes: Images of Disabled People," In *Screening Disability: Essays on Cinema and Disability*, eds. Anthony Enns and Christopher R. Smit. Boston: University Press of America, 2001.

The Making of Beauty and the Beast (1991) Disney Classic. Buena Vista Home Entertainment. youtube.com (accessed 21 April 2010).

Menken, Alan, and Howard Ashman. "Human Again." *Metro Lyrics.* 24 May 2010. http://www.metrolyrics.com/human-again-lyrics-alan-menken.html.

Murphy, Patrick. "'The Whole Wide World Was Scrubbed Clean': The Androcentric Animation of Denatured Disney," in *From Mouse to Mermaid*, 125–136.

Shapiro, Joseph P. *No Pity: People with Disabilities Forging a New Civil Rights Movement.* New York: Three Rivers Press, 1994.

Schickel, Richard. *The Disney Version: The Life, Times, Art and Commerce of Walt Disney.* New York: Simon & Schuster, 1968.

Schweik, Susan M. *The Ugly Laws.* New York: New York University Press, 2009.

Thomson, Rosemarie Garland. *Staring: How We Look.* Oxford: Oxford University Press, 2009.

Wells, Paul. *The Animated Bestiary: Animals, Cartoons, and Culture.* New Brunswick, NJ: Rutgers University Press, 2009.

Zipes, Jack. "Breaking the Disney Spell," in *From Mouse to Mermaid*, 21–42.

SECTION IV—UP AND OUT: ESSAYS ON REIMAGININGS AND NEW VISIONS

Is Disney Avant-Garde? A Comparative Analysis of Alice in Wonderland *(1951)* and Jan Svankmajer's Alice *(1989)*

WILLIAM VERRONE

Disney's *Alice in Wonderland* (1951) is considered a misstep, a film that loses its child-friendly appeal because of its unusual story and source material. The result is a heady mix of exaggerated, diverse, and bizarre characters that, while likable enough, seemed too "odd" a fit for the Disney name. Disney's film of Carroll's allegorical books is somewhat of a departure from the animated films of the Disney canon. Carroll's books ostensibly are about a child's perspective of the irrational and nonsensical world of adults, and *Alice in Wonderland*, the film, eschews Carroll's (supposed) pointed criticism in order to highlight the wonders of childhood—a "fantasyland" that would come to dominate Disney's thinking, in terms of his grandiose theme park—as opposed to the more relevant and important themes of dream and imagination. This does not mean the film is completely bad; in fact, its subversive nature and dark humor make it a worthy case study, I believe, of an atypical Disney film. The Disney version plays upon the tropes of "otherness" and power/subjection, which may explain its lasting appeal inasmuch as it is simply another "Disney cartoon for children." However, Disney did not *intend* for the film to have these themes. Quite unexpectedly as well, the film was somewhat embraced by the counterculture of the 1960s and gained a new, albeit different, audience in the 1970s, who admired the psychedelic "feel" of the film. I would like to discuss the film and another version, Jan Svankmajer's *Alice* (1988), a surreal and disturbing version of the Carroll stories. Svankmajer's *Alice* is a "reimagining" and highly uncompromising avant-garde film. It is an astonishing version of Carroll, and addresses relevant issues of childhood perception, imagination, and dream. Although the films differ considerably in this perspective on a child's insight into her surroundings, they are similar simply and only because the characters in the films are uncanny representations of outsiders. By "outsiders," I mean a group of characters who are either deliberately shunned by society or choose to avoid the dictates of society. They are like "Others" in this regard, characters that are either willingly or unwillingly apart from society. *Alice in Wonderland* presents an interesting quandary. The film is not considered to be one of Disney's best, nor does it receive much general praise. It is eccentric in its structure, which is episodic, and it does not have much to add to Carroll's books (*Alice's Adventures in Wonderland* [1865] and *Through the Looking-Glass* [1871]). In this regard, I would like to discuss the binary nature of the film and what makes it worthy of study: its (inadvertent) theme of Otherness, and the subversive nature of the characters. It has its appeal to children—bright colors, songs, and "weird" creature-characters, but overall, the film lacks depth, and thus seems tiresome and a bit tedious, as opposed to Svankmajer's *Alice*. Disney's film addresses the theme of "otherness," typically understood as "difference" or "being different from" what might be called the status quo or normality. Alice herself is not unusual; it is all the people and creatures she meets in Wonderland who are different, strange, and eccentric, and therefore set apart from the norm. The film does not heighten this awareness to any lengths, choosing to instead "play it safe" by showcasing or displaying the characters' oddness itself.

The professed answer to the question posed in my title is, typically, an emphatic "No," which would be correct. Disney films are not avant-garde in the historical and cultural sense of the idiom, but they do have avant-garde characteristics, particularly in terms of surrealism. The avant-garde is an artistic practice that deliberately seeks alternative forms, styles, and representations of its subject matter. The avant-gardist rejects traditional approaches to literature, film, the visual arts, music—all art forms—in favor of innovation. Avant-garde film advances new techniques, forms of expression, and subject matter, which is the case with Svankmajer's *Alice*. Avant-garde films also typically exist outside the "culture industry," an area where Disney firmly has established itself—and desires to be. Avant-garde filmmakers work in the margins and do not actively seek assurance from the mainstream, unlike Disney. Avant-garde filmmakers are highly independent. Just because *Alice in Wonderland* has an array of fantastical characters, it does not qualify it as an avant-garde film, but these characters do have certain qualities that can be examined in terms of their relations to the avant-garde. What the film does have is the subversity that is characteristic of some avant-garde films. "Subversiveness" implies a desire to overthrow, overturn, or undermine something, and the avant-garde film attempts these things through style, form, and theme. Or, put another way, to be subversive means to highlight the fallacies of the mainstream, in this case, mainstream films, while showcasing the revolutionary, radical, and groundbreaking forms of the film medium itself. Disney's *Alice in Wonderland* has an array of seditious characters who want to undermine authority, if only because they revel in the nonsensical world where they live. They do not necessarily seek assimilation; when Alice arrives in Wonderland, she simply wants to understand or comprehend her surroundings and her newfound predicament rather than becoming fully integrated in the creatures' world.

Disney films have always showcased a certain amount of diversity, but many of the films themselves, as well as the countless instances of "Disneyness" that occur in other films or forms of popular culture, could be considered avant-garde because they are deliberately subversive in style, theme, or attitude (like the pink elephants in *Dumbo*, dancing brooms in *Fantasia*, and an entire plethora of self-reflexive motifs in more recent films). I would like to discuss the potential for avant-garde characteristics of particular moments in *Alice in Wonderland* and use Svankmajer's *Alice* as a counterpoint as most decidedly avant-garde. Svankmajer's film may be little seen, but its imagery and narrative is unique and visionary, and is, admittedly, a far better film and interpretation of Carroll than the Disney (or other) versions. Svankmajer's film has its own sense of "fractured" logic and spatial and temporal dislocation. Given their subject matter, characters, and out of the ordinary locales, Carroll's books that serve as the basis for each film beg to be filmed as strange, bizarre, and fantastic. But there is a key difference between Disney's version and Svankmajer's film: the cartoon world of Disney does not match well with the subject matter; "Carroll is not a kind that translates easily into visual, cartoon form."[1] It is not a children's book per se, and Svankmajer understands this greatly, which is why he uses an actual girl for Alice and his characteristic stop-motion animation of objects and puppets, which breathes new life into *Alice in Wonderland*. Everything in his film is alive in three-dimensions, not flat like Disney's cartoon. Deborah Ross notes the discrepancy between Disney's finished film and the possibility of a more surrealist film, like Svankmajer's. She says,

> The visuals in fact are rather staid and restrained, mainly literal, representational renderings of the story done in the highly finished, realistic style for which the studio was famous. The fall down the rabbit hole, for example, which marks Alice's entry into the dream state, might have lent itself to a surrealistic treatment ... but instead it is simply a serial listing in images of the objects Carroll mentions that Alice sees on her way down.[2]

Svankmajer shows Alice's descent through a school desk drawer, where Alice then goes down the rabbit hole as if in an antiquated pulley system. It is dark and the clacking of the chains makes the scene nightmarish. All of the objects she sees are reproductions of what was in her room, which will later come to life in Wonderland, and sometimes in menacing ways. Svankmajer's stop-motion animation, an extremely difficult process that involves moving real three-dimensional objects just slightly and photographing them frame-by-frame before running the finished frames together to create the sensation of movement, is both eerie and appropriate for the world of Carroll.

Disney's film is structured like a series of episodes of Alice's adventures, which gives it a halting rhythm, most likely due to the fact that thirteen writers worked on the script (including an uncredited Aldous Huxley!). This possibly explains why there is little cohesion to the story. The film comes across as a series of unrelated, "misadventures of Alice"-style wanderings, which have no real sense of connection. Carroll's books were tight and cohesive. Carroll never really meant for his books to be taken simply as children's stories. While appealing to children, they are also satiric and allegorical, while full of logic puzzles, invented words, and general semantic derring-do. Disney alters dialogue and literalizes figurative language so much that the story is less about a child's view of the world, and more a showcase for the strange characters—and, of course, the disastrous songs. But there is a sense of subversive absurdity to how the characters are depicted.

Alice in Wonderland presents several moments of subversive behavior. Tweedledum and Tweedledee, for instance, are illustrated as precocious and slightly obnoxious schoolboys. They are plump, cowardly, yet oddly affectionate with each other. They tell Alice the story of the Walrus and the Carpenter, which in its own way, dramatizes the nature of violence that permeates much of Carroll's story, and the fact that we even see nearly ten minutes of them both subverts the overall narrative (e.g., where's Alice?) and also showcases more subversive characters. Alice leaves them confused; their stories are inconclusive, incomprehensible, and ambiguous (to her), so she moves on to her next episodic encounter. Her encounter with Tweedledum and Tweedledee makes us notice *them* and not her. Their very strangeness elicits our gaze more than Alice, which occurs throughout the film whenever we meet a new creature-character. Alice is also perplexed by the Caterpillar, who exhales vowels and tosses about nonsensical riddles. The hookah-smoking Caterpillar is an authority figure whose words appear meaningless. One surrealist touch occurs when the Caterpillar does blow smoke. The smoke forms words, such as "[k]not," a visual pun that indeed reflects the attitude of the surrealist side of the avant-garde (and also suggests why the film was later applauded by the counterculture). Much of the "adult" content of the book (and to some extent the film) stems from the idea that Alice is adrift in a world where very little makes sense because she encounters representations of the adult world. Both Tweedledum and Tweedledee and the Caterpillar are figures that are subversive because they thwart our expectations by talking nonsense. They also detract from the protagonist, Alice. In terms of the avant-garde, subversion was a catalyst for early attempts at surrealist film. The movement itself, especially in the 1920s and 1930s, was focused on overturning the dictates of the bourgeoisie and the fountainheads of art. Filmmakers as diverse as Luis Bunuel or Jean

Cocteau applauded the irrationality of dream-worlds and the unconscious. Arguably, *Alice's Adventures in Wonderland* is a direct connection to the dream-world. Many avant-garde directors, in fact, used the book as a touchstone for their ideas. Svankmajer greatly admired the book, which is why he wanted to make a film inspired by it. As Peter Hames rightly points out, "Lewis Carroll's *Alice's Adventures in Wonderland* (1865) provided a text admired by the surrealists and a subject very much in line with Svankmajer's own concerns—a dialogue with childhood and the child's world of unrestricted imaginative play."[3] Could this possibly make Disney's film version also somewhat equivalent to a surrealist dream-state? Perhaps, but Walt himself would not agree.

Alice's Adventures in Wonderland is about a young child's imagination, her literal and figurative growth, and the arbitrary rules that govern society. Disney's *Alice in Wonderland* is a codified version, intended to be visually striking in order to placate children. Walt Disney, after previewing the film, said, "The film lacks heart," and, "It is full of weird characters."[4] This sentiment shows his displeasure to the atypical Disney characters in the film. However, it is precisely because the characters in the film are "weird" that it becomes more suggestive of diversity than more recent, contemporary Disney films (which tend to stereotype). To be diverse is to be individualistic; whatever characteristics one has that makes one diverse makes them dissimilar to others, which is *not* a negative thing. Disney's characters seem like people who have been (or could have been) ostracized from society because of their diversity, but it seems to me that their strangeness is what makes them appealing. The unending nonsense of the Mad Tea Party is indicative of the kinds of people that showcase subversive behavior, simply because they act routinized, make babbling generalizations, and are, as the Cheshire Cat tells Alice, completely "mad." The Cheshire Cat's comment is actually very important because he is telling Alice the truth: everyone in Wonderland is somehow off-kilter, slightly deranged, a little unhinged—and she is thrust among them. It should be noted too that "madness" does not equate with "diversity." Being "mad" in Wonderland simply means that things do not make sense to an outsider like Alice. Alice's reply to the Cat is a line direct from Carroll: "But I don't want to go among mad people." The Cat's remark also implies that Alice is the only one in Wonderland who is not mad—she is the only one in Wonderland who is "out of her element." It is to her credit that she can survive; the Queen's wild proclamation of "Off with her head!" finally makes Alice realize that she can stop the madness by telling the Queen her order is "nonsense." She has been the subject of a power domination from her contact with all of the creature-characters in Wonderland. They all exert power over her. Still, by the end, she is timid when it comes to reaching any meaning about her role as the subjugated. It is made much more abundantly clear in Svankmajer's film that by the end, Alice has learned something and that she is the one with power. In it, Alice begins to see that while her imagination may create such a fantastical world, it also will help her rationalize her experience. In Svankmajer's *Alice*, Alice retains control of her environment by the end. When she "awakens," she finds the old pair of scissors and holds them aloft, saying, "Maybe now I'll cut off his head," in reference to the White Rabbit. As Hames says, "It is important to note that the narrative is both imagined and dreamt by Alice and that she remains in control."[5] Disney's *Alice* does not indicate exactly how relevant it is that Alice begins to comprehend her surroundings. It is more a fantasy that inspires wonder, but not the imagination. In discussing Disney's *Alice in Wonderland*, and particularly the Mad Tea Party and its aftermath, Ross notes,

> The storyline ensures that just as [the potential surrealistic] style reaches its climax, Alice is reaching the limits of her fear of imagination. What might have been delightful Daliesque creatures—telephone-ducks, drum-frogs—function rather to frighten the heroine at a point in the plot when she has rejected this "nonsense" and is anxious to get home to write a book about it. Writing a story, she has decided, is much safer than living one.[6]

In fact, by the end of the Disney film, Alice becomes increasingly passive, signified by her waking up—happy and free at last, rid of the imagination. The power plays that occurred in Wonderland still seem to be disadvantageous to Alice. Instead of questioning her position among them all, she is relegated to the passive "other," a reversal that highlights the creature-characters' power, even though they speak irrationalities.

The Mad Tea party is a perfect illustration of the potential for surrealistic imaginings. The tea cups and saucers become alive and flit about the table, much in the same way as the people at the party (except for Alice). They constantly move and multiply, making the scene delirious in its frenetic pacing. It is an avant-garde moment in an otherwise placid film. In comparison, Svankmajer also lets his objects run wild; "His awakening of the stirring in the souls of dormant objects to animate wonderland is Svankmajer's greatest illusion."[7] In Svankmajer's version of the Mad Tea Party, there is a kind of organized chaos. The March Hare and Mad Hatter perform their finite rituals of buttering tin can lids and pouring and drinking tea. Svankmajer's signature rapid and rhythmic editing quickens the pace of the scene. The Mad Hatter speaks in ridiculous riddles and nonsense questions, much like the absent-minded Mad Hatter of Disney (who is not all menacing like Svankmajer's wooden marionette version). Being absent-minded is not a sign of madness. Still, the very idea of speaking in riddles or of constantly questioning one's identity, which happens in Disney's film, can be considered an avant-garde surrealist tendency as well because it thwarts expectations and has the potential for a nonlinear story.

Svankmajer's film draws heavily upon the nature of dream-worlds, particularly in conjunction with how dream influences reality—a key idea in surrealism. Tina-Louise Reid, for instance, suggests, "With *Alice*, Jan Svankmajer maintains his uncompromising vision as he explores a world inspired by Carroll's tales whilst demonstrating the interconnectedness of dream with waking life."[8] Svankmajer accomplishes this by setting the film up as a dream. During the initial credit sequence, Alice, whose mouth is shown in extreme close up whenever she speaks and thus fills the entire frame, tells us, or rather instructs us, "First you must close your eyes, or you won't see anything." This directive has two meanings for the spectator: to dream and to use the imagination. Likewise, Frantisek Dryje says, "This paradoxical sentence from the introduction to Svankmajer's film is an exhortation to dream—to experience something which contains the truth about our lives."[9] After Alice's instruction, the film begins with a survey of her room; it is full of objects that will eventually reappear in Wonderland (and come to life via Svankmajer's masterful animation). In noting the importance of these objects, Roger Cardinal says, "One thing seems clear: the treatment of objects within Wonderland corresponds to the fantastical treatment of dream-work."[10] Because the objects come to life in Wonderland, and in often nightmarish ways, it demonstrates Alice's capacity as an agent of higher imaginative cognition. We get no sense of this in Disney's version. Instead, Alice, in Disney's Wonderland, is acted upon to a much greater degree than she acts or interacts; she more often than not *responds* to people rather than addressing them. The significance of the objects in Alice's room is that they come alive. According to Reid, "Since children instill toys and other objects with life through animation, childhood serves as a potent setting for Svankmajer's resurrections, with Carroll's Wonderland as the most advantageous backdrop."[11] Svankmajer clearly is more attuned to the powers of the imagination than Disney's disciplined version. In Svankmajer's film, Alice throws rocks at the creatures, slams the White Rabbit's hand in a door, and attempts to drown the dormouse. She is not just attempting to maintain control of her environment, but to make sense of it as well, and to shift the power relations among her and the creature-characters.

One important factor concerning the subversive nature of the characters in Disney's *Alice in Wonderland*, is that they could all be considered "outsiders." They exhibit personalities that can be considered diverse, meaning they are somehow poles apart from the mainstream. They are all truly outsiders (just as Alice herself could be, since she is displaced from her normal surroundings). The outsider is often constructed or identified from a distance—a distance created solely to situate the outsider as "Other." Others jeopardize the unity of the community. Strange characters like the March Hare, the Caterpillar, the Cheshire Cat, the Mad Hatter, or even the Queen of Hearts are considered "outsiders" because they are somehow different form societal, cultural, or ideological norms, or are simply too individualistic. All of these outsider characters, though, are perfectly at home in Wonderland. They would never be "at home" anywhere else, but this does not mean their diversity makes them unable to fit in. Rather, in their environment, they are ones who recognize Alice as "diverse"; she becomes the one who does not seem to fit in with her new environment, hence her attempts to control it. Alice's interaction with them displays playfulness on their part, as well as power positions. But the problem lies in the fact that they embody characteristics of the outsider, which means they are not "kid-friendly" fare the likes of Disney would approve. How can anyone—a child specifically—relate to the creature-characters in Disney's Wonderland? Did Disney want to promote anarchy, dissidence, or disobedience? No, but even still, Disney should be applauded (however inadvertently), even though the intent on spotlighting the "Other" was not at all Disney's goal. For instance, while there is some clever wordplay and banter among the characters, the tone certainly is not as aggressive as it should be; it is simply antagonistic, which makes for an easier delineation of Alice (in the "right" or normal) and the others in Wonderland (in the "wrong" or "other") for *children* to recognize.

The duality of these characters, as outsiders yet non-aggressively tame, makes *Alice in Wonderland* an anomaly in the Disney canon. As Sinyard notes, "In his desire to popularize Carroll and perhaps temper his occasional savagery, Disney had succeeded in transforming the malice of *Alice* into crude vaudeville."[12] Perhaps this explains the unpopularity of the film upon its release. The fact that the anarchic characters wield power over Alice signifies the ironic shift from childhood to adulthood, where Alice should be the one in charge since she is dealing with people who are not as clever as she seems to be. Their subversive nature, as creature-characters who represent Otherness, are antithetical to the fairy-tale characters of Disney's other films. Fairy-tale characters have a long tradition in folklore, and their appeal is much more straightforward than the literary characters of *Alice in Wonderland*. Fairy-tale characters are written exclusively for children, which helps explain why Disney has always used them as templates for their successful films. What makes *Alice in Wonderland* unusual, then, is the fact that the characters are drawn from a source that does not translate well into the world of the Disney cartoon.

Svankmajer's *Alice* is an adult film, meant to reflect the importance of connecting with childhood dreams. Because Alice narrates the story Svankmajer allows her to create Wonderland herself. Whenever someone speaks in the film, which is rare, Alice's mouth appears in close-up, saying things like, "...sighed the White Rabbit," or "...cried the Mad Hatter," or even, "...Alice thought to herself." Svankmajer's vision of the child's descent into Wonderland is definitely dark, so it refuses to settle on a Disney-esque style that could render it too civilized. Svankmajer tries to make the visually absurd, irrational equivalent of Carroll's books. Svankmajer himself said, "*Alice* as I filmed it and how, of course, Lewis Carroll conceived it on paper, is an infantile dream. I strictly adhered to its 'logic' when making the film."[13] Svankmajer takes liberties with the source, but he is not so much interested in fidelity than he is the tone, atmosphere, and character of Carroll's stories. He is more interested in depicting the way a child's dream can alter or enhance or influence her immediate, waking life. According to Reid, "Svankmajer engages in a dialogue with dream rather than losing himself in a fantasyland,"[14] which would put him at odds with Disney. Surrealism, in general, is concerned with irrationality, the unconscious, and liberation. Svankmajer's puppets, which he uses in almost all of his films, also suggest a close affinity with childhood imagination. The puppets come to life through animation, but a child's toy comes to life through the imagination. "Svankmajer's use of puppets steeps *Alice* in the realm of magic extending from Carroll, a source rich in irrationality, a quality that exists in magic ritual, dream and child's play,"[15] which also elicits dreams of childhood from the spectator. Svankmajer wants the audience to think about the importance of dream and memory and feel the textures of his animated objects, which, because they are done in striking stop-motion animation, do feel alive. By the end of Disney's version, by contrast, one feels slightly cheated. Ross even says, "All elements [in the film] combine to entrap the unwary viewer: to entice her to fantasize—even to pay money for the privilege—and then to make her feel, like Alice, guilty and ashamed."[16] Indeed, Disney has made the experience less than appetizing.

The stress on childhood really comes from the power to dream and then to realize these dreams—even when they are nightmares. Svankmajer's *Alice* structures itself as a dream, but it is ambiguous as to whether or not it really is a dream, since at the end, Alice sees that the White Rabbit is still missing from its glass enclosure. Since it is gone, we are not quite sure if Alice imagined or dreamt her time in Wonderland. Hames correctly notes, "At the end of *Alice*, when returned to the nursery with all her toys and fantasies apparently in place, Alice finds that the White Rabbit is missing—evidence for the reality of her adventures."[17] Memories that derive from dreams also help structure our understanding of the present, which was one of the key ideas in Carroll's books. Dreams can be a place of childlike innocence, nightmare, or a combination of the two. Alice's innocence is compromised to a certain extent once she enters Svankmajer's Wonderland, which becomes more of a nightmarish world where she must use her wits to survive.

Disney's *Alice in Wonderland* provides a perfect opportunity to consider how Alice's adventures may influence her waking life, but alas, Alice awakens as innocent as before, none the worse for her strange encounters. It is only the perceptive spectator who notices the irony of her encounters with the outsider—as an outsider herself—that can change her. As Deborah Ross suggest, by the end of the film, Alice is at "The center of a self-lacerating musical lament in which [she] abandons for good her fantasy of excitement and power to dwindle into a tiny, forlorn figure in the center of a large, dark frame." She adds, "In the end of the movie, the defiance and assertiveness of the line, 'You're only a pack of cards,' are lost."[18] Again, Disney's focus is more on the happiness of children instead of showing the reality of childhood, where dream

and imagination help create and sustain memory and remembrance. The outsider characters never directly address these issues, and while we may recognize
them, it would be blasphemous for Disney to address them head on. We are
left with our own recognition of the outsider characters, who may be a bit
annoying, but nevertheless are representative of the subversive nature of the
avant-garde. They all could be read as manifestations of unconscious states,
particularly those of childhood and the memories that shape one's cognition
and emotional and physical self. If only Disney recognized this, the potential
could have been enormous.

The many creatures in Svankmajer's *Alice* are also distinguished by their
"otherness." Their diversity stems from their odd construction. For example,
the animals that assist the White Rabbit as he tries to capture Alice are made
of skeletons. As Will Brooker notes, "The representation of the Rabbit and
his skeletal crew—a vicious canine and a team of ill-assembled skeletons, clacking their limbs as they drag mismatched tails behind toothy skulls—only
emphasizes the sadism and violence present in the original story."[19] Disney
completely dissolves the violence (even though Alice is subjected to some
sadistic events, particularly at the end when she runs away from all of the
menacing characters she has encountered in Wonderland). Svankmajer's object
animation emphasizes how it can change the parameters of the everyday, desta-
bilize our accepted ideas of reality, and challenge the conventional understanding of our existence. This is why Alice questions her surroundings in
Wonderland. Svankmajer has said that he believes inanimate objects have their
own lives and that it is part of his filmmaking process to bring their stories
out for others to see and hear, and also for his characters to interact with the
objects' tangible qualities. In *Alice*, for example, tools, rocks, scissors, buttons,
socks, and leaves all become animate and interact with Alice-as-human and
Alice-as-doll (itself an animated object). (Whenever Alice eats the cookie and
shrinks, she becomes a doll, which Svankmajer animates brilliantly.) Svankmajer's understanding of animation and his method of evoking moods and themes
is quite different from Disney. Svankmajer has also made clear his dissatisfaction with the way Disney animation is corruptive. When asked in an interview what he thinks about Disney, Svankmajer gave an eloquent, spirited
reply:

> Disney is among the greatest makers of "art for children." I have always held the
> view that no special art for children simply exists, and what passes for it embod-
> ies either the birch or lucre. "Art for children" is dangerous in that it shares
> either in the domestication of the child's soul ("educational art" = the birch) or
> the bringing up of consumers of mass culture (Disney). I am afraid that a child
> reared on the current produce of Disney will find it difficult to get used to more
> sophisticated and demanding kinds of art, and will easily assume his/her place
> in the ranks of viewers of idiotic TV serials.[20]

Clearly, Svankmajer's take on Disney's world of animated films is in high contrast to what he believes animation should and can accomplish. His animation reveals the mysterious personalities existent in dormant objects. This is entirely an avant-garde motif. As Svankmajer puts it, "I use real animation for mystification, for disturbing the utilitarian habits of the audience, to unsettle them, or for subversive purposes."[21] One thing Svankmajer does have in common with Disney, and especially with *Alice in Wonderland,* is the portrayal of the abnormal characters. The unusual characters of Disney's *Alice in Wonderland* exhibit "difference" in their attitudes toward Alice. Outsiders are usually used in literature or film to shed light on ideological issues such as diversity. In this way, they are meant to instruct us about ourselves, since we, the spectators in this case, are given the subjective perspective of viewing the outsiders of *Alice in Wonderland* from a "safe" environment. Disney, at least, presents them in such a way that makes the fact that they are outsiders relatively normal and acceptable in the world of Wonderland. In other words, being an outsider is tolerable; it is the rest of us—or society—that needs to be more accepting. To some extent, Alice learns this lesson during her adventures, even though the way Disney presents the characters is outlandish, for example, one of buffoonery (the White Rabbit) or forgetfulness (the Mad Hatter) or temperament (the Queen). Alice is constantly ordered by the characters to identify herself. Alice's identity is somewhat in crisis; the constant harangues of the people and critters she meets are meant to strengthen her own subjective perception of herself, and at the same time, provoking her into contemplation of larger issues of diversity.

That said, Disney's version does not overtly mention any of these themes, nor does it aspire to, which is why Alice does not learn from her adventures. As Sinyard notes, "Perhaps the structure is a little too meandering to engage a child's attention all the time ... one admires its cleverness, but its situations fail to move one."[22] But examining the film closely reveals that whether intentional or not, *Alice in Wonderland* is not so much about a girl's adventures than they are about a girl's maturation. Again, Disney does not offer this idea straightforwardly. The setting of Wonderland is symbolic; it is a reflection of the adult world, and therefore a "realistic" world. Wonderland, as depicted in Disney's film, is temporally and physically altered; animals speak (and remain sexless or asexual); people are disproportionate (Tweedledum and Tweedledee, the Red Queen); or Alice herself becomes smaller or larger, making objects or the natural world uneven. She tries to maneuver her way through the world according to irrationality. However, after she flees all of the menacing creatures of her dream-world, she wakes up, and thus is "saved."

The spaces of Svankmajer's Wonderland are claustrophobic, dark, and menacing. Alice's room is the same way—full of intricate and odd objects that create the threatening tone to the film. The confined space of her bedroom becomes the place for Wonderland. It is not a fantasy world of open skies and wooded passages like what we see in Disney. Disney's film does have "darker" colors in some scenes, but the brightly-hued Alice never seems in real threat. In contrast, in one horrific scene in Svankmajer's *Alice*, the skeletal creatures set upon her. The creatures hunt her down and cause her to fall into a pot full of milky-colored water. This graphic scene is Svankmajer's own imaginative way of rendering the violence in Carroll's text in an uncompromising way: in it, the animals hit Alice's face with small stones and the Pigeon "beats her violently with its wings."[23] Svankmajer's Alice is not an innocent victim adrift in a foreign world of typical Disney cutesy characters. Svankmajer recognizes the connection between the objects' world and that of Alice's world. According to Dryje, "The need for aggression, aimed at a certain object, and the need for its adoration are balanced, and this has a certain cathartic effect. The same principal provides the foundation for the emotional (and informational) blueprint of Carroll's *Alice's Adventure sin Wonderland*."[24]

In *Alice*, Svankmajer retells Carroll's stories in his own way. The original stories of *Alice's Adventures in Wonderland* and *Through the Looking-Glass* have encouraged many artists and readers alike to use the imagination as a source of inspiration. As Reid suggests, "The transportation to other nonsensical realms not unlike our own has prompted many artists to filter Wonderland through their own sensibilities."[25] Svankmajer's allegiance to surrealism makes his film avant-garde. According to Chris Jenks,

> Where centuries of classical philosophy, also in pursuit of the truth, had essentially recommended that we "should not let our imaginations run away with us," the Surrealists demanded that we should. Thus imagination (untrustworthy), the unconscious (inarticulate), and desire (unspoken), should now become trustworthy, articulate, and find voice, they should combine as out new mode of cognition and break out from the moral constraints that contemporary classifications of experience have placed upon us.[26]

Svankmajer's *Alice* precisely and deliberately delves into the imagination, the unconscious, and desire, and therefore reflects the avant-garde tendencies of tying dreams to everyday awareness. It is important to also realize that "The dream does not rule over reality, nor reality over the dream; their relationship is dialectical."[27] Thus, in Svankmajer's *Alice*, there is an ongoing investigation of the relationship that the imagination and the dream-world has over normal cognition. The closest Disney's *Alice in Wonderland* (perhaps) comes to this acknowledgement is in its (mis)appropriation as a "drug" movie in the 1970s. Several critics have noted that the film does seem more appropriate to a drug-induced "trip" (a la Alice's "adventures") than other Alice adaptations. Brooker, for instance, writes, "It is Disney's psychedelically multicolored *Alice* that seems most blatantly to invite the reading of Carroll's story as a drug hallucination."[28] If so, it is the only way the film could be mind-expansive on any sort of level. Svankmajer, by contrast, approaches the material in a different way. Reid suggests, "By constructing Wonderland from the recognizable materials of reality and dream, Svankmajer removes the psychedelic reading from Carroll that has been such an easy lapse for other artists."[29] Disney certainly had no intention of making a countercultural film, but the point is that Disney's film could potentially have ties to the workings of dream-states if we want to include the analogy of mind-altering with the avant-garde. It is a stretch, but there again, part of the surrealist wing of the avant-garde was a focus on the expansion of perception via dreams and the unconscious. Disney's diverse array of out of the ordinary characters also helps this argument—if one chooses to follow it.

Disney's *Alice in Wonderland* is not so much an adaptation as it is a dismantling of Carroll's books. This Americanization of Alice, as it were, reeks of popular culture, vaudeville, and sameness, a slight numbing effect that strips the original text of its wonders. Whereas Svankmajer relies upon his own aesthetic to adapt Carroll's ideas of dream and imagination more adequately, "Disney clearly distinguishes Wonderland as fantasy. It promotes Alice as innocent family fun, but cleans up the text, replacing the creatures' rudeness with zaniness, and their wordplay with music-hall pratfalls."[30] Still, should we care at all that Disney has altered the original so much that it becomes sanitized? Shouldn't *Alice in Wonderland* simply be fodder for children, meant to make them laugh as opposed to making them think? After all, "Disney's films offer children opportunities to locate themselves in a world that resonates with their desires and interests."[31] The debate is central to understanding the cultural merit of a film like *Alice in Wonderland*; because the characters in it are so different, we have to investigate their alternativeness.

Disney's undeniably influential animation and consumer-oriented product has predisposed audiences to "lose" themselves in their wondrous worlds. Children are especially appreciative of (susceptible to?) the magic of Disney's entertainment. By resisting the industry standard toward making films for a mature audience, Disney has established itself as a niche player and cornered the market on a loyal demographic. As Henry Giroux notes, "The boundaries between entertainment, education, and commercialization collapse through Disney's sheer reach into everyday life."[32] There will always be new generations who will grow up on Disney and those who are grown up and will return to Disney. Their films are good for "teachable moments," even when, as with the case of *Alice in Wonderland*, the messages in the film are not overly transparent.

Svankmajer's film allows us to recognize the importance of the everyday in our shaping of how we understand the significance of our imagination—to see, that is, how objects interact with themselves and with us when we choose to imagine it. The mundane can become magical. It is a powerful and vital message; what Svankmajer's *Alice* teaches us is how the visions of childhood can commingle with those of the adult world once memory is enacted. Disney's *Alice in Wonderland* prevents the possibility of tapping into the power of memory, simply because the film showcases exciting activity and exploration without linking the use of imagination to dream. According to Giroux, Disney "polices" its products: "The policing of memory erases the emancipatory possibilities of memory."[33] If this is the case, then *Alice in Wonderland* merely becomes nothing more than a "Disney cartoon for children."

Notes

1. Neil Sinyard, *The Best of Disney* (New York: Portland House, 1988), 70.
2. Deborah Ross, "Escape from Wonderland: Disney and the Female Imagination," *Marvels and Tales* 18.1 (2004): 58.
3. Peter Hames, "The Core of Reality: Puppets in the Feature Films of Jan Svankmajer," in *The Cinema of Jan Svankmajer: Dark Alchemy*, ed. Peter Hames (London: Wallflower Press, 2008), 88.
4. Sinyard, *The Best of Disney*, 70.
5. Hames, "The Core of Reality," 88.
6. Ross, "Escape from Wonderland," 58.
7. Tina-Louise Reid, "Alice," in *The Cinema of Central Europe*, ed. Peter Hames (London: Wallflower Press, 2004), 218.
8. Ibid, 215.
9. Frantisek Dryje, "The Force of Imagination," in *The Cinema of Jan Svankmajer: Dark Alchemy*, ed. Peter Hames (London: Wallflower Press, 2008), 156.
10. Roger Cardinal, "Thinking Through Things: The Presence of Objects in the Early Films of Jan Svankmajer," in *The Cinema of Jan Svankmajer: Dark Alchemy*, ed. Peter Hames (London: Wallflower Press, 2008), 75.
11. Reid, "Alice," 217.
12. Sinyard, *The Best of Disney*, 75.
13. Peter Hames, "Interview with Jan Svankmajer," in *The Cinema of Jan Svankmajer: Dark Alchemy*, ed. Peter Hames (London: Wallflower Press, 2008), 114.
14. Reid, "Alice," 218.
15. Ibid, 223.
16. Ross, "Escape from Wonderland," 58.
17. Hames, "The Core of Reality," 98–99.
18. Ross, "Escape from Wonderland," 57.
19. Will Brooker, *Alice's Adventures: Lewis Carroll in Popular Culture* (New York: Continuum, 2004), 216.
20. Hames, "Interview with Jan Svankmajer," 134.
21. Ibid, 120.
22. Sinyard, *The Best of Disney*, 75.
23. Lewis Carroll, *Alice's Adventures in Wonderland* (London: Penguin, 1865), 65.
24. Dryje, "The Force of Imagination," 174.
25. Reid, "Alice," 215.
26. Chris Jenks, *Transgression* (London: Routledge, 2003), 154.
27. Dryje, "The Force of Imagination," 155.
28. Brooker, *Alice's Adventures*, 217.
29. Reid, "Alice," 218.
30. Brooker, *Alice's Adventures*, 218.
31. Henry A. Giroux, *The Mouse That Roared: Disney and the End of Innocence* (Lanham, MD: Rowman and Littlefield, 1999), 91.
32. Ibid, 89.
33. Ibid, 129.

Bibliography

Brooker, Will. *Alice's Adventures: Lewis Carroll in Popular Culture.* New York: Continuum, 2004.

Cardinal, Roger. "Thinking Through Things: The Presence of Objects in the Early Films of Jan Svankmajer." In *The Cinema of Jan Svankmajer: Dark Alchemy*, edited by Peter Hames, 67–82. London: Wallflower Press, 2008.

Carroll, Lewis. *Alice's Adventures in Wonderland*. London: Penguin, 1865.

Dryje, Frantisek. "The Force of Imagination." In *The Cinema of Jan Svankmajer: Dark Alchemy*, edited by Peter Hames, 143–203. London: Wallflower Press, 2008.

Giroux, Henry A. *The Mouse that Roared: Disney and the End of Innocence*. Lanham, MD: Rowman and Littlefield, 1999.

Hames, Peter. "The Core of Reality: Puppets in the Feature Films of Jan Svankmajer." In *The Cinema of Jan Svankmajer: Dark Alchemy*, edited by Peter Hames, 83–103. London: Wallflower Press, 2008.

Hames, Peter. "Interview with Jan Svankmajer." In *The Cinema of Jan Svankmajer: Dark Alchemy*, edited by Peter Hames, 104–139. London: Wallflower Press, 2008.

Jenks, Chris. *Transgression*. London: Routledge, 2003.

Reid, Tina-Louise. "Alice." *In The Cinema of Central Europe*, edited by Peter Hames, 215–223. London: Wallflower Press, 2004.

Ross, Deborah. "Escape from Wonderland: Disney and the Female Imagination." *Marvels and Tales* 18.1 (2004): 53–66.

Sinyard, Neil. *The Best of Disney*. New York: Portland House, 1988.

(Indivi)duality in Return to Oz: Reflection and Revision

ANA SALZBERG

In the last scene of Walter Murch's 1985 film *Return to Oz*, Dorothy Gale (Fairuza Balk) stands before the mirror in her bedroom in Kansas and traces the word *Oz* onto the glass as she whispers the name "Ozma." Immediately, a white light radiates from the mirror, and Ozma (Emma Ridley) herself appears: the young queen of Oz, long banished from her kingdom and only rightfully reinstated by Dorothy in a series of adventures fraught with dark magic and enchantment. Thrilled, Dorothy calls to her aunt to come and see the image of Ozma—who then holds her finger to her lips to caution silence. When Aunt Em (Piper Laurie) finally enters the room, Dorothy hurriedly turns the mirror away and tells her calmly, "It's nothing. Just a reflection." As the audience has learned on this journey to Oz and back, however, Dorothy and Ozma are far more than "just reflections" of each other. Giving form to the intertwining of the realist and fantastic that defines the film itself, the young girls share an inter-subjective dialogue—an existential exchange between two discrete but interconnected entities that exalts the merging of corporeality and ethereality, the natural and the supernatural.

Yet upon the movie's release through Walt Disney Pictures, audiences and critics expressed consternation that *Return to Oz* was itself not "just a reflection" of its classic predecessor, Victor Fleming's *The Wizard of Oz* (1939).[1] Eschewing the musical numbers and chromatic splendor of the earlier film, Murch instead wrote and directed a work that pays homage to L. Frank Baum's original novels, particularly *The Marvelous Land of Oz* (1904) and *Ozma of Oz* (1907).[2] With its diegetic universe bounded by a bleakly realist Kansas (in which Dorothy is prescribed electroconvulsive therapy to treat her "bad waking dreams" of Oz) and a devastated Emerald City, conquered and turned to stone by the evil Nome King (Nicol Williamson), *Return to Oz* offers a dystopic vision of corrupted fantasies and paradises lost. In *The Imaginary Signifier*, theorist Christian Metz describes film as "a beautiful closed object ... whose contours remain intact and which cannot therefore be torn open into an inside and an outside"[3]; yet in his revision-ing of cinematic Oz, Murch reveals the fragmentation of a "beautiful closed" cultural object—or, as he himself termed it, a "cultural artifact"[4]—through an unsettling fairy tale produced, ironically, by the very studio that ensured the iconicity of such mythologies.

With this in mind, *Return to Oz* stands as a radical reflection of not only its classic predecessor but the Walt Disney Pictures canon itself, the strictures of traditional family entertainment challenged by the imaginings of an Oz "torn open." Rejecting the cheerfully-uncanny quality of *Alice in Wonderland* (1951) or the rousing magic of *Bedknobs and Broomsticks* (Robert Stevenson, 1971), for example, Murch's work evokes a supernatural that undermines, rather than ultimately defers to, the dominance of the normative natural realm—and, by extension, the dominance of a normative cultural mythology. Embodying this interplay of reflection and revision are Dorothy and Ozma themselves, doubles in the ever-shifting parameters between the reality of Kansas and the fantasy of Oz, the material and the ephemeral. Through the lens of Dorothy and Ozma's dialogue of subjectivities, then, the film explores the limits of extra- and intra-diegetic (indivi)duality, redefining the "inside and outside" of a theretofore inviolable ideality both within the land of Oz and Disney's Hollywood.

Producing Fantasy: Disney and Oz

Since the beginning of its feature-film production with *Snow White and the Seven Dwarfs* (1937), Disney has ensured the legacy of its animated and live-action filmmaking through an alliance with narratives ingrained within the Western collective cultural consciousness. In this symbiotic relationship, through which Walt Disney Pictures assumes the prestige of classic works whilst enabling their renaissance, fairy tales like *Cinderella* (1950) and *Sleeping Beauty* (1959), and beloved children's books like Johann David Wyss' *The Swiss Family Robinson* (Ken Annakin, 1960) and P.L. Travers' *Mary Poppins* (Robert Stevenson, 1964) comprise a contemporary mythology sustained indefinitely by the Disney franchise. As Jack Zipes writes, "Walt Disney established a dynasty that 'appropriated' classic narratives and 'obfuscated' their original authorship through 'his technical skills and ideological proclivities.'"[5] Appealing to the modern audience's continued fascination with the moving image, Disney Pictures has since become the collective *auteur* of the fairy tale genre for generations of children.

Though not directly associated with *Wizard*, a film emblematic of Metro-Goldwyn Mayer's legendary artistry in the production of studio-era musicals,

Disney nonetheless approached its cinematic retellings with a similar style: the lushness of the images conjuring a realm of thrilling, fantastic possibility; the spirited musical numbers punctuating the progression of the narrative; and the "happy ending" ultimately affirming the supremacy of domestic accord and the triumph over a destabilizing supernatural. Rick Altman has observed that in the fairy tale musical of classic Hollywood, "the love stories ... are never the courtship of a man and a woman alone, they always imply the romance of spectator and image."[6] In the Disney pantheon of fairy tales and its kindred *The Wizard of Oz*, however, the love affair between the audience and the film as—to recall Murch's words—"cultural artifact" has become equally important.

In the early 1980s, Disney pursued an alternative mode of production with dark works like *The Watcher in the Woods* (1982; directed by John Hough and starring Bette Davis) and *Something Wicked This Way Comes* (1983; directed by Jack Clayton and written by Ray Bradbury). Appealing to a more adult audience with their uncanny narratives and imagery, these sinister counterparts to Disney's massive output of wholesome fantasy utilized live-action to recount the often-horrific dramas of human figures placed directly in thrall to destructive supernatural forces. Yet as such unique works, virtually *sui generis* in the world of Disney, the two films did not engage directly with the overdetermined paradigm of family entertainment that preceded *Return to Oz*. In a series of interviews with novelist Michael Ondaatje, Murch explained, "I loved the daring of trying to make a sequel. A little like saying, Let's make a sequel to *Gone With the Wind*."[7] Undaunted by the Technicolor shadow of *The Wizard of Oz* and the expectations of the Disney franchise, Murch explored an altogether different cinematic territory.

Evoking the feminist sensibilities of the original *Oz* novels—as Murch pointed out, "All the really creative, interesting people in [Baum's] books are women"[8]—*Return to Oz* crafts a gothic adventure story centered on two heroines bearing a multi-dimensional impact upon and agency within the cinematic universe.[9] The film opens with a troubled Dorothy, haunted by memories of Oz and unable to make her family believe her accounts of magic and adventure. Taken to a clinic for electroconvulsive therapy, Dorothy is almost "cured" of her visions—but a felicitous lightning storm allows her to escape, with the help of a mysterious young girl later identified as Ozma. Dorothy makes her way to Oz on a raging river, and once there finds the land conquered by doubles for the clinic's doctor and nurse, in the form of the evil Nome King and Princess Mombi (Jean Marsh). With the help of various new friends, Dorothy defeats these enemies and frees Ozma from the enchanted mirror in which she has been trapped by Mombi. Ozma then sends Dorothy back to Kansas, with the promise that she may return to Oz any time she wishes.

Indeed, the movie itself establishes a flux between the registers of time and space—and, most strikingly, between the phenomena of the natural and supernatural. Heightening this union is the interplay between live-action individuals and sophisticated mechanical figures designed for the production. In contrast to other cinematic depictions of Oz that either used make-up and costuming to merge the corporeal and the imaginary (including Fleming's *Wizard*, as well as Sidney Lumet's *The Wiz* [1978]) or straightforward animation (as in 1974's *Journey Back to Oz*, featuring the voices of Liza Minnelli and Mickey Rooney), Murch's film sets in place a complex performance-dialogue between the human and the mechanical that evokes the existential versatility defining Oz itself. Ultimately, rather than ascribe magic to entirely external forces (the witchcraft correspondence courses in *Bedknobs and Broomsticks*; Mary Poppins's flight into and out of the family home), Murch's film offers an a-dichotomous, a-hierarchical universe asserting not the privileging of the real over the fantastic, but the intertwining thereof.

Where the original Dorothy's closing declaration, "There's no place like home," stands as a creed articulating the power of the normative to prevail over the lure of the extraordinary, *Return* instead captures Dorothy's resistance to such divisions. Before leaving Oz, Dorothy tells her friends with plaintive gravity, "I wish I could be in both places at the same time." Through the continuum between magical and actual, corporeal and ethereal established within both the film as a whole and the unique dynamic shared by Dorothy and Ozma, the former's wish does come true—just as, moreover, the dissolved binary between reflection and revision allows *Return to Oz* to assert its autonomy from the very cinematic dynasty it inherited.

Reflection and Embodiment

The title sequence of *Return to Oz* sets forth the union between natural and supernatural that will come to define the film. After an opening shot of a black sky suffused with stars, the camera pulls back steadily until it reveals the frame of a window through which the sky is seen, followed by the surrounding curtains and walls of Dorothy's bedroom itself. Tilted at an angle throughout this panning back, the room seems to drift through the cosmos pictured in the window, in this way creating a not-unpleasant sense of disorientation for the spectator. The continual backward motion of the camera, however, soon adds a further dimension to this suspended spatiality: the frame of a slanted mirror that now contains the image of room and sky. Rather than glimpse the diegetic environment in the immediate actuality offered by a window, then, the audience has gazed upon a reflected reality through a looking glass.

Merging the planes of the material and *im*material, this establishing shot presents a variation on the framing devices (in terms of both narrative structure and *mise en scène*) so often used to place reality and fantasy in opposition. Here, there are no doorways to a Technicolor world as in *The Wizard of Oz*, or enchanted storybooks in which to plunge as in *Bedknobs and Broomsticks*.

Instead, the intrinsically connected succession of frames—those of the window, mirror, and shot itself—convey to the viewer that the actual *is* ethereal; and the supposedly insubstantial, inverted reality of the mirror is, in fact, a *continuation* of the physicality it captures. The following sequences affirm this interplay: Looking into the mirror as she lies in bed, Dorothy sees a shooting star soar across the reflected night sky; the next day, she finds a key bearing the word *OZ* in the fields of the farm. At once, Dorothy knows that her friends have sent it to her on the shooting star—she recognizes, that is, the key as the material trace of an ephemeral dimension ever-present through the mirror-as-channel.

With the looking glass thus depicted as an active mediator of experience rather than a static object, the subsequent introduction of Ozma within a reflection resonates with possibility—the promise of a physical impact wrought by an ethereal energy. Seated in the doctor's study, Dorothy—with eyes red-rimmed from her sleepless nights remembering Oz—gazes upon the machine that will manage what the doctor calls "excess currents" responsible for her memories. Soon the face of a young girl appears in the glass casing of the machine. Dorothy turns to find her smiling through the study window, a serene figure with blonde hair and pale skin standing in contrast to Dorothy's own exhausted form. When Dorothy looks back a moment later, the girl has vanished, but reappears in the following sequence as, again, a reflection in the window of Dorothy's room in the clinic.

Such discussions of reflection and doubling (especially in terms of children) must, of course, address the framework of Lacan's mirror stage. In this paradigm, an infant approaches the mirror and there encounters his/her double, an ideal being that seems endowed with all of the abilities the actual infant lacks. Alternately identifying with the reflection (in a moment of misrecognition) and jealously coveting its capacities, the individual confronts the fundamental dichotomy between a limited reality and an elusive ideality that will haunt him/her throughout existence.[10] Though seductive as a theory, it would nonetheless be simplistic to regard the dynamic between Dorothy and Ozma as a formulaic enactment of the mirror stage. For where Lacan insists upon the reflected other as "a mirage" utterly exterior to the self, within which the individual perceives the cohesion of his discrete corporeal elements,[11] *Return to Oz* depicts Ozma and Dorothy as subjects of commensurate agency moving through and beyond the mirror to influence both the natural and supernatural dimensions. In this film, the mirror is not the exclusive province of the double and her accompanying "psychical realities"[12] but—as asserted in the title sequence—a window between the fantastic and the actual.

Murch himself mused upon the ambiguity of Ozma's identity: "Is she a real person? Or is she an abstract Oz creature, who projected herself into the dimension of the real, in order to influence certain events?"[13] Later, implicitly acknowledging the fluidity of the *Oz* universe, Murch noted, "[T]hat question—Who is Ozma?—is given to the audience to answer. The film doesn't answer it."[14] What the film does declare, however, is that Ozma belongs wholly to the existential continuum set in place within *Return to Oz*, functioning as both an abstraction *and* an embodied figure—as the sequence in which she rescues Dorothy from the clinic definitively expresses. Strapped onto a gurney and wheeled into the operating room, Dorothy only escapes the surge of electricity through a literally last-second bolt of lightning that cuts off the power. The doctor and nurse leave her alone in the darkness, filled with the sounds of winding-down machinery and the screams of tormented patients confined in the depths of the cellar.[15] Noiselessly, the blonde girl appears and frees Dorothy, leading her out of the operating room and down the corridors to flee the clinic.

As they race down the labyrinthine hallways with linked hands, their blurred forms outlined only by flashes of streaming hair and Dorothy's waving arm as she careens in Ozma's wake, the children are virtually indistinguishable from each other. A brief but striking point-of-view shot, filmed with a hand-held camera to capture the panicked rush of the flight, all but insists upon the merging of the girls' identities here as they share bodily agency and subjective perception in a desperate attempt to survive. Finally breaking out of the clinic, the children run through the surrounding woods to a riverbank, followed by the wraith-like figure of the head nurse. With the storm crashing and the nurse shouting after them, the girls have no choice but to plunge into the flooding river; and carried away on the raging tide, both Dorothy and Ozma sink in the water. Only Dorothy emerges. Crawling into a floating crate, she drifts away from the clinic and towards Oz. In contrast to Altman's description of the whimsical "romance of spectator and image" in cinematic fairy tale works, this sequence calls for a more visceral rapport with the viewer (heightened by the resounding minor chords of the musical score): the sensory depth of the branches, rain, and mud through which Ozma and Dorothy struggle, the sheer force of the water that claims Ozma in that moment of wrenching turmoil. The catalyst for Dorothy's return to Oz is not, then, a single event—a strictly natural disaster like the original tornado—but rather an extended alignment of oneiric terror and sensual gravity.

In her phenomenological study of cinema, theorist Vivian Sobchack relates such on-screen sensory suffusions to the embodied experience as a whole. She defines embodiment as a "condition of human being that necessarily entails both the body and consciousness, objectivity and subjectivity, in an *irreducible ensemble*."[16] Embodied existence, then, calls for the cohesion between the registers of experience—an acceptance of, rather than a resistance to, the ever-present interplay between the corporeal and the psychical. With this in mind, Ozma and Dorothy's fusion in the hyper-sensory escape sequence presents a realization of their dialogical identities, the affirmation of each child's mutually invested consciousness and physical form. Ozma is not a mere reflection of Dorothy's desire for an ideal double, just as Dorothy is not simply the bodily counterpart to an ethereal projection. To paraphrase Murch's remark, Ozma and Dorothy are *both* "real people" and the inhabitants of an abstract realm. Together, they represent figures of versatile dimensionality, comprising not only body and consciousness but the possibilities of the supernatural within the context of the natural It is such an intertwining between the material and the ephemeral that, as the subsequent discussion will detail, founds Murch's approach to—his revised reflection of—the land of cinematic Oz itself.

A New Kind of Mirror

In his analysis of the Lacanian imaginary in the experience of cinema, Metz describes an on-screen image as "not really the object" it attempts to capture but "its shade, its phantom, its double, its *replica* in a new kind of mirror."[17] If one applies the Metzian paradigm of the vexed relationship between reality and filmic imaginary to the notion of a cinematic sequel, *Return to Oz* stands as a "new kind of mirror" in its rapport with the original "object" of *The Wizard of Oz*. For Murch's film rejects any characterization as a one-dimensional "shade, phantom, double" of the work so embedded in cultural consciousness—it claims, instead, a discrete identity complementary to, but not dependent upon, its antecedent. This approach was, however, fairly controversial; as Murch remarked, the public demanded, "How dare you make a sequel to *The Wizard of Oz*? And how dare you make it in the way you made it?"[18]

Perhaps most shocking to audiences were the images of an Oz in ruins: the iconic Yellow Brick Road destroyed; the Ruby Slippers stolen by the Nome King; the Emerald City and its inhabitants turned to stone; and the beloved Scarecrow transformed into an ornament in the evil king's collection. Following the Nome King's *coup*, the only animate entities remaining in Oz are supporters like Princess Mombi, a shape-shifting witch, and the Wheelers, frightening half-men who stalk Dorothy on arms and legs made of wheels. In an article discussing the franchise of the *Oz* books and their subsequent cinematic representations, Richard Flynn mentions *Return to Oz* only to disparage the tableau of the desolated Yellow Brick Road as "emblematic of the film's failure."[19] But contrary to this facile condemnation, the Oz imagery in Murch's film triumphs in its creation of a landscape of purely suspended animation—an environment in which the beings are not dead, but waiting to be brought back to life.

As Dorothy wanders through the courtyard of the Emerald City, the bleak surroundings seem to vibrate with the sensory echo of once-vital ladies and gentlemen—and, especially poignantly, the Cowardly Lion and Tin Man—who now linger in an extended, collective pause. Ostensibly, the scene depicts a vast lifelessness in an Oz made uncanny; but more than this, it evokes the land's inherently ambiguous relationship to questions of mortality. Murch reminds us, "There's an ambivalence about the fact that in Oz nothing ever dies.... It's a world in which there is dismemberment but no death."[20] As this sequence demonstrates, it is also a world in which there is existential suspension rather than death. In a particularly affecting shot capturing this melding of sentient flesh and frozen stone, a close-up frames the face of one of the women. Mouth open, eyes wide in distress, her expression of alarm seems to reach beyond the confines of her static condition to warn Dorothy of coming danger. To paraphrase Metz's terms, this woman and her fellow inhabitants are beautiful closed objects on the verge of breaking open—like the cultural artifact of cinematic Oz itself.

Through the character of Princess Mombi, however, *Return to Oz* explores the dangers of remaining a beautiful closed object, the threat of producing only simulacra of an original being. Residing in a palace paneled entirely in mirrors, Mombi focuses much of her substantial powers on the transformation of her physical form—a pursuit made possible through her possession of a collection of heads, stolen from the young dancing girls of the Emerald City. In a variety of countenances—all lovely, all animate—the heads of the women are kept in cabinets lining the walls of a long corridor; and as Mombi walks down the hall, each watches and waits for the witch to select her chosen incarnation. Mombi also seeks to make Dorothy vulnerable to these machinations, deciding to imprison the girl in a tower until her own "certain kind of prettiness" emerges and the witch may take her head.

Rather than represent an exaltation of what Sobchack describes as the lived-body's "excessive and ambiguous ... materiality, ... polymorphism, and ... production of existential meaning,"[21] Mombi's shape-shifting stands as a corruption of the embodied experience—the appropriation of another's physical form in order to realize the infinite variety of her ideal selves. Mombi's is a decadent dark magic, a supernatural force consumed with the gratification of narcissistic desires; and in reducing these individuals to objects of self-obsessed aestheticism, Mombi renders the heads a collective simulacrum of her own identity. In a troubling inversion of the mirror's significance in the dialogue of subjectivities between Dorothy and Ozma, Mombi's own head resides in the only mirrored cabinet on the corridor—languishing on a shelf containing the discarded accoutrements of her magic. In Cabinet 31, the looking glass conceals, rather than adds dimension to, the actual self that lies on the other side of the reflection.

The violation of the medium of the mirror, emblematic of the depth of Mombi's villainy, bears dire consequences for Ozma herself. Banished by the Nome King and cursed by Mombi to an exile in the mirrors of the palace, Ozma lives as a green flash fluttering desperately from one panel to another. Through this spell, Ozma finds herself suspended within the veneer of a surface reflection, a mockery of the very element that had served as her window to the material realm. Recalling Metz's terms, Mombi has succeeded in making Ozma a "shade, phantom, double" in a kind of mirror decidedly unnatural within the universe of *Return to Oz*: one that limits, rather than expands, the existential situation of the characters, severing the fusion between the registers of experience that has guided Dorothy and Ozma. The witch attempts, then, to reduce the "irreducible ensemble" of that cohesive embodied existence described by Sobchack, to restrict the "excessive and ambiguous" possibilities of the lived-body to the confines of a shallow mirror and a narrow cabinet.

Yet the fundamental unity between body and consciousness proves its resilience. As Dorothy tries to flee the palace, she loses her way in the mirrored interior and cannot find a way out. Suddenly, a flickering opalescence appears upon one of the walls, briefly taking shape as the hazy image of a young girl beckoning to Dorothy. Following the direction of the projection, Dorothy exits the hall through a door concealed by the surface of the mirror. Just as in the clinic sequence, Ozma again saves Dorothy's life. Prevailing against the reductive power of a sinister looking glass, the dynamic engagement between Dorothy and Ozma asserts that the greatest magic lies within the intrinsically connected elements of corporeal form and ethereal subjectivity. Dorothy may have to fight to preserve her bodily identity from Mombi's covetous narcissism, and Ozma may wander in her *im*material exile, but it is only the witch herself who is truly trapped within the cursed mirror.

If Mombi's hall of heads and mirrored palace make manifest the dangers of a myopic preoccupation with the reproduction of an ideal image, the adherence to the dictates of a "beautiful closed object," then Dorothy and Ozma's transcendent communication within that realm of dark magic affirms *Return to Oz*'s own identity as a "new kind of mirror" of cinematic Oz. As if in articulation of the film's radical project, the sight of Ozma projected onto the mirror recalls the Technicolor splendor of MGM's *Wizard* as it unreels—only to give way, as Dorothy literally goes through the looking glass, to a world beyond the seemingly-insulated "screen." Evoking an Oz not explored by the original, canonical film, *Return to Oz* defines itself as a film-as-mirror reflecting the alternative possibilities of that legendary land rather than its immediate iconic associations.

Through the Looking Glass

The last of the Oz sequences does, however, present a land more in keeping with the audience's traditional conceptions. After Dorothy has reclaimed the Ruby Slippers and reanimated the Emerald City, the people of Oz celebrate in a grand parade that leads to Princess Mombi's now-cheerful palace. It is an illustrious fete, filled with classic figures from the original film: the Munchkins make an appearance, as do the Scarecrow, Tin Man, and Cowardly Lion. In a final gesture of victory, guards carry a caged Mombi through the crowds.

Her magical powers taken from her, she is now, as she concedes, "a miserable creature indeed." Though meant to represent the joyful ending to Dorothy's quest, the triumphant return of the familiar, the scene nonetheless bears a quality incongruous to the greater film itself. In this self-conscious rendering of the iconic Oz, the viewer recognizes the "shade, phantom, double" of *Wizard* from which *Return to Oz* consistently differentiates itself; the infusion of a merry fantastic belonging more to the "wonderful world of Disney" than to the unsettled/ing universe of a revision-ed Oz. Rather than detract from the happy ending to Dorothy's harrowing adventures, however, this juxtaposition serves to emphasize the affective power of the Oz in which the audience heretofore found itself immersed. The brief reconstruction of the cultural artifact, that is, emphasizes how successfully it has been altered.

The final sequence also captures a climactic encounter between Dorothy and Ozma, those dual subjectivities so crucial to the project of the film. After Dorothy refuses the title of Queen of Oz, declaring that she has "to go back" but longs to be in Kansas and Oz "at the same time," the Ruby Slippers she is wearing glow brightly. Immediately, the green flash that is Ozma appears in the mirrored wall and, finally, takes form as a girl in royal dress. In a medium long-shot, the camera frames a tableau in which Dorothy and her friends face the expanse of the looking glass—only to see Ozma standing in Dorothy's place in the otherwise faithful reflection of the palace scene. After both children walk up to their respective sides of the mirror with symmetrical precision, Dorothy recognizes Ozma as her savior from the clinic; Ozma only replies, "Help me step through the glass, Dorothy." Reaching up to touch the looking glass, the girls link hands as the mirror begins to shimmer, and Ozma leaves the realm of the ethereal to join Dorothy in the material.

Crystallizing the issues of actuality and fantasy, corporeality and ethereality that have shaped the relationship between the girls, these images address the fundamental question that Murch himself posed: *"Who is Ozma?"*[22] With this mystery in mind, does the scene, in which Ozma literally takes Dorothy's place in the world of the mirror, contend that the two are in fact the same entity? That they are, ultimately, interchangeable? In a diegetic world that rejects the polarization of experience, however, the answer to Ozma's identity cannot be defined in terms of the absolute. Instead, it lies in the mirror itself, that ethereal continuation of a physical dimension providing a channel between natural reality and supernatural potential. As Ozma stands in regal splendor, directly facing Dorothy's humbler aspect, the mirror fulfills its role as a window framing yet another alternate world—one in which Ozma has been restored to her rightful place as ruler and stands before her loyal subjects. And just as Dorothy needed Ozma's aid in order to escape the clinic, Ozma now calls upon Dorothy's kindred presence in order to realize this vision of Oz's future.

Highlighting this mutuality is composer David Shire's scoring of the scene. Throughout the film, Dorothy and Ozma's respective themes—the former's a sweetly melancholy melody, the latter's a grave, grand work—suffuse the aural space of the soundtrack in a musical evocation of the narrative's pathos. Indeed, Shire's score presents a lyrical complement to the diegetic soundtrack, creating a rich aural dimensionality resonating with moments of mournful strings and footsteps on the stones of the Emerald City; somber brass and the sound of Mombi's key turning in the locks of her cabinets. Engaging with the actual and the ethereal like Dorothy and Ozma themselves, Murch and Shire's sound-dialogue further affirms the film's guiding concern with the continuum between natural and supernatural. In this defining moment before the mirror, with Ozma's theme representing what Murch calls a "musical inversion" of Dorothy's,[23] the melodies intertwine in an orchestral union that heightens—reflects—the embodied harmony between both sides of the looking glass.

    In his discussion of Ozma, Murch went on to suggest, "[M]aybe she's a projection of some aspect of Dorothy. But maybe it's the opposite."[24] Or perhaps it is both. Each giving form to elements of the abstract and the actual, Dorothy and Ozma are not interchangeable or, to return to the line of dialogue that opened this essay, "just reflections" of each other. Instead, they *co*-exist as discrete but reciprocally invested beings, engaging in an existential exchange that asserts the interconnectedness of the body and consciousness, the natural and the supernatural—with the mirror forming a channel between flesh and spirit. Neither Dorothy nor Ozma is an authentic original in contrast to the other as shadowed reflection; nor, indeed, is *Wizard* placed in sacrosanct opposition to its successor. For in that a-dichotomous, a-hierarchical realm constructed in *Return to Oz*, each is a beautiful *open subject*.

The Return

    Throughout the film, a subtle but substantial threat to Oz provides an unsettling undercurrent in the narrative: the act of forgetting—the land of Oz itself, its inhabitants, and the halcyon days before the Nome King's revolution. First faced by Dorothy in the electroconvulsive-therapy sequence, the peril of the eradication of memory is entirely associated with the forces of dark magic; and as such, it provides a source of delight for the Nome King and Mombi. After plotting an elaborate game for turning Dorothy and her friends into ornaments for his collection, the King exclaims, "Soon there'll be no one left who remembers Oz"; and as she watches Ozma flutter desperately from one mirror to another, Mombi taunts the exiled queen, "There's nobody left who even knows *who* you are." In a final challenge to Dorothy's honor, the Nome King—like the clinic doctor for whom he is a double—attempts to cajole her into abandoning her friends to their frozen fates: "Forget about them." Even in Oz, a world of immortality ostensibly challenged only by in-animation, the act of forgetting represents the phenomenon closest to death: the withdrawing of one's subjective awareness from another living entity—the separation of a consciousness and a body.

In relating such notions to the process of making *Return to Oz* itself, one could argue that the question of memory stands as an especially complex issue. With *Wizard* and the Disney canon of family-fantasy ubiquitous in the collective consciousness of the audience, *Return to Oz* from its inception met with the expectations imposed by these paragons. To diverge from such an institutional memory was perceived as a nearly blasphemous act of forgetting—a willful turning away from the history of family entertainment. Truly, in its revision-ing of cinematic Oz, an exploration founded in re-creation rather than reflection, *Return to Oz* represents a moment of expansion for Walt Disney Pictures. More than merely rebel against its antecedents, the production of the film insisted that audiences actively engage with their established understanding of the cultural artifact of Oz; and in this way, the movie constructed a universe appealing to renewed perceptions rather than gratified preconceptions. In an extra-diegetic variation on the sinister electroconvulsive therapy sequence, the film bespoke a *reinvigoration* of memory rather than the negation thereof—testing the boundaries of the culturally revered in a stimulating challenge to passive remembrance. In the context of Murch's work, then, it is far more dangerous to let Oz languish as a beautiful closed object; to allow Ozma to remain in the mirror, or the Scarecrow as an ornament, for fear of shattering the object and revealing an alternative entity.

The unique cinematic being that is *Return to Oz* concludes with Dorothy's return to Kansas. Found on a riverbank, Dorothy learns that the clinic from which she escaped burned down in the lightning storm, and that the doctor lost his life trying to save his machines. Yet even in the safety of Aunt Em's embrace, Dorothy cannot truly evade the traces of the supernatural that still suffuse the natural of Kansas. Stunned, she sees the nurse, who had been reincarnated in the form of Mombi, mysteriously imprisoned in the back of a police wagon trundling down the road in an eerie reprise of the parade in the Emerald City. In another infusion of the fantastic into the actual, this image signals to both Dorothy and the audience that though Oz itself has been liberated, the realm of reality remains under its spell. This enchantment, of course, finds a far more poignant realization in Ozma's appearance in Dorothy's mirror. As discussed earlier, Ozma's presence in the domestic space of Kansas offers a final affirmation of the continuum between the supernatural and natural, as well as the kinship between the two young girls who are so much more than "just reflections" of each other. Though the movie ends with Dorothy playing outside with Toto on a sunny day, what lingers as the film ends is the wistfulness of her expression when she turns back to the mirror—only to realize that Ozma has, for the moment, vanished.

Although her reflection is fleeting, Ozma and the land she rules remain with Dorothy in a more material way. Before Aunt Em and Uncle Henry find

Dorothy on the riverbank, she lies on the ground alone. In an expression of what Martine Beugnet has termed a "body-landscape" effect, or a shot that explores the surface and texture of a corporeal figure,[25] an extreme close-up frames Dorothy's eye as she gazes straight ahead. Grounded in the physical, the image indeed creates a landscape of Dorothy's skin and eye, the elements of her visage filling the screen as completely as the vistas of the Kansas prairies or the expanse of night sky which opened the film. Dorothy's eye itself, however, is a green as vivid as the verdant flash so associated with Ozma's presence. It is, in fact, emerald.

In this ultimate fusion of the ethereal and the physical, the shot proclaims Dorothy's literal incorporation of the fantastic dimension to which she and Ozma equally belong—the embodied conjunction of an otherworldly vision and a mortal form. Like the audience itself, Dorothy bears a gaze that will not forget the return to Oz.

Notes

1. As Janet Maslin wrote in her review for *The New York Times*, "Return to Oz is the work of ingenious technicians who seem either not to know what gave the original film its magic, or not to care. Instead of ... [a] sequel ... [Murch's film] is more of a grim variation."

2. A renowned film editor and sound engineer, Murch has contributed to a myriad of important works, including *Apocalypse Now* (Francis Ford Coppola, 1979) and *The English Patient* (Anthony Minghella, 1996); and in 1998, he re-edited Orson Welles's *Touch of Evil* (1958) in accordance with the director's original vision. To date, *Return to Oz* is the only film that he has directed.

3. Christian Metz, *The Imaginary Signifier: Psychoanalysis and the Cinema*. Trans. Celia Britton, Annwyl Williams, Ben Brewster, and Alfred Guzzetti (Bloomington: Indiana University Press, 1977), 94—95.

4. In Michael Ondaatje, *The Conversations: Walter Murch and the Art of Editing Film*. (London: Bloomsbury Publishing, 2002), 285.

5. Jack Zipes, "Breaking the Disney Spell," in *From Mouse to Mermaid: The Politics of Film, Gender, and Culture*, eds. Elizabeth Bell, Lynda Haas, Laura Sells (Bloomington: Indiana University Press, 1995), 21.

6. Rick Altman, *The American Film Musical* (Bloomington: Indiana University Press, 1989), 153.

7. Ondaatje, 285.

8. Ondaatje, 290.

9. Disney's engagement with young female protagonists continued in the live-action film *The Journey of Natty Gann* (directed by Jeremy Kagan), also released in 1985. In this work, a teenage girl crosses Depression-era America to find her father.

10. Jacques Lacan, *Ecrits*. Trans. Bruce Fink. (New York: W.W. Norton, 2006.) 77.

11. Lacan, 76.

12. Lacan, 77.

13. Ondaatje, 105.

14. Ondaatje, 107.

15. In a letter to the *Journal of Biological Psychiatry*, John Hodgkinson (on behalf of The Manic-Depressive Association) decried the film's depiction of electroconvulsive therapy. Moreover, he called for a campaign to convince Disney to either withdraw the movie from distribution or edit the sequence at the clinic. (*Biological Psychiatry* 21 [May 1986]: 578.)

16. Vivian Sobchack, *Carnal Thoughts: Embodiment and Moving Image Culture* (Berkeley: University of California Press, 2004), 4.

17. Metz, 45.

18. Ondaatje, 285.

19. Richard Flynn, "Imitation Oz: The Sequel as Commodity," *The Lion and the Unicorn* 20 no. 1. (June 1996): 127.
20. Ondaatje, 289–290.
21. Sobchack, *The Address of the Eye: A Phenomenology of Film Experience* (Princeton: Princeton University Press, 1992), 144.
22. Ondaatje, 106.
23. Ondaatje, 107.
24. *Ibid.*
25. Martine Beugnet, "Close-Up Vision: Re-Mapping the Body in the Work of Contemporary French Women Filmmakers," *Nottingham French Studies* 45, no. 3 (Autumn 2006): 28.

Bibliography

Altman, Rick. *The American Film Musical.* Bloomington: Indiana University Press, 1989.

Beugnet, Martine. "Close-Up Vision: Re-Mapping the Body in the Work of Contemporary French Women Filmmakers." *Nottingham French Studies* 45, no. 3 (Autumn 2006): 24–48.

Flynn, Richard. "Imitation Oz: The Sequel as Commodity." *The Lion and the Unicorn* 20, no. 1 (June 1996): 121–131.

Hodgkinson, John. "Correspondence." *Biological Psychiatry* 21 (May 1986): 578.

Lacan, Jacques. *Ecrits.* Translated by Bruce Fink. New York: W.W. Norton, 2006.

Maslin, Janet. "Review of *Return to Oz,* directed by Walter Murch." *The New York Times* 21 June 1985.

Metz, Christian. *The Imaginary Signifier: Psychoanalysis and the Cinema.* Translated by Celia Britton, Annwyl Williams, Ben Brewster, and Alfred Guzzetti. Bloomington: Indiana University Press, 1977.

Ondaatje, Michael. *The Conversations: Walter Murch and the Art of Editing Film.* London: Bloomsbury Publishing, 2002.

Sobchack, Vivian. *The Address of the Eye: A Phenomenology of Film Experience.* Princeton: Princeton University Press, 1992.

_____. *Carnal Thoughts: Embodiment and Moving Image Culture.* Berkeley: University of California Press, 2004.

Zipes, Jack. "Breaking the Disney Spell." In *From Mouse to Mermaid: The Politics of Film, Gender, and Culture,* edited by Elizabeth Bell, Lynda Haas, Laura Sells. Bloomington: Indiana University Press, 1995.

Securing the Virtual Frontier for Whiteness in Tron

MICHAEL GREEN

Tron (1982), directed by Steven Lisberger, was Disney's attempt to have a Star Wars-style triumph, particularly needed during a downtime for the company's film fortunes. The sustained success of Disney's new live action wing, Touchstone, was a few years away and the company's animated film renaissance which, like *Tron*, would rely partially on advances in computer technology, was almost a decade away with *The Little Mermaid* (1989).[1]

Like most of Hollywood at the time, Disney believed that the holy trio of innovative special effects technology, new synergy/marketing tactics and blockbuster filmmaking was the road back to relevance and profits after the economic downturn of the early 1970s. The most financially successful films of the several years prior to *Tron*'s release were fantasies that had been married to groundbreaking new developments in special effects, marketed as brands, and aimed at teenagers: not only George Lucas's *Star Wars* (1977) and its sequels, but *Close Encounters of the Third Kind* (1977), *Superman* (1978), *Star Trek: The Motion Picture* (1979), *Raiders of the Lost Ark* (1981), and others.[2] Disney had tried and failed to get into the blockbuster game with *The Black Hole* (1979). Not without experience making successful science fiction films— *20,000 Leagues Under the Sea* (1954), *Son of Flubber* (1963)—and keen to appease its stockholders, the studio would try again with *Tron*.[3]

Despite the Herculean efforts that went into the pioneering production— the invention of sustained, immersive CGI; imagining and designing the virtual world—*Tron* was far from the success that the studio was hoping for, either critically/artistically or, especially, financially.[4] Of the major science fiction movies of the summer of 1982, *E.T.* ran away with the box office and the Oscar nominations; *Star Trek II: The Wrath of Khan* was a solid hit and a critical darling; *Blade Runner* (1982) has emerged as a cult classic and made its way into cinema's canon. *Tron* never found love with either audiences or critics, both of whom found the story uninvolving and the characters bland.[5] Unlike *Blade Runner*, it has not had a critical or cult renaissance, though Disney is hoping that at the least the brand name conjures up enough nostalgia to spark interest in the long-in-coming sequel, *Tron Legacy* (2010).

What the movie is largely remembered for is its tie-in with the popular arcade game that it spawned—which, like the movie, featured the famous "light cycle" sequence—and with the relatively brief golden age of arcade games in general.[6] *Tron* tried to capitalize on the video game craze both at the level of merchandising/marketing (again following in the trailblazing steps of George Lucas and company) and within the narrative itself, as the movie's hero, Kevin Flynn (Jeff Bridges), survives and eventually triumphs within the virtual world largely because of his skills at arcade games.[7]

Not surprisingly, given Hollywood's inclination towards formula, the parallels between *Tron* and *Star Wars* go beyond the movies' innovation of special effects technology and merchandising tie-ins. Like Lucas's groundbreaker, *Tron* attempts to marry the new effects to classical sci-fi themes and narrative features, including good vs. evil; class struggle; revolt against totalitarianism; and the quest story. Like *Star Wars*—and a lot of science fiction, including Cyberpunk, one genre to which *Tron* belongs—the movie is schizophrenic in its approach to technology (particularly advanced weaponry). It fetishizes it at the same time that it spins a cautionary tale about its dehumanizing dangers; it vilifies it but asserts it as a necessary tool of the Eurocentric West to maintain liberal democracy over Totalitarianism.[8]

Though *Star Wars* takes place in a "galaxy far, far away" and *Tron* is set largely in a virtual world inside a computer, both narratives concern three scrappy heroes—two young men and a young woman—who embark on a journey to battle an evil overlord and make the galaxy/virtual world safe for regular freedom-loving folk. Though I will later show that, despite the nominal story of class conflict, *Tron*'s heroes are actually fighting to preserve advanced capitalism for *whiteness*, which in this essay is being used as a critical category and discussed as a cultural construct that "secures its dominance by seeming not to be anything in particular," as Richard Dyer writes.[9] Building on Dyer's work, George Lipsitz argues

> white Americans are encouraged to invest in Whiteness, to remain true to an identity that provides them with resources, power and opportunity. This whiteness, of course, is a delusion, a scientific and cultural fiction that like all racial identities has no foundation in biology or anthropology. Whiteness is, however, a social fact, an identity created and continues with all-too-real-consequences for the distribution of wealth, prestige and opportunity.

In asserting how whiteness is represented in *Tron*, I argue that the movie perpetuates Hollywood's traditional approach to representing race and gender norms in cinema. These traditional ideas feature white powerful males at the center of the narrative; characters of other races and ethnicities are marginalized, vilified, stereotyped, absent, or some combination thereof; and the pattern of representation is repeated so often throughout Hollywood history that it is made to seem "normal," thus striving to permanently equate whiteness with both superiority and "normality." The idea of "normality" also mandates that protagonists are heterosexual, non-disabled and typically middle class (or at least subscribe to middle class values).

Star Wars essentially updated Flash Gordon and other early science fiction serials that relocated the Western to outer space with these ideas of the "norm" intact. The space operas culled narrative and other formal features from the Western, and those features were inextricable from racist and sexist representation that was part and parcel of the genre: white settlers/colonists in conflict with racial and ethnic Others at the frontier; women supporting and being protected by men or else being punished for sexual independence.

But Star Wars went into production in the mid 1970s and the movie's hero, Luke Skywalker, still had a touch of the 1960s about him: he wore his hair long, espoused youthful naïveté and rebelled against his family's conservative wishes for his future: he wanted to join the revolution. Tron, on the other hand, went into production at a time when political and cultural conservatism had firmly reasserted influence over a mainstream America anxious and uncertain over the threat of global nuclear war (constantly imagized and narrativised by the government and the media); over the lingering anguish of Vietnam and the fear that America had been diminished both militarily and morally; and over the ever stronger push for equal rights by women, racial and ethnic minorities and gays and lesbians, which could no longer be ignored or put down. Hollywood responded to all this by churning out cinematic comfort food in the form of 1930s and '40s style genre throwbacks by Spielberg, Lucas, et al. These movies—Raiders of the Lost Ark is particularly representative— were being updated with period racism and sexism intact, to reassure the dominant mainstream whose superiority and centrality Hollywood had insisted upon for so long.[10]

Tron sits at the intersection of all these cultural and industrial elements: anxiety over technology, national identity, and perceived encroaching Otherness both from without and from within; and a film industry bent, as always, on marrying new technology to traditional conservative representation. In this way, Tron, like all movies, is a product of its specific historical moment. But, as noted, the movie also takes its place in a long line of like-minded Hollywood science fiction movies that perpetuate Eurocentric, patriarchal hegemony. At the level of hoary science fiction themes and race and gender representation, the movie doesn't play much differently than Flash Gordon. Given what many critics and moviegoers have found to be its generally uninvolving characters and narrative, it might hardly seem worthy of study over any other middling science fiction movie of the era.

Yet *Tron* brought several historic firsts. Most significantly, it was the first feature film to substantially integrate computer-generated special effects, which of course would revolutionize the film and media industries.[11] It was the first film to represent virtual reality, in which humans interact inside digital worlds.[12] It was, along with *Blade Runner*, released a few weeks earlier—the first "Cyberpunk" film. Though literary science fiction had already imagined the Internet and virtual reality, neither loomed large in the popular consciousness of the time. Both were essentially new frontiers for humans in 1982, in real life and in the movies.

In terms of representation this is significant because, even despite the freshness of *Star Wars*, the Western and the space opera had exhausted stories in which white American men righteously claim traditional frontiers. These stories had long been a staple narrative for Disney as well, particularly for their live-action entertainments. Leading up to *Tron*, movies on the subject included *20,000 Leagues Under the Sea* (1954), *Westward Ho* (1956), *Old Yeller* (1957), *The Light in the Forest (1958), Ten Who Dared* (1960), *The Adventures of Bullwhip Griffin* (1967), *The Black Hole* (1979), and many, many others. On television, Fess Parker helped Disney spin the American frontier saga over and over again by playing Davy Crockett and Daniel Boone in made-for-television movies and hundreds of hour-long episodes. Disney also ran the *Man in Space* series in the mid 1950s, chronicling the American achievements and goals at that frontier.

Finally, of course, Disneyland itself was a virtual Frontier world, featuring "Adventureland," "Frontierland" and "Tomorrowland," among others. All of these "lands" are strategically situated around "Main Street USA," suggesting that the American dominion stretched out infinitely in all directions from its cozy home base of security and Puritan values.[13] Together, all of this popular material strongly perpetuated the myth of manifest destiny—of frontiers as the righteous domain of Anglo Americans—and was committed to essentially effacing America's bloody history of Colonialism.[14]

But despite the success of the post-war Disney frontier narratives, the claiming of such frontiers by white men had begun to be seen—in academic circles and to some extent in popular culture—as colonial and immoral, an attitude reflected in the revisionist cinema of the late 1960s and '70s. Films such as *Little Big Man* (1970), *Billy Jack* (1971) and *One Flew Over the Cuckoo's Nest* (1975), for example, were manifesting white liberal guilt about historical treatment of Native Americans, and major stars such as Marlon Brando and George C. Scott were publically supporting the issue as well.[15] In the face of diminishing acceptance of traditional Eurocentric colonialism, Disney needed new—and subtler—cinematic arenas in which to reassert the superiority of the white patriarchal self and its perceived "rightful" dominion. In addition to its other historic firsts, and despite the fact that the movie never caught on with audiences, *Tron* broke new ground in that, through the burgeoning genre of Cyberpunk, it claimed two new cinematic frontiers for Whiteness and its associated systems of colonialism and capitalism: CGI and virtual space.

Genre and Representation

Save for perhaps the first half of *Wall-E*, Disney films have not been in the business of representing dystopias. And though with its chirpy heroes and bright cinematographic pallet, *Tron* may seem to be the generic opposite of a dystopic vision such as *Blade Runner*, both films actually belong to the early 1980s sub-genre known as Cyberpunk. Though *Tron* was not deliberately evoking Cyberpunk as such—it wouldn't become known as a genre for several years after the movie's release, it is certainly among the handful of novels, stories and films from the early 1980s that would, taken together, manifest enough similarities to later help create and be grouped into that genre.[16]

Like *20,000 Leagues Under the Sea* or *The Black Hole*, Cyberpunk stories are frontier stories, but the frontiers are not the traditional sci-fi frontiers of the ocean or beneath the earth or other worlds or universes. In Cyberpunk, the frontiers are close to home: the near rather than distant future; virtual reality; and transcendent new possibilities of Posthumanism (often referred to as transhumanism), which concerns humans interfacing with or combining with computers and other advanced technology (cybernetics), or sending their detached consciousnesses inside virtual spaces.[17]

The stories are set within a breakdown in the social order that results in decaying, post-industrial dystopias that offer few choices for human happiness or freedom. Cyberpunk plots often feature anti-heroes as protagonists: young rogues, criminals and hackers, who, while flawed and anti-social, are shown to heroically oppose oppressive, dehumanizing systems such as artificial intelligences, giant corporations and systems of totalitarianism (or some combination thereof). The anti-heroes traffic in technology and often innovate uses for which the technology was not intended, but which allows them to survive and sometimes prevail over the malevolent forces.[18] Class conflict is also a theme, with the young anti-heroes scrambling for socioeconomic survival in the face of vastly wealthy corporations who are sucking up every resource.[19] Movie examples of Cyberpunk include *Blade Runner, Johnny Mnemonic* (1995), *Strange Days* (1995), *eXistenZ* (1999) *The Matrix* (1999), and *Anime* films such as *Akira* (1988) and *Ghost in the Shell* (1996).

Tron, though not often grouped together with these films, nevertheless manifests most of their genre tropes, including the advanced science and the breakdown of the social order. Kevin Flynn, the young hacker/hero, is a brilliant computer programmer who uses advanced technology to become Clu—his avatar inside the virtual world—and battle the dehumanizing megacorporation/artificial intelligence that has marginalized Flynn in the "real world" by stealing his ideas for programs and forcing him out of his research position at ENCOM Corporation. He is alienated now from his former career and from his former colleagues at ENCOM, Alan (Bruce Boxleitner) and Dr. Lora Baines (Cindy Morgan), who discover him living "on the edge of society," in a small apartment above the video arcade he runs which features games he has created.[20]

Posthumanism is of course, a major element of *Tron*'s virtual world, as Flynn, through "invasive modification of the human body," is beamed into the movie's virtual world to become a sort of organic/digital hybrid.[21] Posthumanism is significantly a condition of the movie's "real" world as well. Dillenger (David Warner), the corporate boss of ENCOM, has become a slave to the Artificial Intelligence known as the Master Control Program (MCP), whose goal is to take over the Pentagon. Finally, the interface between the video games and the teenagers at Flynn's arcade represents contemporary posthumanism, (albeit not in a way that most people think about it).

Though *Tron* does not imagine a dystopia in conventional Cyberpunk fashion, the fact that the movie's "real" spaces are entirely contained to Flynn's arcade and the corporation—its scientific and computer labs, offices and its roof—does imply that comfortable middle-class existence has vanished. Signs of typical American life are absent in *Tron*, or at least the typical American life that was routine in Hollywood movies in 1982, ala *E.T.*, *Tootsie* or *Fast Times at Ridgemont High*. There are no suburban breakfast tables, schools, malls, restaurants, police stations, courthouses or other signs of a "functioning" society, i.e., one that is perpetuating and protecting the status quo that is typically portrayed in Hollywood movies. Further, the sense of urgency displayed by Flynn, Alan and Lora in their defiance of Dillenger's corporate dictatorship; Flynn's (self) alienation; the jeopardy in which the characters feel they are in; and the fact that none of them interact in the larger society; all signal that the world is no longer safe for their kind, which the movie will make more and more clear means white, straight, young, able-bodied, non-ethnic middle class Americans.

Cyberpunk and Racial Anxiety

Tron manifests some of the racial anxiety and xenophobia that scholars have argued are typical of Cyberpunk, the narratives of which tend to reflect concerns over multiculturalism and miscegenation, or racial mixing. The anxiety of posthumanism is partly an fear of merging with the "Other" in whatever form. In the genre's dystopian future, Western powers and white heroes are often shown to be under siege, particularly by Asians, who were considered an economic threat to the United States in the early 1980s. Timothy Yu writes,

[Cyberpunk] portraits of the postmodern city expose the extent to which the imagining of postmodernism has been grounded in Orientalism and racial anxiety ... at times they also propose in response a recolonization that reasserts the hegemony of the white Western subject.²²

Stephen Hong Sohn similarly argues that Cyberpunk stories are sites for "the projection of futuristic anxieties..." and that Orientialism "troubles the possibility that the West can retain or recover a nostalgically configured purity."²³ Crucial to my argument, Chun asserts, "Faced with a 'Japanese future,' [stories of] high tech Orientalism resurrects the frontier—in a virtual form—in order to secure open space for America ... [and] offers representations of survivors, of savvy-navigators who can open closed [cyber] spaces."²⁴ This is seen in *Neuromancer* and, I argue, in *Tron*, as Flynn opens, "navigates" and finally secures the new frontier of cyberspace for his vision/version of America.²⁵

Though *Tron* does not depict a multicultural "actual" world—or indeed any non-white characters at all (save for one black extra in the opening scenes)—it is nonetheless conspicuous by its absence. As with *Blade Runner*, the skyscraping corporate roof in *Tron*, again, one of the few "real" spaces shown, signals a deliberate distance from the multicultural "dirty" reality on the ground. Whereas *Blade Runner* clearly represents this multi-ethnic threat and sends Whites into towers and "off-world" to escape it, *Tron* elides representation of the multicultural world but nevertheless implies the threat by creating urgency for "white flight" into the "open spaces" of virtual reality. As Chun writes, "[Cyberspace] narratives imagine a world dominated by 'global' difference in order to dispel the hostility and invasiveness of such a world."²⁶

The very first scene inside the virtual world of *Tron* establishes the dangers to middle class capitalist patriarchy by this "invasive global difference." A computer program co-opted/enslaved by the Master Control Program is given the virtual avatar of a middle-aged white man. "Hey look," he says, as he is being "imprisoned" by guards with black holes where there faces should be, "This is all a mistake. I'm just a compound interest program. I work at a savings and loan. I can't play these video games." The program could conceivably take any form—including that of an African American inner-city schoolteacher, a Latina social worker, a Polish-American unionized dockworker, a Cuban American house wife and mother of four, etc. But *Tron* signals its anxieties of these groups and the progressiveness and need they represent by making this avatar an extension of Wall Street and corporate capitalism, which the "black" guards threaten, and whose (upward) mobility they limit.

"It's murder out there," says another captured program/white male avatar. "You can't even travel around your own microcircuit without permission from Master Control Program." He says this not in a voice tinged with fear, though his life is presumably in danger, but rather with distaste and resentment. Later

Tron says, "My user has information that would make this place a free system again ... and no MCP looking over your shoulder!" He also says his goal is to "erase the MCP and change the system."[27] MCP gives the "programs" inside the virtual world the choice to renounce their white "users," and join him, or be eliminated in gladiatorial contests. Given what we have seen at this point of Cyberpunk in general and *Tron* in particular, the fear being allegorized here is the fear of forced multiculturalism, having to share the power and dwindling resources of the world with the Other, in whatever threatening form.[28] During an idyll in their adventures, when three young white men are alone together, they revitalize themselves by drinking from a digital stream, after which Tron says, "Boy, you forget how good the power feels, when you get to a purer source." In the context of the movie so far, "purity" takes on troubling racial and cultural associations.

Further establishing this, even ethnic working class whites will have no place in the virtual world. The first task given to Flynn by Dillinger, after he is beamed inside the virtual world and takes the form of Clu, is to defeat a program whose avatar is a "program" with a vaguely Italian, working class accent. Though Flynn refuses to kill this character as a way of setting up his virtue, the character is nonetheless purged from virtual space and the movie as soon as the point is made about Flynn's character. Hypocritically, despite sparing this character, Flynn will nevertheless go on to eradicate all Others inside the virtual world. This early scene sets up the goal of Flynn/Clu, Alan/Tron and Lora/Yori—and by extension the movie—which will be to purge and homogenize the virtual frontier, and then seal and protect its borders before the New World becomes contaminated in the way that the "old" New World has been.

With this narrative set-up, *Tron* manifests the multicultural anxiety of the neo-conservative era, when, among other indicators of the cultural and political mood, the Reagan Administration worked to roll back Affirmative Action; dry up tax dollars to the crumbling inner cities and their largely non-white populations; promote deregulation; and generally protect and expand Wall Street and corporate America, both of which were practically the exclusive domain of white men in the early 1980s.

Whiteness and Ideology

Hollywood has long equated Whiteness with heroism, virtue and morality, while non-white characters—black, red, yellow, brown—have been historically represented as falling short of, if not outright failing in contrast to, the white ideal. When Flynn refers to Alan and Lora approvingly, if somewhat mockingly, as a "clean-cut young couple," the movie is reinforcing what it considers the accepted norm for movie protagonists.[29]

Though *Tron* does not feature any non-white characters with speaking parts, the movie, consistent with Hollywood traditions, does use color as a way of demarcating between heroes and villains. Blue equals whiteness inside the virtual world: it is the color of the glowing virtual uniforms of Clu, Tron, Yori, Ram, the wise old Obi-Wan Kenobi-style wizard Dumont, and the aforementioned "middle class" slave programs, all played by white American actors. Conversely, red represents evil—it is the color of Sark, his minions and Master Control—and even being touched by a "red" villain is enough to render a blue character compromised, weak and impure. In one scene, Tron does not even recognize a temporarily "reddened" Flynn as a "good guy," and almost destroys him. The only way for a compromised character to reverse this stain of miscegenation is to touch a pure "blue" hero. Once reunited and melded with a pure blue hero, the "contamination" fades away and the formerly afflicted character regains strength and fortitude.

Although Dillenger/Sark is European and white, some of his qualities still signify him as "Other"—his British accent, his cowardice, his age (in Hollywood blockbusters, older people are invariably vilified or marginalized). Sark is also linked with blackness. His evil tanks are black; the "faces" of his minions are pitch black, signifying their racial Otherness. Significantly, David Warner, the actor who plays Dillenger/Sark also plays Master Control. Master Control takes the form of a giant digital face whose wide nose, wide lips and deep baritone voice are phenotypes (physical characteristics) typically associated with African Americans. Having Warner play all three characters is the movie's shorthand for correlating villainy with blackness. Further, Master Control, especially through his voice, clearly evokes Darth Vader, another black villain. Especially given *Tron*'s many other parallels with *Star Wars*, the average 1982 moviegoer would almost certainly associate the redness and blueness of the movie's characters with the red and blue lightsabers used by Darth Vader and Luke Skywalker in *Star Wars* and *The Empire Strikes Back* (1980). The shades in both movies match each other almost exactly and signify evil and virtue, respectively. The connection here for the viewer is clear, if only unconsciously: redness equals Darth Vader equals blackness equals villainy in Hollywood sci-fi representation.

By contrast, the movie associates Whiteness with courage, heroism and even Godliness by setting up Flynn as a white Messiah character.[30] The human users of *Tron* are set up as Gods/controllers to their avatars inside the virtual world. Once MCP digitizes him, Flynn becomes the only human/user inside the Virtual World, making him in a sense a deity among mortals, and as such he is capable of Godlike feats. In one scene he saves the protagonists from a fatal encounter with the villains by using his body as a conduit to shift the high-powered energy beams on which their ship is traveling. Later he resuscitates a dying Yori. Finally, in the movie's climax, he somehow leaps into MCP and uses his User powers to transform the AI's red color to blue, thus liberating the virtual world for Blueness.

The movie sets up Flynn's savior/messiah status even before he enters the virtual world. He is referred to as the "best programmer Encom ever saw"—preternaturally intelligent and gifted. Alan even likens Flynn to "Santa Claus," which doesn't quite seem to apply in the context of their conversation, except as a way of associating him with Eurocentric, capitalist, patriarchal authority.

Moreover, a character speaks of Flynn as "playing space cowboy," which here not only refers to virtual space, but also evokes associations with Westerns and Western inflected science fiction such as *Flash Gordon* and *Star Wars*. Significantly, it also evokes the idea of the "imperial imaginary," which refers to the cinematic representation of the colonizing actions of white, male Europeans and Americans. In these stories, colonizers "tame" and conquer the frontier and the savages that live beyond it, securing the space for Empire, while whooping it up like adventuring boys.[31] By "playing space cowboy"–space refers here to virtual space, not outer space—Flynn takes his place in a long line of cinematic imperial adventurers at the Western frontier—in this case, the virtual frontier.

Technology and Representation

Perhaps the biggest indicator that the movie intends to equate virtue and strength with whiteness is that it designs the faces of the heroes inside the virtual world to look like silent movie stars. This silent movie parallel is established right away in the first scene in which *Tron's* virtual world is introduced—two white faces in close-up, which, in their formal likeness to early film characters, could easily be right out of D.W. Griffith.

I make the connection to Griffith's characters not arbitrarily, but to describe the link between form and representation in *Tron*. Scholars have argued that Griffith—and other early filmmakers—did not just innovate film technology and then, separately, employ it in the service of stories that featured white racism and white supremacy such as *The Birth of a Nation* or Griffith's Biograph shorts. Rather, form and content evolved together so that the very language of filmmaking—narrative, mise-en-scene, cinematography and editing—was inextricably bound up with the cinematic advancement of white supremacy. As early directors standardized early formal techniques, they standardized a representation of white supremacy for a century of filmmaking. Bernardi writes,

> Griffith ... helped develop parallel editing and other stylistic techniques in support of storytelling, but also ... perpetuated a discourse supported by racist practices—which is to say that Griffith's articulations of style and of race are involved in the same cinematic and discursive processes; pragmatically, they co-constitute the filmmaker's narrative system.

This narrative system, argues Bernardi, articulates "an ideology of race that positions 'whites' as normal and superior and 'non-whites' as deviant and infe-rior."[32]

Considering this, the silent movie faces of *Tron*'s white heroes not only evoke the age when white racism was overt and ugly in American filmmaking and when—with a few exceptions, such as Griffith's own (problematic) *Broken Blossoms* (1922)—only whites could be heroes. They are also the filmmakers' winking acknowledgement that they, like the early filmmakers, are engaged in the work of innovating a new cinema of storytelling, in this case CGI, which is arguably the most important cinematic innovation since color.

Now to the point: when *Tron* uses CGI to not only advance a discourse of whiteness, but to represent white characters to appear *exactly as they did in the work of Griffith and other silent filmmakers*, an agenda emerges that is larger than just perpetuating representational norms, à la the typical Hollywood film. It is, as Bernardi argues of Griffith, to re-set ideological standards in an age of conservative racial anxiety by marrying white supremacy to brand new tech-nology—not only to advance white supremacy through new artistic techniques, but to continue to evolve form and content simultaneously so that they would be inextricable from each other.

By linking patriarchal white supremacy with CGI (along with virtual space and Cyberpunk), *Tron* was, in essence, a new dawn for Hollywood in terms of perpetuating race and gender norms. Given how patriarchal whiteness has been positioned in Hollywood's biggest and most groundbreaking CGI films since—which have been, not coincidentally, Hollywood's biggest films: *Jurassic Park* (1993), *The Lion King* (1994), *Forrest Gump* (1994), the new *Star Wars* films (1999–2005), *Spiderman* (2002), *Harry Potter* (2001–2009), *The Lord of the Rings* (2001–2003), *Avatar* (2009), all films that feature white male heroes and marginalize women and people of color—one can argue that *Tron* has been successful in setting the template. Had *Tron* instead featured African American, Native American, gay, disabled or female protagonists (among other possibilities), it is perhaps more likely (if not highly likely) that the association between CGI and representation would have evolved differently. The initial model for other filmmakers would have looked different and perhaps began to (slowly) help reverse a history of institutionalized cinematic racism.[33]

Conclusion

The apotheosis of the red/blue racial coding in *Tron* is reached at the movie's climax when Clu, Tron and Yori defeat Master Control and blue beams sweep over the world, eradicating Otherness, homogenizing the virtual envi-ronment, making it safe for all of Hollywood's norms: white, middle-class, youthful, heterosexual, athletic, patriarchal. This is sealed by Tron and Yori's kiss. Hollywood's ideal union can be safely consummated now in the newly clean virtual space, which has been preserved for Eurocentric dominance on the inside and cut off from the multicultural "pollution" on the outside. The "open spaces" imagined by Cyberpunk have indeed granted sanctuary to besieged whiteness in the late 20th century. The "video warriors," as they are called in the movie, have conquered the new frontier—the virtual frontier. "Every tower is lighting up," says Dumont in the last shot inside the virtual world, signifying that the "light" of Western civilization has replaced the former barbarism at the frontier. His power as a white patriarch has been restored now that Flynn and Tron have rescued "The fate of both the electronic world and the real world."

In homage to *The Wizard of Oz* (1939), the film vanquishes threats inside a fantasy world to make the "real" world safe again for the traditional nuclear family. In the final scene Flynn, newly anointed as the corporate boss, swoops down in the corporate helicopter to meet Alan and Lora on ENCOM's roof. Again, their position atop the skyscraper keeps them safe and separate from the multicultural world; they are restored on the outside to the position of the Anglo heroes in "imperial imaginary" stories, lording it over the natives below. Taking their place in a long line of Disney heroes, they have conquered the new frontier virtual world and now control the technologically advanced portal *between* the worlds as well; the helicopter also signals their rule of the air far above the "real" world, as well as the technology that allows for its safe and easy navigation. As in real life, reducing multiculturalism depends on controlling both the ability to travel and the borders that allow mobility.

The final shot fades out on the "real" city, photographed to look like a grid from inside *Tron*'s virtual world: clean, fast-moving, pure and unmarred by complication, need or conflict, suggesting that, despite the multicultural threat, despite mainstream anxiety of the new technological world with its easy travel and porous borders, the Eurocentric mainstream is still dominant and in control. The ostensible class war in *Tron*—with the protagonists battling evil corporate power—turns out to be a red herring. Unlike, the narrative of the original *Star Wars* trilogy, which truly seems to want to make the working-class universe safe from aristocracy, *Tron*'s narrative merely transfers power—social, cultural, economic, technological—from the "evil" co-opters to the "rightful" holders (my quotes). As Chun writes, Cyberspace "reinvigorates capitalism" and it reinvigorates if for youth.[34] In *Star Wars*, the protagonists return from their triumph to be hailed as heroes by their working class brethren; at the conclusion of *Tron*, Flynn is now the corporate leader, re-affirming the race and gender hierarchies in patriarchal capitalism advocated by Reagan-era politics and policies—and by Disney movies. The only question left for them is which frontier to conquer next.[35]

Notes

1. Douglas Gomery, "Disney's Business History," in *Disney Discourse: Producing the Magic Kingdom*, ed. Eric Smoodin (New York: Routledge, 1994), 78–79.

2. Justin Wyatt, *High Concept: Movies and Marketing in Hollywood* (Austin: University of Texas Press, 1994), 2–22.

3. Brian Attebery, "Beyond Captain Nemo: Disney's Science Fiction," in *From Mouse to Mermaid: The Politics of Film, Gender and Culture*, ed. Elizabeth Bell, Lynda Haas, and Laura Sells (Bloomington: Indiana University Press, 1995), 150–151.

4. AP Byline, "Stock Decline After Screening of *Tron* Irks Disney Studio," *The New York Times*, July 9, 1982, Business section, late edition.

5. Roger Ebert, summing up the critical consensus towards the movie, wrote, "It is not a human interest adventure in any generally accepted way.... It's brilliant at what it does, and in a technical way maybe it's breaking ground for a generation of movies in which computer-generated universes will be the background for mind-generated stories about emotion-generated personalities."

6. Arcade games were at their peak in the late 1970s and early 1980s when they began to be marginalized by home console games.

7. The producers no doubt hoped that teenagers would imagine their own skills put to heroic use, indulging the fantasy that they weren't wasting an inordinate amount of their free time.

8. In this way *Tron* also has much in common with *Wargames* (1983) and other nuclear war–themed movies of the period such as *Mad Max* (1979), *Superman III* (1983), *Testament* (1983), *Terminator* (1984), *Real Genius* (1985), *Spies Like Us* (1985), *The Manhattan Project* (1986), and many others.

9. Richard Dyer is a pioneering whiteness scholar, whose essay "White," published in a 1988 issue of the British film journal *Screen*, and subsequent 1997 book of the same title, laid the groundwork for Whiteness as a study of fertile cultural inquiry.

10. Robert Sklar, *Movie Made America: A Cultural History of the American Movies* (New York: Vintage Books, 1994), 339–356.

11. Ellen Wolff, "*Tron*: Then and Now," *Millimeter*, July 1, 2007, 30.

12. Though CGI had been used briefly in such films as *Looker* (1981) and *Star Trek II: The Wrath of Khan*, *Tron* was the first film to use CGI extensively—the movie features 15 fully computer generated minutes—and to use it to represent a fully immersive character experience.

13. Davy Crockett movies included *Davy Crockett at the Alamo* and *Davy Crockett and the River Pirates* (both 1955). Daniel Boone ran for 159 episodes between 1964 and 1970.

14. Frontier narratives as a Disney staple have continued long after *Tron* as well. Such movies include *Pocahontas* (1995), *Tarzan* (1999), *Atlantis* (2001), *Treasure Planet* (2002), *Wall-E* (2008), *Up* (2009) and many others.

15. Robert F. Berkhofer Jr., *The White Man's Indian: Images of the American Indian from Columbus to the Present* (New York: Knopf, 1978), 108.

16. Bruce Bethke's 1983 short story "Cyberpunk" gave the genre its name and William Gibson's 1984 novel *Neuromancer* became its defining text.

17. Stories from the science fiction literature movement from the 1960s known as the New Wave, which featured seminal sci-fi texts from such authors as Phillip K. Dick and Samuel R. Delany and often dealt with posthuman themes, preceded and greatly influenced Cyberpunk.

18. Lawrence Person, author of "Notes Towards a Postcyberpunk Manifesto," summarizes "Classic Cyberpunk characters [as] marginalized, alienated loners who lived on the edge of society in generally dystopic futures where daily life was impacted by rapid technological change, an ubiquitous datasphere of computerized information, and invasive modification of the human body." http://slashdot.org/features/99/10/08/2123255.shtml

19. Though not as pertinent to *Tron*, the genre often strongly evokes Film Noir and hard-boiled detective fiction, particularly in its evocation of alienated heroes who, stripped of their illusions, are forced to confront the grim truth of human existence.

20. Person, Lawrence. "Notes Towards a Postcyberpunk Manifesto."

21. Person, Lawrence. "Notes Towards a Postcyberpunk Manifesto."

22. Timothy Yu, "Oriental Cities, Postmodern Futures: *Naked Lunch*, *Blade Runner*, and *Neuromancer*," *MELUS* 33.4 (Winter 2008): 48.

23. Stephen Hong Sohn, "Introduction: Alien/Asian: Imagining the Racialized Future," *MELUS* 33.4 (Winter 2008): 7.

24. Wendy Hui Kyong Chun, "Othering Cyberspace," *The Visual Culture Reader*, ed. Nicholas Mirzoeff (New York: Routledge, 1998), 251.

25. Cyberpunk also represents racial anxiety beyond the "the yellow peril." Sandy Rankin argues that Walter Mosley's short story collection *Futureland* co-opts the genre tropes as a way to criticize its visions, including its racist subtexts, by creating Cyberpunk stories that are populated by black people, and that replace dystopic xenophobic visions with more utopian ones.

26. Wendy Hui Kyong Chun, "Othering Cyberspace," *The Visual Culture Reader,* ed. Nicholas Mirzoeff (New York: Routledge, 1998), 250.

27. Surely, it's only a coincidence that Master Control could stand for another M.C.—multiculturalism, or the big government legislation, loathed by conservatives, that has enabled it.

28. The place for women suggested by *Tron* is, if anything, even more cut and dried than the place suggested for minorities. The movie signals its ideas about gender by putting a woman in a scientific laboratory, and then giving her virtually nothing to do there other than to look utterly unconvincing in her oversized prop glasses—subtle mockery of women as scientists—and a starched and brilliant white lab coat that's clearly never been exposed to the messy, hard work of real science. Her job in the movie's opening scenes is that of flirt and enabler. Later, she takes on the obligatory Hollywood female roles of victim, sex object (in her skin-tight outfit) and object for the men to fight over and be admired by.

29. *Tron*'s all-white cast is not only typical of Hollywood moviemaking in the early 1980s, but also of the live-action Disney features of the several decades preceding it: *Old Yeller, Herbie, The Shaggy Dog,* etc.

30. Hernán Vera and Andrew Gordon, *Screen Saviors: Hollywood Fictions of Whiteness* (Lanham, MD: Rowman and Littlefield, 2003), 33–34.

31. Ella Shohat and Robert Stam, "The Imperial Imaginary," *Unthinking Eurocentrism: Multiculturalism and the Media* (London, Routledge: 1994), 100—136.

32. Daniel Bernardi, "The Voice of Whiteness: D.W. Griffith's Biograph Films (1908 -1913)," *The Birth of Whiteness: Race and the Emergence of United States Cinema,* ed. Daniel Bernardi (New Brunswick, NJ: Rutgers University Press, 1996), 104.

33. One could argue that 27 years later, James Cameron's *Avatar* has is the next step in this evolution of cinema that links new film technology with a discourse of whiteness.

34. Wendy Hui Kyong Chun, "Othering Cyberspace," *The Visual Culture Reader,* ed. Nicholas Mirzoeff (New York: Routledge, 1998), 246.

35. The winter 2010 release of *Tron Legacy*'s previews make it look as though it is in line with the familiar race and gender representation of the original. The only speaking parts in the trailer go to white men and the brief shots of women show them as highly sexualized. There are no nonwhite characters in the trailer. The detailed casting available on IMDB shows the same—an almost completely white cast. The one black actress, Yaya DaCosta, is billed as a "siren." It seems as though the *Tron* brand is revisiting its legacy in more ways than one.

Bibliography

AP Byline. "Stock Decline After Screening of *Tron* Irks Disney Studio," *The New York Times,* July 9, 1982, Business section, late edition.

Attebery, Brian. "Beyond Captain Nemo: Disney's Science Fiction." In *From Mouse to Mermaid: The Politics of Film, Gender and Culture,* edited by Elizabeth Bell, Lynda Haas, and Laura Sells, 148–160. Bloomington: Indiana University Press, 1995.

Berkhofer Jr., Robert F. *The White Man's Indian: Images of the American Indian from Columbus to the Present.* New York: Knopf, 1978.

Bernardi, Daniel. "The Voice of Whiteness: D.W. Griffith's Biograph Films (1908–1913)." In *The Birth of Whiteness: Race and the Emergence of United States Cinema,* edited by Daniel Bernardi, 103–128. New Brunswick, NJ: Rutgers University Press, 1996.

Chun, Wendy Hui Kyong. "Othering Cyberspace." *The Visual Culture Reader,* edited by Nicholas Mirzoeff, 243–54. New York: Routledge, 1998.

Dyer, Richard. "White." *Screen* 29.4 (Fall 1988): 4.

Ebert, Roger. "Review of *Tron*." *Roger Ebert's Video Companion,* 1995 Edition, 746–747. Kansas City: Andrews and McMeel, 1995.

Gomery, Douglas. "Disney's Business History." In *Disney Discourse: Producing the Magic Kingdom*, edited by Eric Smoodin, 71–86. New York: Routledge, 1994.

Lipsitz, George. *The Possessive Investment in Whiteness: How White People Profit from Identity Politics*. Temple University Press: Philadelphia, 1998.

Rankin, Sandy. "The (Not Yet) Utopian Dimension and the Collapse of Cyberpunk in Walter Mosley's Futureland: Nine Short Stories of an Imminent World." In *New Boundaries in Political Science Fiction*, edited by Donald M. Hassler and Clyde Wilcox, 315–338. Columbia: University of South Carolina Press, 2008.

Shohat, Ella, and Robert Stam. "The Imperial Imaginary." *Unthinking Eurocentrism: Multiculturalism and the Media*. Routledge: London, 1994.

Sklar, Robert. *Movie Made America: A Cultural History of the American Movies*. New York: Vintage Books, 1994.

Slashdot, "Notes Towards a PostCyberpunk Manifesto," by Lawrence Person. http://slashdot.org/features/99/10/08/2123255.shtml

Sohn, Stephen Hong. "Introduction: Alien/Asian: Imagining the Racialized Future." *MELUS* 33.4 (Winter 2008): 5–22.

Vera, Hernán, and Andrew Gordon. *Screen Saviors: Hollywood Fictions of Whiteness*. Lanham, MD: Rowman and Littlefield, 2003.

Wolff, Ellen. "*Tron*: Then and Now." *Millimeter*, July 1, 2007.

Wyatt, Justin. *High Concept: Movies and Marketing in Hollywood*. Austin: University of Texas Press, 1994.

Yu, Timothy. "Oriental Cities, Postmodern Futures: *Naked Lunch*, *Blade Runner*, and *Neuromancer*." *MELUS* 33.4 (Winter 2008): 45–71.

A Womb with a Phew!:
Post-Humanist Theory
and Pixar's Wall-E

WALTER C. METZ

This essay seeks to understand the significance for disability studies of Disney/Pixar's *Wall-E* (2008), an animated blockbuster about a wheelchair-like robot who helps guide wheelchair-using humans back to a devastated Earth. While Wall-E is indeed isolated for the first twenty minutes of the film on an otherwise lifeless planet, I do not offer disability studies in the tradition of Martin F. Norden's *The Cinema of Isolation* (1994), the foundational text in studies of film and disability. Instead, I turn for methodology to a more recent reader, *Screening Disability: Essays on Cinema and Disability* (2001), in which Thomas B. Hoeksema and Christopher R. Smit advocate for a balancing of film studies with disability studies:

> While a posture of disability activism ... has helped Disability Studies gain status similar to that of Women's and African American Studies in the humanities, it has not encouraged a stylistic, analytical or structural study of these films as cinematic expressions.... Cinematic depictions of people who live with disability have been enormously diverse.... We believe that it is inaccurate and insufficient to characterize cinematic depictions of disability as primarily negative and stereotypic. We also think that taking an activist, advocacy perspective when critiquing disability cinema risks missing insights that may be obtained by reviewing films using additional tools from the field of Film Studies.[1]

Such a fluid view of disability studies and its application to film is supported by Christopher R. Smit and Anthony Enns in the introduction to the anthology: "[D]isability itself has no easily recognizable form.... The disabled experience, defined only in relation to a perceived lack of human potential, becomes

253

significant as a distorted mirror image of what we take to be 'human' and thereby reveals our culture's preconceived notions of normalcy."[2] My approach to *Wall-E* positions the film's representation of wheelchairs within the theoretical tools of film studies. If disability is a continuum, and most of us are, like me, a "temporarily able-bodied person (TAB),"[3] then what does *Wall-E* teach us about our past, present, and future on this continuum? As a fantasy film, *Wall-E* is able to pose questions about these important topics in nimble and productive ways. While Wall-E begins the film isolated, he uses his love of cinema in order to find love with Eve, and leads human beings out of their wheelchairs and back to Earth.

Screening Disability ends with provocative essays about the spectacle of disability in various contemporary fantasy films. Smits and Enns summarize the argument made by Susan Crutchfield in "The Noble Ruined Body: Blindness and Visual Prosthetics in Three Science Fiction Films": "Disability then becomes 'a rhetorical figure for the postmodern norm of human/technology interfaces,' and Crutchfield concludes that film itself serves as one such human/technology interface which interpolates the spectator into the ideology of the prosthetic."[4] *Wall-E* shatters the ideology of the prosthetic by foregrounding a completely robotic entity's ability to process the joys of human activity as a way of teaching the wheelchair-bound humans that they can be more than their technological interfaces have allowed them to imagine.

Screening Disability concludes with a terrific study by James L. Cherney of the erotic politics of David Cronenberg's 1996 film adaptation of J.G. Ballard's 1973 novel, *Crash*. Cherney uses the critical theory of Donna Haraway— particularly her influential essay, "A Cyborg Manifesto" from *Simians, Cyborgs and Women: The Reinvention of Nature*—to argue that "cyborg theory undermines the ideological foundations of ableist culture."[5] In studying the characters in *Crash*, who express themselves erotically with the prosthetics resulting from car crashes, Cherney argues, "The blasphemous transgression makes the biological fact of distinctiveness between different kinds of humans seem practically irrelevant."[6] My essay proposes that *Wall-E* is an even further abstraction away from the embodied nature of disability toward an interrogation of the larger theoretical terrain of post-human theory, emerging from Haraway's cyborg manifesto, as expressing the struggles and triumphs of the human condition.

Wall-E and the Post-Human Spork[7]

A theoretical concept for understanding culture, adapted from Haraway's brand of post-structural science and technology studies, post-human theory seeks to understand the relationship between a technological culture and the human body. In the late 1980s, critical theorist Donna Haraway argued that feminism needed to shed its Luddite perspective. In formulating a new theoretical concept of the cyborg, Haraway argued for the transformative vision of a new human through which technology became a pathway, not to oppression, but to a progressive politics. *Wall-E* features such a cyborg, whose job is to construct large buildings out of human garbage in an abandoned New York City.

Since the publication of Haraway's manifesto, other critical theorists have forwarded her arguments about the post-human cyborg in diverse areas such as systems theory, narrative, biotechnology, and, indeed, disability studies. Simultaneously, the post-structuralist dismantling of humanist philosophy begun in the late 1960s by Michel Foucault and Jacques Derrida has dovetailed with Haraway's understandings of the cyborg. That is to say, post-structuralist philosophy postulates that human beings are *constructed* into subjectivity, rather than being *born* individuals possessing free will as Enlightenment humanism had suggested for hundreds of years. Haraway's cyborg is thus a gender-inflected version of a larger post-structural turn in philosophizing about the interconnected, rather than the oppositional, relationship between the human and the machine. Naming this new strand of understanding the post-human puts into sharp focus the massive shift implied by both philosophy (post-structural theories of subject construction) and new technology (new media technologies, biomedical surgeries, and the like).

In short, a development in critical theory postulating a post-human identity within the domain of post-humanist philosophy has found traction in a culture in which technology is enacting these theoretical suppositions. Cinema, and not only science-fiction cinema, is at the forefront of embodying the cultural repercussions of this theoretical shift. Wall-E the robot is thus an emblem of this post-human identity. To pun *Blade Runner* (1982), Wall-E is, by the end of his film, "more post-human than human."

Furthermore, Wall-E has agency in a way denied by the dystopic *Blade Runner*. Early on, the robot passes by huge television screens owned by Buy 'N' Large (BNL), the corporate masters who destroyed the Earth. In cheery commercials, BNL assures the American populace that they will clean up the mess while people lounge in spacecraft resembling the Love Boat. *Blade Runner*, of course, first featured these floating, giant television screens—"A new home awaits you off-world"—advertising leaving the poisoned earth as cavalierly as Coca-Cola spots advocate refreshment. Here, Pixar's *Wall-E* far transcends the at best liberal ethos of the Disney Corporation's other environmental cinema. Like its ilk on the Discovery Channel and PBS's *Nature*, contemporary Disney nature productions, like Disneynature's inaugural project, *Earth* (2007), revel in a pornographic display of the beauty of the animal world, completely ignoring the human, political context, futile posturing by politicians while the Earth's climate irrecoverably sinks into collapse. *Wall-E* refuses this folly, instead showing humans the direct result of inaction: global devastation.

The academic literature for understanding the interrelated phenomena

implied by post-human and post-humanist philosophy is expanding exponen-
tially. Floyd Merrell's *Sensing Corporeally: Toward a Post-Human Understanding*
(2003) is one such work of academic philosophy. Bruce Clarke pushes the
application towards film and literature in *Posthuman Metamorphosis: Narrative
and Systems*, connecting via narrative and systems theory diverse texts like *The
Fly* (1986) and Toni Morrison's *Beloved*. The largest concentration of such
work, of course, is to be found in science-fiction studies. Daniel Dinello's
Technophobia!: Science Fiction Visions of Posthuman Technology uses post-human
theory as a frame for understanding the history of cinema, from interpretations
of Mary Shelley's 1818 novel *Frankenstein* and the landmark science fiction
film *Metropolis* (1927) to *The Terminator* (1984) and *The Matrix* (1999). In *The
Postmodern Humanism of Philip K. Dick*, Jason P. Vest examines the most likely
candidate in the history of science fiction writing for mining the tensions
between humans and machines. In *Supermen: Tales of the Posthuman Future*,
Gardner Dozois collects a wider set of science fiction short stories which have
historically and variably engaged the post-human.

Studying the post-human has become a cottage industry, with the use-
fulness of the term spilling out from philosophy and textual study into all
aspects of cultural studies. Chris Hables Gray sees the post-human politically,
in *Cyborg Citizen: Politics in the Posthuman Age*, while Francis Fukuyama tracks
the concept more practically in *Our Posthuman Future: Consequences of the
Biotechnology Revolution*. *Mechademia, Volume 3: Limits of the Human* applies
the theory to Japanese manga comic books and anime cinema. Here, I will
analyze Pixar's recent animated film blockbuster *Wall-E* via the framework of
post-human theory.

Obviously, highly commercial Hollywood cinema is not designed to
engage contemporary philosophy, but instead to make money. However, it
seems precisely because of this contradiction that Pixar's project is significant.
Being about a robot with whom kids and their parents are meant to fall in
love, *Wall-E* is by definition a film which foregrounds a superficial plot devoted
to heteronormative identity: the clearly male Wall-E falls in love with the
clearly female Eve. However, Pixar's *Wall-E* is not like other banal ventures
by the Disney Corporation into science fiction, films such as *The Black Hole*
(1979) and *Tron* (1982). While *Tron* engaged in representations of human/com-
puter interfaces of potential interest to post-human philosophy, it did so merely
to foreground its then cutting-edge special effects, choosing as a narrative
housing a bland story of corporate skullduggery within the computer. *Wall-E*
grapples with the post-human at a far greater level of theoretical complexity:
since robots do not have gender, these two characters are not bound by human
biology. Both of them, for example, have wombs. *Wall-E*'s genius lies in its
ability to both engage the human (we care about his humanity: will his love
for Eve be returned?) and the post-human (he is a tiny machine meant to clean
up the Earth after humans have destroyed it, rebuilding the skyline of Man-

hattan with gigantic trash skyscrapers). Wall-E has skills that humans do not; it seems the emotional message of the film might be, in a post-human sense, that *so do we*.

At the beginning of the film, the friendly robotic trash compactor finds a plastic utensil amidst the rubble of an abandoned Earth, the result of an environmental catastrophe. When he brings the object to his home, an abandoned machine, a larger version of himself, a WALL-R, he cannot decide whether to file the spork with his other plastic forks or spoons. Not easily deterred, he places his beloved object in between. This moment, resplendent with contemporary gender philosophy, allegorizes the significance of post-human theory for the film's gender representations. Wall-E, a robot coded male by his voice (that of legendary *Star Wars* sound designer Ben Burtt) who loves musicals, and Eve, his beloved with a feminine voice (that of Elissa Knight) but a death-dealing laser ray gun arm, are post-gendered in the most fruitful ways.

Intriguingly, *Star Wars: A New Hope* (1977), the original film on which Burtt served as dialogue and sound effects editor, serves as a principal case study for the conclusion to Norden's *The Cinema of Isolation*. Norden sees Darth Vader, "a walking wonderland of bionic effects,"[8] as one of Hollywood's deep-rooted negative stereotypes of people with disabilities, the "Obsessive Avenger."[9] Norden claims, "The filmmakers underscored the evil Vader's unnatural qualities by supplementing his commanding voice and black-robed presence with the sounds of labored breathing emanating from a mask-like respirator that looks out impassively from beneath a Nazi-esque helmet."[10] *Wall-E* is not indicative of any of the negative stereotypes Norden analyzes. He is certainly no "Obsessive Avenger" like Darth Vader; he shares some qualities with the "physically-disabled High-Tech Guru,"[11] but Wall-E's central presence in the film as both helpmate to disabled humans, and the film's central character, make Wall-E so much more than a stereotype. In my argument, then, *Wall-E* is both methodologically and narratively an undoing of the classical representation of disability in American cinema.

Most significantly for the argument that Wall-E and Eve are productive cyborgs, both have wombs (Wall-E's for compacting trash to build skyscrapers to clean up the Earth, and Eve's for holding the plant which represents our planet's botanical hope for re-forestation). Indeed, by following this train of thought, *Wall-E*'s narrative is built on re-imaging the concept of the womb. First, in a New Age sense, in the back story of the film, humans did not treat Mother Earth well, fouling her productive womb to the point that they had to abandon the toxic planet altogether. Seemingly the only surviving entity on the planet, Wall-E uses his womb, his trash compactor belly, to crush detritus into skyscrapers of garbage. His womb, seeing as Disney definitely wants to construct him as the film's romantic male lead, is surprisingly productive.

Off-handedly, Wall-E discovers a plant alive inside an abandoned refrigcrator. This plot device serves as the motor for the rest of the film. Eve, a robot designed to return to Earth from the humans' refugee spaceship in order to seek out signs of life on the abandoned planet, finds the plant when Wall-E presents it to her out of his womb. This activates Eve's programming, causing her to mechanically shut down her personality and return to the ship with the plant safely monitored in her high-tech womb. Thus, in the span of a few minutes of screen time, the plant has transited from an accidental, deactivated refrigerated womb to Wall-E's equally low tech, and non-biological womb, to Eve's womb, a technological wonderland of plant-sustaining circuitry.

However, when Eve successfully returns to the *Axiom*, a philosophically significant name for a space ship if there ever was one, all is not well with humanity. Having lived in space for 700 years, the people's bodies have atrophied, lying around in self-propelled Barcaloungers all day. Their ship, voiced by Sigourney Weaver, she of non-procreative, hard-bodied 1980s feminine Ripley fame from Ridley Scott's *Alien* (1979), has become a toxic womb, stifling humanity's ability to do anything for itself. Compounding the problem, something has gone wrong with the computer controlling the ship, Auto, who, like HAL from Stanley Kubrick's *2001* (1968), seeks to keep the humans stifled in their womb-like state, drifting in space.

Wall-E and Eve unite with Captain McCrea (voiced by Jeff Garlin) to defeat Auto and return the humans to Earth. When McCrea shuts down Auto, he moans quietly, grinding down like HAL did in *2001*. The references to *2001* in *Wall-E* are sculpted to reiterate the plot of Kubrick's film. When we first meet Auto, the Captain claps his hands to turn on Johann Strauss' "Blue Danube Waltz," which *2001* used to celebrate the technical precision of space flight. Later in *Wall-E*, when the Captain gets out of his wheelchair to relieve Auto of duty, Stanton accompanies the scene with Richard Strauss' "Also Spoke Zarathustra," *2001*'s musical ode to the triumphant birth of the star child at film's end. In both films, the toxic wombs provided by computer-driven ships are abandoned as humanity re-asserts its need to take voluntaristic action.

All this talk about wombs is crucial for understanding the post-human, and disability studies, dynamics of *Wall-E*. In 1985, Gena Corea unearthed the 20th century medical history of the artificial womb. In *The Mother Machine: Reproductive Technologies from Artificial Insemination to Artificial Wombs*, Corea details how patriarchal doctors from the 1920s to the 1960s, assuming that the female womb was a dirty place, dangerous to children, set about to invent a clean, antiseptic, mechanical womb which would replace natural maternity. The projects were, of course, shocking failures. The feminist revolution would be largely built upon discussing the implications of the failure, resulting in such massive sea changes as a return to breastfeeding instead of reliance on scientifically engineered baby "formulas."

Second wave feminist discourse about motherhood is a useful frame for thinking about post-humanism.[12] Feminists argued for both the importance of natural childrearing as a defense of womanhood, as well as the possibility that modernity could allow for a moving beyond the discursive shackling of women to maternity. In this light, one cyborg possibility lies in using technologies not to replicate patriarchy (a practice which undergirded the quest for the artificial womb), but instead to move beyond what limits human beings, such as rigidly defined gender roles. It is for this reason that I emphasize the Utopian possibilities of the gender representations in *Wall-E*.

It is not that *Wall-E* is an obviously defensible film politically. Clearly it is designed to encourage spectators to see Wall-E as a cute male lover and Eve as a traditional heroine in a romantic comedy, at first resistant to Wall-E's advances, but in the end falling in love with him because of his obvious charms: robot boy meets robot girl, robot girl leaves robot boy, and then robot girl marries robot boy. My point instead is that the implications of the representational practices of *Wall-E* overflow beyond the profit dynamics of the film. The fact that both Wall-E and Eve have productive wombs means that the facile gender identification encouraged by the film is simply untenable. The gendering of the relationship between Wall-E and Eve implies that they will both create a future together which is distinctly non-hierarchical.

The ending of the film further complicates a stable reading. Due to Wall-E's and Eve's heroics, the humans land the *Axiom* back on the Earth. Without any denouement to speak of, the end credits roll. Using a completely different stop-motion, hand-drawn two-dimensional animation style than the rest of the film (which is done in Pixar's now famous three-dimensional CGI style), the credits relate to us the happy ending story of the humans' recovery of the Earth. Nothing we have seen before prepares us for this happy ending, and thus it is unconvincing in a Sirkian, Brechtian way. Wall-E's experience on the planet was one of stark survival: when his radar indicated that a gigantic dust storm was coming to swallow New York City, he retreated to his machine enclosure to ride out the horror."

The humans who have been entombed on the *Axiom* have no demonstrable survival skills: they believe pizza is a plant! Thus, when the credits depict the return of agricultural civilization to the Earth, the non-animated, two-dimensional presentation strikes the appropriate chord: it is flat and unbelievable. Set to the tune of Peter Gabriel's "Down to Earth," the end credits depict various historical painting styles, including the Impressionists' flowers, as a way of sugar coating the redemption of humanity. However, it seems likely that, should there be a *Wall-E, Part Two*, we would see Wall-E and Eve existing amidst a pile of human bones, long since destroyed by the violent storms of an Earth they had abandoned for its still-present toxicity. The only reason the plant survived in the first place was that it was protected by the refrigerator's, Wall-E's, and then Eve's wombs. We are given no indication that the human beings' wombs even work: a purportedly humorous shot on the *Axiom* shows robots taking care of human infants, straight out of Aldous Huxley's dystopian novel, *Brave New World*. Indeed, the last image of Wall-E's credits features Wall-E and Eve alone, holding hands in front of a tree, the roots of which are attached to the boot in which the film's original plant grew, with no human beings in the image at all.

In short, Wall-E and Eve serve as the post-human avatars of *Wall-E*. Their hybridization of human traits (he loves musicals, she loves him for being kind) with their mechanical bodies (wombs which accomplish important tasks) represent the future of humanity. As Haraway suggested long ago, if theorized correctly, this might not be all that bad of a thing. Technology could symbolically represent a path beyond the ailments of gender oppression that biological bodies have bequeathed to us as a previously insoluble problem. This is a matter as productive for Disability Studies as it is for genre studies of science-fiction cinema.

Wall-E and Intertextuality

Wall-E is built around a collision between two films from the late 1960s, not just the science fiction film *2001* but also the Hollywood musical *Hello, Dolly!* (1969). Midway through *Wall-E*, the robot lovers leave the Earth to join the exiled humans. On the *Axiom*, they find themselves at war with the ship's autopilot, a malevolent pacifier of human freedom, culled from *2001*'s HAL. However, whereas Kubrick's film is interested in documenting the devolution of humanity to robotic inanity, *Wall-E* generically fuses its dystopian science fiction to the optimism of the Hollywood blockbuster musical. Wall-E's and Eve's love is built around a mutually developed understanding of singing and dancing human lovers, Irene Molloy (Marianne McAndrew) and Cornelius Hackl (Michael Crawford). While *Hello, Dolly!* nostalgically looks back to a pre-industrial 1890 New York City, *Wall-E* envisions a future Earth restored to a pastoral garden in which the robots' love guides the humans back to the planet. They become, oddly, a singing and dancing cyborg Adam and Eve.

Wall-E is the post-human mirror of *Hello, Dolly!*. In 1969, *Hello, Dolly!* dreams of returning to the 19th century, to a New York City which is not yet the city to which Henry James returned in horror in 1905, filled with monstrous high rises such as the Flatiron Building. *Hello, Dolly!* ends with a stunning quadruple wedding on the shores of the Hudson River, a bucolic celebration of the Earth's natural bounty. Such a vision of New York is laughable to a film like *2001*, made just a year earlier in 1968, in which human cities orbit the Moon, and are made out of brightly-colored plastic, to chromatically enhance the bland humans who inhabit them. *Wall-E* begins at a subsequent place in history, the world of *Blade Runner*, in which human cities are about to collapse due to overpopulation, or *Escape from New York* (1981), for which *Wall-E* seems a post-human antidote: If human beings are going to ruin their cities by becoming murderous thugs, post-human robots like Wall-E and Eve can carry on the best of our culture, such as performing Hollywood musical numbers, with no need of death-dealing guns.

When Eve first arrives back on Earth, her first instinct is to shoot anything that moves with her laser gun, a metallic Annie Oakley. She almost accidentally kills both Wall-E and his cockroach companion in this fashion. However, Eve learns from Wall-E the power of the Hollywood musical to replace guns with love. The film's bleak ending for humans, despite its attempt to soothe the kids (and the adults for that matter) with Peter Gabriel, leaves us with little else in which to believe. The love shared between Wall-E and Eve, given their exquisite understanding of *Hello, Dolly!*, might just be enough.

In this sense, Pixar's *Wall-E* engages in the tradition of the contemporary Disney animated feature's representation of modern love. From *Beauty and the Beast* (1991) through *The Princess and the Frog* (2009), the Disney film has attempted to undo its company's attachment to the passive young heroine from fairy-tale romance. In an anthem to this revision, *Beauty and the Beast* begins with a fabulous assault on the passive female's stultifying small-town life. In a song which bears her name, with music and lyrics by Alan Menken and Howard Ashman, Belle (Paige O'Hara), seemingly doomed to marry the boorish Gaston (Richard White), belts out her passionate desire to transcend the provincial life which has been assigned to her. In *Wall-E*, Eve starts with a productive, purposeful life, searching the galaxy for plant life. As with most romances—and yet she significantly takes on the role of the male adventurer— Eve stumbles by accident upon the loving Wall-E, and on a discarded Earth where a nostalgic, provincial life would seem tremendous progress.

Wall-E's intertextual engagement with *Hello, Dolly!*, therefore, is more than just a convenient way for the film to wordlessly develop character, as director Andrew Stanton proposes. In an interview with the Associated Press, Stanton states that he used the tunes "Put On Your Sunday Clothes" and "It Only Takes a Moment" to "express the psyche of the love-starved trash compacting robot." But much more than this, the use of Jerry Herman's music offers an historical rebus, in which an evacuated 20th century subtends how *Hello, Dolly!* nostalgically longs for a return to the 19th century, highlighting *Wall-E's* very different futurist project, in which an ecological disaster in the 22nd century has nearly obliterated the human cultural artifacts on Earth.

In their article "From Environmental Adaptation to Sentimental Nostalgia," Robin L. Murray and Joseph K. Heumann capture the historicity of *Wall-E's* project when they use its references to the silent film comedies of Charlie Chaplin, Buster Keaton, and Harold Lloyd in order to argue for the film as an evolutionary comedy. Drawing on the ecocriticism of Joseph Meeker, they propose that Wall-E teaches the humans on the *Axiom* to be nostalgic for the green Earth that once was. Using Meeker's theory that evolutionary theory expresses the basic impulse of comedy (because we only can see the evidence of successful biological adaptations, evolution is a theory of happy survivability), Murray and Heumann observe the similar path *Wall-E* charts for robots aiding humans to re-discover their place in the natural world. In short, Wall-E and Eve evolve into new post-human newlyweds who transcend the human limitations of the four pairs who find themselves married at the conclusion of *Hello, Dolly!* on the gloriously green shores of the Hudson River. That is, Dolly Levi (Barbra Steisand) and Horace Vandergelder (Walter Matthau) are a conventional gender-bound human couple—Horace sings "It Takes a Woman" about why women are so much better at tasks requiring social skills, and Dolly sings "Call on Dolly" and "Motherhood March" which confirm Horace's sexist essentialism—whereas Eve carries a gun and Wall-E watches musicals all day, while both produce out of their wombs.

In their most astute observation, Murray and Heumann notice that the first image the ship's computer shows Captain McCrea is the opening and closing shot from D.W. Griffith's *A Corner in Wheat*:

> Images from D.W. Griffith's *A Corner in Wheat* (1909) show a lone farmer sowing seeds, while foregrounding the connection between humans and nature and the possibilities that remain after a corporation has taken control of agricultural industries. The collective eco-memories on display there become the captain's individual nostalgic yearnings, all because Wall-E found a plant and brought soil to Axiom's sterile world [12].

A Corner in Wheat is not merely a reference to capture film scholars into the world of *Wall-E*. Instead, it is a profound political historical reference. Despite his otherwise conservative Victorian values, Griffith in *A Corner in Wheat* ironically shows the results of an America that has refused farmers having the same opportunity for success as corporate big shots. *Wall-E* is a similar political critique of the world of corporate capitalism.

In its referencing, *Wall-E*, of the 21st century, skips back across the destruction of the 20th century, not to nostalgically retreat to the pastoral ideal of the 19th century, but to exorcise it from our experience. The world of *Hello, Dolly!* that so enamors Wall-E is so abstracted in the clips of the film he is able to record off of his iPod screen, that the original film's message is all but obliterated. For instance, Wall-E literally consumes the film, watching it from an old VHS tape which he keeps in his toaster, projected through an iPod, magnified artificially by a lens, more detritus Wall-E has salvaged from the abandoned streets of Manhattan. While the film is most obviously a critique of Americans' excessive consumption, Wall-E productively consumes *Hello, Dolly!* after popping it out of his toaster, in order to redeem humanity via the film's message of love. Stanton's use of the musical, then, implies instead a future in which Wall-E's and Eve's love teaches us not about how much better it was in the past, but instead, how much better we can be in the future, if we only learn to love instead of to waste our potential.

Gene Kelly's film begins with a black and white still photograph of Manhattan in 1890. Horses on the street mix with steam train engines. After coloring the image first blue and then green, the full color range of the film is put back into the image. In the very background of a dense image of city life, an elevated train starts moving, which we first hear chugging away on the soundtrack. An optical wipe moves semi-circularly across the image from the upper right hand corner, bringing the entire scene to life. We follow people's legs as they walk down the streets of the city. The music at this point expresses the synchronicity between the rhythms of city life and that of the human inhabitants. The social world of humans and the natural world around them (both the green of Central Park and the built environment of the city) are in perfect harmony.

However, this grandiose set, constructed at 20th Century–Fox, making *Hello, Dolly!* one of the most expensive films of the 1960s, is not just of any Manhattan space, but is central to our memory of a functional city. In the left foreground of the image, between 23rd Street and Fifth Avenue, is the V that forms Broadway, forming the basis of the south, downtown end of Madison Square. In twelve years' time, the building we see in *Hello, Dolly!*, a two-story brownstone, would be razed and replaced by the Flatiron Building. In 1902, this Daniel Burnham designed Beaux-Arts building with its neo-classical impulses would come to define the so-called "New New York," replacing the 19th century with its skyscraper modernity. *Hello, Dolly!'s* nostalgia for the 19th century is produced by the structuring absence of the Flatiron Building, its deletion a marker of the superiority of the past.

This gesture is the central move in Henry James' travelogue, *The American Scene*, first published in 1907.[13] After having lived as an expatriate in Europe for many years, James returned to the United States, publishing the book as a critical travelogue of his experiences seeing the country with fresh eyes. The section on New York City is the book's hallmark, in which James laments the loss of "Old New York," replaced by a world of gargantuan skyscrapers. In the section, "New York Revisited" (72), James writes of his astonishment that the skyscrapers have produced a "terrible town" in which the organic unity of the 19th century has been overshadowed by the tall buildings, beasts of commerce. He laments that he can no longer see Trinity Church in the skyline: "Beauty indeed was the aim of the creator of the spire of Trinity Church, so cruelly overtopped and so barely distinguishable, from your train-bearing barge, as you stand off; it is abject helpless humility.... It aches and throbs, this smothered visibility.... We commune with it, in tenderness and pity" (78). James thus argues that the skyscrapers, "those monsters of the mere market," destroy his ability to see the humanity of the city: "It is the fault of the buildings whose very first care is to deprive churches of their visibility" (80).

James comes close to defining the very space of *Hello, Dolly!'s* opening shot in his rabid critique of modernity: "It was to speak to me audibly enough

... through the thick of that frenzy of Broadway just where Broadway receives from Wall Street the fiercest application of the maddening lash."[14] *Hello, Dolly!* cites 1890 because it precedes the construction of the Flatiron Building as a "maddening lash" across the country/city hybridity of 19th century New York City, a happy duality most famously celebrated by Walt Whitman in "Crossing Brooklyn Ferry" : "I too lived, Brooklyn of ample hills was mine, / I too walk'd the streets of Manhattan island, and bathed in the waters around it."[15] *Hello, Dolly!* and *The American Scene* nonetheless share a nostalgic mode. Both Gene Kelly and Henry James long for a New York before the disaster that is sky-scraper modernity.

   Wall-E, then, becomes a different sort of adaptation of Henry James than that offered by *Hello, Dolly!* There is no Flatiron Building in *Wall-E* because the toxicity of the 21st century has destroyed the skyscraper altogether. Instead, *Wall-E* answers the grandiosity of *Hello, Dolly!'s* opening shot with its own spectacular imagery. In a vicious reversal of the Utopian cosmic zoom which begins Carl Sagan's *Contact* (1997), in which the camera follows *centrifugally* the trajectory of radio waves leaving the solar system carrying 20th century human civilization, *Wall-E* begins with a *centripetal* zoom, from starry outer space, through the detritus of ruined orbiting satellites long since junked, to a panoramic sweep through what conventionally seems to be the Manhattan skyline. However, these are mere simulacra of skyscrapers. The Flatiron Build-ing and its ilk have been replaced by built piles of garbage from Wall-E's womb. The initial shot of the film thus parodies not only *Contact's* Utopianism, but many romantic comedies' clichéd sweeps of Manhattan as a place where true love will be found within the Hollywood genre film. The world of both James' Old New York and the New New York of the romantic comedy has been reduced to rubble by the time *Wall-E* begins.

   And yet, rather than retreating into the solipsism of James' and *Hello, Dolly!'s* nostalgia for an impossible past, Wall-E adapts the present conditions to a possible future. As Murray and Heumann argue, *Wall-E* resists sentimental nostalgia via an evolutionary theory of adaptation. *Wall-E's* post-human cap-ture of the beautiful music from *Hello, Dolly!*, without its reliance on a particular spatial geography, leads the film to envision the continuation of precious human values. *Hello, Dolly!*, while playing with temporality (reconstructing 1890 New York in 1969 Hollywood), is like Henry James' *The American Scene*, a text from a spatially-obsessed civilization. The unrequited lovers leave Yonkers, the sticks in 1890, but no longer so in 1969, to go to Manhattan to find true love, as Hol-lywood romantic comedies have been suggesting is the only way to find it for the past 100 years. After many comic foibles, four couples do find their soul mates, and return to the bucolic countryside to get married and procreate within nature's bounty.

   However, *Wall-E* suggests that the spatial metaphors that subtend Henry James and *Hello, Dolly!*—there is a stable nature, inherently defensible, and an urban space of dubious merits—are, if not already destroyed in 2008, about to be. *Wall-E* then, becomes a film obsessed not with space but with time. With human history destroyed, the film looks to the future to imagine, not so much a return to the American garden, but the need for complex human emotions to find expression somehow. Wall-E learns love not from a mother and father, but from isolated film clips, ripped out of their original narrative and spatial contexts. The importance of his tectonic work, then, becomes not the rebuilding of skyscrapers out of trash, but of a filmic mashed-up text that he can show Eve so that they can learn how to fall in love together. The fact that *Wall-E* can only truly imagine these emotions being expressed by the post-human— it is the robots, and not the humans, who love the cinema—is the film's great radical invention. While the Earth is a disaster, the film's happy ending rings true: a new, non-Biblical Eve, who is not going to be cast out of Eden for eating an apple, and Wall-E make a home for themselves with their step-children, the adopted humans who will need them, like a father and mother, to survive.

It is with this observation, of Andrew Stanton's little robot as a parental cinephile, with which I will conclude this admittedly unconventional Disability Studies analysis of *Wall-E*. On the continuum of temporarily able-bodied people, I see Wall-E as sharing most of my traits. While I do not wheel myself around Earth as does Wall-E, both he and I address our bodily limitations— both physical and mental—in the same way. Most of my life is devoted to using the cinema to fight the pain of living. At home, I show movie clips to my kids to teach them what sort of productive, intellectually-engaged life is worth living. In my work, my classroom, I do the same with university students. Wall-E is, above all, a really great film professor. He shows Eve that the joy in being in love is to watch clips of the singing and dancing in *Hello, Dolly!* Martin Norden describes the third phase of representations of disability in the Hollywood cinema, beginning in the 1970s, thusly: "Rehabilitative struggles, which took center stage during the second period, began giving way to other concerns: pursuing a career, fighting for social justice, sexually expressing oneself, simply getting on with everyday life."[16] These are the things which Wall-E struggles to do (he pursues his love for Eve, he fights with computers to allow humans to return to Earth), which I struggle to do (in my family life, in my job). For me, that's enough. I'd rather see Wall-E's love of the Hollywood musical serving as a blueprint for the future than *2001*'s horrific star child— the size of a planet with an emotional brain the size of Dave Bowman's—any day of the week, especially when I have my Sunday clothes on.

Notes

1. Hoeksema and Smit, 35.
2. Smit and Enns, ix.
3. Norden, 19.

4. Smit and Enns, xvi.
5. Cherney, 170.
6. Cherney, 169–170.
7. Many of the ideas for this reading of *Wall-E* first came to mind during my discussions with Charles Dye, on whose MFA committee I served as chair at Montana State University. I am deeply grateful for the many conversations with Charles about the ecological dimensions of *Wall-E*.
8. Norden, 293.
9. *Ibid.*, 22.
10. *Ibid.*, 293.
11. *Ibid.*, 298.
12. While first wave feminists were focused on basic human rights, such as voting, the second wave approach expanded the quest for equality to such issues as the responsibility for child-rearing. As I discuss later, second wave feminist Gena Corea studied the ways in which patriarchal culture demeans women's bodies as inferior to science in relation to reproduction.
13. My sincere thanks to Robert Bennett, Professor of English at Montana State University, for his erudite analysis of the cultural history of New York City.
14. James., 80.
15. Whitman, 146.
16. Norden, 23.

Bibliography

Cherney, James L. "Sexy Cyborgs: Disability and Erotic Politics in Cronenberg's *Crash*," *Screening Disability*. Eds. Smit and Enns. 165–180.

Clark, Bruce. *Post-human Metamorphosis: Narrative and Systems*. New York: Fordham University Press, 2008.

Corea, Gena. *The Mother Machine: Reproductive Technologies from Artificial Insemination to Artificial Wombs*. New York: Harper & Row, 1985.

Crutchfield, Susan. "The Noble Ruined Body: Blindness and Visual Prosthetics in Three Science Fiction Films," *Screening Disability*. Eds. Smit and Enns. 135–150.

Dinello, Daniel. *Technophobia! Science Fiction Visions of Posthuman Technology*. Austin: University of Texas Press, 2005.

Dozois, Gardner (Ed.). *Supermen: Tales of the Posthuman Future*. New York: St. Martin's Griffin, 2002.

Fukuyama, Francis. *Our Post-human Future: Consequences of the Biotechnology Revolutions*. New York: Picador, 2002.

Gray, Chris Hables. *Cyborg Citizen: Politics in the Post-human Age*. New York: Routledge, 2001.

Halberstam, Judith, and Ira Livingston. *Post-human Bodies*. Bloomington: Indiana University Press, 1995.

Haraway, Donna. "A Cyborg Manifesto: Science, Technology, and Socialist-Feminism in the Late Twentieth Century," *Simians, Cyborgs and Women: The Reinvention of Nature*. New York: Routledge, 1991. 149–181.

Hayles, N. Katherine. *How We Became Post-human: Virtual Bodies in Cybernetics, Literature and Informatics*. Chicago: University of Chicago Press, 1999.

"*Hello Dolly!* Inspires *Wall-E* Romance." http://cnn.com. 2008. Accessed: November 11, 2008.

Hoeksema, Thomas B., and Christopher R. Smit. "The Fusion of Film Studies and Disability Studies," *Screening Disability*. Eds. Smit and Enns. 33–46.

Huxley, Aldous. *Brave New World*. New York: Harper Perennial, 2010.

James, Henry. *The American Scene*. http://www2.newpaltz.edu/~hathaway/american-scene.html. Accessed September 28, 2009.

Lunning, Frenchy (Ed.). *Mechademia 3: Limits of the Human.* Minneapolis: University of Minnesota Press, 2008.

Meeker, Joseph W. "The Comic Mode," *The Ecocriticism Reader: Landmarks in Literary Ecology.* Eds. Cheryll Glotfelty and Harold Fromm. Athens: University of Georgia Press,1996. 155–169.

Murray, Robin L., and Joseph K. Heumann. "*Wall-E:* From Environmental Adaptation to Sentimental Nostalgia." *Jump Cut: A Review of Contemporary Media.* 51. [Spring 2009].

Norden, Martin F. *The Cinema of Isolation: A History of Physical Disability in the Movies.* New Brunswick, NJ: Rutgers University Press, 1994.

_____. "The Hollywood Discourse on Disability: Some Personal Reflections," *Screening Disability.* Eds. Smit and Enns. 19–32.

Smit, Christopher R., and Anthony Enns (Eds.) *Screening Disability: Essays on Cinema and Disability.* Lanham, MD: University Press of America, 2001.

_____. "Introduction: The State of Cinema and Disability Studies," *Screening Disability.* Eds. Smit and Enns. ix–xviii.

Toffoletti, Kim. *Cyborgs and Barbie Dolls: Feminism, Popular Culture and the Posthuman Body.* London: IB Tauris, 2007.

Vest, Jason P. *The Postmodern Humanism of Philip K. Dick.* Lanham, MD: Scarecrow Press, 2009.

Whitman, Walt. "Crossing Brooklyn Ferry," *Leaves of Grass.* New York: Signet, 1955. 144–149.

Home Is Where
the Heart Is: Pixar's Up

DENNIS TYLER

On March 7, 2010, the movie *Up* took home Pixar Animation Studios' fifth Best Animated Feature Academy Award; very few people were surprised that *Up* won. Indeed, all seven Pixar films that had been released since the award was first given in 2001 had been nominated and, with the exception of *Monsters, Inc.* (2001) which lost to *Shrek* (2001) and *Cars* (2006) which lost to *Happy Feet* (2006), Pixar had not only won the award, but also had been the strong favorite in the category. The website, *Rotten Tomatoes*, which collects and categorizes movie reviews, had given *Up* a 98% Fresh rating as of April 5, 2010. The critical "consensus" on *Rotten Tomatoes* is quoted as "[a]nother masterful work of art from Pixar, *Up* is an exciting, hilarious, and heartfelt adventure impeccably crafted and told with wit and depth."[1] Obviously, in the minds of critics, Pixar is doing something right, but *Up* also garnered impressive box office receipts, out-performing all other films in its opening weekend, to bring in $68,108,790. As of February 2010, the film had made over $720 million worldwide.[2] This box office success surpassed all other Pixar films except *Finding Nemo* (2003).

As with all other Pixar feature films, there was general anticipation prior to release, but critic Doug Creutz was not alone in suggesting a concern about the commercial potential of *Up*. Cruetz said that each of Pixar's films "seem to be less commercial than the last."[3] Richard Greenfield of Pali Research also expressed concern about *Up*'s commercial viability, but after the remarkable first week's returns, acknowledged he was "dead wrong."[4] Concerns like Creutz's and Greenfield's were reflected in Thinkway Toys, which has produced toys for most Pixar films, not producing any toys for the film.[5] Initially only a handful of novelizations, children's books, and plush toys of the main dogs in the film were produced. Compared to other Disney and Pixar features, the marketing for *Up* is remarkably sparse. As detailed in the Pixar Blog, *Up*'s commercial success has led to more marketing, but it's still a far cry from other Disney-Pixar films.[6] In one of the few mentions of *Up* in criticism, M. Keith Booker suggests that there is "room seriously to question whether *Up* is a children's film at all given the number of serious issues" it addresses.[7] Despite these concerns, *Up* is generally considered a children's movie.[8] What Booker, Cruetz, and Greenfield are all suggesting is that Pixar, essentially, does not make "children's films" or at least not films *just* for children, which presupposes the representation of reality that is appropriate for a children's movie.[9]

Up has been both a commercial and critical success, as have, generally speaking, all of Pixar's feature films to date. This record of success has created a substantial body of work with a supposed intent to entertain children and families. As the Movieguy says to John Lasseter, the chief creative officer for Pixar, in an interview on *Cars*, only Disney and Pixar are producing child friendly entertainment that is suitable for the entire family.[10] This essay explores two related questions: first, how has Pixar achieved this success? As David A. Price demonstrates throughout the first half of *The Pixar Touch*, computer animation had generally been thought of as lifeless and cold before Pixar. With their early shorts, Pixar began to study techniques to bring "life" or "heart" to their animation.[11]

Second, what reality is Pixar representing? I will argue that Pixar studied, adopted, and adapted the techniques of Disney's animators in bringing an "illusion of life" to their animation but, in doing so, they were self-aware of some issues of representation and have striven to represent a reality that is remarkably different than Disney in some respects. Pixar's films may be "family friendly," but this notion calls into question what a family is. Throughout the Pixar canon, "the family" is not simply the biological entity of the nuclear family, but rather a grouping of individuals who care for each other whether technically related or not. Though heavily invested in representing "safe" family values, Pixar, nonetheless, has managed to respond to the current cultural landscape and the changing nature of family and family relationships. In the fifties and sixties, Disney could casually expect heteronormative nuclear families; even Disney animated features as late as *Chicken Little* (2005) and *Meet the Robinsons* (2007) deploy this family structure (though there are signs of other affective affiliations in the unpopular crowd that befriends Chicken Little or the extended kinship of the Robinson clan). From *Toy Story* forward, the "family" does not just refer to the heteronormative nuclear family, but to a wide ranging affective network.[12] Thus, in *Up*, though all the major characters come from various broken home environments, they find together a family of individuals whose concern for each other bonds them and brings them together. Though *Up* would thus seem to hold some promise of a progressive representation of difference, in the end, it capitulates to foregrounding and valorizing the white patriarch's story as the "story." Ultimately, it becomes a conservative and conserving narrative of containment.

In 1941, the influential Russian filmmaker and theorist, Sergei Eisenstein, apparently had the intent to write an essay on Walt Disney and began taking notes and drafting his thoughts, but they were not published in his lifetime. Eisenstein described Disney's animated features as being "like direct embodiment[s] of the method of animism." He goes on to note how we feel that "*if* it moves, then it's alive." Even though "we *know* that they [animated characters] are drawings and not living beings ... projections of drawing on a screen ... [and] miracles and tricks of technology[,] we *sense* them as alive ... as moving, as active ... as existing and even thinking."[13] Here then, in a way of speaking, lies an issue for representation in animation; the characters on the screen are not being portrayed by an actor whose actual body must, in some sense be seen, but by a representation that takes on the semblance of reality that is granted to it by the animator's technique. Though all film is in some senses manufactured illusions of reality, animators have to go a step further and create the illusion of solidity and materiality out of drawn lines, spaces, and colors.

In 1995, Ollie Johnston and Frank Thomas published the book on the technique of Disney animation that is generally regarded as definitive: *Disney Animation: The Illusion of Life*. Johnston and Thomas detail twelve principles of Disney animation:

1. Squeeze and stretch
2. Anticipation
3. Staging
4. Straight ahead action and pose to pose
5. Follow through and overlapping action
6. Slow in and slow out
7. Arcs
8. Secondary action
9. Timing
10. Exaggeration
11. Solid drawing
12. Appeal[14]

One key aspect of what Johnston, Thomas, and Disney's other "Nine Old Men" discovered in devising these twelve principles is that for animation to appear lifelike, it must obey certain laws of the physical universe. Matter has weight and inertia, so all actions have corresponding reactions; in order to depict these in an animated reality, at the extremes of motion, shapes have to be distorted. As examples, the Disney animators would draw a flour sack in various poses so as to get the feel of real weight, or draw a simple bouncing ball to learn to depict the way objects "squeeze and stretch" as they encounter the various forces of their movement.[15] A second key insight was in storytelling to ensure that the audience could follow the pertinent action; animators began to make storyboards and rough drawings of an action sequence to ensure the right angle and character poses from which to draw it. Additionally, a proper amount of anticipation and follow through made the action more believable. Disney animators also learned to look toward Nature and study reality before drawing. Animators would film actors reading their lines or acting out various events and use these as guides to animating characters, scenes, and actions. Study trips were arranged to study specific locations and animals were brought in the studio and studied in order to replicate their movements.[16] In general, however, what the Disney animators discovered is that the key to successful animation was a certain amount of exaggeration: the mass of objects was exaggerated to give them physicality; the character traits of actors were exaggerated to give the animated characters the quirky individuality of "real" people; and the movements of animals were exaggerated so that their species identity was explicit. At their best, following these principles allowed Disney to produce animated characters that became iconic for their verisimilitude to material beings; at their worst, they produced gendered, racial, and cultural stereotypes. In *Snow White* when Dopey's head is clanged between two cymbals, he can briefly become an Asian stereotype; or in *Bambi*, when puppy love is depicted between Thumper and a young female rabbit, stereotypes of human femininity are portrayed in the drawings and actions of his love interest; Robin Hood and Maid Marion are represented as a wily fox and a sexy vixen in *Robin Hood*.

Even though we *know* these are just drawings, these and many other examples throughout Disney's canon illustrate how these animation techniques can easily tap into and make use of cultural stereotypes and reinforce them by sensually embodying what was, perhaps, only a vague notion before. We may recognize the stereotype of the crafty fox, but not fully realize that in watching *Robin Hood* (1973) we are treated to a visualized materialization of that idea. Perhaps most tellingly, in this regard are Disney's princesses, who with excesses of femininity, an innate connection with nature, impossible thinness, beautiful flawless skin, and perfect hair, attire, and poise, always manage to get the prince and "live happily ever after." Likewise, Disney villains are often misshapen, have speech impediments or racially charged accents. Their "evilness" is a palpable emanation that depends on any number of stereotypical notions of what it means to be "evil." Because animators are not constrained by the material reality of the actresses who voiced these princesses or the actors and actresses who voiced these villains, they have given them idealized forms so that even though we *know* they are just drawings, they *seem* real; they become them.[17]

Thinking through animated representations leads Eisenstein to suggest that "Disney's works themselves strike [him] as the same kind of drop of comfort, an instant of relief, a fleeting touch of lips in the hell of social burdens, injustices and torments, in which the circle of his American viewers is forever trapped."[18] This sense of escaping life, this "obliviousness" that Eisenstein sees, is at once the potential and the danger of animation. "And Disney, like all of them, through the magic of his works and more intensely, perhaps, than anyone else, bestows precisely this upon his viewer, precisely obliviousness, an instant of complete and total release from everything connected with the suffering caused by the social conditions of the social order."[19] When this technique can be used to envision escape from oppression, it would serve a progressive purpose in giving encouragement to those whose social circumstances themselves seem to provide little hope; however, pushed too far, this would be an invitation to delusion. In *The Little Mermaid* (1989), for instance, Ariel's defiance of her father's wishes can seem remarkably progressive, suggesting that a sixteen year old girl knows her heart better than her father *and* should follow it. In *The Rescuers* (1977), Penny's rescue by two mice might teach us that we are never too small to offer assistance. Both "lessons," however, are just as easily distorted. Tyrannical fathers are real, but few daughters have to contend with the god of the sea for a father; likewise, few people can really be helped by a few mice and assorted swamp creatures.

Much of the same pedagogical expectation has been placed on Pixar, but as John Lasseter explains in a 2007 interview with Tavis Smiley about the movie *Cars*, Pixar is sensitive to more than just this element of an animated feature: "We make movies for the kind of movies we like to watch. We're reasonably intelligent up there at Pixar. But we love movies, and we love taking our kids to the movies. And to me, there's so often I've been to a movie for my kids that I'm bored to death. And I said, 'I don't want that to happen in our movies.'"[20] Lasseter goes on to say that, "It's not just about the cynicism, or getting humor from putting somebody else down. That doesn't happen in a Pixar film. It's about heart." "Heart" is at the heart of what Johnston and Thomas have to say about Disney's animation technique; at its best, what the illusion of life means is that the audience believes the animated character on the screen has "heart" even though we also know it is just a drawing. Lasseter says, "[c]haracter animation is when an object moves like it is alive, when it moves like it is thinking and all of its movements are generated by its own thought processes.... It is the thinking that gives the illusion of life."[21] Though Lasseter does not credit Johnston and Thomas, it is clear he is referencing their ideas. In *Up*, care is taken to suggest not only that the characters are acting, but that they are thinking, receiving mental feedback on their environment and adjusting their actions accordingly. Though there are numerous examples, perhaps the most telling is when Carl imagines lowering Russell from the floating house. The entire sequence is a visualization of his daydream that depicts in a graphic way the choices Carl faces.

In a computer-animated film, much of what the Disney animators had to learn to draw can be handled by algorithms that treat an animator's drawing as a three-dimensional virtual object. Thus, for Pixar, one of the major challenges of making movies was not just understanding how to draw using principles like the ones Disney used, but figuring out the math involved so it could be programmed into a computer and rendered correctly in the film. In *Toy Story* (1995), care had to be taken so that wooden and plastic toys both remained toys but also had believable emotions and movements; in *Monsters, Inc.*, the monsters had to be scary enough to believably be embodiments of children's nightmares, but human enough for Boo not to fear Sully.[22] Pixar has breathed emotion into computer-animated ants, monsters, cars, fish, rats, and robots. And most famously, the Luxo lamp that is their trademark. In *The Pixar Touch*, Price quotes Ralph Guggenheim, a Pixar executive, as saying that, "several of [Disney's] senior execs admitted to me by the end of *Toy Story* production that Pixar had made a film that contained more of the 'heart' of traditional Disney animated films than they themselves were making at that time."[23] Pixar has produced this "heart" by placing the ideas, concerns, and props of children's lives front and center; broadly speaking, very much like Disney, they have animated the fantasies of children.

Up departs slightly from this approach in focusing its attention on the life of Carl Fredricksen, an elderly widower who chooses to finally pursue a childhood dream. This departure from form is, of course, the basis of the industry's concerns and the critical acclaim the film has earned. The film begins with Carl and Ellie as children in a fairly typical "cute meet." Ellie is the proactive and energetic one while Carl is passive. These traits play out again shortly later in their wedding and the montage of their life together that follows. Carl's family is quiet, Puritanical, and inexpressive. Ellie's family is loud, raucous, and clearly enthusiastic about the wedding. Once married, Carl and Ellie both seem to settle, literalized in the different armchairs that they inhabit. Their zoo jobs are not ambitious and their income moderate. They are the depiction of normalcy—a white middle income couple. They are "safe," non-subversive. Though we get no sense of their politics or sexuality, nothing stands out about them; but it is this very comfortable normality that is one of the representational problems of *Up*. Ellie was a spirited out-spoken child who barely gave Carl time to speak. At their wedding, Ellie leapt on *him* and kissed the *groom*, visibly embarrassing him and clearly not amusing his staid family who look as if they are dressed in mourning while her family just as clearly approves.

Just as in *Blackstone's Commentary* where a wife is "covered" by her husband, so Ellie's spirit seems to be tamed or covered by Carl's more practical and phlegmatic nature.[24] Her chair is flamboyant, with impractical curves and decorative wings, but her life has been contained, her voice silenced. Her dream is Paradise Falls; his, as we see them looking up at clouds—fatherhood. As they each describe various things in the clouds above them, he sees a baby; and then all the clouds are babies. His vision takes over and becomes their vision; his quiet unassuming manner becomes hers, and when they prove to be an infertile couple, it is apparently a failing in her. As she sits in the backyard letting the breeze blow over her, Carl brings Ellie her childhood *Adventure Book*, wordlessly saying that now they can focus on taking a trip. But her dream, a woman's dream of adventure, is a dream deferred, again and again. It was first superseded and erased by the expectation of parenthood and now every practical use of money—defined in terms of their relationship—must come first. Ellie's body defines her; she is the catalyst of Carl's sexual awakening, the would-be womb for his child, and at last, her body succumbs to age just before his grand gesture of tickets to Paradise Falls. In an irony of which the film-makers seem unaware, in Ellie's final note that indicates she has felt fulfilled with her life, it is Carl's dream that has satisfied him while she is asking him to go and fulfill hers. By the film's end, Carl and Russell are sitting outside Fenton's Ice Cream Parlor sharing ice cream and a game that Russell used to play with his father. This surrogate-fatherhood is what completes the cycle of Carl's life, returning him to the "spirit of adventure," the name of the blimp that hovers over them and the words written on the balloon that first creates a connection with Ellie. By living her adventure, his failed dream of fatherhood is also realized. There is little doubt that we are to see that they loved each other and his attachment to her after death is his guilt for not helping her to realize her dream, but Pixar's depiction as an equal love story leaves something to be desired in that the woman's dream, which turns out to encompass both his and her wishes, is deferred beyond her ability to pursue it. In its place is substituted a lifelong pattern of repetitive domestic service—she must help him dress—that is presented as fulfilling.[25]

Ellie's note truly *is* a loving gesture, however, and the film does acknowledge that. Releasing Carl from his guilt places her at the heart of *Up* and breathes life into it. Ellie and Carl are both aware that her life did not turn out as she had hoped. But, apparently, while in the hospital, knowing she will die, she has completed her *Adventure Book* as a gesture of compassion for her husband. It is significant that Carl, unaware of this gesture, brings his guilt, literalized as the house, with him to Paradise Falls. He fails to read her *Adventure Book* until then, and then only by chance. In fact, her dying wish for him is fulfilled only by the happenstance of gentrification and urbanization in the first place. Though Ellie's spirit may be covered by Carl's, hers is the true "spirit of adventure" in the film, and though the adult Ellie does not have a line—no voice actress was even hired—her voice speaks throughout the movie as home.

If gender difference in *Up* is conspicuous mostly by its absence, what can be said of race? While the main conflict of the story may be between two Caucasian men, other racial representations populate the margins of this story. Russell, voiced by Jordan Nagai, is an Asian American boy who belongs to the Wilderness Explorers (ironically abbreviated as WE). In *The Politics of the Visible*, Eleanor Ty refers to the "visible hieroglyphs imprinted on our eyes, our black hair, our noses, our faces, and our bodies, the resonance of another tongue, the haunting taste of another culture, as well as the perception, real or imagined of being from another place."[26] Ty's point is that Asians in America are marked as Other by their bodies and speech, often negatively. Though voiced by an Asian American actor, Russell has no noticeable Asian-inflected speech patterns. Docter says he picked Nagai for the part because his voice "is appealing and innocent and cute and different from what I was initially thinking."[27] His heavy-set body is based on Peter Sohn, a Pixar animator. Russell's skin tone and facial features are only vaguely "Asian" in appearance.[28]

While it is encouraging that Pixar did not rely on racially charged stereotypical features in their representation of an Asian American character, there is another assumption here, which is perhaps equally troubling: the assumption of whiteness. In discussing whiteness, George Yancy says, "Whites have a way of speaking from a center that they often appear to forget forms the white ideological fulcrum upon which what they say (do not say) or see (do not see) hinges."[29] This "forgetfulness" of Whites results in anything not specifically marked out as non-white to be White, thus Russell's lack of obvious Asian marking causes him to appear to be "white." Since Carl and Ellie are white, Russell becomes covered by Carl, racially. And by the house that represents Ellie and the guilt that Carl has brought with him. Like a long line of white men before him, Carl enlists others in his projects. His "white man's burden" is the *raison d'etre* and central burden in the journey not only for him, but also for Kevin and Dug as well. The patriarch's concern has covered not only the woman (Ellie), the racial Other (Russell), but domesticated nature (Dug) and the untamed wild nature (Kevin). Just as Ellie's dreams were deferred throughout their life together, so Carl pays lip service to Russell's concern for Kevin, Kevin's concern for her babies, and Dug's interest both in Kevin and in being his master. The white man must rule them all and his irrational desire to put his house next to Paradise Falls must become their desire as well. This house is for them merely a house, but for him, it is home.

If a distinction is drawn between the notions of "home" and "house," "home" is clearly a more intimate, and therefore, potentially a more fraught space. "Home" is an ideological space of (dis)comfort, while "house" is merely one's abode. Though Russell, Kevin, and Dug share quarters under the house with Carl, only for Carl is it a "home" and therefore a space that has expectations beyond that merely of shelter. Nonetheless, as Gaston Bachelard points out in *The Poetics of Space*, all houses have an intimacy to them. Bachelard says that "the house image would appear to have become the topography of our intimate being."[30] The "house shelters day dreaming, the house protects the dreamer, the house allows one to dream in peace."[31] Russell chooses the moment when they are sheltering under the house to share with Carl an intimate detail of his life: his parents are separated and his dad lives with another woman, Phyllis.[32] Carl, thinking too typically, refers to Phyllis as Russell's mother, only to have him reply, "Phyllis is not my mom." Carl's quiet "Oh" and embarrassed silence replace any explanation. We are never told what Russell's home life is really like because he is to find another kind of family with Carl. This quiet moment is the moment when Carl and Russell first bond and start becoming family. Like nearly all other families in the Pixar canon, however, this family cannot be fit into the traditional[33] nuclear family mode. It will expand to include the others sleeping under the house—Dug and Kevin.

Because they are not human, Pixar can endow Dug and Kevin with characteristics inappropriate to humans. Dug speaks his mind in the most literal of fashions, to the point of absurdity. Kevin, though wordless, is expressively flamboyant.[34] Not only is this family unrelated, they cannot be recontained in the nuclear family as a model, except in that it is a Patriarchal model. There is an unwritten assumption that the white human man will rule this little clan, an assumption that is bolstered by his being the only adult human in the group. Kevin cannot speak and Dug is a willing slave. Both Kevin and Dug show unrelenting love and care for Carl and Russell, even to the point of risking their lives. It is only through these nonhuman companions that Carl learns to become fully human himself. The moment of his realization comes through Ellie's final note to him in her *Adventure Book*, but in turning to risk (and lose) his house to save Kevin, he demonstrates the family connection that has been made. He realizes the "cross your heart" vow he has made to Russell should carry at least as much weight as the one he had made to Ellie; by honoring his vow to Russell, he is honoring his memory of Ellie better than in his self-absorbed moping. *Up* ensures that we are likely to identify with Carl and his change of heart through not only the techniques of Disney life-like animation, but through clever use of what Scott McCloud refers to as icons.

In *Understanding Comics*, McCloud analyzes the use of realistic vs. cartoon drawing techniques in comic art, and that when a drawn character is too photorealistic, the ability of the reader to identify is hampered; as an example, he presents the classic Hegré comic strip *Tintin*'s use of "clear-line" style, where a cartoonish character is presented against a realistic background. Disney, he says, has "used it with impressive results for over 50 years."[35] And Pixar is clearly following suit. The tepui-inspired backgrounds of Paradise Falls are beautiful and lush, detailed as only computer animation makes possible; Pixar followed Disney's process of location scouting, sending artists to the tepuis of Venezuela to research them. The point of placing cartoonish, iconic characters in an otherwise realistic universe, McCloud claims, is to encourage readerly self-identification with the cartoon character: "when you look at a photo or realistic drawing of a face you see it as the face of another ... but when you enter the world of the cartoon you see yourself."[36] McCloud bases this theory on the notion that since we do not have our own face constantly in view, we rely on a more generalized or iconic representation of our own features as we converse and interact with others, but since we have their faces in view, we ascribe more photorealistic features to them; thus, any character made up of iconic lines more easily can represent us.

McCloud's theory skirts issues of stereotypical representation, marginalization, and exclusion. However, McCloud's reading of iconic cartoon characters suggests that the drawing of a character is more than just a matter of stylistic choice; it can tell us something of who the animator is envisioning as audience for the comic (or film). Though McCloud's analysis would suggest that anyone can more easily identify with a character that is drawn as a cartoon than a realistic figure, it would also follow that it is easier for someone who is closer to the character being represented to make this identification. I have already mentioned Ellie's problematic marginalization in *Up*; if we are to think of Kevin as female, then the main female character in this movie is a squawky bird whose coloration is apparently based on the male Himalayan Monal Pheasant.[37] With the notable exception of *The Incredibles* (2004), however, the lack of substantial female roles seems to be something of a Pixar standard.[38] There is less in Pixar films and in *Up* in particular for women than men to latch onto. There is a sense in which the repetition of a male-centered story throughout the majority of the Pixar canon cannot be seen as incidental, but as telling us something about the stories Pixar finds compelling. It is as notable as Disney's fascination with Princess stories has been. Recently, Disney has even tried to update and diversify their depiction of the "princess" with an African American princess in *The Princess and the Frog* (2009); however, despite being set in the Southern past, issues of race-based social marginalization are muted at best if not outright ignored. Though we are supposed to identify with her story, the lack of social realism in Tiana's story, the skirting of the realities of historical racism, and the sloppy stereotypical depictions of African American spiritualities deracialize Disney's African American princess to the point where it is difficult to see anything news or different here from other Disney princesses other than skin color. Her race is incidental and plays no significant role in the story.

Though given little narrative space, African Americans in *Up* are also depicted in roles in which race seems to be simply incidental: one of the attendants for Shady Oaks; the girl who watches the house fly by her window; several of the boys at the end receiving a badge next to Russell. These roles are all drawn with a greater degree of realism than the main characters and thus, though seemingly progressive in their everydayness, they remain part of the background of the story. The contrast I would make with *The Princess and the Frog* is that we are not "supposed" to identify with the African American characters in *Up*; this is a white guy's story, after all. Of course, it's not just *any* white guy, however. Carl's childhood hero—Charles Muntz—is one of the villains of the story. Muntz, like most minor characters, is drawn more realistically and less iconically than Carl, Dug, and Russell. The same is true of his dogs;

while Dug is a generic cartoon mutt, Alpha, Beta and Gamma are all recognizable breeds. Muntz, tall, gaunt and angular, contrasts with Carl's squat, stocky body. Like the construction foreman—the other villain of the movie—Muntz's lean form signals his allegiance to an adult world of business and prestige and are deliberately alienating, particularly for the children in the audience. In contrast, Carl's square jaw, Russell's comically large neck and upturned nose, the cartoony flamboyancy of Kevin, and the larger-than-life snout of Dug encourage the audience to place themselves in these characters' positions and therefore become sympathetic to their position in the film.

It is the dogs (mostly Dug) that were expected to appeal to young viewers. The negative appraisals of *Up*, it seems, were predicated only on the expectation that Pixar intended young viewers to find identification with Carl, but the end of his "life montage" as he rides a chair downstairs and goes out to sit on his porch are, like Dug's doggy attributes, the sorts of activities young viewers are likely to associate with their own grandfathers. *Up* begins as nostalgia for lost childhood. Disney has done this as well, presenting a nostalgic childhood is from generations earlier. *Pinocchio* (1940), *Peter Pan* (1953), *Alice in Wonderland* (1951), and all the princess films are clearly set in the past, invoking a time when things were, perhaps, different (i.e., better). *Up* begins with this gesture, but brings its character into the nasty, greedy present. Though brief, the conflict with the contractors who are remaking Carl's neighborhood into another urban block of office buildings is a clear indication of the thoughtless, faceless greed of modern capitalist America. The boss is clearly motivated by profit and his drumming fingers on Carl's fence post signify all we need to know of him: his interests are evil and possessive. Again, this is something that the adults in the audience can identify with; evil corporate bureaucrats who take people's homes away from them are common enough in popular culture. *Monsters, Inc.*, *The Incredibles*, and *Ratatouille* (2007) all contain moments of the same sort of boss. In contrast, Disney villains are more often motivated by straight evil, a personal power trip or an attempt to deliberately thwart the destiny of the hero/ine than they are by greed. Even Muntz is not motivated specifically to thwart Carl but opposes him through a differing sense of priorities.

By bringing the idealized past into a contrast with the present, *Up* achieves what *Enchanted* (2007) in a different way accomplished and must, like *Enchanted*, chart a way back to the world of fantasy. In this case, it is the flying house, a nice sideways tribute to *The Wizard of Oz* (1934) (note, that like in *Oz*, characters seem to be constantly stuck under the house, but rather than being flattened, they are brought in to safety). It is in this fantastical moment of flight that *Up* takes on a different character, a change that is signaled by the introduction of Russell shortly before. Until this point, *Up* has been relentlessly about Carl, and indeed, his quest will continue to dominate, but something unique and different begins to enter the movie with Russell and is reinforced with Dug and Kevin. The white man's burden simply will not do;

in this way, *Up* gestures toward relinquishing this burden and opening up to the concerns of the racial/sexual other, though the white man's story co-opts and contains all other narratives. Kevin's protection falls to Carl and Russell's and Dug's stories are "solved" not by a direct approach, but by their assistance to Carl. *Up* stops short of allowing these narratives of Otherness to speak in their own right.

And so the magic moment of the flying house as the multicolored balloons cast shadows over the bedroom of a young African American girl at play. It is a brief moment, but a signal of unimaginable hope and wonder; the house, multicolored, is a dream home, a house in which there are dreams of what America could have been and of what is was/is. It is the burden of the past we must carry with us whether we will or not. It invokes its Victorian A-frame past as burden. To the girl, standing in the window, it is wondrous. In this moment, *Up* achieves a brief identification with the non-white/non-male/non-adult Other. This girl *is* the audience, enthralled. She is us. And we, like her, in this moment can envision anything. Though *Up* will recapitulate and recontain the energy of this moment, collapsing all story into the narrative of Carl, we are given here just a glimpse of what the future could hold. For her, the girl at play, this cannot be her adventure, but she can also be inspired, perhaps. How quickly does Pixar switch to a typical white heteronormative family window-shopping.

This moment is the crux of the reality *Up* is depicting; which side of the window are we on? Are we the girl, startled in her play, looking out the window in wonder, washed by a rainbow of possibility or are we the window-shopping family, seeing the house reflected in a pane of storefront glass, flying away above and beyond us? *Up*, like all art, is a window on reality, and it serves at once to both reflect the social milieu from which it springs and to construct an idealized world of its own.

On one level, *Up* is Carl's flight of escape from social problems, but he cannot leave them behind. They follow him and in the world of Paradise Falls, he must come to grips both with all he has left behind and with all he might wish for the future. Though he loved Ellie, her life was voiceless; her act of grace gives him a second chance. As he sits in front of Fenton's with Russell, her gift has given him the spirit of adventure he always desired but did not possess. Carl must do more than window shop. Ironically, he takes his house with him to Paradise Falls only to leave it there and return to the city to face new adventures with Dug and Russell. It is a family of care not kin. It is family of choice and a family of heart. Though there is potential to read into *Up* some subversion of white patriarchal centrality, this subversion is safely silenced by the movie's end. It may be a family of choice, but it is a family based on what is comfortable and familiar to the patriarch and his concerns, ultimately, trump those of anyone else.

Notes

1. http://www.rottentomatoes.com/m/up/
2. http://www.the-numbers.com/movies/2009/UP.php.
3. http://www.nytimes.com/2009/04/06/business/media/06pixar.html. Some later Pixar films such as *Wall-E* (2008), *Ratatouille* (2007), and the *Cars* films have also had detractors. For *Wall-E*, see Stephanie Zacharek's review for Salon.com at http://www.salon.com/entertainment/movies /review/2008/06/27/wall_e/; for *Ratatouille*, see JoBlo's Movie Emporium review: http://www. joblo.com/index.php?id=16543; and for *Cars*, see Anthony Lane's review for the *New Yorker*: http://www.newyorker.com/archive/2006/06/19/060619crci_cinema. Each of these reviews is notable for suggesting that with the movie in question, Pixar has finally hit a dry spell of creativity. In any case, predicting the end of Pixar's remarkable successful run has proven to be a hazardous enterprise for film critics.
4. http://mediadecoder.blogs.nytimes.com/2009/07/08/wall-street-analyst-belatedly-sees-the-up-side/
5. http://pixarblog.blogspot.com/2009/02/up-toys-and-merchandise.html
6. The Pixar Blog can be found at: http://pixarblog.blogspot.com/2009/02/up-toys-and-merchandise.html. Disney's online Toy Store which sells Disney and Pixar Toys can be found at http://www.disneystore.com/. A cursory search for any other Pixar film will amply demonstrate the phenomenon. *Up* has one page of merchandise, most of which are books and T-shirts.
7. Booker, 110.
8. See http://en.wikipedia.org/wiki/List_of_children%27s_films#2009. Though Wikipedia is not highly regarded critically, it does a good job of representing prevailing public opinion and is cited here for that purpose alone. Alternatively, Pixar's films have been described as "family films." In an interview with Chuck the Movieguy, John Lasseter comments that his wife tells him to make movies not just for an initial viewing, but for "100th time a parent has to suffer through them." See http://www.youtube.com/watch?v=D9ak_e3U8PI (0:38).
9. Children's films have received less attention than films for adults, it seems, but *The Antic Art: Enhancing Children's Literary Experiences Through Film and Video* (1995) by Lucy Rollin and Ian Wojcik-Andrew's collection, *Children's Films: History, Ideology, Pedagogy, Theory* (2000) seem the places to begin. See also Booker's *Disney, Pixar, and the Hidden Messages of Children's Films* (2009) for application to Pixar's film specifically.
10. See http://www.smileyyoutube.com/vid.aspx?id=799391.
11. See Price throughout, but particularly pages 1–117 for the prehistory of Pixar Animation Studios. Price provides a detailed history of the major creative forces behind Pixar's evolution into an animation studio and the creative and technological struggles they faced.
12. *The Incredibles* is a notable exception to the pattern.
13. Eisenstein on Disney, 55.
14. These principles are first listed on page 15 without commentary and then explored over the remainder of the book with numerous examples and illustrations of how the Disney style evolved over time.
15. Thomas, 17, 19.
16. These various points are illustrated throughout *The Illusion of Life*; roughly speaking, pgs 303–18 illustrate the importance of anticipation and follow through; and pages 319–66 depict the use of animals and human actors in Disney animation.
17. In passing, let me note that I have picked these examples practically at random as the examples in Disney's canon are practically endless. Nevertheless, it is not my purpose to demonize Disney or these animation principles. All animated films have made use of them and arguably, must. For all the flawed applications such techniques may be prone to, when used with more sensitivity and care, they have proven to be just as useful in dispelling stereotypes as reinforcing them. Dreamworks' *Shrek* is a well known example of using animation to subvert the stereotypical fairy story narrative.
18. Eisenstein, 7.
19. *Ibid.*, 8.
20. lhttp://www.pbs.org/kcet/tavissmiley/archive/200701/20070124_lasseter.html.
21. Price, v.
22. See Price throughout, particularly chapters 6–8.

23. Qtd. in Price, 155–6.

24. This is from Book 1 Chapter 15, pg. 430 of *Blackstone's Commentaries on the Law of England*: "By marriage, the hufband and wife are one perfon in law 1 : that is, the very being or legal exiftence of the woman is fufpended during the marriage, or at leaft is incorporated and confolidated into that of the hufband : under whofe wing, protection, and cover, fhe performs every thing ; and is therefore called in our law-french a feme-covert ; is faid to be covert-baron, or under the protection and influence of her hufband, her baron, or lord ; and her condition during her marriage is called her coverture. Upon this principle, of an union of perfon in hufband and wife, depend almoft all the legal rights, duties, and difabilities, that either of them acquire by the marriage." From http://avalon.law.yale.edu/18th_century/blackstone_bk1ch15.asphttp://avalon.law.yale.edu/18th_century/blackstone_bk1ch15.asp.

25. In all fairness to Pixar, a similar, but reversed moment occurs in *The Incredibles* when Mr. Incredible tells his wife that she and their kids have been his greatest adventure.

26. Ty, 3–4.

27. http://articles.latimes.com/2009/may/28/entertainment/et-jordanpete28.

28. Interestingly, both I and a colleague have noted that over repeated viewings of *Up*, Russell appears more Asian. Also, it is worth noting that in other depictions, he also seems more Asian. In *Wild Life*, a coloring book version of *Up* that tells the story from Russell's point of view, Russell's features are much more noticeably Asian.

29. Yancy, 1

30. Bachelard, xxxvi.

31. *Ibid.*, 6.

32. *Up* never clarifies what the relationship is, whether Russell's parents married and divorced or what relationship if any pertains between Russell and his mother.

33. What I mean by "traditional" is a family consisting solely of a male father and a female mother and their direct offspring. It my contention that with the notable exception of *The Incredibles* this traditional family model is not represented in Pixar. See Lawrence Stone's *The Family, Sex and Marriage in England, 1500–1800* for an exhaustive look at where this "traditional" family arose. Though it is out-of-date and occasionally reaches conclusions that are no longer critically salient, Stone's work has yet to be superseded in its scope.

34. The website Slashfilm makes the suggestion that Kevin is "a nod to the LGBT community" because of her gender ambiguity in the movie. See http://www.slashfilm.com/2009/06/09/is-kevin-the-tropical-bird-in-pixars-up-a-nod-to-the-lbgt-movement/. I originally intended to read Kevin's gender as ambiguous as well, contending that we have no evidence of her gender—men must father children, after all, so the existence of babies means little; however, in researching this paper, I came across the coloring book *Wild Life* in which the reader is asked to decipher a special message to Russell about Kevin. This message is "Kevin is a girl." See Hands, pg. 27.*Wild Life* is, of course, separate from the movie, but it is an official *Up* product. What is troubling about this identification is that the only evidence of Kevin's gender is the babies, thus strongly associating femininity with children.

35. McCloud, 43.

36. *Ibid.*, 36.

37. See http://wiki.answers.com/Q/What_type_of_bird_is_Kevin_from_up. This claim is not based on any statement of fact from the makers of the film, but if it is true, it recomplicates Kevin's gender.

38. There are female sidekicks, such as Dory in *Finding Nemo* and Jesse in *Toy Story II*, but in these two films the plotlines are clearly male-oriented. *Finding Nemo* is very much about the father-son bond and about how a boy becomes a man; Dory is more comedy relief. Jesse's role in *Toy Story II* is slightly more central, but the thrust of the story is clearly the same as *Toy Story*—the importance of "buddies," the homosocial bond between men. At the time of this writing, only in *The Incredibles* of the Pixar canon had a female role been given priority in determining the plot. In *A Bug's Life*, even the queen and princess ants are essentially subsidiary characters; the feminine circus bugs, such as the caterpillar and lady bug are played almost as men in drag and the black widow spider is, like Dory, clearly not the focal point of the story in any way. *Cars* and *Monsters, Inc.* both potentially have love interests, but, again, the plot of these movies centers on the issues of the main male character.

Bibliography

Answers.com. "WikiAnswers–What type of bird is Kevin from up?" Answers.com. http://wiki.answers.com/Q/What_type_of_bird_is_Kevin_from_up.

Avalon Project. "Avalon Project—Blackstone's Commentaries on the Laws of England—Book the First : Chapter the Fifteenth : Of Husband and Wife." Avalon.law.yale.edu. http://avalon.law.yale.edu/18th_century/blackstone_bk1ch15.asp.

Bachelard, Gaston. *The Poetics of Space*. Translated from the French by Maria Jolas. Foreword by Étienne Gilson. New York: Orion Press, 1964.

Barnes, Brooks. "Pixar's Latest Film Has Wall Street on Edge." NYTimes.com. http://www.nytimes.com/2009/04/06/business/media/06pixar.html.

_____. "Wall Street Analyst Belatedly Sees the *Up*-side—Media Blog Decoder—NYTimes.com." NYTimes.com. http://mediadecoder.blogs.nytimes.com/2009/07/08/wall-street-analyst-belatedly-sees-the-up-side/.

Booker, M. Keith. *Disney, Pixar and the Hidden Messages of Children's Films*. San Francisco: Praeger, 2010.

Disney Store. "Disney Store | Official Site for Disney Merchandise." The Disney Store. http://www.disneystore.com/.

Eisenstein, Segei. *Eisenstein on Disney*. Ed. Jay Leyda. Trans. Alan Upchurch. Introduction by Naum Kleiman. Calcutta: Seagull Books, 1986.

Gillam, Ken and Shannon R. Wooden. "Post Princess Models of Gender: the New Man in Disney/Pixar." *Journal of Popular Film and Television* 36.1 (2008): 2–8.

JoBlo. "Review: *Ratatouille*—JoBlo.com." The JoBlo Movie Network. http://www.joblo.com/index.php?id=16543.

King, Susan. "Jordan Nagai, *Up*—*Los Angeles Times*." Latimes.com. http://articles.latimes.com/2009/may/28/entertainment/et-jordanpete28.

Lane, Anthony. "Engine Trouble: *The New Yorker*. "Newyorker.com. http://www.newyorker.com/archive/2006/06/19/060619crci_cinema.

McCloud, Scott. *Understanding Comics: The Invisible Art*. Northampton, MA: Tundra Pub, 1993.

Price, David A. *The Pixar Touch: The Making of a Company*. New York: Vintage, 2008.

Rotten Tomatoes. "*Up* Movie Reviews, Pictures." http://www.rottentomatoes.com/m/up/.

Smiley, Tavis. "Tavis Smiley . Shows . John Lasseter . January 24, 2007." Pbs.org. http://www.pbs.org/kcet/tavissmiley/archive/200701/20070124_lasseter.html.

Smiley You Tube. "*Cars* blu ray: John Lasseter interview for the Blu Ray Disc *Cars*." Smileyyoutube.com. http://www.youtube.com/watch?v=D9ak_e3U8PI.

Stephenson, Hunter. "Essay: Is Kevin, the Tropical Bird in Pixar's *Up*, a Nod to the LGBT Movement?" Slashfilm.com. http://www.slashfilm.com/2009/06/09/is-kevin-the-tropical-bird-in-pixars-up-a-nod-to-the-lbgt-movement/.

The Numbers. "Movie *Up*—Box Office Data, News, Cast Information." http://www.the-numbers.com/movies/2009/UP.php.

The Pixar Blog. "The Pixar Blog: *Up* toys and merchandise [UPDATE: Adult Tees, pins, Kevin plush]." The Pixar Blog. http://pixarblog.blogspot.com/2009/02/up-toys-and-merchandise.html.

Thomas, Frank, and Ollie Johnston. *Disney Animation: The Illusion of Life*. New York: Abbeville Press, 1984.

Ty, Eleanor Rose. *The Politics of the Visible in Asian North American Narratives*. Buffalo: University of Toronto Press, 2004.

Wikipedia. "List of Children's Films—Wikipedia, the free encyclopedia." Wikipedia. org. http://en.wikipedia.org/wiki/List_of_children%27s_films#2009.

Yancy, George, ed. *What White Looks Like: African American Philosophers on the Whiteness Question.* New York: Routledge, 2004.

Zacharek, Stephanie. "Stephanie Zacherek—Salon.com." Salon.com. http://www. salon.com/entertainment/movies/review/2008/06/27/wall_e/.

Filmography

The Adventures of Bullwhip Griffin (1967), directed by James Neilson (Burbank, CA: Walt Disney Home Entertainment, 2005), DVD.

"*Africa Before Dark*" (1927), In *Walt Disney Treasures_The Adventures of Oswald the Lucky Rabbit*, directed by Walt Disney, Ub Iwerks (Burbank, CA: Walt Disney Home Entertainment, 2007), DVD.

Akira (1988), directed by Katsuhiro Ôtomo (Akira Committee Company Ltd., 2001), DVD.

Aladdin (1992), directed by Ron Clements and John Musker (Burbank, CA: Walt Disney Home Entertainment, 2004), DVD.

Alice in Wonderland (1951), directed by Clyde Geronimi, David Hand, Hamilton Luske, Robert Florey, and Wilfred Jackson (Burbank, CA: Walt Disney Home Entertainment, 2010), DVD.

Alice (1989), directed by Jan Svankmajer (Zurich, Switzerland: Channel Four Films, 2000), DVD.

Alien (1979), directed by Ridley Scott (Century City/Los Angeles, CA: 20th Century–Fox, 1999), DVD.

The Aristocats (1970), directed by Wolfgang Reitherman (Burbank, CA: Walt Disney Home Entertainment, 2008), DVD.

Atlantis: The Lost Empire (2001), directed by Gary Trousdale and Kirk Wise (Burbank, CA: Walt Disney Home Entertainment, 2002), DVD.

Avatar (2009), directed by James Cameron (Century City/Los Angeles, CA: 20th Century–Fox, 2010), DVD.

Bambi (1942), directed by James Alger (Burbank, CA: Walt Disney Home Video, 2005). DVD.

Beauty and the Beast (1991), directed by Gary Trousdale and Kirk Wise (Burbank, CA: Walt Disney Home Entertainment, 2002), DVD.

Beauty and the Beast (1989), 10th Anniversary Edition, directed by Kirk Wise and Gary Trousadle (Burbank, CA: Walt Disney Home Entertainment, 1999) DVD.

Bedknobs and Broomsticks (1971), directed by Robert Stevenson (Burbank, CA: Walt Disney Home Entertainment, 2009), DVD.

La Belle et la bête (1946), directed by Jean Cocteau (Paris, France: DisCina, The Criterion Collection, 2003), DVD

Billy Jack (1971), directed by Tom Laughlin (Burbank, CA: Warner Home Video, 2000), DVD.

The Birth of a Nation (1915), directed by D. W. Griffith (Hollywood, CA: David W. Griffith Corp/Epoch Producing Corp., 1998), DVD.

The Black Hole (1979), directed by Gary Nelson (Burbank, CA: Walt Disney Home Entertainment, 2002), DVD.

Blade Runner (1982), directed by Ridley Scott (The Ladd Company and Warner Brothers Pictures, 1999), DVD.

The Blind Side (2009), directed by John Lee Hancock (Burbank, CA: Warner Home Video, 2010), DVD.

"Bright Lights" In *Walt Disney Treasures_The Adventures of Oswald the Lucky Rabbit* (1927), directed by Walt Disney, Ub Iwerks (Burbank, CA: Walt Disney Home Entertainment, 2007), DVD.

Broken Blossoms (1919), directed by D. W. Griffith (Century City/Hollywood/Los Angeles, CA: United Artists/Paramount, 1999), DVD.

Brother Bear (2003), directed by Aaron Blaise and Robert Walker (Burbank, CA: Walt Disney Home Entertainment, 2004), DVD.

Cars (2006), directed by John Lasseter, Joe Ranft (Emeryville/Burbank, CA: Pixar Animation/Walt Disney Home Entertainment, 2006), DVD.

Chicken Little (2005), directed by Mark Dindal (Burbank, CA: Walt Disney Home Entertainment, 2006), DVD.

A Christmas Carol (1938), directed by Edwin L. Marin (Burbank, CA: Warner Home Video, 2005), DVD.

Cinderella (1950), directed by Clyde Geronimi, Wilfred Jackson, and Hamilton Luske (Burbank, CA: Walt Disney Home Entertainment, 2004), DVD.

Cinderella II: Dreams Come True (2002), directed by John Kafka (Burbank, CA: Walt Disney Home Entertainment, 2002), DVD.

Cinderella III: A Twist in Time (2007), directed by Frank Nissen (Burbank, CA: Walt Disney Home Entertainment, 2007), DVD.

City Lights (1931), directed by Charlie Chaplin (Burbank, CA: Warner Home Video, 2004), DVD.

Close Encounters of the Third Kind (1977), directed by Steven Spielberg (Los Angeles, CA: Columbia Pictures, 2007), DVD.

"Commando Duck" (1943), directed by Jack King. In *Walt Disney on the Front Lines* (Burbank, CA: Buena Vista Home Entertainment, 2003), DVD.

Contact (1997), directed by Robert Zemeckis (Burbank, CA: Warner Home Video, 2009), DVD.

Coraline (2009), directed by Henry Selick (New York, NY: Focus Features, 2010), DVD.

"A Corner in Wheat" (1909), directed by D.W. Griffithin *Biograph Shorts: Griffith Masterworks* (1912) (Waterbury, VT. King Video, 2010), DVD.

Crash (1996), directed by David Cronenberg (Toronto, Ontario: Alliance Communications Corporation, 2003), DVD.

Davy Crockett and the River Pirates (1956), directed by Norman Foster. In *Davy Crockett—Two Movie Set* (Burbank, CA: Walt Disney Home Entertainment, 2004), DVD.

Davy Crockett at the Alamo (1956), directed by Norman Foster. In *Davy Crockett—Two Movie Set* (Burbank, CA: Walt Disney Home Entertainment, 2004), DVD.

Disney's Earth (2009), directed by Alastair Fothergill and Mark Linfield (Burbank, CA: Walt Disney Home Entertainment, 2009), DVD.

Dr. Seuss' The Cat in the Hat (2003), directed by Bo Welch (Universal City, CA: Universal Studios, 2004), DVD.

Dominick and Eugene(1988), directed by Robert M. Young (Los Angeles, CA: MGM, 2001), DVD.

Dondi (1961), directed by Albert Zugsmith (Los Angeles, CA: Allied Artists Pictures, 2006), DVD.

Down Argentine Way (1940), directed by Irving Cummings (Los Angeles, CA: 20th Century–Fox, 2006), DVD.

DuckTales The Movie: Treasure of the Lost Lamp (1990), directed by Bob Hathcock (Burbank, CA: Walt Disney Home Entertainment, 2006), DVD.

Dumb and Dumber (1994), directed by Bobby and Peter Farrelly (Los Angeles, CA: New Line Cinema, 2006), DVD.

Dumbo (1941), directed by Ben Sharpsteen, Bill Roberts, Jack Kinney, John Elliotte, Norman Ferguson (Burbank, CA: Walt Disney Home Video, 2011), DVD.

E.T. (1982), directed by Steven Spielberg (Universal City, CA: Universal Pictures, 2002), DVD.

The Emperor's New Groove (2000), directed by Mark Dindal (Burbank, CA: Walt Disney Home Entertainment, 2001), DVD.

The Empire Strikes Back (1980), directed by Irvin Kershner (San Francisco/Century City/Los Angeles, CA: Lucasfilm/20th Century–Fox, 2004), DVD.

Enchanted (2007), directed by Kevin Lima (Burbank, CA: Walt Disney Home Entertainment, 2008), DVD.

Escape from New York (1981), directed by John Carpenter (Los Angeles, CA: MGM, 2000), DVD.

eXistenZ (1999), directed by David Cronenberg (La Crosse, WI: Echo Bridge Home Entertainment, 2011), DVD.

Fantasia (1940), directed by James Algar, Samuel Armstrong, Ford Beebe, Norman Ferguson, Jim Handley, T. Hee, Wilfred Jackson, Hamilton Luske, Bill Roberts, Paul Satterfield, Ben Sharpsteen. (Burbank, CA: Walt Disney Home Entertainment, 1991).

Fantastic Mr. Fox (2009), directed by Wes Anderson (Los Angeles, CA: 20th Century–Fox, 2010), DVD.

Fast Times at Ridgemont High (1982), directed by Amy Heckerling (Universal City, CA: Refugee Films/Universal Pictures, 1999), DVD.

Finding Nemo (2003), directed by Andrew Stanton, Lee Unkrich (Emeryville/Burbank, CA: Pixar Animation/Walt Disney Home Entertainment, 2003), DVD.

Flash Gordon (1936), directed by Frederick Sephani (Universal City/Hollywood, CA: Universal Pictures/King Features Productions, 2002).

The Fly (1986), directed by David Cronenberg (Toronto, Ontario: Alliance Communications Corporation, 2005), DVD.

Forrest Gump (1994), directed by Robert Zemeckis (Hollywood, CA: Paramount, 2001), DVD.

"Der Fuehrer's Face" (1943), directed by Jack King. In *Walt Disney on the Front Lines* (Burbank, CA: Buena Vista Home Entertainment, 2003), DVD.

Full Metal Jacket (1987), directed by Stanley Kubrick (Burbank, CA: Warner Home Video, 2007), DVD.

The Geisha Boy (1958), directed by Frank Tashlin (Los Angeles, CA: Paramount, 2012), DVD.

Ghost in the Shell (1996), directed by Mamoru Oshii (Tokyo, Japan: Bandai Visual Company/Kodansha/Production I.G., 2005), DVD.

Gone with the Wind (1939), directed by Victor Fleming (Burbank, CA: Warner Home Video, 2006), DVD.

The Green Berets (1968), directed by John Wayne, Ray Kellogg (Burbank, CA: Warner Home Video, 2007), DVD.

The Grocery Boy (1932), directed by Walt Disney, Wilfred Jackson. In *Walt Disney Treasures_Mickey Mouse in Black and White*. (Burbank, CA: Walt Disney Home Entertainment, 2002), DVD.

The Hand that Rocks the Cradle (1992), directed by Curtis Hanson (Burbank, CA: Walt Disney Home Entertainment, 1998), DVD.

Harry Potter series (2001–2009), (complete 8 film collection), directed by Chris Columbus, Alfonso Cuaron, Mike Newell, David Yates (Burbank, CA: Warner Home Video, 2011), DVD.

Harvey (1950), directed by Henry Koster (Universal City, CA: Universal Studios, 2001), DVD.

Hell to Eternity (1960), directed by Phil Karlson (Los Angeles, CA: Allied Artists Pictures, 2007), DVD.

Hello, Dolly! (1969), directed by Gene Kelly (Century City/Los Angeles, CA: 20th Century–Fox, 2003), DVD.

"How to Be a Sailor" (1943), directed by Jack King. In *Walt Disney on the Front Lines* (Burbank, CA: Buena Vista Home Entertainment, 2003), DVD.

The Hunchback of Notre Dame (1923), directed by Wallace Worsley (Universal City, CA: Universal Pictures, 2007), DVD.

The Hunchback of Notre Dame (1996), directed by Gary Trousdale and Kirk Wise (Burbank, CA: Walt Disney Home Entertainment, 2002), DVD.

The Incredibles (2004), directed by Brad Bird, Bud Luckey, Roger Gould (Emeryville /Burbank, CA: Pixar Animation/Walt Disney Home Entertainment, 2005), DVD.

The Jazz Singer (1927), directed by Alan Crosland (Burbank, CA: Warner Home Video, 2007), DVD.

Johnny Mnemonic (1995), directed by Robert Longo (Culver City, CA/Montreal, Quebec: Tri-Star Pictures/Alliance Communications Corporation, 1997), DVD.

Journey Back to Oz (1974), directed by Hal Sutherland (Minneapolis, MN: BCI Eclipse, 2006), DVD.

The Jungle Book (1967), directed by Wolfgang Reitherman (Burbank, CA: Walt Disney Home Entertainment, 2007), DVD.

Jurassic Park (1993), directed by Steven Spielberg (Universal City, CA: Universal Pictures/Amblin Entertainment, 2000), DVD.

Lady and the Tramp (1955), directed by Clyde Geronimi, Hamilton Luske and Wilfred Jackson (Burbank, CA: Walt Disney Home Entertainment, 2006), DVD.

Lady and the Tramp II— Scamp's Adventure (2001), directed by Darrell Rooney and Jeannine Roussel (Burbank, CA: Walt Disney Home Entertainment, 2001), DVD.

The Light in the Forest (1958), directed by Herschel Daugherty (Burbank, CA: Walt Disney Home Entertainment, 2003), DVD.

The Lion King (1994), directed by Roger Allers and Rob Minkoff (Burbank, CA: Walt Disney Home Entertainment, 2003), DVD.

The Lion King, 1 1/2 (2004), directed by Bradley Raymond (Burbank, CA: Walt Disney Home Entertainment, 2004), DVD.

The Lion King II: Simba's Pride(1998), directed by Darrell Rooney and Rob LaDuca (Burbank, CA: Walt Disney Home Entertainment, 1998), DVD.

Little Big Man (1970), directed by Arthur Penn (Los Angeles, CA: Paramount, 2003), DVD.

The Little Mermaid (1989), directed by Ron Clements and John Musker (Burbank, CA: Walt Disney Home Entertainment, 2006), DVD.

Looker (1981), directed by Michael Crichton (Beverly Hills/Burbank CA: The Ladd Company/Warner Brothers Home Video, 2007), DVD.

The Lord of the Rings trilogy (2001–2003), directed by Peter Jackson (Los Angeles, CA: New Line Cinema, 2006), DVD.

The Love Bug (1968), directed by Robert Stevenson (Burbank, CA: Walt Disney Home Entertainment, 2003), DVD.

Mad Max (1979), directed by George Miller (Beverly Hills, CA: MGM, 2002), DVD.

The Manhattan Project (1986), directed by Marshall Brickman (Santa Monica/Los Angeles, CA: Gladden Entertainment, 2002), DVD.

Mary Poppins (1964), directed by Robert Stevenson (Burbank, CA: Walt Disney Home Entertainment, 2009), DVD.

The Matrix (1999), directed by Andy Wachowski and Lana Wachowski (Burbank, CA: Warner Home Video, 2007), DVD.

Metropolis (1927), directed by Fritz Lang (Hollywood, CA: Paramount, 2003), DVD.

Mickey Mouse Monopoly (2002), directed by Miguel Pickler (Northampton, MA: Media Education Foundation, 2002), DVD.

Monsters, Inc. (2001), directed by David Silverman, Lee Unkrich, Pete Docter, Ralph Eggleston, Roger Gould (Emeryville/Burbank, CA: Pixar Animation/Walt Disney Home Entertainment, 2002), DVD.

Mulan (1998), directed by Tony Bancroft and Barry Cook (Burbank, CA: Walt Disney Home Entertainment, 2004), DVD.

Of Mice and Men (1939), directed by Lewis Milestone (Culver City, CA: Hal Roach Studios [Image Entertainment], 1998), DVD.

Old Yeller (1957), directed by Robert Stevenson (Burbank, CA: Walt Disney Home Entertainment, 2002), DVD.

Oliver and Company (1988), directed by Charles A. Nichols, Clyde Geronimi, George Scribner (Burbank, CA: Walt Disney Home Entertainment, 2002), DVD.

One Flew Over the Cuckoo's Nest (1975), directed by Milos Forman (Burbank, CA: Warner Home Video, 2006), DVD.

Orphans of the Storm (1921), directed by D.W. Griffith (Philadelphia, PA: Alpha Video, 2003), DVD.

Peter Pan (1953), directed by Hamilton Luske, Clyde Geronimi, Wilfred Jackson (Burbank, CA: Walt Disney Home Entertainment, 2007), DVD.

Pinocchio (1940), directed by Norman Ferguson, T. Hee, Wilfred Jackson, Jack Kinney, Hamilton Luske, Bill Roberts, and Ben Sharpsteen (Burbank, CA: Walt Disney Home Entertainment, 1999), DVD.

Pocahontas (1995), directed by Mike Gabriel and Eric Goldberg (Burbank, CA: Walt Disney Home Entertainment, 2000), DVD.

Precious (2009), directed by Lee Daniels (Santa Monica, CA: Lionsgate Entertainment, Corp., 2010), DVD.

The Princess and the Frog (2009), directed by Ron Clements, John Musker (Burbank, CA: Walt Disney Home Entertainment, 2010), DVD.

Raiders of the Lost Ark (1981), directed by Steven Spielberg (San Francisco/Hollywood, CA: Lucasfilm/Paramount, 2003), DVD.

Ratatouille (2007), directed by Brad Bird Jan Pinkava (Emeryville/Burbank, CA: Pixar Animation/Walt Disney Home Entertainment, 2007), DVD.

Real Genius (1985), directed by Martha Coolidge (Culver City, CA: Sony Pictures Home Entertainment, 2002), DVD.

The Reluctant Dragon (1941), directed by Alfred L. Werker, Hamilton Luske, Jack Cutting, Ub Iwerks and Jack Kinney. In *Walt Disney Treasures_Behind the Scenes at the*

Walt Disney Studio (Burbank, CA: Walt Disney Home Entertainment, 2002), DVD.

The Rescuers (1977), directed by John Lounsbery, Wolfgang Reitherman, Art Stevens (Burbank, CA: Walt Disney Home Entertainment, 2003), DVD.

Return to Oz (1985), directed by Walter Murch (Burbank, CA: Walt Disney Home Entertainment, 2004), DVD.

Robin Hood (1973), directed by Wolfgang Reitherman (Burbank, CA: Walt Disney Home Entertainment, 2006), DVD.

Sagwa, the Chinese Siamese Cat (TV Series), produced by Léon G. Arc, George Daugherty and David Ka Lik Wong (San Francisco, CA: Industrial FX Productions Inc., 2001), DVD.

Saludos Amigos/Three Caballeros (released as dual DVD set) (1942/1944), directed by Wilfred Jackson, Jack Kinney, Hamilton Luske (as Ham Luske) and Bill Roberts (*Saludos*); Norman Ferguson, Clyde Geronimi, Jack Kinney, Bill Roberts and Harold Young (*Caballeros*) (Burbank, CA: Walt Disney Home Entertainment, 2008), DVD.

The Secret of Kells (2009), directed by Tomm Moore (Paris, France: Les Armateurs, 2010), DVD.

The Shaggy Dog (1959), directed by Charles Barton (Burbank, CA: Walt Disney Home Entertainment, 2006), DVD.

Shrek 2 (2004), directed by Andrew Adamson, Kelly Asbury, Conrad Vernon (Universal City, CA: Dreamworks Animated Studios, 2004), DVD.

Sleeping Beauty (1959), directed by Clyde Geronimi (Burbank, CA: Walt Disney Home Entertainment, 2008), DVD.

Sling Blade (1996), directed by Billy Bob Thornton (Santa Monica, CA: Miramax Studios, 2005), DVD.

Snow White and the Seven Dwarfs (1937), directed by Ben Sharpsteen, David Hand, Larry Morey, Perce Pearce, and Wilfred Jackson (Burbank, CA: Walt Disney Home Entertainment, 2001), DVD.

Something Wicked This Way Comes (1983), directed by Jack Clayton (Burbank, CA: Walt Disney Home Entertainment, 2004), DVD.

Son of Flubber (1963), directed by Robert Stevenson (Burbank, CA: Walt Disney Home Entertainment, 2004), DVD.

Song of the South (1946), directed by Harve Foster and Wilfred Jackson (Dahlongha, GA: Classic Reels & Broadcasts Co., 2010), DVD.

Spiderman (2002), directed by Sam Raimi (Culver City, CA: Columbia Pictures, 2002), DVD.

Spies Like Us (1985), directed by John Landis (Burbank, CA: AAR Films/Warner BrothersHome Video, 1998), DVD.

Star Trek: The Motion Picture (1979), directed by Robert Wise (Hollywood, CA: Century Associates/Paramount, 2001), DVD.

Star Trek II: The Wrath of Khan (1982), directed by Nicholas Meyer (Hollywood, CA: Paramount, 2000), DVD.

Star Wars [A New Hope] (1977), directed by George Lucas (San Francisco/Century City/Los Angeles, CA: Lucasfilm/20th Century–Fox, 2004), DVD.

Star Wars (Prequel Trilogy) (1999–2005), directed by George Lucas (San Francisco/Century City/Los Angeles, CA: Lucasfilm/20th Century–Fox, 2008), DVD.

"Steamboat Willie" (1932), directed by Walt Disney, Ub Iwerks. In *Walt Disney Treasures_Mickey Mouse in Black and White* (Burbank, CA: Walt Disney Home Entertainment, 2002), DVD.

Strange Days (1995), directed by Kathryn Bigelow (Santa Monica/Los Angeles CA: Lightstorm Entertainment, 2002), DVD.

Superman (1978), directed by Richard Donner (Burbank, CA: Warner Home Video, 2006), DVD.

Superman III (1983) (, directed by Richard LesterBurbank, CA: Warner Home Video, 2006), DVD.

The Swiss Family Robinson (1960), directed by Ken Annakin (Burbank, CA: Walt Disney Home Entertainment, 2004), DVD.

The Sword in the Stone (1963), directed by Les Perkins, Wolfgang Reitherman (Burbank, CA: Walt Disney Home Entertainment, 2001), DVD.

Tangled (2010), directed by Nathan Greno, Byron Howard (Emeryville/Burbank, CA: Pixar Animation Studios/Walt Disney Home Entertainment, 2011), DVD.

Tarzan (1999), directed by Chris Buck and Kevin Lima (Burbank, CA: Walt Disney Home Entertainment, 2005), DVD.

Ten Who Dared (1960), Directed by William Beaudine (Burbank, CA: Walt Disney Home Entertainment, 2009), DVD.

The Terminator (1984), directed by James Cameron (Los Angeles, CA: MGM, 2001), DVD.

Testament (1983), directed by Lynne Littman (Hollywood/Los Angeles, CA: Paramount/ American Playhouse, 2004), DVD.

That Night in Rio (1941), directed by directed by Irving Cummings (Los Angeles, CA: 20th Century–Fox, 2007), DVD.

Tonka (1958), directed by Lewis R. Foster (Burbank, CA: Walt Disney Home Entertainment, 2009), DVD.

Tootsie (1982), directed by Sydney Pollack (Culver City/Los Angeles, CA: Columbia Pictures/Punch Productions, 2001), DVD.

Toy Story 3 (2010), directed by Lee Unkrich (Emeryville/Burbank, CA: Pixar Animation Studios/Walt Disney Home Entertainment, 2010), DVD.

"Trader Mickey" (1932), directed by Walt Disney, David Hand. In *Walt Disney Treasures_Mickey Mouse in Black and White* (Burbank, CA: Walt Disney Home Entertainment, 2002), DVD.

Treasure Planet (2002), directed by Ron Clements and John Musker (Burbank, CA: Walt Disney Home Entertainment, 2003), DVD.

Tron (1982), directed by Steven Lisberger (Burbank, CA: Walt Disney Home Entertainment, 2002), DVD.

Tron Legacy (2010), directed by Joseph Kosinski (Burbank, CA: Walt Disney Home Entertainment, 2011), DVD.

20,000 Leagues Under the Sea (1954), directed by Richard Fleischer (Burbank, CA: Walt Disney Home Entertainment, 2004), DVD.

2001: A Space Odyssey (1968), directed by Stanley Kubrick (Burbank, CA: Warner Home Video, 2007), DVD.

Up (2009), directed by Bob Peterson and Pete Docter (Emeryville/Burbank, CA: Pixar Animation/Walt Disney Home Entertainment, 2009), DVD.

Wall-E (2008), directed by Andrew Stanton (Emeryville/Burbank, CA: Pixar Animation Studios/Walt Disney Home Entertainment, 2008), DVD.

Walt Disney Treasures_The Adventures of Oswald the Lucky Rabbit (1927), directed by Walt Disney, Ub Iwerks (Burbank, CA: Walt Disney Home Entertainment, 2007), DVD.

Wargames (1983), directed by John Badham (Beverly Hills, CA: MGM/United Artists, 1998), DVD.

The Watcher in the Woods (1982), directed by John Hough (Burbank, CA: Walt Disney Home Entertainment, 2004), DVD

Weekend in Havana (1941), directed by Walter Lang (Los Angeles, CA: 20th Century–Fox, 2006), DVD.

Westward Ho: The Wagons (1956), directed by William Beaudine (Burbank, CA: Walt Disney Home Entertainment, 2011), DVD.

Who Framed Roger Rabbit? (1988), directed by Robert Zemekis (Burbank, CA: Walt Disney Home Video, 2003), DVD.

The Wiz (1978), directed by Sidney Lumet (Universal City, CA: Universal Pictures, 2004), DVD.

The Wizard of Oz (1939), directed by Victor Fleming (Burbank, CA: Warner Home Video, 2009), DVD.

About the Contributors

Kimiko **Akita** is an associate professor in the School of Communication at the University of Central Florida in Orlando, where she teaches international and intercultural communication and a cultural studies honors seminar in *manga* and *anime*.

Tammy **Berberi** is an assistant professor of French at the University of Minnesota, Morris. She is interested in the representation of disability in 19th-century French literature and the history of caricature and pathology. She coedited, with Elizabeth Hamilton and Ian Sutherland, *Worlds Apart: Disability and Foreign Language Learning* (Yale University Press).

Viktor **Berberi** teaches Italian at the University of Minnesota, Morris. His publications include essays on Italian modernist poetry, theories of metaphor, and contemporary Italian migration literature.

Natchee **Blu Barnd** is an adjunct professor of critical studies at California College of the Arts. He is a comparative ethnic studies scholar interested in the intersections between ethnic studies, cultural geography and indigenous studies. He also actively works with cultural centers in California, where he combines scholarship, mentoring and community-building.

Johnson **Cheu** is an assistant professor in the department of Writing, Rhetoric and American Cultures at Michigan State University. He has published scholarly work in disability studies and popular culture studies. His poetry and creative essays have also appeared widely.

Danielle **Glassmeyer** is an assistant professor at Bradley University where she teaches 20th-21st century American literature and film. Her research focuses on Cold War texts that re-think gender, social, and political boundaries, and on the structures by which trauma narratives are organized.

Karen S. **Goldman** is the assistant director for outreach for the Center for Latin American Studies and a research associate for the Department of Hispanic Languages and Literatures at the University of Pittsburgh.

Michael **Green** is a lecturer in film and media studies at Arizona State University, where he teaches courses in screenwriting and film studies. He has published articles in the *Journal of Film and Video* and *Bright Lights Film Journal*, among others. He has completed his first novel, *The Sepulchral City*.

Nancy Hansen is the director of the interdisciplinary master's program in disability studies at the University of Manitoba in Winnipeg, Manitoba, Canada. She is interested in disability history, geography of disability, disabled women's issues, disabled people's access to health care and disability and the media.

Rick Kenney is an associate professor at the Florida Gulf Coast University in Fort Myers, where he teaches journalism and conducts research in media ethics. He is also an Ethics Fellow with the Poynter Institute for Media Studies.

Gwendolyn Limbach earned her B.A. in English literature and her master's degree from Pace University. She has published essays on popular texts and feminism. She teaches in New York City.

Zana Marie Lutfiyya is a professor and the associate dean of Graduate Studies and Research at the University of Manitoba in Winnipeg, Manitoba, Canada. She is interested in the factors that help or hinder the social integration and participation of individuals with intellectual disabilities into community life.

Walter C. Metz is the chair of the Department of Cinema and Photography at Southern Illinois University. He is the author of two books: *Engaging Film Criticism: Film History and Contemporary American Cinema* (Peter Lang, 2004) and *Bewitched* (Wayne State University Press, 2007).

Martin F. Norden teaches film history/theory/criticism and screenwriting as a professor of communication at the University of Massachusetts–Amherst. He is the author of *The Cinema of Isolation: A History of Physical Disability in the Movies* (Rutgers University Press, 1994) and numerous other publications.

Prajna Parasher began her career as a filmmaker in Paris, France, and earned her Ph.D. from Northwestern University. She has several films which address political, economic and philosophical concerns. She is a professor, chair of the Art, Design and Communication Department and director of the Film and Digital Technology program at Chatham University.

Amanda Putnam is an associate professor who teaches interdisciplinary humanities courses at Roosevelt University in Chicago. She specializes in women's literature with a specific focus on transnational black women's literature. Her scholarly interests include the racial and gendered spaces of television and film.

Ana Salzberg received her Ph.D. in film studies from the University of Edinburgh. She has published articles on Hitchcock's *Vertigo* and stars like Rita Hayworth and Marilyn Monroe, and is completing a book on studio-era stardom. Her research interests include classic Hollywood cinema, psychoanalytic and feminist film theory, and the intersection between old and new media.

Karen D. Schwartz received her Ph.D. in inclusive special education and currently works as a research facilitator for the University of Manitoba in Winnipeg, Canada. She is interested in the issues facing people with intellectual disabilities, with a focus on the role that various discourses play in conceptualizing these individuals.

Gael **Sweeney** teaches in the writing program at Syracuse University and has published and given papers on topics from Elvis and White Trash, *Queer as Folk* and Sherlock Holmes fandoms, Lena Horne, Judy Garland, and Maureen O'Hara, to the cultural significance of *A Christmas Story* and *As the World Turns*.

Sarah E. **Turner** is a senior lecturer at the University of Vermont, where she teaches courses on race and ethnic literary studies and race and television, among many others. She is co-editing a scholarly collection on colorblind racism in film and television, as well as working on a collection on Disney television.

Dennis **Tyler** is a scholar and creative writer, with an interest in 19th-century fiction and issues of domesticity and cultural spaces. He has published short stories and poems. He has lived in many areas of the United States, and teaches at Henderson Community College in Kentucky.

William **Verrone** teaches film and literature at the University of North Alabama where he founded and chairs the film studies minor. He has written extensively on different film directors, genres, and aesthetics, and in 2009 was the executive director and convener of the Conference on Global Film.

Kheli R. **Willetts** is an assistant professor of African American art history and film in the Department of African American Studies at Syracuse University and is executive director of the Community Folk Art Center, a community service-based unit of the African American Studies Department.

Index

297

.